Modern Challenges to Islamic Law

The diversity of interpretation within Islamic legal traditions can be challenging for those working within this field of study. Using a distinctly contextual approach, this book addresses such challenges by combining theoretical insights with empirical explorations into how vernacular understandings of Islamic law impact on the application of law in the daily life of Muslims. Engaging with topics as diverse as Islamic constitutionalism, Islamic finance, human rights and internet *fatawa*, Shaheen Ali provides an invaluable resource for scholars, students and practitioners alike by exploring exactly what constitutes Islamic law in the contemporary world. Useful examples, case studies, a glossary of terms and the author's personal reflections accompany rigorous academic critique. The book offers the reader a unique and discerning discussion of Islamic law in practice.

Shaheen Sardar Ali is Professor of Law, University of Warwick, UK; formerly Vice-Chair of the United Nations Working Group on Arbitrary Detention (2008–2014). She has served as Professor II University of Oslo, Norway, Professor of Law, University of Peshawar, Pakistan, as well as Director Women's Study Centre at the same university. She has served as the first woman cabinet Minister for Health, Population Welfare and Women Development, Government of the Khyber Pukhtunkhwa Province of Pakistan and first Chair of Pakistan's National Commission on the Status of Women. She served on the Prime Minister's Consultative Committee for Women (Pakistan), and the Senate National Commission of Enquiry on the Status of Women (Pakistan). Professor Ali has received a number of national and international awards including the Public Sector Award (Asian Women Achievements Awards) 2005, the British Muslims Annual Award at the House of Lords, 2002, Star Woman of the Year 1996 in the field of law (Pakistan), the Presidential Award (Aizaz-i-Fazeelat) in 1992 for contribution to the teaching and research in higher education (Pakistan), and an honourable mention in the UNESCO Prize for the Teaching of Human Rights in 1992. In 2012, she was named one of the 100 most influential women of Pakistan. Professor Ali has published extensively in a number of areas including Human Rights, Women's Rights, Children's Rights, Islamic Law and Jurisprudence, International Law, and Gender Studies.

The Law in Context Series

Editors: William Twining (University College London),
Christopher McCrudden (Queen's University Belfast) and
Bronwen Morgan (University of Bristol).

Since 1970 the Law in Context series has been at the forefront of the movement to broaden the study of law. It has been a vehicle for the publication of innovative scholarly books that treat law and legal phenomena critically in their social, political and economic contexts from a variety of perspectives. The series particularly aims to publish scholarly legal writing that brings fresh perspectives to bear on new and existing areas of law taught in universities. A contextual approach involves treating legal subjects broadly, using materials from other social sciences, and from any other discipline that helps to explain the operation in practice of the subject under discussion.

It is hoped that this orientation is at once more stimulating and more realistic than the bare exposition of legal rules. The series includes original books that have a different emphasis from traditional legal textbooks, while maintaining the same high standards of scholarship. They are written primarily for undergraduate and graduate students of law and of other disciplines, but will also appeal to a wider readership. In the past, most books in the series have focused on English law, but recent publications include books on European law, globalisation, transnational legal processes, and comparative law.

Books in the Series

Diduck: *Law's Families*

Fortin: *Children's Rights and the Developing Law*

Ghai & Woodman: *Practising Self-Government: A Comparative Study of Autonomous Regions*

Glover-Thomas: *Reconstructing Mental Health Law and Policy*

Gobert & Punch: *Rethinking Corporate Crime*

Goldman: *Globalisation and the Western Legal Tradition: Recurring Patterns of Law and Authority*

Haack: *Evidence Matters: Science, Proof, and Truth in the Law*

Harlow & Rawlings: *Law and Administration*

Harris: *An Introduction to Law*

Harris, Campbell & Halson: *Remedies in Contract and Tort*

Harvey: *Seeking Asylum in the UK: Problems and Prospects*

Hervey & McHale: *European Union Health Law*

Hervey & McHale: *Health Law and the European Union*

Holder and Lee: *Environmental Protection, Law and Policy*

Jackson and Summers: *The Internationalisation of Criminal Evidence*

Kostakopoulou:*The Future Governance of Citizenship*

Lewis: *Choice and the Legal Order: Rising above Politics*

Likosky: *Transnational Legal Processes*

Likosky: *Law, Infrastructure and Human Rights*

Maughan & Webb: *Lawyering Skills and the Legal Process*

McGlynn: *Families and the European Union: Law, Politics and Pluralism*

Moffat: *Trusts Law: Text and Materials*

Monti: *EC Competition Law*

Morgan: *Contract Law Minimalism*

Morgan & Yeung: *An Introduction to Law and Regulation: Text and Materials*

Norrie: *Crime, Reason and History*

O'Dair: *Legal Ethics*

Oliver: *Common Values and the Public–Private Divide*

Oliver & Drewry: *The Law and Parliament*

Picciotto: *International Business Taxation*

Probert: *The Changing Legal Regulation of Cohabitation, 1600–2010*

Reed: *Internet Law: Text and Materials*

Richardson: *Law, Process and Custody*

Roberts & Palmer: *Dispute Processes: ADR and the Primary Forms of Decision-Making*

Rowbottom: *Democracy Distorted: Wealth, Influence and Democratic Politics*

Sauter: *Public Services in EU Law*

Scott & Black: *Cranston's Consumers and the Law*

Seneviratne: *Ombudsmen: Public Services and Administrative Justice*

Siems: *Comparative Law*

Stapleton: *Product Liability*

Stewart: *Gender, Law and Justice in a Global Market*

Tamanaha: *Law as a Means to an End: Threat to the Rule of Law*

Turpin and Tomkins: *British Government and the Constitution: Text and Materials*

Twining: *Globalisation and Legal Theory*

Twining: *Rethinking Evidence*

International Journal of Law in Context: A Global Forum for Interdisciplinary Legal Studies

The International Journal of Law in Context is the companion journal to the Law in Context book series and provides a forum for interdisciplinary legal studies and offers intellectual space for ground-breaking critical research. It publishes contextual work about law and its relationship with other disciplines including but not limited to science, literature, humanities, philosophy, sociology, psychology, ethics, history and geography. More information about the journal and how to submit an article can be found at http://journals.cambridge.org/ijc

Modern Challenges to Islamic Law

SHAHEEN SARDAR ALI

University of Warwick

CAMBRIDGE
UNIVERSITY PRESS

CAMBRIDGE
UNIVERSITY PRESS

University Printing House, Cambridge CB2 8BS, United Kingdom

Cambridge University Press is part of the University of Cambridge.

It furthers the University's mission by disseminating knowledge in the pursuit of education, learning, and research at the highest international levels of excellence.

www.cambridge.org
Information on this title: www.cambridge.org/9781107033382

© Shaheen Sardar Ali 2016

This publication is in copyright. Subject to statutory exception and to the provisions of relevant collective licensing agreements, no reproduction of any part may take place without the written permission of Cambridge University Press.

First published 2016

Printed in the United Kingdom by Clays, St Ives plc

A catalogue record for this publication is available from the British Library.

ISBN 978-1-107-03338-2 Hardback
ISBN 978-1-107-63909-6 Paperback

Cambridge University Press has no responsibility for the persistence or accuracy of URLs for external or third-party internet websites referred to in this publication and does not guarantee that any content on such websites is, or will remain, accurate or appropriate.

To Ali
For a lifetime of love, trust, encouragement and support

To Zareen
For teaching us to believe and persevere as we grieve for loved ones.
You will always live in our hearts.

To Gulsanga, Isfandyar, Zara, Abbas, Sara, Asfundyar, Hussain,
Khadeeja, Virdan, Behram, Zardad
For being there for me, making me a proud and happy mother and
grandmother. God bless you All.

Contents

Acknowledgements

Attempting to acknowledge the debts of gratitude in a work informed by a lifetime of teaching, research and activism in Islamic law is truly overwhelming as it is impossible to mention everyone who contributed to this project. Family, friends, colleagues and thousands of students whom I have been privileged to tutor over thirty-nine years have all individually and collectively nurtured and nourished my thoughts and writing, an enrichment for which I shall forever carry an unrepayable debt. But most of all, *Modern Challenges to Islamic Law*, as an idea and project, is indebted to Professor William Twining. I thank him for believing in the project and in my ability to take it to fruition. Professor Twining is an institution of solidarity and support, sincere guidance and inspiration and one would wish for more selfless academics of his ilk.

I have been blessed with an exceptional family who have encouraged and supported me through thick and thin, believe in me and respect my passion for teaching and research. First and foremost and leading the brood is my husband Sardar Ali, who is my best friend, mentor and guide, and without him at my side I would have been unable to undertake my personal and intellectual journey, especially during the final months of writing after we lost our beloved granddaughter Zareen. Following in their father's footsteps, our three children, Gulsanga, Isfandyar and Zara are solid rocks of support, ever appreciative, making me grateful, humble and proud. We have been equally fortunate in their loving spouses – Abbas, Sara and Asfundyar – who evince a keen interest in my work, finding time to discuss it and give me feedback. Our grandchildren are my inspiration, putting smiles on my face and spurring me on – Hussain, Khadeeja, Virdan, Behram, Zardad and little Zareen (from her place in heaven). So thank you all!

Writing *Modern Challenges to Islamic Law* has been a steep learning curve gathering my life experiences as a Muslim woman with multiple identities and experiences and bringing them together in an academic format and expression. I am grateful to the anonymous reviewers of the book proposal for suggesting inclusion of a wide range of themes and topics. Challenging at the time, I believe it has made *Modern Challenges* a book that will hopefully evoke interest among a broad and varied readership. The range of themes covered would not have been possible had I not received generous periods of study leave and fellowships to undertake the research and writing. I am fortunate in the institutional support and encouragement offered to me. My home institution – Warwick University and Warwick Law School – approved study leave; the Lichtenberg Kolleg, Göttingen University and the Max Planck Institute of Private International and Comparative Law, Hamburg offered fellowships. At Göttingen, Professor Schneider and colleagues of the Lichtenberg Kolleg provided valuable forums to present work in progress and constructive comments. In Hamburg, my 'Islamic law family', as I call it, provided an inspirational space in which my work flourished. Led by Dr Nadjma Yassari, this group of amazingly motivated and meticulous scholars offered me a place in their midst, making it the most memorable research leave ever! Thank you Nadjma Jan, Eman, Lena-Maria, Tess and all the interns.

At the United Nations in Geneva, the library staff facilitated archival research, providing useful tips on how to access relevant materials. My colleagues Jolene Tautakitaki and Ikinasio Tautakitaki provided exemplary support in accessing the archival material on the drafting process of CEDAW and deserve a special thank-you.

Many friends and colleagues supported this project and enriched my understandings by discussing and reading draft chapters and providing valuable feedback: Anne Hellum, Nadjma Yassari, Tess Chemnitzer, Lena-Maria Moller, Shirin Rai, Jeremy Roche, Abdul Paliwala, Lena Rethal, Mike Saward, Eleanor Nesbitt, Eric Heinze, Irene Schneider, Gaenor Bruce, Barbara Roberson, Gillian Douglas, Alan Norrie, Rebecca Probert, Paul Raffield, Dora Kostakopolou, Ming-Sung Kho, Raza Saeed and Sheharyar Hamid.

My 'shining stars', as I call my doctoral candidates and students who over the years have provided inspiration and research assistance remain my solid support and inspirational base. Ayesha Shahid, Mamman Lawan, Musa Abubakar, Sahar Maranlou, Shahbaz Cheema, Riaz Walji, Hashim Bata, Rajnaara Akhtar, Bayan Al-Shabani and Arjumand Bano Kazmi are gratefully acknowledged for making *Modern Challenges* possible. A number of dedicated persons extended much-needed research assistance, which is greatly appreciated. These include Asfundyar Yousaf, Rukhshanda Raz, Menaal Munshey, David Jones, Sajila Sohail Khan, Taslim Asif, Isfandyar Ali Khan and Amna Cheema.

Editorial support is always critical to a project of this duration and intensity, and through these years the editorial team at Cambridge University Press has been exemplary. Sinead Maloney supported me through the initial period when the book proposal was being reviewed and revised. Finola O'Sullivan, Marta Walkowiak, Valerie Appleby, Emma Collison, John Gaunt, Tamzen Le Blanc and Rebecca Roberts made me feel comfortable and supported me during the final reviews and edits and I remain grateful to them for making this an enjoyable process. Last but certainly not least is my pleasure to thank Liam Brown, without whom I would be still struggling with draft chapters. His meticulous editing has brought us to the point where I am typing these lines!

I wish to acknowledge that Chapter 3 was previously published in Nadjma Yassari's edited volume *Changing God's Law: The Dynamics of Middle Eastern Family Law* (2016) Abingdon: Routledge pp. 34–67.

Thank you all.

Glossary

adah	see *'urf*
'adat	customary practices, custom
'adl	justice
aalim	scholar (plural *ulema*)
aman	protection
ansar	hosts – in early Islamic history refers to the people of Medina who hosted the migrant Muslims from Makkah
asal	capital
awliya	guardians
bay' mu'ajjal	credit sale
bay'ah	oath of allegiance
bida'	(reprehensible) innovation in Islamic law or teaching
burqa/burka	full-body covering worn by women, including the face
chador	covering worn over clothes by women
dar-al-Harb	land(s) of war
dar-al-Islam	land(s) of peace
dar-al-sulh	land(s) of (negotiated) peace
daraba	contested term in relation to verse 4:34 of the Qur'an, normally used to denote hitting/to strike
darshal	Pashto word for *dihliz*
darura	necessity
dawla	state
dihliz	threshold, inter-space, in-between place
din	religion
Eid-Milad-un-nabi	birth anniversary of the Prophet Muhammad
faqih	jurist
faskh	a judicial decree of divorce
fatwa	opinion (plural *fatawa*)
fiqh	jurisprudence
fiqh al-aqalliyat	jurisprudence of minorities
gharar	uncertainty, risk, speculation

hadd	prescribed limit (plural *hudud*), used in Islamic criminal justice to denote the mandatory offences/punishment set in the Qur'an and Sunna
hadith	the recorded statements or actions of the Prophet Muhammad (plural *ahadith*)
halala	see *tahlil*
hijab	headscarf worn by women
hijra	migration
hiyal	legal fiction
ibadaat	lit. 'worship'
iddat	prescribed minimum waiting period between marriages for Muslim divorced/widowed women
ifta	the institution of *fatwa*
ijara	lease
ijma	consensus of opinion among Muslim jurists on a particular question of law
ijtihad	lit. 'exertion', and technically the effort of a jurist to arrive at a response to a legal question through independent reasoning
ikhtilaf	diversity of opinions
ikhtilaf al-fuqaha	diversity of opinions among jurists
ikrah	duress
imam	leader, employed in various contexts including a prayer leader
imama	religious leadership
imambargah	mosque/congregation hall of Shia Muslims
istisna	commissioned manufacture
izzat	honour
jihad	lit. to exert, struggle, including, as a last resort, armed struggle
jirga	council of elders/decision-making assembly
kafir	infidel, non-believer
khilafa	caliphate
khul'	divorce initiated by the wife in return for relinquishing her *mahr*
maddhab	school of juristic thought in Islam
mahajir	migrant; in Islamic history, denotes the first migrant Muslims from Makkah to Medina
mahr	marriage gift by husband to wife at the time of marriage
mahram	close male relative
majlis	gathering, for example for commemorating the martyrdom of the grandson of the Prophet Muhammad at Karbala (plural *majalis*)
maqasid-al-sharia	'objectives of *sharia*'

maslaha	the public good/welfare
muamalat	socio-economic relationships
mubara't	divorce by mutual consent
mudaraba	profit sharing
mufti	A *fatwa*-giving scholar
muhallil	a man who marries a woman and divorces her so she can remarry her first husband; see *tahlil*
muharram	the first month of the Islamic calendar
mujtahid	one who is qualified to make *ijma/ijtihad*
mu'minin	faithful covenanters (in the context of the Medina Charter), normally used to denote Muslims/the faithful
murabaha	a form of short-term financing
musharaka	joint partnership
mustafti	*fatwa*-seeker
nikah	the ceremony where the 'Islamic' marriage contract is signed
niqab	face veil
nushuz	rebellious disobedience
panchayat	village council
pir	religious person
qadi	judge
qanun	state law, also used in the sense of secular law
qard hasan	charitable loan with no expectation of return on the part of the person loaning the money
qawwamun	provider/protector, someone who looks after and is responsible for (usually) the family
qiwama	the concept of male as protector and provider
qiyas	analogical deduction
Qur'an	the religious text and primary source of Islamic law believed by Muslims to be the word of God
riba	excessive interest, usury
risala	God's message to humankind
riwaj	custom
salam	a form of sale using advance payment for goods that need not be in existence at the time of payment to be delivered on a fixed future date
sharia	principles of Islamic law
shura	consultation, also a consultative body when used as a noun
siyar	Islamic international law
siyasa sharia	*Sharia* as enacted in state law through statutory ordinances
sood	interest on capital
Sunna	the words and deeds of the Prophet Muhammad recorded as *hadith* for posterity and as a source of Islamic law

ta'amul	see *'urf*
tahlil	intervening marriage enabling remarriage between divorced couples
takaful	'Islamic' insurance
takhayyur	juristic choice
talaq	pronouncement of divorce by the husband
talaq al-bida	(also called *talaq-i-bain* and triple *talaq*) a contested form of delivering *talaq* – three pronouncements in one sitting
talaq-i-ahsan	mode of delivering *talaq* where husband makes one pronouncement refraining from sexual relations thereafter for a prescribed period of time, leaving room for reconciliation
talaq-i-hasan	mode of delivering *talaq* – comprises three pronouncements in three consecutive months without sexual contact; room for reconciliation
talaq-i-tafwid	the right to pronounce divorce upon a husband, delegated by him to his wife or third party
talaqnama	divorce deed
talfiq	lit. 'patchwork'; as a legal term, the putting together of a rule based upon diverse opinions from various schools of juristic thought in Islam
taqlid	duty to follow
tawarruq	a form of *murabaha* contract involving buy-back of a commodity
tawhid	oneness of God
taysir	the 'making easy' of practising Islam
ulema	religious scholars (plural)
umma	universal nationhood of Muslims
'urf	customary practices
usul-al-hukm	principles of government
usul-ul-fiqh	principles of jurisprudence
wali	guardian, also used in relation to marriage guardianship
wilaya	guardianship
wilayat al-ijbar	marriage guardianship with power of coercion; see *wali*
zakat	annual mandatory tax on unspent wealth beyond a prescribed minimum for the poor and needy, generally 2.5%, 5–10% on harvest

Table of Cases

Table of Legislation

Introduction

Poised at the *dihliz*[1]

Life, I sit at your *dihliz*,
Hands holding the bowl of endeavour.[2]
In my eyes are desires for a flower-filled spring,
On my lips lie grievances of the indifference of time.
Life, I sit at your *dihliz*.

The word *dihliz* is common to Arabic, Turkish, Persian and Urdu, those great languages of the Muslim world, with cognates in many related languages besides (in my native Pashto, the word is *darshal*). A literal, albeit inadequate, English translation might be 'threshold' or 'vestibule' – the *dihliz* is an 'inter-space' or an 'in-between place'. As a metaphor, though, the *dihliz* has a deep cultural significance that goes well beyond its bare translation, encompassing a passage or corridor connecting and disconnecting spaces, places and buildings; a notional path that connects and frames other spaces.

Much like the poet, I am poised at a *dihliz*, exploring conceptual and analytical tools to contextualize and write about Islamic law, a subject that constitutes both a personal and a professional journey. How do I link theoretical perspectives of a discipline to its lived reality in language that resonates with readers across cultures, geographies and knowledge systems? In seeking an appropriate vantage point from which to engage with the Islamic legal traditions, the metaphor that comes to mind is of being poised at the *dihliz*. This in-between place or threshold is also imagined as a passage or corridor connecting and disconnecting spaces, places and buildings. Located at the *dihliz*, one is simultaneously inside and outside the broader frameworks of life and knowledge. Conscious of

---

[1] The translation here from Urdu is my own; it is not literal, but I have attempted to convey the underlying meaning of the verses. As *Modern Challenges* was nearing completion I discovered that Ebrahim Moosa had named his website *Dihliz*, reflecting there on the meanings of the word. I gratefully acknowledge his insights (see also E. Moosa, *Ghazali and the Poetics of Imagination* (Chapel Hill: University of North Carolina Press, 2005)). *Dihliz* is pronounced deh-leez in Urdu and dih-leez in Arabic.

[2] The bowl is commonly used as a metaphor for a space wanting or needing to be filled; holding a bowl signifies both impoverishment and a desire for fulfillment. Those who seek something also arrive at the *dihliz*, where they hope to fulfil their desires and achieve their purpose.

competing experiences and contexts, at the *dihliz* one is offered multiple panoramic visions dotted on the horizons beyond one's immediate proximity. From its vantage point, I position myself to explore and expose multiple interpretations of Islamic law as well as the complexity inherent in handling plural normativity. *Modern Challenges to Islamic Law* aims to bring to the fore the diversity within Muslim communities and the various cultural and linguistic lenses through which they perceive and experience their religious traditions. At the level of state and government, it aims to demonstrate how Islamic law is served up rhetorically and selectively for popular consumption and for the retention of authority.

Modern Challenges has as its background four decades of professional engagement with the Islamic legal traditions, augmented by six decades of personal experiences as a woman with multiple identities: a Pashtun from the Swat Valley who is Muslim, Pakistani and British. Exposed to both Western and non-Western educational and legal systems, and having lived and worked in Asia, Europe and beyond, I find myself adept at perceiving many different visions and realities simultaneously. However, I would like to make clear that my main experience and knowledge is with Commonwealth jurisdictions and common law legal systems and does not extend to, for instance, Indonesia and other South East Asian Muslim jurisdictions.[3] Likewise, whilst I am deeply aware of the role and contribution of Shia perspectives on jurisprudence, as well as more recently on state and government, my personal and research experiences are confined to Sunni Islam.[4]

Multiple locations both geographical and intellectual inform my perspectives and approaches to the Islamic legal traditions. Based on these varied experiences, I am able to bring to the present project a variety of conceptual and interpretative tools to engage with the globalizing and transformative impacts that are affecting subjects as disparate as Islamic finance, Internet *fatawa* and women's rights movements. The manner in which Muslim state practices are negotiating new challenges also forms part of my contemplations at the *dihliz*. This is a position that fosters inclusivity, in that it acknowledges that there is no single, definitive position on any given aspect of the legal traditions in Islam. Aware of any number of equally compelling views in and around the *dihliz*, those so positioned are seldom dismissive of others' perspectives. Presenting one's position without apology or dismissal of others' viewpoints is the balancing act performed at

---

[3] I recognize that Indonesia is the largest Muslim country in the world and requires close attention, but it is beyond my areas of expertise and the remit of this book. This does not preclude me from including its system of *zakat* in Chapter 4, along with other Muslim countries where appropriate.

[4] A highly sophisticated body of work has emerged over the years in this field of scholarship. Most prominently, in the areas of state and government, the Iraqi scholar Muhammad Baqer as-Sadr has been hugely influential in shaping Ayatullah Khomeini's idea of the Islamic Republic. See Chibli Mallat, *The Renewal of Islamic Law: Muhammad Baqer as-Sadr, Najaf and the Shi'i International* (Cambridge: Cambridge University Press, 2004).

the *dihliz*. It is both the centre and the margins of tradition and modernity – moving, fluid and dynamic, much like the Islamic legal traditions.

The inter-disciplinary and cross-cultural approach adopted in *Modern Challenges* reflects the *dihliz* where various disciplines and knowledge traditions meet, cross paths, and engage in meaningful conversations. It is a metaphor that may usefully be employed when placing the Islamic legal traditions in conversation with their Western counterparts. I believe in engaging with both Muslim and Western traditions as well as with my own ethnic, racial and linguistic identities as the tools of this inter- and intra-cultural conversation. The terms 'Islamic' and 'Western' are employed while bearing in mind that neither is a monolithic concept and that both traditions have a vast range of variations within their folds. I do not set out to 'prove' or 'disprove' any particular narrative, because I believe that where there are multiple narratives each must be heard and respected.

Being positioned at the *dihliz* also signifies awareness of paradox and contradictions, subjectivity and objectivity. Throughout *Modern Challenges*, we are confronted with the paradoxes and contradictions reflected in the theory and practice of Islamic law in various and varying communities, states and governments.[5] Equally challenging when situated at the *dihliz* are the negotiation, contestation and struggle with past and present, with hegemonic and colonial knowledge traditions. Reflexivity is inherent in positioning oneself at the *dihliz*; developing the ability to be self-critical is imperative in understanding the Islamic legal traditions. Moosa sums this up rather well in his use of *dihliz* to analyse Al-Ghazali's work when he observes, 'This attempt to foster a conversation among iterations of different intellectual traditions aims to advance an emancipatory and humane discursive tradition, one to which the Muslim intellectual legacy can make a meaningful contribution'.[6]

On the Terminology in This Book

I am conscious of the variety of meanings ascribed to key terms in this work – 'modernity', 'tradition', 'Islamic law', *sharia*, 'Western' and 'Westernization', to name but a few – and it is appropriate to present my reasons for appearing to privilege these over other comparable terms.

As the ethicist Jeffrey Stout observes, 'No categories require more careful handling these days than *tradition* and *modernity*.'[7] In popular use, these two

---

[5] Saudi Arabia, for instance, described by some as the 'Vatican of Sunni Islam', actively avoided using the term 'Islamic' in describing its banking and financial sector, whereas the British prime minister David Cameron readily declared his aspiration to make Britain a 'hub of Islamic finance'.

[6] Moosa, *Ghazali*, p. 35.

[7] Jeffrey Stout, 'Commitments and Traditions in the Study of Religious Ethics', *Journal of Religious Ethics* 25(3) (1998) 25th Anniversary Supplement, 23–56 at 49, original emphasis.

terms may denote a dichotomous construction of meaning, but it is increasingly recognized that neither term is monolithic. Tradition need not always be opposed to modernity and change and may even facilitate it.[8] I use 'modern' to imply present, current or contemporary,[9] yet with caution, as I am aware of the problem of 'periodizing' time. When, for a start, does the past end and the present begin? There are ruptures and new beginnings, the ebbs and flows of eras, and fragments of continuity that link the past to the present and future. Some aspects of modernity can be found in every past and some traditions in every present. Muslim communities have perceived 'modernity' in different ways, including its relevance to and compatibility with the Islamic traditions; it has been perceived as synonymous with Westernization, hence resistance to the term in some Muslim constituencies.

Why 'Islamic law' rather than '*sharia* law' or 'Muslim law'?[10] Adding 'law' to *sharia* implies that *sharia* constitutes law in the sense of legally enforceable rules akin to black-letter law, so reducing its scope and meaning. But such law is only one of many components of *sharia*, which covers all aspects of human life, and so '*sharia* law', I submit, would be misleading. Further, I consider *sharia* to be the principles of Islamic law,[11] as well as a moral, ethical, normative framework encompassing both the divine texts and human understandings and articulations. 'Muslim law' refers to those aspects of the law that are understood by Muslims to be Islamic; it would arguably include '*urf* – customary practices that do not strictly fall within Islamic law but which some Muslims follow.[12] 'Muslim law' and 'Islamic law' are used interchangeably by some authors,[13] but

---

[8] Muhammad Qasim Zaman, *The Ulama in Contemporary Islam: Custodians of Change* (Princeton: Princeton University Press, 2007), p. 3.

[9] Two interesting and important edited collections on the subject employ the term. See, for instance, Yvonne Yazbeck and Barbara Freyer Stowasser (eds.), *Islamic Law and the Challenges of Modernity* (Walnut Creek: Altamira Press, 2004); Muhammad Khalid Masud, Armando Salvatore and Martin van Bruinessen (eds.), *Islam and Modernity: Key Issues and Debates* (Edinburgh: Edinburgh University Press, 2009).

[10] Or indeed 'Muhammadan law', the description of the Islamic legal traditions as understood by British colonial administrators.

[11] I adopted this position in my monograph Shaheen Sardar Ali, *Gender and Human Rights in Islam and International Law: Equal before Allah, Unequal before Man?* (The Hague: Kluwer, 2000).

[12] For instance, traditional Islamic law prohibits adoption (as the term is understood in Western jurisdictions), yet South Asian Muslim communities have long 'adopted' children, with childless couples skirting around Islamic rules of inheritance to make sure such children were provided for. See Shaheen Sardar Ali, 'A Comparative Perspective of the Convention on the Rights of the Child and the Principles of Islamic Law', in *Protecting the World's Children: Impact of the Convention of the Rights of the Child in Diverse Legal Systems* (Cambridge: Cambridge University Press, 2007), pp. 142–208. Until 1962, customary practices depriving women of their inheritance rights (contrary to Islamic law) prevailed. See M. A. Mannan (ed.), *D. F. Mulla's Principles of Mahomedan Law* (Lahore: PLD Publishers, 1995). At 519, the author states, 'Where custom is given priority by legislation over general Muhammadan Law, a special family or tribal custom of adoption will, if proved, prevail.'

[13] 'Muslim law' and 'Islamic law' have been employed in the title of monographs as well as edited collections, including the following: David Pearl and Werner Menski, *Muslim Family Law*, 3rd

understandings of what constitutes 'Muslim' as opposed to 'Islamic' law is not and cannot be uniform, as Islamic law does not have a static, fixed content, extrapolated as it is from a range of sources by different juristic schools.

And so 'Islamic law' – a term constructed in colonial times – is the one I prefer to employ, conscious, of course, that this too may be understood differently by different people. In *Modern Challenges*, 'Islamic law' encompasses the law's theoretical framework, its sources in the Islamic legal traditions and its interpretative discourse, as well as the legislative enactments of Muslim jurisdictions.[14]

Modern Challenges to Islamic Law: Multiple Narratives from the *Dihliz*

Modern Challenges forms a narrative of my continuous pursuit of understanding the nature and scope of Islamic law and its efficacy and application in the contemporary world. As a Muslim student of law and society,[15] an activist for women's rights and a woman besides, I have grappled with questions arising from over forty years of engagement with Islamic law. There is a rich body of existing literature in English on various aspects of the Islamic traditions, including the social, legal, political, economic and moral, to which I too have made my small contribution. While perspectives vary, many accounts of Islamic law and its interface with society have enhanced our understandings, and critical arguments over theory and practice have been debated and developed. The Islamic legal traditions are neither linear nor monolithic, and, as Asad observes, Islam is a discursive tradition and must be approached as such.[16] *Modern Challenges* likewise adopts a contextual and discursive approach to Islamic law, offering insights into how local understandings transform its scope and application in the daily lives of Muslims in the contemporary world.

edition (London: Sweet and Maxwell, 1998). Ziba Mir-Husseini employs 'Muslim' law as well as 'Islamic' law in, for instance, her celebrated monograph *Marriage on Trial. A Study of Islamic Family Law: Iran and Morocco Compared* (London: I. B. Tauris, 1993); and Ziba Mir-Husseini, Kari Vogt, Lena Larsen and Christian Moe (eds.), *Gender and Equality in Muslim Family Law: Justice and Ethics in the Islamic Legal Tradition* (London: I. B. Tauris, 2013); also Anver M. Emon, *Islamic Natural Law Theories* (Oxford: Oxford University Press, 2010); and Mathias Rohe, *Islamic Law in Past and Present* (trans. Gwendolin Goldbloom) (Leiden: Brill, 2014).

[14] I am aware that this definition too will invite some criticism on the basis that the term 'Islamic law' creates the expectation of a uniform body of regulatory norms in statutory formulation, a position few scholars on the subject would be willing to support. Islamic law must combine jurisprudence (*fiqh* and *usul-ul-fiqh*) *and* law, as one leads to the other. Second, and more importantly, the 'law' in Islamic law should not be understood as the sole authoritative voice of black-letter law as conceptualized in Western legal systems.

[15] I was brought up to believe that one always remains a student – a *taalib-e-ilm* (seeker of knowledge).

[16] Talal Asad, *The Idea of an Anthropology of Islam*, Occasional Papers (Washington, DC: Center for Contemporary Arab Studies, 1986), p. 14; Talal Asad, *Genealogies of Religion: Discipline and Reasons of Power in Christianity and Islam* (Baltimore: Johns Hopkins University Press, 1993), p. 28.

As this narrative will show, very rarely do scholars and jurists agree on a legal outcome or rule as being the 'definitive' Islamic response. Writing a book on Islamic law, then, is a challenging project, not least due to questions of authority and legitimacy of substance, content and context, as well as the sheer diversity of interpretations and understandings of Islam's religious texts. What are Muslims' understandings of what constitutes Islamic law, and from where do these understandings purport to derive their legitimacy? Are legitimacy and authority based upon legal and juristic perspectives from within the Islamic legal traditions, or have Muslim communities developed these understandings based upon their lived experiences? Standing at the *dihliz*, privileged to see and live within more than one Muslim community, it is enlightening to perceive a continued diversity of thought and practice. Looking eastward towards my place of birth and early life, I perceive the robust challenge being mounted by Muslim women for their inheritance rights. They do so on the basis of rights inherent within the Qur'an and Sunna and are not afraid of advancing those claims in a patriarchal society that believes in land as belonging solely to male heirs.[17] Looking westwards, among Muslim communities in Europe and North America, the burning issue for Muslim women is not inheritance but recognition of marital status and the right to divorce.[18]

Likewise, I see contradictions and paradoxes in various aspects of life as led by Muslims. Growing up in the conservative Swat Valley of northwest Pakistan, I often heard a saying that described grandparents' affections: 'children are *asal* [capital]; grandchildren are *sood* [interest]. Needless to say, *sood* is sweeter than *asal!*' At the time it never occurred to me that Islam most unequivocally forbids interest; how, then, could this saying have any meaning? If Muslims were not meant to take or give interest, how did they know it was sweet? Never once did I hear the unacceptability of interest raised.

In my many roles I have confronted many questions. Does Islamic law protect the equal rights of men and women to marry persons of their own choosing? How might it permit polygamy without infringing women's rights? How does it respond to the contemporary issue of child marriages? What is the religious justification for migration to non-Muslim countries? What is the impact on Islamic law of the diversity of legal opinions? Are human rights an integral component of the Islamic legal tradition, and, if so, are they different to those emanating from the West? Such questions are important not only to lay Muslims at a personal level, but also to the study of law and social science, to researchers, and to policy- and law-makers. I contribute to these debates as a student of law and society, provide critical responses where I can, and raise questions that need further investigation. As a contribution to these debates, *Modern Challenges*

---

[17] Interestingly, a similar resistance was not seen when women claimed land as part of their *mahr* (dower). Was it the fact that *mahr* was seen as an undertaking – a word of honour – demanding fulfilment, whereas the male heirs to land considered it their birthright? This selective use of Islam and Islamic law permeates all aspects of life.

[18] See my discussion on *Sharia* Councils and women's right to divorce in Britain in Chapter 7.

relates theory to context and practice and looks at how Islamic legal systems are responding to contemporary issues such as globalization and scientific and technological development. It looks at how, and to what extent, Islamic legal traditions and Muslim communities locally and globally perceive, construct, interpret and respond to these challenges. To give a nuanced understanding of the legal traditions, I present a contextual and personal narrative of how I have lived, practised and reflected upon Islamic law. I have experienced this mainly in my native Pakistan but have continued to do so in Britain and those several other countries and cultures where I have lived and worked.

My own life is a case in point of the complex identities any single Muslim may have in the contemporary world, and of how they impact on their understanding and practising of Islamic law; I have the perspective of an insider who has experienced the interface between its fixed and moving aspects. Though my own story is one of countless valid narratives, it demonstrates the importance of exploring the transformative nature of Islamic law as Muslims experience it.

I was born to a Punjabi mother and Pashtun father and raised in the Pashtun culture of the remote mountains of Pakistan's Swat Valley. My education was in the Roman Catholic Sacred Heart High School, run by the Sisters of Charity of Jesus and Mary, in the Punjabi city of Lahore, followed by the University Degree College for Women and the University of Peshawar,[19] and finally I studied for my LLM and PhD in international law at Hull University in the UK. So I have been negotiating competing layers of religious, cultural and legal normative frameworks since the age of five. This has meant a lifetime of exposure to the plurality of understandings within the Islamic legal traditions that are at play in the lives of citizens of an ostensibly 'Islamic' state which is in reality highly differentiated by ethnicities, languages and cultures; a rural/urban divide; and class distinctions. Simultaneously I have experienced life in the British, Norwegian and North American Muslim diasporas and grappled with Islamic law issues as debated in those various communities. My own life has exemplified this plurality and been witness to considerable change: Lahore, my home during my formative years, is an urban reflection of a rich Punjabi culture that has cut across religion, caste and class. Yet Lahore, home to a number of the saints of Islam's esoteric Sufi tradition, was also the home of the Muslim League and the city where, before Partition, Islam became the slogan and *raison d'être* for the creation of an independent nation.

In my own country, 400 miles from home, from a young age I found myself upon a steep learning curve on Islam and Muslims. As a five-year-old from the Swat Valley and the only Pashtun student at the Sacred Heart convent, Lahore's Punjabi culture and language were almost totally alien to me, despite my being born to a Punjabi mother. Since at the time I had only experienced the Swat Pashtuns' relatively functional practice of Islam, as a young girl my

---

[19] Later renamed the Jinnah College for Women, the University Degree College for Women formed part of the University of Peshawar.

ignorance of what to my Punjabi classmates were well-known festivals and religious practices even led them to suspect my religious affiliation. Coming from a Sunni family, I was surprised by the Lahore Shias' practice of marking the month of *Muharram*[20] by wearing black clothes and participating in religious meetings and rituals.[21] I would ask myself the question, if their Qur'an and their Prophet were the same, then why were the laws based on their texts different?[22] This was a plurality to which I had not been exposed.[23] The day-to-day Islam of the people, be it in Swat or Lahore, was coloured by cultural understandings and not by dogmatic Islam. True, there were those at the extremes – Sunnis who felt the Shias were bordering on being non-Islamic; Shias who felt the Sunnis had been disloyal to the family of the Prophet – but how interesting that at a personal and community level the division that led to parallel histories, laws, politics and more was lived out in such benign co-existence.[24]

Living in Pakistan in the 1970s, I saw a slow change come about in the self-perception of Muslims regarding both the sect (either Sunni or Shia) and the juristic school (i.e. Hanafi, Maliki, Shafi'i, or Hanbali) they followed. In an increasingly globalized world, two events especially lent impetus to this, not simply in Pakistan but the world over. The 1979 Soviet invasion of Afghanistan ushered in a fundamentalist, literalist, Wahabi Islam;[25] the Iranian revolution of

---

[20] The first of the Islamic year, whose first ten days mark the Battle of Karbala where the grandson of the Prophet Muhammad and many of his family were martyred. The schism between Sunni and Shia Muslims was deepened, never to be bridged again.

[21] Such meetings (*majalis*; singular *majlis*) during *Muharram* mostly took place in the *imambargah* – congregation halls or mosques of the Shias, although smaller ones were also organized in private homes. Interestingly, significant numbers of Sunnis too would attend. In Peshawar, I have seen Sunnis make a wish (a *mannat*) on an aspect of their lives that they wanted resolved and give an offering signifying their gratefulness if the *mannat* was fulfilled.

[22] For example, Sunnis require at least two witnesses to a marriage contract, while Shias hold that a marriage conducted without witnesses is still valid. Nevertheless, written marriage contracts duly attested are the norm among Shias. Laws of inheritance differ too: where a Shia father dies without leaving a male heir, the estate is divided among his female heirs; with Sunnis, after giving a portion to the widow and daughters of the deceased, the remainder goes to the nearest male agnate. Shias hold that *zakat* is an act of personal worship and that the state cannot intervene and collect charitable money for distribution; Sunni Islam is ambivalent on this point, but some Sunni governments have collected *zakat*.

[23] As a child I was unaware of the divisions within Sunni Islam into Hanafi, Maliki, Shafi'i and Hanbali.

[24] Swat had no Shias, hence my ignorance that Muslims could be other than what I thought was simply 'Muslim'. That said, *Muharram* was even for us Sunni Pashtuns the month of sombre grieving at the martyrdom of the Prophet's family. I remember how a woman was 'commissioned' by my grandmother to live in our family home for the first ten days of *Muharram* and recite the story of the Battle of Karbala every evening to the ladies of the household.

[25] It was not until the mid-1980s that, as a university lecturer in Peshawar, I first saw a woman fully covered in a black *burqa*, in temperatures of 47 °C (I was familiar only with the traditional Pashtun *chador*, or what we called a 'shuttlecock' *burqa*). Such Arab women had accompanied husbands who were supporting the Afghans in fighting the Soviets. The *burqa* proved contagious and it is now a common sight to see Pashtun and other Pakistani women in this Arab garb: the Arabization of Islam and the undermining of 'cultural' Islam had begun.

the same year did likewise for a militant and radical Shia Islam.[26] The poisonous seeds of intolerance and militancy were sown and an emphasis placed on public ritual in an increasingly antagonistic atmosphere: witness the Sunnis' *Eid Milad-un-Nabi* marking the Prophet's birth, and the Shias' processions marking the martyrdom of Hussain and his household at Karbala.

Returning to Swat after university, I experienced Islamic law as it was lived in the family sphere of millions of other Pashtuns. I had been engaged during childhood to a paternal cousin, and our marriage ceremony reflected how state-legislated Islamic family law is so often sidelined in favour of centuries-old traditions and custom: amongst other things, the Pashtun tradition of conducting the marriage ceremony in the groom's home would have been considered sacrilege by most Muslims.[27] Like everyone else's, our marriage ceremony was conducted orally, and even today, after forty years, we do not have a written document to prove it! Yet the stipulations in that marriage contract were honoured meticulously, and my husband did not rest until he had fulfilled the pledge entered into therein by our grandfather.[28]

Such is the diversity of the experience which forms the foundation of my outlook. It is such multi-layered, plural, complex legalities, both formal and informal, which have enabled me to experience and explore Islam and Islamic law from a highly personal perspective. Throughout decades of academic study of, and personal interaction with, Islamic law, I have been asking questions: what *is* this phenomenon? Whence does it acquire its legitimacy and authority? Who interprets its divine primary and secondary sources? Is its remit strictly and simply to follow a literal interpretation and application of the text, drawing upon seventh-century examples and contexts? Or might we justifiably acknowledge that the rules found in the Qur'an and Sunna are by no means exhaustive or prescriptive, and that it is Islamically legitimate to develop others which are adaptable to changing needs? Is it 'law' in the Western sense of legally enforceable rules, or is it something more, or something less?

The question of Islamic law's compatibility with ever-changing, evolving and interdependent societies is not new. For decades, academics, religious scholars and Muslim (as well as non-Muslim) communities have sought to resolve the tensions between sources perceived as immutable and their application to changing times and places. I have consistently argued – as have others – that the Islamic legal tradition is not a monolithic entity; hence my conscious

---

[26] Prior to the Iranian revolution, one was unable to distinguish between a Sunni scholar (*alim*) and a Shia. The revolution ushered in a new 'dress code' for Shia clergy, who took to the headgear and robes worn by their Iranian counterparts.

[27] Pakistan's Muslim Family Laws Ordinance 1961 had not been extended to Swat, and customary laws, informed by principles of Islamic family law, prevailed.

[28] In Pashtun communities at the time, it was representatives of the bride and groom who took the vows on their behalf: the groom was not expected to be present at his own marriage! The only time our oral tradition caused us anguish was at the British Embassy in Brussels when applying for visas; the immigration officer asked for proof of marriage and would not believe us when we said our marriage had been conducted orally.

adoption of the phrase 'Islamic legal traditions'.[29] The principles of Islamic law and *sharia* are inherently dynamic, sensitive and susceptible to changing needs. *Modern Challenges* advances this argument by demonstrating Islamic law as an evolutionary, dynamic, responsive and multidimensional phenomenon capable of generating responses from within its varied and rich traditions, highlighting its plurality and its inbuilt transformative processes.

Contemporary demands by Muslims for 'Islamic' responses to social and scientific developments increasingly involve returning to the original sources of law to ascertain whether a given practice is legitimate or runs counter to understandings of Islam. As for many years the only woman legal academic at Peshawar University Law School, I would often be approached by women (and sometimes men) asking for 'Islamic legal advice' on contemporary questions: did scientific methods of ascertaining pregnancy have implications for *iddat*, the minimum 'waiting period' for women between marriages? What were the possible contemporary responses to the calculation of minimum and maximum gestation periods and paternity in the Islamic legal traditions? Engagement with Islamic law was for me more than an academic post, with implications for the lives and relationships of those who turned to me for possible solutions.

Many claim to be, as Dr El Fadl so aptly describes it, *Speaking in God's Name*.[30] There are ultimately as many expressions of Islam as there are Muslims. Each school of thought claims authenticity over competing interpretations, and no individual scholar can claim a definitive view on Islamic law encompassing all possible perspectives. What I therefore aim to do in *Modern Challenges* is offer my personal and academic insights into the subject as I have experienced it; as I have read, researched, taught and applied it in my political activism. Like all Muslims, I believe in the Qur'an as the word of Allah revealed to the Prophet Muhammad. As a Muslim academic I also believe in questioning and challenging certain formulations of Islamic law, and it is this belief which informs the discussion and analysis in this book. The accounts that I have chosen by way of developing this personal narrative through an academic lens are helpful in determining the contours of evolving legal traditions.

In choosing the subject matter of the various chapters, I have been guided by my personal and professional experiences but also attempted to cover varying aspects of Islamic law. Conscious that a single monograph could not encapsulate the entire range of themes within the Islamic legal traditions, I have taken the liberty of limiting *Modern Challenges* to subjects with which I have been closely involved. In other words, this is an attempt to give a scholarly account of some modern challenges from the point of view of a scholar fortified by the inside knowledge of one who has had the privilege of a wide range of practical experience. For instance, rather than exploring the various sources

[29] Ali, *Gender and Human Rights*, p. 3.
[30] Khalid Abou El Fadl, *Speaking in God's Name: Islamic Law, Authority and Women* (Oxford: One World, 2001).

of Islamic law as a departure point for *Modern Challenges*, I present my own personal conceptualization employing the metaphor of the flowing stream to denote *sharia*. Likewise, my (brief) time as Cabinet minister brought home the importance of exploring (Islamic) constitutionalism(s) as a critical aspect of state and government in Muslim jurisdictions – in terms of both presence and absence. I then provide a case study of law reform in post-colonial Muslim jurisdictions to highlight the dynamics between Muslim attempts at constitutionalism and law reform. The subject of Islamic finance was included in *Modern Challenges* in view of the critical role of finance and banking in the lives of Muslims and non-Muslims alike and of interest to the wider world. My personal interest led me to explore the social justice and welfare arm of Islamic finance, focusing on *zakat*. I then move to areas of women's rights and human rights and chose CEDAW as the focus of Chapters 5 and 6. I wanted to bring into the public domain the processes of treaty-making in national and international institutions and the role of religion within these processes through archival research, as well as my own personal involvement in Pakistan's accession to CEDAW. Chapter 5 is an example of how Muslim women navigate the 'in-between' spaces of the various *dihliz* they find themselves in – women, Muslim and representatives of their governments within an international environment. Chapter 7, exploring the role and rationale of *Sharia* Councils in Britain, is singled out in view of my own status as a British Muslim of Pakistani origin and (potentially) affected by informal dispute-resolution forums in the British diaspora. Finally, Chapter 8, interrogating Internet *fatawa*, represents an important and contemporary modern challenge to traditional articulations of Islamic law. As a Muslim woman, the subject matter of these *fatawa* on women and gender are of huge significance to how I engage with the Islamic legal traditions in an increasingly globalized environment. Conversely, these discussions impact on how Muslim women are perceived more broadly within family and society; hence my reason for choosing this as one of the chapters for *Modern Challenges*.

The novelty of this book is that it speaks to a wide range of themes in a single authorial voice and tries to link theory to practice. A brief overview of the various chapters will provide a flavour.

A discussion on Islamic law will always have *sharia* as its focus. As the opening chapter in *Modern Challenges*, the 'flowing stream' conceptualizes *sharia* as currents of dynamic, responsive, renewable, flowing water – the currents representing its various components. Bearing in mind that *sharia* has fourteen centuries of history behind it, it is not the intention here to engage in a straight historical account. This chapter is not about Islamic *fiqh* (jurisprudence). Instead, the insights presented here are meant as signposts to how *sharia* is understood and employed by Muslim states and governments, and in the lived realities of Muslims at an individual and collective level. Chapter 1 thus highlights the discursive nature of the *sharia*, evolving and resilient in the face of challenges and questions posed to it by tradition and modernity.

Chapter 2 explores whether constitutional developments in Muslim-majority jurisdictions point to the presence of an 'Islamic constitutionalism'; applies historical notions of Islamic constitutionalism to contemporary challenges; and looks at how the rise of the nation state, colonialism and globalization have forced the normative framework of the polity to evolve and emerge in ways not envisaged by thinkers of the classical period of Islamic law. As in most areas of the Islamic legal traditions, opinion on Islamic constitutionalism is far from unanimous, with wide gaps between rhetoric and reality. Most legal scholars agree that 'constitutional law (*usul-al-hukm*) is one of the most underdeveloped areas of Islamic law and jurisprudence'.[31] The Qur'an and Sunna provide elements on which the structure of constitutionalism might be built, including *shura* (consultation), *bay'ah* (allegiance), principles of justice and the accountability of rulers. The Medina Charter is cited in support of the historical beginnings of an Islamic constitutionalism. Some writers on Islamic law and politics, including Maududi, initiate their discussions on the assumption that there is no separation between religion (*din*) and state (*dawla*). My own journey through the public sphere, though, has taught me that narratives of the inseparability of religion and state are not fully reflective of the lived experiences of Muslims in many parts of the world: there are a myriad subtle linkages and connections, overlaps and disjunctures. A selective use of Islam and Islamic law is evident in virtually all spheres of life in Muslim countries, but nowhere is this selectivity more pronounced than in the arena of state and politics, constitutionalism and governance.

The place of Islam and law in the public and private lives of Muslim communities and states has been the subject of study in both Western and non-Western academia, and my choice of the subject is not novel. What *is* novel is my insider's perspective on the issues arising not only from the 'ought' but also the 'is' of politics and law. As a Cabinet minister in the Islamic Republic of Pakistan, I was advised in confidence by a civil servant to keep religion and politics separate.[32] Sitting at the seat of governance, I never heard anyone mention or even allude to the Islamic obligations of those in power: injunctions in the Islamic traditions regarding the accountability of those in positions of authority remained confined to textbooks. Whereas in Islam rulers were responsible for the welfare of everyone within the jurisdiction, this was an obligation that was dispensed with by most.

---

[31] Muhammad Hashim Kamali, 'Constitutionalism in Islamic Countries: A Contemporary Perspective of Islamic Law', in Rainer Grote and Tilmann Röder (eds.), *Constitutionalism in Islamic Countries: Between Upheaval and Continuity* (Oxford: Oxford University Press, 2012), p. 19.

[32] This advice was tendered after I had wondered aloud why, despite their regular prayers and fasting, our personnel shirked work and sometimes risked lives by their indifference to official obligations. They clearly did not see the connection between being good Muslims and being conscientious civil servants.

Chapter 3 proceeds to investigate a further example of colonial influence on Islamic law by contextualizing family law reforms in the Muslim world. It is an example of the journey of Islamic family law and the transformative impact of colonization on it. Initially the result of colonial authorities trying to make sense of a fluid, plural Islamic law by legislating some aspects as 'Anglo-Muhammadan law', family law reform soon became an indigenous Muslim demand. The subject represents a fascinating example of the ongoing contestations between contemporary notions of justice, equality and human rights on the one hand and established understandings of Islamic jurisprudence (*fiqh*) on the other. Two contesting environments and understandings of law reform are in evidence: on the one hand, there are a host of laws that are a result of 'woman-friendly reform'. These include attempts at 'neutralizing' some of the unfettered male power within the institutions of marriage and divorce without displacing or challenging what are perceived as immutable religious texts. Simultaneously however, where 'Islamist' parties or individuals have come into power in post-colonial states (for instance Nimeiri in Sudan, Imam Khomeini in Iran and Zia-ul-Haq in Pakistan), they engaged in law reform based on different readings of those same texts, leading to changes in the law adversely affecting women in these jurisdictions.

Chapter 3 examines the genealogy of the terms 'Muhammadan law' and 'Islamic law' as colonial constructs that were limited to just one version of Islamic family law. Whilst generally woman-friendly, the general premise underlying Islamic family law is that society consists of male-headed households where men hold authority and provide and protect vulnerable, weak and dependent females who are in their charge. In other words, family law reform implicitly assumes the supremacy of a *wilaya–qiwama* ('guardian–provider') nexus; that is to say, a connection between men's authority over women and their obligation to protect and maintain them. The main dynamic of law reform is the challenge mounted to this nexus by some societal constituencies. 'Complementarity' rather than 'equality' informs measures for law reform, in the belief that distinctions between the positions of men and women (regarding, for example, polygamy, inheritance rights and wardship) are defined by the Qur'an and Sunna and are therefore unquestionable. Although diversity in interpretations of the primary sources allows for woman-friendly juristic opinions, the opposite trend also continues, particularly at the societal level.

A distinctive feature of family law reform in Pakistan is its embeddedness within the common law colonial legacy of 'Anglo-Muhammadan' as well as Islamic law. Courts today continue to rely heavily on collections of law compiled during colonial times, minimally modified through statute and case law. Whilst both statute law and court judgments are informed by Islamic law, they do not always reinforce one another, resulting in less coherence and continuity than is desirable.

This chapter contextualizes family law reform within the plural legalities operating in post-colonial Pakistan. In the zealously guarded domain of the

'Muslim' family, law reform is an almost imperceptible process filtering through a maze of cultural norms and prevailing political compulsions. The result has been half-hearted, piecemeal and incoherent reform in a top-down legislative process with minimal impact and implementation on the ground.

In a similar vein, Chapter 4 on Islamic finance highlights that Islamic law in its colonial and post-colonial variants is a modern phenomenon. The inevitable outcome of historical, socio-economic and political processes, Islamic law as generally experienced today exemplifies continuities, discontinuities and ruptures. Modernity, globalization and the nation state increasingly interact with tradition, religion, diverse cultures and legal orders both official and unofficial, resulting in synthetic phenomena such as modern Islamic finance and banking.

In the popular consciousness, Islamic finance is equated with the prohibition of usury, speculative risk and games of chance. In theory, engaging in religiously permissible, non-exploitative, equitable and ethical activities forms the cornerstone of Islamic finance; in practice, for centuries the reality has been otherwise and the vast majority of the Muslim world has engaged with conventional, interest-based regimes in one form or another.

Both institutionally and on an intellectual level, knowledge and evolution of Islamic finance long remained stagnant, and only in the twentieth century was this aspect of the legal traditions revived. From the 1970s, modern Islamic finance set out with a desire for the re-Islamization of finance as a reactive strategy to Western colonial domination. Purporting to offer an alternative to conventional financial regimes, Islamic norms were reinterpreted and a strictly formal approach adopted (partly by employing legal fictions), adhering closely to the wording of traditional interpretations. Both strategies remain contested, and they form the focus of analysis in a chapter which offers a contextual perspective on the complexity, diversity and interpretative plurality of Islamic finance. On the one hand, Islamic finance is attempting to legitimize itself to a Muslim constituency; on the other it seeks to convince the wider world of a viable alternative to conventional regimes.

Chapters 5 and 6 are inspired and informed by my experiences as a member of the human rights and women's rights movements in Pakistan. They focus on the drafting and ratification processes of the UN Convention on the Elimination of All Forms of Discrimination against Women (CEDAW), drawing on opportunities that arose to represent Pakistan at human rights conferences and events (as a member of the Prime Minister's National Consultative Committee I advised the government of Pakistan on ratification).[33] CEDAW was ratified by 188 states, but it attracted the largest number of reservations of any UN convention. Amongst states entering reservations, some Muslim states

---

[33] This treaty, adopted by the UN in 1979, has been hailed as an 'international bill of women's rights'. As part of my lobbying, I wrote *A Comparative Study of the United Nations Convention on the Elimination of all Forms of Discrimination against Women: Islamic Law and Laws of Pakistan* (Peshawar: Shaheen, 1995).

specifically mentioned Islam and Islamic law, whilst others did not invoke religious grounds. Other Muslim states ratified without entering any reservations at all, or entered reservations regarding Article 29 alone, whilst Iran and Somalia have neither signed nor ratified. In keeping with the interpretative plurality of the Islamic legal traditions, there is little uniformity in the positions adopted by Muslim states towards CEDAW.

The literature on CEDAW in relation to Muslim states focuses almost entirely on their reservations. There is sparse critical engagement with the drafting processes and interventions by representatives of Muslim states, and little is mentioned of the role played by Muslim delegates towards including a developmental perspective on women's human rights in collaboration with other states from the developing South. From the summary records of drafting sessions, I analysed the inputs of Muslim women. The variety of positions adopted, invoking multiple identities and an autonomous approach towards women's rights, are fascinating. As is persistently argued in *Modern Challenges*, Islamic law is seen, understood and practised through the lens of particular cultural traditions and is not always the same as that prescribed in juristic articulations or governmental manifestations. Chapter 5 thus contributes to the CEDAW literature by linking the inputs of Muslim delegates during the drafting process to the subsequent reservations entered by their governments. More specifically, it brings to the fore the active contribution of Muslim women who went beyond their assigned roles to advance women's rights. These delegates were present as active participants; skilful navigators of the religious, cultural, social and political; and able to negotiate North–South and East–West divisions. Unlike stereotypical images of Muslim women as oppressed and voiceless, they played a remarkable role as part of a multi-layered process of diplomacy, alliance-making and consensus-building.

Once ratified, how did CEDAW fare on the domestic front? As a member of the women's and human rights movement I had personally campaigned for its ratification in seminars and workshops; as a member of the Senate Commission of Inquiry for Women,[34] and the Prime Minister's National Consultative Committee, I was privy to discussions leading to the Cabinet's decision to ratify. After its ratification I was Cabinet minister for health, population, and women's development in the government of the North-West Frontier Province,[35] and was the first chair of the National Commission on the Status of Women. I have also had discussions and personal communications with members of the Pakistani NGO community, in particular those involved in the 2007 CEDAW Committee where Pakistan's Country Reports were being looked at.

Chapter 6, then, proceeds from an insider's perspective to investigate the extent to which CEDAW finds a place in policy documents, legislation, judicial

---

[34] Leading to the Commission's 1997 Report of the Commission of Inquiry for Women in Pakistan.

[35] Now the Khyber Pukhtunkhwa.

decisions, governance structures and institutions in Pakistan. It asks whether CEDAW's pre- and post-ratification processes and attendant discourse have 'domesticated' it within state, government and society. Have constituencies taken ownership of the treaty and contextualized it within indigenous frameworks? Did the government of Pakistan accede to CEDAW just to 'look good', or did it believe in such formulations of women's rights? Are there indications that CEDAW has found a place within the wider population? In a country where pluralism is deeply embedded in legal culture as well as in religious and cultural norms, human rights instruments in general and CEDAW in particular have received an ambivalent and mixed reception as the newest layer of plural legalities.

A major turning point in my life came when I migrated to a non-Muslim jurisdiction, put down roots, and made Britain my home. For twenty years now I have witnessed the role of a Muslim diaspora within a changing Islamic legal tradition. Building on earlier work,[36] Chapter 7 deals with the role of the diaspora in an evolving Islamic law in a non-Muslim context, outlining some of the evolutionary aspects primarily linked to the presence of diaspora communities in non-Muslim countries.

The first of three themes looks at how the concept of *hijra* ('migration') linked to persecution has been reformulated as a search for economic prosperity, and how economic migration is justified in religious terms despite the fact that it goes against the classical bipartite division of the world into 'the abode of Islam' (*dar-al-Islam*) and 'the abode of war' (*dar-al-harb*). But this divide is itself derivative of state practices in the classical Islamic period, is evolutionary in nature, and is not categorically prescribed by the Qur'an. The current trend of economic migration and its subsequent religious rationalization sufficiently evidence the evolutionary nature of understanding of such dictates.

A further illustration of the evolutionary dimension of Islamic law is the novel phenomenon of *fiqh al-aqalliyat*, or 'Muslim minority jurisprudence', which deals with the specific issues faced by Muslims living in non-Muslim countries. Critics of *fiqh al-aqalliyat* argue that this development makes rules that were permissible as exceptions into general rules of application – essentially a change in God's law. While it is true that *fiqh al-aqalliyat* is to some extent stretching jurisprudential boundaries, at the same time such pragmatism provides Muslims with opportunities to live in overwhelmingly non-Muslim countries while observing religious dictates, allowing them to put down roots in host societies.

As time has gone on, Muslim diasporas have started to establish their own judicial mechanisms. These are provided with functioning space by the host

---

[36] Shaheen Sardar Ali, 'Religious Pluralism, Human Rights and Citizenship in Europe', in M. L. P. Leonon and J. E. Goldschmidt (eds.), *Religious Pluralism and Human Rights in Europe* (Antwerp: Intersentia, 2007); 'Authority and Authenticity: Sharia Councils, Muslim Women's Rights and the English Courts', *Child and Family Law Quarterly* 25(2) (2013), 113–37; 'From Muslim Migrants to Muslim Citizens: Islamic Law and Muslims in a Multi-faith Britain', in R. Griffiths-Jones (ed.), *Islam in English Law: Rights and Responsibilities and the Role of Shari'a* (Cambridge: Cambridge University Press, 2012), pp. 157–75.

states, though often not without debate. While there are critics of this development, my main contention is that it demonstrates how Islamic law evolves as the diaspora responds to its immediate needs. But this evolution is not predetermined to have a positive impact: while diaspora Muslims can feel welcomed by host societies' allowing them space to administer their own affairs according to their religious precepts, quasi-judicial institutions can support worryingly isolationist tendencies. In the UK, *Sharia* Councils have been criticized for violating women's rights, and in the present political climate they are expected to be the subject of close governmental scrutiny.

Islamic law and the Muslim diaspora represent one of the most challenging areas of engagement in my endeavour to discover how Islam manifests itself in a non-Muslim environment. Never before has the migration of people ascribing to one single religion caused such anxiety, tension and concern. From the perspective of host communities, there is a lack of integration. Opinions are voiced that 'Muslim culture' subscribes to oppressive practices, and that Muslim countries implement laws of apostasy, are sympathetic to armed struggle (often considered synonymous with *jihad*), and challenge Western concepts of human rights. Muslim communities in Europe are also said to endorse parallel, informal structures in the area of family law. Yet diaspora communities often feel they are living in a culturally, linguistically and religiously alien environment where local influences are undermining their Islamic identity and social fabric: witness objections to sex education, pre-marital sex and 'Western' notions of gender equality. A wave of regulations on Muslim dress and a lack of recognition for Islamic law are held up as examples of disregard for Muslims. This, then, is the background to Chapter 7, which advances the argument that, despite their apparently irresolvable nature, all of these issues are susceptible to resolution. Neither the Islamic tradition nor the traditions of host communities preclude dialogue and negotiation, but the framework must be undertaken in an ethos of egalitarianism. A methodology for resolving issues must be skilfully crafted through the interaction of plural norms rooted in the indigenous normative systems of both host and Muslim communities. This chapter assesses and evaluates Muslim dispute-resolution forums and mechanisms such as *Sharia* Councils, Muslim Arbitration Tribunals, and the European Council of Fatwa and Research, against the backdrop of the emerging discourse on *fiqh al-aqalliyat* jurisprudence as a possible integrationist strategy for European Muslims. I focus on the role and rationale of *Sharia* Councils, considering their authority and authenticity from an Islamic jurisprudential perspective. These councils have been established on the premise that they are manifestations of the diaspora's need for forums adjudicating on Islamic law. In practice, however, 95 per cent of their caseload is women seeking divorce, predominantly women in unregistered *nikah* marriages who have no recourse to the courts to dissolve their union since their marriage was never valid under English law. But since Islamic laws are susceptible to interpretative plurality, who determines what constitutes an 'authentic' Islamic legal requirement in the absence of an identifiable authority? Critical questions in this chapter contribute to contemporary debates on the limits of liberal multiculturalism in Britain.[37] I argue that acceding to demands for diverse religious and cultural traditions is a slippery slope, since the ingredients of accommodation are contested, undefined and boundary-less. From a feminist perspective, the multiculturalist agenda is dominated by those in positions of authority within traditions which have historically excluded women. Who speaks for whom, and who defines culture, religion and tradition, are all questions of power play and domination. The very existence of *Sharia* Councils, and lack of Islamic alternatives,[38] pressurizes women to use such forums to obtain acceptance from their families and communities.

On a visit to the US in 2009, some young Muslim women introduced me to the 'Internet *muftis*' who had become the first port of call for their questions and clarifications regarding Islamic family law and women's rights and obligations. A random survey of such websites brought up a phenomenal list of questions and answers, and I was fascinated by the idea of casting the *fatwa*, a centuries-old method of legal interpretation, in a new mould for young diaspora Muslims. In Chapter 7 I approach the relatively well-trodden subject of Islamic family law in a novel way, through the eyes of contemporary *fatwa*-seekers who pose questions regarding issues deeply entrenched in classical understandings but with significant implications for contemporary society.

One of the main arguments advanced in *Modern Challenges* is the inherent dynamism of the Islamic legal traditions and their responsiveness to social realities through various juristic techniques and mechanisms. Historically, one such has been *fatawa* – non-binding responses on specific issues, flexible vehicles of legal interpretation, reflecting evolving norms in language comprehensible to lay Muslims. *Ifta* (the act of issuing *fatawa*) has undergone significant transformation in the Internet age whilst retaining its core function, and this institution as an interpretative and pedagogical tool and a virtual, discursive space is an ever-expanding field for investigation. Chapter 8 therefore looks at the idea that, in employing a combination of traditional *ifta* tools and the virtual environment of the World Wide Web, Internet *fatawa* simultaneously challenge tradition and modernity: tradition is being challenged by a fragmentation of authority and a democratizing of knowledge; modernity is being challenged in the way Internet *fatawa* are legitimating and reviving historical

---

[37] There is a rich and ever-growing body of literature on multiculturalism. Some of the work upon which this chapter draws includes W. Kymlicka, *Multicultural Citizenship: A Liberal Theory of Minority Rights* (Oxford: Clarendon Press, 1995); B. Parekh, *Rethinking Multiculturalism: Cultural Diversity and Political Theory* (Cambridge, MA: Harvard University Press, 2002); A. Shachar, *Multicultural Jurisdictions: Cultural Differences and Women's Rights* (Cambridge: Cambridge University Press, 2005); A. Phillips, *Multiculturalism without Culture* (Princeton: Princeton University Press, 2007); T. Modood, A. Triandafyllidou and R. Zapata-Barrero (eds.), *Multiculturalism, Muslims and Citizenship* (Oxford: Routledge, 2006); T. Modood, *Multiculturalism* (Themes for the 21st Century Series) (Cambridge: Polity Press, 2007).

[38] For instance, inserting a *talaq-i-tafwid* clause in a marriage contract, giving the wife the right to divorce.

formulations of legal interpretations. Drawing upon a selection of Internet *fatawa* on women, gender and family law norms, this chapter concludes that they have led to a dislocation of traditional forms of legal authority and are enabling and empowering women to decide for themselves how to act (even if they are not necessarily being liberated from patriarchal interpretations of law).

As Muslims seek online answers from within the legal traditions, Internet *fatawa* are proving to be a modern manifestation of the ever-present tension between 'doctrinal' law from above and 'living' law from below. Increasing access to the Internet is challenging the historical conception that only states and governments are the legitimate arbiters of legal disputes, and that the traditional sources of interpretative authority – the local *aalim* or the *imam* of the neighbourhood mosque – are the only repositories of Islamic law. *Modern Challenges* is reflective of the numerous challenges, complex diversities and irrepressible pluralities that any student of the Islamic legal traditions grapples with and seeks answers for. Its distinctiveness lies in its engagement with Islamic law as understood and applied by Muslim communities – individually, collectively and at the levels of state and government. By examining contemporary global and local aspects of law otherwise approached as discrete disciplines by academic authors, *Modern Challenges* is, I believe, distinctly different from other approaches. I have very much relished the opportunity which writing this book has given me to look at fresh sources in English, Arabic and Urdu (three of the languages through which I have personally experienced Islamic law) and to reflect on decades of interactions with Islam at all levels of my professional and home life. I hope that readers will find it equally interesting and challenging.

1

Sharia: The Flowing Stream

1.1 Introduction

The focus of any discussion on the Islamic legal traditions within Muslim communities is *sharia*.[1] The very word evokes radically different responses from different constituencies: while the vast majority of Muslims perceive it as a path of guidance, some Muslims, and the popular Western media, ascribe to it mostly negative meanings, often confining it to the field of criminal justice, the use of brutal punishments and the oppression of women.[2] At an ideological level, some consider its application a panacea for all the ills befalling Muslims, whereas others regard it as the main obstacle to progress.[3] As to its scope, it is believed by some to be the equivalent of 'Islamic law', and by others to be an all-encompassing framework for how Muslims ought to lead their lives, extending well beyond the legal realm. One of the main questions that arise from this, then, is what precisely do those various protagonists understand by *sharia*?[4] Bearing in mind that *sharia* has fourteen centuries of history behind it, it is not my intention here to engage in a straight historical account.[5] I am

---

[1] *Sharia* also forms part of the debate as to how the non-Muslim public, courts, policy-makers and legislators comprehend Islam and Islamic law: see, for example, the negative, reductive and simplistic perception regarding *sharia* in the 2001 ECtHR case of *Refah Partisi (The Welfare Party) and Others v. Turkey* (41340/98, 41342/98, and 41344/98), para 70.

[2] As Mathias Rohe observes regarding the views of some, '*sharia* stands only for harsh penal sanctions, for unequal treatment of sexes and religions, and for a non-democratic organization of the state under the rule of Islam.' '*Sharia* and the Muslim Diaspora', in R. Peters and P. Bearman (eds.), *The Ashgate Research Companion to Islamic Law* (Farnham: Ashgate, 2014), p. 261.

[3] J. S. Nielsen, '*Sharia* between Renewal and Tradition', in J. S. Nielsen and L. Christoffersen (eds.), *Sharia as Discourse: Legal Traditions and the Encounter with Europe* (Farnham: Ashgate, 2010), p. 1.

[4] Yvonne Y. Haddad and Barbara F. Stowasser, 'Islamic Law and the Challenge of Modernity', in Haddad and Stowasser (eds.), *Islamic Law and the Challenges of Modernity* (Walnut Creek: Altamira Press, 2004), p. 4; Nielsen, '*Sharia* between Renewal and Tradition'.

[5] There exists a wide range of English-language scholarship tracing the origins of *sharia*. All scholars, both Muslim and non-Muslim, agree that *sharia* developed during the first few centuries of Islam. Thereafter, considerable diversity of viewpoints is evident, especially regarding the process of development, influences impacting on *sharia*, and so on. See K. Vikor, 'Origins of the Sharia', in Peters and Bearman, *The Ashgate Research Companion to Islamic Law*, p. 14.

aware of the jurisprudential complexities arising from multiple interpretations of the Qur'an and Sunna, from the origins and development of the various schools of juristic thought in Islam, and their bearing on *sharia*. This chapter is not about Islamic *fiqh* (jurisprudence). Instead, the insights presented here are meant as signposts to how *sharia* is understood and employed by Muslim states and governments, and in the lived realities of Muslims at an individual and collective level.

Divine injunctions and human endeavours have together created an evolving set of regulatory norms for all aspects of Muslim life. Themes such as pluralism, tradition, modernity, contestation over authority and authenticity, fragmentation of authority, and globalization have informed this evolution and underlie the various chapters of *Modern Challenges*. Each demonstrates aspects of the discursive nature of the *sharia*, evolving and resilient in the face of challenges and questions posed to it by tradition and modernity. What, for instance, are the mechanisms applied to understanding the *sharia*? Has the *sharia* undergone a reductive process whereby its moral and ethical dimension has been sidelined and legal elements placed centre stage, or vice versa? How have tradition and modernity impacted on *sharia*? Is it possible to create authority and legitimacy for *sharia* within a plural Islamic tradition, and, if so, who is authorized to do so? How does *sharia* operate in a globalized world? Can (and should) there be a formal authority or institution to interpret and implement *sharia*?[6] Is it even feasible? Such questions will be touched upon throughout *Modern Challenges*.

This present chapter portrays *sharia* not as a static entity but as a stream, forever flowing onward, its currents intertwining, giving rise to legally enforceable rules, principles of morality and principles of governance and social justice. New currents – technologies, globalization, the nation state, Muslim diasporas . . . – have only recently entered the stream to become part of its ever-moving waters; long-established currents such as *ifta* (the issuing of a *fatwa*) have been refigured with the advent of the Internet, radio and television *fatawa* and the judgments of Islamic finance advisory boards. Yet the absence of a central authority capable of granting 'Islamic legitimacy' has led to a fragmentation of authority and a clash of currents in the flowing stream – we might think of these as patches of rough water. A state's legislation might clash with its judicial institutions in declaring certain laws Islamic or otherwise. The latest current to enter the flowing stream is that of lay Muslim populations, who, with increasing access to 'Islamic' knowledge, are raising questions and challenging certain formulations of Islamic law and *sharia*. Other recent currents – the rise of the modern nation state and its appropriation of legislative power, colonialism and globalization – have irrevocably transformed the *sharia*. Exemplifying

---

[6] I recall here the position adopted by A. A. An-Na'im, who believes that the *sharia* cannot and ought not to be implemented by the state and must be left to the personal choice of Muslims (*Islam and the Secular State: Negotiating the Future of Sharia* (Cambridge, MA: Harvard University Press, 2008)).

Islam's inherent pluralism, the currents of *sharia* lie behind the contestation and negotiation we see at various historical junctures. Forever overcoming these challenges, *sharia* continues to sustain, manifest, transform and even challenge itself within a globalized world. Each generation of Muslims continues to contribute to a dynamic ebb and flow that oscillates between multiple traditions and modernities.

1.2 *Sharia, Fiqh,* and Islamic Law

> Then We put you, [O Muhammad], on an ordained way concerning the matter [of religion]; so follow it and do not follow the inclinations of those who do not know.   Qur'an 45:18

The core concepts or constructs in the study of Islamic law are *sharia* and *fiqh*. Let us take *sharia* first. Its centrality to the Islamic legal traditions and – due to its contested nature – its broader implications for how Muslims lead their lives cannot be overstated. The Qur'an describes *sharia* as the 'ordained way', asking the Prophet Muhammad to follow it. In popular understandings, as well as in the opinion of some scholars on the subject, *sharia* and Islamic law are considered synonymous – a definition unduly limiting and limited.[7] Some believe it to be a 'well-defined, wholesome entity' that has been pushed to the back burner, waiting to be nudged back as a discrete legal code.[8] Such simplistic perceptions of *sharia* ascribe to it the legendary and vaguely panacea-like aura of a divinely sanctioned code. It has stimulated some Muslims to demand the introduction of *sharia* as formal law in Muslim jurisdictions – not recognizing that *sharia* is not a code of law in the modern sense.[9] The scope of *sharia* has also been broadened to include all human actions – legal, social, political, economic and moral – as the product of history constructed over centuries by Muslim jurists.

My personal position, to be distinguished from other writers on the subject, is to see *sharia* as the overarching umbrella of rules, regulations, values and normative frameworks, covering all aspects and spheres of life for Muslims, as developed over time. It comprises elements informed by the religious texts of Islam as well as human interpretations by generations of Muslim jurists and scholars. *Sharia* therefore denotes the principles of Islamic law, rather than the

---

[7] See Rohe, *Islamic Law in Past and Present*, p. 10. Hallaq also refers to 'Islamic law' as '*sharia*': W. Hallaq, *An Introduction to Islamic Law* (Cambridge: Cambridge University Press, 2009), p. 1; the opening line of M. Masud, B. Messick and D. Powers, 'Muftis, Fatwas, and Islamic Legal Interpretation', in M. Masud, B. Messick and D. Powers (eds.), *Islamic Legal Interpretation: Muftis and Their Fatwas* (Karachi: Oxford University Press, 2005), p. 3, states, 'of the *shari'a*, or Islamic law'.

[8] Hallaq critiques those who believe in this description of *sharia*: W. Hallaq, 'Can the *Sharia* Be Restored?', in Haddad and Stowasser, *Islamic Law*, p. 21.

[9] The Nizam-i-Mustafa movement against Pakistan's first elected prime minister Zulfiqar Ali Bhutto demanded the introduction of a social system where *sharia* was the supreme law of the land.

law per se. *Sharia* encapsulates the rules of rituals and worship (*ibadaat*) and of social relations (*muamalat*). Not all of *sharia* is legally enforceable in a court of law; some remains in the moral/ethical domain, and our human understandings of its requirements and our actions in relation to these are to be judged in the hereafter.

The *sharia* certainly has a strong religious foundational basis, as reflected in the viewpoint of a number of scholars. Rahman notes,

> At the very root of the Muslim conception of law lies the idea that law is inherently and essentially religious. That is why, from the beginning of Islamic history, law has been regarded as flowing from or being part of the concept of *sharia* (the divinely ordained pattern of human conduct).[10]

Kamali too reiterates the divine and religious nature of *sharia*: 'Notwithstanding the fact that human reason has always played an important role in the development of Shariah . . . the Shariah itself is primarily founded on divine revelations.'[11] In Hamoudi's view, *sharia* refers to 'the corpus of extensive, overlapping and oft conflicting rules developed by Muslim jurists, medieval and modern, from Islam's sacred foundational texts, the Qur'an, as revealed word of God, and the Hadith, or statements, utterances, and actions of the Prophet Muhammad'.[12] An-Naim, on the other hand, is of the view that *sharia*

> refers to the general normative system of Islam as historically understood and developed by Muslim jurists, especially during the first three centuries of Islam – the eighth to tenth centuries CE. In this commonly used sense, *sharia* includes a much broader set of principles and norms than legal subject matter as such.[13]

Rahman, Kamali and Hamoudi, then, flag up the divine and religiously ordained origins and nature of the *sharia*, whereas An-Naim's emphasis lies in the role of Muslim jurists in constructing it. All are in agreement, though, that *sharia* is not simply law but an overarching set of principles and rules governing human conduct, some of which is recommendatory, an act of worship or a moral principle. Whilst all actions are, from a religious point of view, injunctions to be carried out for fear of God, not all of them are legally enforceable or mandatory, in the sense that a court of law will not sentence one for their omission.

Etymologically, the term *sharia* can be understood to mean 'the path to be followed to reach a watering place in the desert' – the path to a flowing

---

[10]   Fazlur Rahman, *Islam*, 2nd edition (Chicago: The University of Chicago Press, 1979), p. 68.
[11]   M. H. Kamali, *Principles of Islamic Jurisprudence*, 3rd edition (Cambridge: Islamic Texts Society, 2003), p. xix.
[12]   H. A. Hamoudi, 'The Impossible, Highly Desired Islamic Bank', *William & Mary Business Law Review* 5 (2014), 105.
[13]   A. A. An-Naim (ed.), *Islamic Family Law in a Changing World: A Global Resource Book* (London: Zed Press, 2002), pp. 1–2; also A. A. An-Na'im, *Towards an Islamic Reformation: Civil Liberties, Human Rights and International Law* (Syracuse: Syracuse University Press, 1990), p. 185.

stream where animals and humans come to drink life-giving water. Just as stagnant water is not life-giving, so *sharia* is not an unchanging path.[14] Its purpose is to lead the way to what gives life, not to be the destination in and of itself. It may be argued that, by its definition as a changing pathway, *sharia* has evolution built into its meaning and cannot be rigid and determinate. A useful way to understand *sharia* is to visualize it as a single, flowing stream composed of different currents. Taking the analogy further, the flowing stream of *sharia* is fed and sustained – and at times overwhelmed – by other streams entering its path. More subtle impacts on the flowing stream consist in the terrain through which it makes its way – the cultures and traditions of the communities interacting with *sharia*. Imperceptibly, the flowing stream has drawn into itself varying influences from the soil it has traversed over time, and indeed is still traversing. '*Angrezi* (i.e. English) *sharia*' is an example of how British Muslim versions of *sharia* have adopted elements of English law and society.[15] Conversely, the terrain too absorbs water from the flowing stream and in so doing an interaction between differing normative environments occurs. As the ebb and flow of currents propels the flowing stream through time, it changes hue, speed, depth and breadth. Yet all the while the waters of the *sharia* flow on, negotiating and overcoming whatever they encounter along their path.

An important reason for the fluidity, evolution and plurality of *sharia* lies in the fact that its sources, too, demonstrate attributes of plurality in how they have been understood and applied over the centuries. *Sharia* (and its constituents, including Islamic law) is based upon primary sources – the Qur'an[16] and Sunna[17] – and secondary sources, including *ijma*[18] and *qiyas*.[19] But the story does not end there, for alongside the primary and secondary sources are the juristic techniques of the Islamic tradition, which, again, allow for great fluidity and evolution: *ijtihad, taqlid, ikhtilaf, takhayyur, talfiq, maslaha, darura, maqasid-al-sharia*, and '*urf*.

---

[14] For a discussion, see Ali, *Gender and Human Rights*, pp. 23–24. Contrast the views of some earlier orientalists, who advanced the argument that, after the formative and classical periods of development, the *sharia* tended to stagnate: J. Schacht, *Introduction to Islamic Law* (Oxford: Clarendon Press, 1964); N. J. Coulson, *A History of Islamic Law* (Edinburgh: Edinburgh University Press, 1964). In a later work, Coulson argued that *sharia* was more dynamic than he had earlier appreciated: *Conflicts and Tensions in Islamic Jurisprudence* (Chicago: The University of Chicago Press, 1969).

[15] See Chapter 7 below on *Sharia* Councils and British Muslims' understandings of *sharia*.

[16] The Qur'an, with its 6,666 verses in 114 chapters, is believed by Muslims to be the word of God revealed to the Prophet Muhammad through the Angel Gabriel over a period of twenty-two years, two months and twenty-two days.

[17] Sunna (the words and deeds of the Prophet Muhammad) are compiled as *hadith* (pl. *ahadith*). A *hadith* is composed of the *matn* (text) and the *isnad* (chain of transmitters).

[18] *Ijma* is 'consensus' or 'agreement' among Muslim jurists at any particular time on a question of law.

[19] As a source of law, *qiyas* ('deductive analogy') comes into operation in matters that are neither covered by an express text of the Qur'an or Sunna nor dealt with by *ijma*: the law deduced by application of what has already been laid down by these three sources is *qiyas*.

Ijtihad ('utmost effort') denotes the exercising of independent reasoning to provide answers when the Qur'an and Sunna are silent on a particular issue. A person qualified to undertake *ijtihad* is known as a *mujtahid*, and there are specific requirements for a person to be acknowledged as such. These vary between Sunni and Shia Islam, but in general one must have a very detailed knowledge of Arabic, of the primary sources of *sharia*, and of *fiqh* jurisprudence. *Taqlid* ('duty to follow') is generally considered the opposite of *ijtihad*, hence it is 'emulation', the acceptance of the authority of a ruling by a *mujtahid* without examining how it was arrived at. Yet even then, while *taqlid* obviously has the potential to be inhibitive of independent legal formulations, still it allows for choice from among the variant views of different *mujtahid* of different schools of thought as recorded in authoritative texts.

By applying the juristic technique of *ikhtilaf* ('unity in diversity'), jurists and practitioners arrived at positions that were representative of diverse viewpoints. Seen as 'alleviating earlier polemical and intolerant attitudes' among the jurists of different schools of thought,[20] *ikhtilaf* is supported by a *hadith*: 'Difference among my community is a sign of the bounty of God.'[21]

Takhayyur ('process of selection') is used to consider possible alternatives from a range of juristic opinions on a particular point of law, with the intention of applying the least restrictive legal principles to issues arising. For example, regarding how a woman may seek dissolution of her marriage, the Hanafi school of juristic thought (for which see below) is restrictive, whereas the Maliki school is more flexible, allowing a wife to rely on her husband's cruelty (a position incorporated into a number of Muslim personal-status laws). Likewise, the Hanbali doctrine of abiding by stipulations (based on *ahadith*) led this school to declare that the marriage contract could stipulate the husband's monogamy, the wife's choosing the place of residence, and so on. *Takhayyur* has been of enormous significance in developing a number of woman-friendly family law codes in Muslim jurisdictions.[22]

Talfiq ('patchwork') implies the process whereby jurists construct legal rules through the combination and fusion of opinions derived from different schools of thought on a particular issue. A fascinating example is the 1864 landmark case of *Muhammad Ibrahim* v. *Gulam Ahmed*, where an Indian girl brought up within Shafi'i tradition married without her father's consent. In court, she declared that she had chosen to adopt the Hanafi school's tradition, as this allowed an adult woman to marry without the consent of her guardian.

Maslaha ('public interest') is a technique propounded by the founder of the Maliki school, who allowed 'a deduction of law to be based on general

---

[20] H. P. Glenn, *Legal Traditions of the World: Sustainable Diversity in Law* (Oxford: Oxford University Press, 2000), p. 207.

[21] Coulson, *History of Islamic Law*, p. 102.

[22] Examples of *takhayyur* include the Dissolution of Muslim Marriages Act 1939, the Moroccan Code of Personal Status 1858, the Jordanian Law of Family Rights 1951, the Syrian Law of Personal Rights 1953, the Ottoman Law of Family Rights 1917, and most recently the Moroccan Family Code (Moudawana) 2004.

considerations of the public good'. There is evidence that *qadis* (judges) and jurists have employed *maslaha* to override problems arising out of adherence to strict doctrines enshrined in the classical legal texts; in a modern context, we might see this in terms of jurists reconciling modern cultural norms with the more 'traditional'. *Darura* ('necessity') is another technique that can be applied where it becomes imperative to make what is prohibited permissible (for example, violating a prohibition in order to avoid starving to death, the latter option itself being contrary to the objectives of *sharia*). And *maqasid-al-sharia* ('objectives of *sharia*') itself is increasingly being invoked by individuals as well as institutions to overcome formalistic obstacles in implementing Islamic law.

The last but certainly not the least in the armoury of juristic techniques is *'urf* ('custom').[23] It being held that what the people in general consider to be good is also considered to be good by Allah, long-standing and widely practised custom can be acceptable in Islamic law. By way of example, the wearing of gold by men might be ruled *haram*, but how is 'gold' to be defined? Local custom might permit men to wear low-carat gold, in which case the application of *'urf* allows for this.

Even to the casual observer of Islamic law, then, it should be clear that the manner in which law is generated within the Islamic legal traditions is most definitely pluralist, with the inherent capacity for alternative legitimate conceptions of what constitutes law and permissible action. Linked closely to the sources and evolution of Islamic law and *sharia* is the fact that Muslims are divided into Sunni and Shia, who have each developed their own particular schools of jurisprudence. Sunni follow four main juristic schools of thought or *madahhab* (sing. *madhhab*) – Hanafi, Maliki, Shafi'i and Hanbali; Shia are sub-divided into three main schools – Ja'fari, Ismaili and Zaidi.[24]

The Hanafi school is named after the eighth-century Iraqi jurist Abu Hanifa Al-Nu'man. It is distinct for upholding individual judgments or opinions (*ahl-al-raiy*), giving preference to *qiyas* over *ahadith*, laying emphasis on the principle of *istihsan* (juristic equity), believing that *ijma* is valid in every age, and recognizing *'urf* as a source of law. Numerically the largest school, it extends to Iraq, Turkey, Syria, Afghanistan, Turkish Central Asia, India, Pakistan and Bangladesh. The Maliki school is named after the eighth-century Medina jurist and traditionalist Malik ibn Anas and is more inclined towards jurisprudence based on the Qur'an and *ahadith*. When confronted with conflicting *ahadith*, Malik depended upon *ijma* of the *mujtahids* of Medina to resolve the conflict. Followers of this school are found in North and West Africa. Muhammad Idris

---

[23] At times controversial, this source of law and juristic technique plays an important role in the growth of the Islamic legal tradition as it speaks to the commonly held beliefs and convictions of communities. Thus some communities of South Asia have relied upon *'urf* to interpret Muslim laws of inheritance.

[24] The scope of this chapter and of *Modern Challenges* generally is confined to the more prevalent Sunni sects in Islam.

ibn Al-Shafi'i, founder of the Shafi'i school, is considered the 'creator' of the classical theory of Islamic jurisprudence (*usul*) and remembered for developing *ijma* as a source of law. Al-Shafi'i was responsible for the doctrine of *qiyas* but ruled that it may be based on the Qur'an, *ahadith*, or *ijma*. Shafi'is are to be found on the littoral of Arabia, India, Lower Egypt, East Africa and South East Asia. The ninth-century Ahmed bin Hanbal, founder of the Hanbali school, perfected the doctrine of *usul-ul-fiqh* ('principles of jurisprudence'). Hanbalis place a literal and narrow interpretation on *ahadith* and give a narrow margin to *ijma* and *qiyas*. The school represents an extreme reaction to the Hanafis' upholding of individual judgments, and is found in Central Arabia, Syria and Palestine. The mid-eighteenth-century Wahabi movement of Muhammad ibn Abd-ul-Wahab seeks inspiration from this school, which continues to dominate in the Arab Gulf states.

That *sharia* has been historically constructed by generations of jurists through their individual and collective understanding of the religious text in Islam is well documented,[25] and even this briefest overview of the four Sunni *madahhab* is enough to give a taste of the plurality within the Islamic legal traditions and to show why the flowing stream of *sharia* and Islamic law are inherently pluralist. As a sophisticated and complex moral–legal project, *sharia* served Muslim communities exceptionally well for much of their history. Yet it has been observed that it

> collapsed under the weight of European colonialism and all its consequences, including the creation of modern states in the Muslim world. The foundations of the shari'a, especially the independent jurists who developed the doctrines of God's will as expressed in the sources of the law and articulated them for rulers and peoples alike, were swept away in the nineteenth and twentieth centuries. This destruction was total, and the resurrection of the classical shari'a is an impossible task.[26]

This will prove to be an overly stark assessment of what are no doubt the outcomes of major transformative processes: imagining *sharia* instead as a flowing stream allows us to recognize that events such as European colonialism have reduced its flow and narrowed its path, but did not (and indeed cannot) dam its source or remove its objective. *Sharia* has sustained itself through new forms,

---

[25] For further details on this subject, see An-Na'im, *Islamic Family Law in a Changing World*, pp. 1–2; Rahman, *Islam*; and Hallaq, *Introduction to Islamic Law*.

[26] M. D. Welton, 'Review of Hallaq's *The Impossible State: Islam, Politics, and Modernity's Moral Predicament*', *Middle East Journal* 67(3) (2013), 492–3. Also see Hallaq, *Introduction to Islamic Law*, pp. 8–9. Hamoudi alludes to a similar outcome: 'Of all of the myths relating to the Muslim state in our times, none is more persistent than that its legitimacy, and the legitimacy of the law it pronounces, depends on the imprimatur of *shari'a* . . . While there is something romantic, and almost touching, in the notion that the Muslim world is somehow different from the rest of the globe in the primacy it affords to God's law in establishing the rules of the legal order, it has no basis in fact.' See H. A. Hamoudi, 'The Death of Islamic Law', *Georgia Journal of International and Comparative Law* 38 (2010), p. 293; University of Pittsburgh Legal Studies Research Paper No. 2010-02.

clothed in new garb. *Sharia* was never a homogeneous entity; it always contained within itself a rich array of concepts, methods and interpretative mechanisms. In *Modern Challenges*, examples are presented of the evolving forms of what may be described as modern articulations of *sharia*. These emerging aspects reflect popular understandings of Islamic law as well as governmental approaches, influenced by the lived experiences of individuals and states.[27]

Like *sharia*, the concept of *fiqh* (jurisprudence) is sometimes translated as 'Islamic law' – an inadequate translation with implications for the nature of both concepts and their potential development. As we have seen, *sharia* comprises the divine injunctions of the Qur'an and the divinely inspired injunctions of the Sunna, alongside human understandings of these so as to arrive at legally enforceable norms. *Fiqh*, on the other hand, is entirely a human effort 'concerned with the knowledge of the detailed rules of Islamic law . . . *Fiqh*, in other words, is the law itself'.[28] Yet since *sharia* and *fiqh* drew heavily upon the Qur'an and Sunna for their formulations, over time their corpus became prone to elevation to the parallel status of immutable divine law, beyond evolution and change, and with interpretative rights belonging to a restricted class of scholars. Elevating *fiqh* to the status of *sharia* imports into its nature an unjustifiable immutability that only results in the fossilization of the Islamic legal traditions.[29]

Fiqh (literally 'understanding')

> connotes the efforts and activities, largely on the part of qualified scholars, to discover and give expression to the many facets of Qur'an- and Sunna-derived principles of [*shari'a*] law. While *sharia* is a focus of the faith, *fiqh* is esteemed mainly as an intellectual literary tradition and/or the sophisticated product of centuries of Islamic high legal culture.[30]

Summarizing the distinction between *sharia* and *fiqh*, El-Fadl makes the following observation: 'Sharia'h is the Divine ideal, standing as if suspended in mid-air, unaffected and uncorrupted by the vagaries of life. The *fiqh* is the human attempt to understand and apply the ideal. Therefore, Sharia'h is immutable, immaculate and flawless – *fiqh* is not.'[31] Haddad and Stowasser highlight the human input into both *sharia* and *fiqh* by explaining how 'religious scholars combined

---

[27] Muslim states have signed up to a wide range of treaties on human rights, trade, arms, military exercises, terrorism and so on. These obligations, too, impact on how individuals and states interact with the wider world, and feed into understandings of a modern *sharia*.

[28] Kamali, *Principles*, p. 2. Others too have noted the distinction between *sharia* and *fiqh*, including F. E. Vogel and S. L. Hayes, *Islamic Law and Finance: Religion, Risk and Return* (London: Kluwer, 1998), pp. 23–4; A. Quraishi, 'What if Sharia Weren't the Enemy? Rethinking International Women's Rights Advocacy on Islamic Law', *Columbia Journal of Gender and Law* 22 (2011), 203.

[29] This is not my personal interpretation of *sharia*, which I take not to be divine law but a human understanding of the divine alongside human interpretative endeavour.

[30] Haddad and Stowasser, 'Islamic Law and the Challenge of Modernity', p. 5.

[31] K. A. El-Fadl, 'The Centrality of Shariah to Government and Constitutionalism in Islam', in R. Grote and T. Röder (eds.), *Constitutionalism in Islamic Countries: Between Upheaval and Continuity* (Oxford: Oxford University Press, 2012), p. 57.

rationalist readings of Quran and Sunna with the specialists' knowledge of previous and contemporaneous juristic opinions that incorporated time-specific preferences and public policy options on the part of their framers'.[32] The vast body of classical *fiqh* resulting from these endeavours was stated and recorded in the form of innumerable legal points, many of them contradictory. The classical *madahhab* schools of *fiqh* developed sophisticated principles and rules, but this body of knowledge remained discursive: 'What constituted the law was rarely made explicit as the rules and principles are not only legal but moral, defeating at times any hope of legalistic precision.'[33]

Over a millennium, from roughly the year 800 to 1800, classical *fiqh* jurists developed an extensive corpus of legal opinions, as well as branches of law broadly divided into *ibadaat* (worship, rituals) and *muamalat* (social relations). Although perceived as an intellectual elite, it would not be true to say that jurists were completely isolated from the social, political and economic realities of their time. New problems continued to inform their legal formulations, and the body of precedent-driven legal maxims and specific details continued to evolve. Overall, however, the main emphasis of jurists was to perpetuate a largely inherited, tradition-based moral vision through their professional monopoly over *ijtihad*.[34] Classical *fiqh* literature is an ongoing moral discourse of scholars of theology and jurisprudence rather than a record of legal practices. The arrival of the European-style nation state into the Muslim world transformed this legal landscape and affected how *sharia* and *fiqh* were to be used. Jurists had remained independent of the state and had developed law in an autonomous environment; the corpus of *fiqh* was a mass of disparate legal compendia, difficult for most to comprehend, let alone implement. The arrival of colonialism undermined the place of the jurist as the authoritative law-maker. The Ottoman rulers were the first to bring tradition closer to modernity by a codification of laws akin to European law-making: their civil code of 1876, the *Majalla*, was the first Middle Eastern codification, representing as it did the rewriting of large parts of the Hanafi legal tradition in a modern format.[35]

1.3 The Currents of the Flowing Stream

The foregoing, then, gives an idea of the inherently protean nature of *sharia* and its jurisprudence. The remainder of this first chapter looks at some of the characteristics which throughout *Modern Challenges* endow *sharia* with such mutability.

---

[32] Haddad and Stowasser, 'Islamic Law and the Challenge of Modernity'. Also N. Calder, 'Law', in *Oxford Encyclopaedia of the Modern Islamic World*, vol. 2 (New York: Oxford University Press, 1995), p. 452.

[33] Vogel and Hayes, *Islamic Law and Finance*, p. 28, cited in Haddad and Stowasser, 'Islamic Law and the Challenge of Modernity', p. 5.

[34] Haddad and Stowasser, 'Islamic Law and the Challenge of Modernity', p. 5.   [35] Ibid., p. 6.

A characteristic current of the flowing stream is its pluralism. Legal plural-ism, specifically, is well-trodden terrain, amenable to various meanings and perspectives. An explanation of how it has been conceptualized and employed in *Modern Challenges* is therefore in order.

Societies and legal systems generally are not 'closed-off, impervious entities that can be adequately studied in isolation to understanding a wide range of "legalities" that affect societies' relations both internally and externally.'[36] In an increasingly globalized environment, there is a proliferation of 'official and unofficial legal orders in any polity', resulting in the coexistence of multiple bodies of law in the same social field.[37] The nation state does not hold a monopoly over law-making, as other regulatory norms operate in the same space, impacting on how people order their lives.

European colonization of Muslim-majority parts of the globe created hybrid legal systems comprising indigenous laws (religious as well as customary) upon which were superimposed colonial, state-based legal systems. Thus, in Indone-sia, local customary practices (*adat*) were applied alongside Islamic law and the statutory law promulgated by colonial rulers. In South Asia, customary law and practices (*riwaj*), personal-status laws applicable to religious denomina-tions and statutory laws operated in parallel and in hierarchies.[38] Regional-ization, globalization and transnational regulatory frameworks have resulted in societies and social spaces becoming subject to highly complex normative orders with multiple pluralities in play.[39] Social fields – including the political systems, cultures and traditions of a place – do not operate as watertight com-partments and, despite often appearing systemically closed, are in actual fact cognitively open. Local, national and global normative orders interact simulta-neously. Porous boundaries are susceptible to interaction with 'other referents in highly complex and heterogeneous ways . . . which may come to mimic, resemble or define themselves in opposition to each other.'[40]

One variant of legal pluralism is the global legal pluralism resulting from the collisions between multiple and contradictory normative frameworks, both structural and ideological, and giving rise to innumerable heterogeneous legal orders – a so-called 'poly-contextualisation of the law'.[41] As Sousa Santos sug-gests, postmodernity propelled legal pluralism into a new phase: 'Not the legal

---

[36] J. Ercanbrack, *The Transformation of Islamic Law in Global Financial Markets* (Cambridge: Cambridge University Press, 2015), p. 7; W. Twining, *Globalisation and Legal Theory* (London: Butterworths, 2000), p. 51. See also B. de Sousa Santos, *Toward a New Common Sense* (New York: Routledge, 1995), p. 385.

[37] Ercanbrack, *Transformation*, p. 8; G. R. Woodman, 'The Idea of Legal Pluralism', in B. Dupret, M. Berger and L. Al-Zwaini (eds.), *Legal Pluralism in the Arab World* (The Hague: Kluwer, 1999), p. 10.

[38] See Chapter 3 below on law reform.

[39] S. E. Merry, 'Legal Pluralism', *Law & Society Review* 22 (1988), 873.

[40] See Chapter 4 below on Islamic finance; also Ercanbrack, *Transformation*, p. 8; Twining, *Globalisation*, p. 85; Sousa Santos, *Common Sense*, p. 270.

[41] Ercanbrack, *Transformation*, p. 9, fn. 49.

pluralism of the traditional legal anthropology in which the different legal orders are conceived as separate entities coexisting in the same political space, but rather the conception of different legal spaces superimposed, interpenetrated, and mixed in our minds as much as in our actions.'[42] In *Modern Challenges*, the existence of such legal pluralism is the background against which multiple legalities are observed to operate within the Islamic legal traditions: Sunni and Shia Islam operate side by side; within Sunni tradition, pluralism is at play where the Hanafi, Maliki, Shafi'i, and Hanbali operate separately while also interacting with each other; simultaneously in Shia tradition the three main *madahhab* have evolved, sometimes at variance, sometimes heading in similar directions. These multiple pluralities, as well as the gap between textual law and its practical application, bring to mind Dupret, who observes a difference in how some authors assume legal pluralism where they perceive 'a gap between legal practices and formal textual legal provisions. Ought these practices to be seen as effects of inefficiency of law or positive manifestation of their conformity to other legal orderings?'[43]

Sharia as the overall normative regulatory framework for Muslims was neither conceived nor put into practice in a vacuum. Its seeds were sown in a soil replete with pre-existing legal orders both formal and informal, including the robust tribal customary regime of seventh-century Arabia. Islam did not completely wipe out these pre-existing orders, but set about to reform and modify some practices and prohibit others. *'Urf* was acknowledged as a valid source of law so long as it was not violative of *sharia*. Simultaneously, Islam introduced elements of an equal-rights regime, and rights for women, children and the disabled. In Medina further rules of coexistence emerged, displacing earlier modes. The phenomenal spread of Islam thereafter resulted in the close inter-action of *sharia* and Islamic law with local regulatory frameworks, giving rise to plural legal systems that continue to the present day and allow communities the opportunity for selectivity in which set of 'laws' to apply and follow.

Another recurring theme in *Modern Challenges* is the gap between what is stated in the textual sources of the Islamic legal traditions and how it is applied in daily life. In some jurisdictions, for example, inheritance laws have been modified so as to accommodate the offspring of a person's pre-deceased children.[44] Setting a very high *mahr* (dower) for a wife in the marriage contract to inhibit subsequent polygamy by the husband is common practice among some South Asian communities. Courts in some jurisdictions, meanwhile, have favoured patriarchal interpretations of law and superimposed local customary practices to the detriment of women: in the landmark 'Saima Waheed case', it was ruled that the marriage of an adult woman was void without her male guardian's

---

[42] B. de Sousa Santos, 'Law: A Map of Misreading: Towards a Postmodern Conception of Law', *Journal of Law & Society* 14 (1989), 297–8.

[43] B. Dupret, 'Legal Pluralism, Plurality of Laws, and Legal Practices: Theories, Critiques and Praxeological Re-specification', *European Journal of Legal Studies* 1 (2007), 6.

[44] E.g. s. 4 of Pakistan's Muslim Family Laws Ordinance 1961.

consent, disregarding centuries of established Hanafi jurisprudence.[45] *Modern Challenges* demonstrates this gap between form and substance with an account of how 'supremacy of *sharia*' clauses have been imported into constitutional texts but disregarded in practice. We also see how, despite laws prohibiting the so-called 'triple *talaq*' divorce, the practice continues; and how, despite national courts requiring governments to prohibit *riba* interest in financial transactions, governments have failed to comply.

Challenging though these examples are to Islamic tradition, the reality is that 'living' law on the ground appears not to be what the sources of Islamic law say it 'should' be. Selective use of Islam and Islamic law is evident in all the chapters of *Modern Challenges*. We do not need to delve too far into the practices of Muslims around the world to uncover great heterogeneity, little uniformity, and a lack of coherence in how communities engage with Islamic law. One reason for this is the existence of the distinct schools of juristic thought and, with the passage of time, the widening gap that has opened between sources of law and their many possible interpretations. There being no Muslim equivalent of Roman Catholicism's Pope, there are multiple centres of authority; neither, in Sunni Islam, is there an organized clergy; and neither are Muslims required to follow any single *madhhab* uncritically. The lay population is now increasingly vocal in articulating questions and seeking answers. With increased access to knowledge through the Internet, television, radio and print media, individuals can be more proactive in how they engage with law.

1.4 New Exegeses: Challenging Readings of the Qur'an

Each generation of Muslims reads the Qur'an through the lens of its individual and collective perspectives, sometimes reinforcing existing tradition, sometimes displacing it. The departure point for challenge to both tradition and modernity is the Qur'anic text, on the basis of which varying positions are adopted. Discussion of whether, for example, there is support for constitutionalism within the Islamic traditions, of whether modification to Islamic family law is justified, and of the range of readings relating to the meaning and scope of the term *riba* all invoke Qur'anic verses. Legitimacy is sought by appropriating the 'superior location' through relevant Qur'anic injunctions.

As the primary source upon which the edifice of *sharia* and Islamic law has been and is being constructed, the Qur'an has been the focus of attention for scholars and lay Muslims for fourteen centuries, and their endeavours to understand and apply the Qur'an to their lived realities have blossomed into myriad

---

[45] On appeal the decision was reversed by a full bench of the same court, but the dissenting judges retained their earlier observations regarding the presence and consent of the father as her *wali*. See S. S. Ali, 'Is an Adult Muslim Woman *Sui Juris*? Some Reflections on the Concept of "Consent in Marriage" without a *Wali* (with Particular Reference to the Saima Waheed Case)', *Yearbook of Islamic and Middle Eastern Law* 3 (1996), 156–74.

interpretations specific to context, time and place. Much of this interpretation focuses on the position of women and their role in society. Since the context of Muslim communities remains largely patriarchal, male-led readings of the Qur'an have inevitably created gender hierarchies, while the analytical, inter-pretative and conceptual tools of Islamic jurisprudence have perpetuated this trend.

But these hierarchies are not going unchallenged from within the Islamic traditions.[46] Bringing with it the new social perspectives of the late twentieth and early twenty-first centuries, a robust and vibrant scholarship has emerged, focusing on Qur'anic interpretation through the lens of female experience.[47]

1.4.1 Verse 4:34

Attempts to displace traditional interpretations of verse 4:34 of the Qur'an are a case in point. With much of *Modern Challenges* addressing issues relating to women, it is worthwhile using this verse – arguably responsible more than any other for creating and entrenching male superiority – as an example of how multiple, contestable positions are generated from a single source.[48] The verse states,

> Men are the protectors and maintainers of women, because Allah has given the one more [strength] than the other, and because they support them from their means. Therefore the righteous women are devoutly obedient, and guard in [the husband's] absence what Allah would have them guard. As to those women on whose part ye fear disloyalty and ill-conduct, admonish them [first]. [Next], refuse to share their beds, [and last] beat them [lightly]. But if they return to obedience, seek not against them means [of annoyance]. For Allah is Most-High, Great [above you all].[49]

In other English translations, the verse begins: 'Men are in charge of women',[50] 'Men have authority over women because Allah has made one superior to the other',[51] 'Men are the ones who support women since God has given some persons advantages over others',[52] and 'Men are the managers of the affairs of

---

[46] See, for instance, Chapter 8 below on Internet *fatawa*.

[47] To name just a few of the Muslim women engaged in reinterpretation and rereading of the Qur'an from a female perspective, we have Riffat Hassan, Amina Wadud-Muhsin, Aziza Al-Hibri, Fatima Mernissi, Asma Barlas and Ziba Mir-Husseini.

[48] A detailed analysis was presented in an earlier work of verses that create and reinforce gender hierarchies, and I do not propose to rehearse that entire argument here: Ali, *Gender and Human Rights*, pp. 42–88.

[49] Trans. Yusuf Ali.

[50] M. Pickthall, *The Meaning of the Glorious Koran: An Explanatory Translation* (London: Knopf, 1930).

[51] *The Koran* (trans. A. J. Arberry) (London: George Allen and Unwin, 1966).

[52] *The Qur'an: Basic Teachings* (trans. and ed. T. B. Irving, K. Ahmad and M. M. Ahsan) (Leicester: Islamic Foundation, 1979).

women'.[53] These readings all place women as a class in need of protection and providing for, while men as a class are given the role of protectors and providers. Such variant, yet valid, interpretations of the seventh-century Arabic have historically been the subject of enthusiastic debates, and Muslim women scholars have, for the most part, mounted a robust challenge to the accepted paradigm of male superiority. How, then, can a Qur'anic verse be read differently?

Barbara Stowasser, in her study of the status of women in early Islam, argues that such verses have fallen prey to exegetes who, in their enthusiasm to ensure maximum application of Qur'anic provisions, attempted to place 'a fence about the law by requiring a precautionary margin in order to ensure the entire fulfilment of its dictates, so the interpreters of the *Quran* demanded more than the original'.[54] She cites a number of commentaries, demonstrating how each successive commentator became more restrictive of women's rights until, by the seventeenth century, women had been completely excluded from all spheres of public life. The earliest commentary cited is from the tenth century,[55] and it endows men with authority over their women in the family setting, coupled with the obligation to provide for them by way of material support. A commentary from the thirteenth century, however, is more detailed and more restrictive: men are 'in charge of women as rulers are in charge of their subjects':

> Allah has preferred men over women in the completeness of mental ability, good counsel, complete power in the performance of duties and the carrying out of [divine] commands. Hence to men have been confined prophecy, religious leadership, saintship, the performance of religious rites, the giving of evidence in law courts, the duties of the Holy War, and worship [in the mosque] on Friday, etc., the privilege of electing chiefs, the larger share of inheritance, and discretion in matters of divorce, by virtue of that which they spend of their wealth, in marrying [the women] such as their dowers and cost of their maintenance.[56]

The verse had been interpreted so as to bring within its ambit a woman's entire legal personality, denying her independent personhood. In the seventeenth century, this exegesis was further refined when a later scholar stated that plain 'religious leadership' (*imama*) referred to the roles of both prayer-leader (*imama kubra*) and spiritual leader of the whole nation (*imama sughra*). The earlier 'saintship' (*wilaya*) was interpreted as the wholesale assumption of responsibility (*tawallin*) for women in matters of marriage.[57] How does one begin to challenge such restrictive interpretations?

---

[53] *The Holy Qur'an: English Translation of the Meanings and Commentary* (Mecca: Presidency of Islamic Researches, Ifta, Call and Guidance, 1411 AH).

[54] B. Stowasser, 'The Status of Women in Early Islam', in F. Hussain (ed.), *Muslim Women* (New York: St Martin's Press, 1984), p. 25, citing R. Levy, *The Social Structure of Islam*, reprint (Cambridge: Cambridge University Press, 1979), p. 126.

[55] By Abu Jafar Mohammed Jarir al-Tabari. Stowasser, 'Status of Women in Early Islam'.

[56] By Nasir al-Din Abu al-Khayr 'Abd Allah ibn Umar al-Baydawi. Stowasser, 'Status of Women in Early Islam', p. 26.

[57] By Ahmad ibn Mohammed al-Khafaji. Stowasser, 'Status of Women in Early Islam', p. 25.

Aziza Al-Hibri argues that the problematic concept is the word *qawwamun*, which is difficult to translate: while some exegetes understand it as making men the 'protectors' and 'maintainers' of women, she points out, the basic notion involved is one of moral guidance and caring.[58] The 'traditional' interpretation has men as being in charge of women's affairs because men were created by Allah as superior to woman (in strength and reason) and because they provide for women (i.e. they spend their money on them). This interpretation, though, Al-Hibri argues, is unwarranted and inconsistent with other Islamic teachings.[59] She points out that there is no reference in the verse to men's physical or intellectual superiority, nor are men as a class *qawwamun* over women as a class. At most, a man is entitled to care for a woman and provide her with moral guidance: 'It is worth noting that the passage does not even assert that some men are inherently superior to some women. It only states that in certain matters some men may have more than some women.'[60] Al-Hibri also makes the point that, by her interpretation, no one has the right to counsel a self-supporting woman, and since 'Islam emphasises democracy and enjoins Muslims to counsel each other in making decisions, this resolution falls totally within the spirit of Islam'.[61]

In arguing that the 'traditional' interpretation is inconsistent with other Islamic teachings, Al-Hibri cites verse 9:71: 'The believers, men and women, are *awliya*, of one another.' *Awliya*, conceptually quite similar to *qawwamun*, may be translated as 'protectors', 'in charge', 'guides' and so on: 'How could women be *awliya* of men if men are superior to women in both physical and intellectual strength? And, how could women be in charge of men who have absolute authority over them?'[62]

Riffat Hassan, sometimes called 'the first Muslim woman theologian',[63] adopts a different and innovative interpretation. She observes,

> In simple words what this passage is saying is that since only women bear children ... a function whose importance in the survival of any community cannot be questioned – they should not have the additional obligation of being

---

[58] A. Al-Hibri, 'A Study of Islamic Herstory: Or How Did We Ever Get into This Mess?', *Women's Studies International Forum* 5(2) (1982), 217.

[59] Ibid.   [60] Ibid., p. 218.   [61] Ibid.

[62] Ibid. Al-Hibri also quotes a saying of the Prophet Muhammad in favour of equality of the sexes: 'All people are equal, as equal as the teeth of a comb. There is no claim of merit of an Arab over a non-Arab, or of a white over a black person, or of a male over a female. Only God-fearing people merit a preference with God'.

[63] I had the pleasure and privilege of working with Dr Hassan during my research with Women Living under Muslim Laws on a project on Women and Laws in the Muslim World. She has written prolifically on the subject of Qur'anic interpretation from the perspective of Muslim women, including 'The Role and Responsibilities of Women in the Legal and Ritual Tradition of Islam', paper presented to the Trialogue of Jewish–Christian–Muslim scholars at the Joseph and Rose Kennedy Institute for Ethics, Washington, DC, 1980; 'On Human Rights and the Quranic Perspective', in A. Swidler (ed.), *Human Rights in Religious Traditions* (New York: Pilgrim Press, 1982), pp. 51–66; 'An Islamic Perspective', in J. Belcher (ed.), *Women, Religion and Sexuality* (Geneva: WCC, 1990), pp. 93–128.

breadwinners whilst they perform this function. Thus during the period of a woman's child-bearing, the function must be performed by men (not just husbands) . . . It enjoins men in general to assume responsibility for women in general when they are performing the vitally important function of child-bearing.[64]

So Hassan sees the verse as a safety net for child-bearing and child-rearing women, who should not have to fend for themselves, and as a protective right for women, obligating communities to support them. She establishes the link with child-bearing by taking the word *salihat* (generally translated as 'righteously obedient') to denote 'capability' or 'potentiality', and proceeds to argue that the word *qanitat* (translated normally as 'obedience') suggests a 'water container', a metaphor for the womb. Thus if all women refuse to procreate, it is the community, and not husbands, who have the right to discipline them.

But verse 4:34 has not only traditionally been used to give women a lower status than men; it also appears to legitimize violence against women. The most contentious word in the verse is the term *daraba*, commonly translated as 'striking' or 'hitting'. So how does one go about rereading this apparently clear meaning?

Hassan argues that in a legal context *daraba* denotes 'holding in confinement'. Shahab argues that the word also means 'to prevent', which would give us: 'leave [their wives] alone in their beds and prevent them going outside their houses'.[65] Wadud takes issue with privileging *daraba* with the sole meaning of hitting when it can equally well mean 'to set an example' (another exegete similarly appears to take *daraba* to denote 'example', 'simile' or 'parable');[66] she also argues that *daraba* is intended to be distinguished restrictively from *darraba* ('to strike repeatedly'), and reads the verse as 'prohibiting unchecked violence against females'. Barlas, citing verse 38:44, in which Allah asks Job to 'take in thy hand a little grass, and strike [i.e. *daraba*] therewith', argues that the use of *daraba* is symbolic,[67] pointing out that all explanatory commentaries in *hadith* and *fiqh* literature emphasize that the strike should not cause bodily harm. Furthermore, in a time when men did not *need* permission to strike their wives, verse 4:34 could only be restrictive rather than prescriptive.[68]

Does the background to the revelation of verse 4:34 shine light on how it might be understood? A husband had hit his wife on the face, upon which she, accompanied by her father, had complained to the Prophet Muhammad. He had replied that she should have retaliation, and they had risen to leave but were called back when the Prophet said that Gabriel had come to him and asked

[64] R. Hassan, extract from a paper presented at a Qur'anic interpretation meeting held in Karachi, 8–13 July 1990, under the auspices of Women Living under Muslim Laws.

[65] R. Shahab, *Muslim Women in Political Power* (Lahore: Maqbool Academy, 1993), p. 231.

[66] I am grateful to Professor Jorgen Nielsen, who supervised Dr Fino for her doctoral project at the University of Birmingham, for this information.

[67] A. Barlas, *Believing Women in Islam: Unreading Patriarchal Interpretations of the Qur'an* (Austin: University of Texas Press, 2002), p. 188.

[68] Ibid.

him to suspend his decision before revealing this verse. The incident reveals at least the unacceptability of physical violence against a wife: had this not been the case, the father would not have reacted by accompanying his daughter to complain to the Prophet. All this, then, leaves us with a strikingly different range of alternative interpretations of verse 4:34, and provides a good example of how challenges may be mounted from within the Islamic legal traditions to arrive at contemporary readings of the Qur'an.

1.5 The Fragmentation of the Authority of *Sharia* and Islamic Law

Straddling both tradition and modernity, Islamic law – and, more broadly, *sharia* – maintains its continuous and oscillatory journey of evolution, continuity and rupture.[69] In recent times, though, modernity has exerted a much more significant influence over tradition. An unprecedented pace of social change has arrived with the development of new technologies. The global reach of this change is without parallel as it has brought within its fold the most far-flung areas of the world in hitherto unimaginable ways.[70] Aspects of modernity have generated wholly novel institutions such as the nation state, the corporation and the specialization of production and knowledge, to all of which the Muslim world has subscribed.[71] Yet the authority of tradition remains paramount for many in Muslim communities, and it is here that the traditional knowledge base accrued through centuries of jurisprudence is critical. This knowledge has impacted upon the challenges of (post-)colonization and globalization and has led to new modes of self-identification (in e.g. Muslim diasporas) and new articulations of legal sources. Simultaneously – and reliably – tradition is challenging expressions of modernity: witness Maududi's writings, and the emergence of such movements as the Taliban and Al-Qaeda.

Fatawa can be seen as a modern manifestation of historical challenges to formal authority. In two areas at least, the traditional institution of *ifta* has made a comeback, albeit in modern forms. In the field of Islamic finance, the search for certainty and uniformity in the adaptation of classical *sharia* to modern purposes is playing an important part in a new and rapidly developing transnational legal system. *Sharia* advisory bodies placed within Islamic finance institutions play a central role in assessing and declaring products to be *sharia*-compliant or not. Unlike traditional *fatawa* that were advisory in nature, these

---

[69] Historically, tradition has been challenged by modernity many a time. The early classical era of Islam, for example, witnessed the rise of 'people of independent reasoning', who were forced to retreat in the face of rising traditionalism. Tradition also triumphed over modernity by declaring the 'closure of the gates of *ijtihad*' until, in the twentieth century, scholars such as Iqbal rebutted this (in *Reconstruction of Religious Thought in Islam*). Law reform in the Muslim world since the codifications of the late nineteenth century is one example of modernity's comeback and the retreat of tradition.

[70] Ercanbrack, *Transformation*, p. 6.

[71] Ibid. Ercanbrack also refers to A. Giddens, *The Consequences of Modernity* (Cambridge: Polity Press, 1990), p. 6.

fatawa of financial regulation are legally binding. On the Internet, meanwhile, *fatawa* are being handed down as responses to challenging questions posed by a virtual, globalized community. Yet accessing the Internet and choosing a *mufti* whose *fatwa* can, after all, be disregarded makes this process an enabling and empowering one for lay Muslims; *fatawa* appear as sources of authority and legitimacy, and rival *fatawa* as sources of contestation.

Referring to Islamic scholars he encountered on a visit to Al-Azhar University in Cairo in 1892, Muhammad Shibli Nu'mani once remarked that 'those people who have been once as much as touched by traditional education, remain forever irreconcilably estranged from modern learning'.[72] *Plus ça change* – contestation between 'traditionalists' and 'modernists' today resounds in Muslim communities around the globe. Modernity is challenging tradition as never before. Historically, jurists trained in the intricacies of classical *fiqh* possessed enormous power and authority and defined the authenticity of what constituted 'real' Islamic law. The nation state, by appropriating legislative power, displaced the traditional loci of law-making and interpretation: the *aalim*, the *faqih* and the *mufti*. In the Muslim world, therefore rival loci of authority, authenticity and legitimacy of law-making emerged – a struggle that is ongoing.

1.6 Globalization

'Since every country belongs to God, so it is mine', wrote the poet–philosopher Dr Muhammad Iqbal, who is credited with the idea of a Muslim homeland in the 1930s.[73] This particular line summarizes the universalist aspects of the Islamic traditions, recalling its extra-territorial and autonomous nature and bringing to mind the concept of the global *umma*. How do concepts of globalization and *umma* relate to each other, and what are the implications of globalization for Islamic law and *sharia*? Both concepts have common attributes in that they transcend territorial boundaries and work across cultures, religions and traditions. Both undermine the nation state, challenging and transforming sovereign authority.

Globalization also brings to the fore other realities and ways of being and doing. In *Modern Challenges*, the effects of globalization's interaction with plural communities come to light. The drivers of globalization – migration, Internet and media – prompt Muslim communities to see Islam and Islamic law in all its diversity and plurality; conversely, globalization also connects diverse communities, opening up possibilities of a reimagined *umma* in what was previously seen as a utopian ideal. This reimagined reality is experienced as a social resonance with the Qur'anic injunction to 'get to know one another'. These two strands of globalization also point to the translocal and transnational nature of Muslim communities and how they perceive and apply *sharia* and

---

[72] M. S. Nu'mani, *Safarnama* (Lahore: Ghulam Ali and Sons, 1961), pp. 285–6.
[73] The translation from Persian is mine and is not a literal one.

Islamic law. Multiple belongings – to diaspora and to homeland – have resulted in cultural hybridization.[74]

As the study of Internet *fatawa* in *Modern Challenges* shows, globalization and its drivers have facilitated debates within Muslim communities from different juristic schools. This has led to a rethinking of Islam and Islamic law by the lay population in the diaspora and also in their homelands. A wandering, borderless Islam has emerged, fragmenting traditional loci of authority: witness the UK's *Sharia* Councils, the European Council of Fatwa and Research, and the numerous organizations that have mushroomed in response to the needs of Western diaspora Muslims.

Yet although, as a community of believers in Allah and in the Prophet Muhammad as His last prophet, all Muslims are said to constitute one *umma* regardless of distinctions, the reality is somewhat different. In practical terms, Muslims first and foremost owe allegiance to their nation states and not to a theoretical *umma*; hence the requirements of visa formalities between Muslim states. Non-Arab Muslims might live all their lives in the Arab Middle East, but they are rarely granted full citizenship rights in their host nations. Despite a collective voice in the Organisation of Islamic Cooperation, very rarely do Muslim states vote in unison at forums such as the UN.

1.7 Concluding Reflections

Sharia, with its plurality developed as it was by the jurists of various *madahhab* over so long a time, defies definitive categorization. Over the centuries, Muslims have continuously engaged with their legal traditions, answering questions and raising others that might never be answered. The flowing stream of *sharia* has enfolded within itself currents from every age and place. The stream is best approached as a discursive tradition comprising a wide range of regulatory norms and some distinctly legal rules.

Some Muslims have interpreted *sharia* mainly in opposition to Western legal frameworks, others with a view to arriving at understandings relevant to modernity, or to the position of women. The Sudanese scholar Abdullahi Ahmed An-Naim has proposed dialogue within and among Muslim communities so they might reach a common understanding on aspects of Islamic law and *sharia* and confront some of their more difficult and disturbing elements from within the Islamic traditions: for it is from within that challenges must come.

Within contemporary Muslim states and communities, the prime strategy or mechanism for legitimizing laws lies in invoking their 'Islamicity'; yet the

---

[74] South Asian British Muslims, for example, have two sets of wedding celebrations: a *nikah*, where they sign the Islamic contract of marriage and where the bride wears traditional clothes, and a registry wedding where she mostly wears an outfit which in South Asian culture would be inappropriate (as it is a pale colour, whereas traditional South Asian brides wear red). At the height of a meal of *pulao* and chicken tikka, a wedding cake emerges and is cut by the bride and groom – something completely alien to South Asian culture.

reality is that the legal formulations of classical *sharia*[75] are no longer the sovereign law of most countries of the Muslim world: by the end of the 1800s, Muslim rulers had almost wholly discarded *sharia* and the state had begun to assume the power to determine its sovereign laws.[76] Islamic law as we now approach it is a modern concept and a product of modernity. On the one hand, it actively generates rules and regulations, customs and symbols; on the other, it is cognitively open and vulnerable to rules and influences emanating from the wider world. It is a dynamic, fluid and evolving normative framework that generates and is generated by social, political, cultural and economic factors and compulsions. It is not dependent upon territory. By equating Islamic law with *sharia*, and by conceptualizing *sharia* exclusively as the law of Allah, its human dimension is undermined or even excluded, and its scope shrunk to enforceable rules and confined within the narrow boundaries of black-letter law. This approach disadvantages both *sharia* and Islamic law and masks the ongoing socio-legal, political and economic journey that the text has undertaken to arrive at legal formulations as we understand them today. *Sharia* is much more than legally enforceable rules, drawing within its ambit ethics, morality, religious injunctions and sociopolitical norms. In relation to this, it can be noted that, over the centuries, *sharia* has afforded states the right to legislate for their populations using laws inspired by *sharia* and determined through human deliberation. Yet this process does not make those laws 'un-Islamic' – a distinction that has thus far not been acceptable to the vast majority of the Muslims. In the succeeding chapters, this distinction will be made clearer.

[75] I.e. from before the early nineteenth century, when Islamic law was displaced by Western-based legal systems.

[76] W. Hallaq, *Sharia: Theory, Practice, Transformations* (Cambridge: Cambridge University Press, 2009), p. 443.

2

An Elephant in the Room or a Needle in a Haystack? Searching for 'Islamic' Constitutionalism(s)

2.1 Introduction

A key challenge in the study of Islamic law is how to approach modern concepts that do not readily avail themselves of comparators within the Islamic legal traditions. This inquiry assumes a more complex nature when those conceptual comparators themselves are evolving, contested and open to varying definitions. Constitutionalism is one such concept which has become the subject of increasing scrutiny challenging traditional conceptions of Muslim state and government.[1]

---

[1] Scholars have written on aspects of Islamic constitutionalism from a variety of perspectives. These include, to name a few, K. A. El Fadl, *Islam and the Challenge of Democracy* (Princeton: Princeton University Press, 2004); and 'The Centrality of Shariah'; M. Ahmad (ed.), *State, Politics, and Islam* (Indianapolis: American Trust Publications, 1986); D. Ahmed and Gouda, 'Measuring Constitutional Islamization: The Islamic Constitutions Index', *Hastings International & Comparative Law Review* 38(1) (2015), 1–76; M. S. Al-Awa, *On the Political System of the Islamic States* (Indianapolis: American Trust Publications, 1980); A. A. An-Na'im, *Islam and the Secular State: Negotiating the Future of Shari'a* (Cambridge, MA: Harvard University Press, 2008); An-Na'im, *African Constitutionalism and the Role of Islam* (Pennsylvania: Philadelphia University Press, 2006); S. A. Arjomand, 'Religion and Constitutionalism in Western History and in Modern Iran and Pakistan', in Arjomand (ed.), *The Political Dimensions of Religion* (Albany: State University of New York Press, 1993), pp. 69–99; Arjomand, 'The Constitution of Medina: A Sociolegal Interpretation of Muhammad's Acts of Foundation of the Umma', *International Journal of Middle East Studies* 41 (2009), 555–75; Arjomand, 'Islamic Constitutionalism', *Annual Review of Law and Social Sciences* 3 (2007), 115–40; M. Asad, *The Principles of State and Government in Islam* (Kuala Lumpur: Islamic Book Trust, 1980); N. J. Brown, *Constitutions in a Non-constitutional World: Arab Basic Laws and the Prospects for Accountable Government* (Albany: State University of New York Press, 2002); N. J. Brown and A. O. Sherif, 'Inscribing the Islamic Shari'a in Arab Constitutional Law', in Haddad and Stowasser, *Islamic Law*, pp. 55–80; Grote and Röder, *Constitutionalism in Islamic Countries*; Haddad and Stowasser, *Islamic Law*; N. Hosen, *Shari'a and Constitutional Reform in Indonesia* (Singapore: Institute of South East Asian Studies, 2007); Hosen, 'In Search of Islamic Constitutionalism', *American Journal of Social Sciences* 21(2) (2004), 1–24; Kamali, 'Constitutionalism in Islamic Countries'; C. Mallat (ed.), *Islam and Public Law: Classical and Contemporary Studies* (London: Graham & Trotman, 1993); A. A. Maududi, *Political Theory of Islam* (Lahore: Islamic Publications, 1985); I. Rabb, '"We the Jurists": Islamic Constitutionalism in Iraq', *Journal of Constitutional Law* 10(3) (2008), 527–79; N. Sultany, 'Religion and Constitutionalism: Lessons from American and Islamic Constitutionalism', *Emory International Law Review* 28 (2014), 345–424; C. B. Lombardi, *State Law as Islamic Law in Modern Egypt: The Incorporation of the Shari'a into Egyptian Constitutional Law* (Leiden: Brill, 2006); K. A. Stilt,

In its earlier, liberal conceptions, 'constitutionalism' was broadly defined and built upon three pillars: upholding the rule of law, the enforcement of effective limitations on governmental powers, and the protection of fundamental rights. This was essentially the model received in the Muslim world, upon which Islamic law was grafted so as to 'Islamize' constitutional texts and constitutionalism.[2] But modern constitutionalism presents itself in various forms and raises many different challenges and potential contradictions within itself. Constitutionalism and democracy, for instance, appear 'intimately related yet intrinsically opposed',[3] giving rise to much debate regarding 'constitutional democracy'. Loughlin and Walker alert us to the paradox of constitutionalism in the tensions generated by the power inherent in the people on the one hand and in constitutional forms on the other, through which alone it may be exercised.[4] Other issues at the centre of debates on constitutionalism include the impact of global, transnational and international law and governance networks. The constitutionalization of international law,[5] as well as the pluralist nature of domestic legal structures, poses a threat to the very existence of constitutionalism in its classical form.[6]

As in most areas of the Islamic legal traditions, opinion on Islamic constitutionalism too is far from unanimous. Most Islamic law scholars agree that 'constitutional law (*usul-al-hukm*) is one of the most under-developed areas of Islamic law and jurisprudence'.[7] Some Qur'anic verses and the Sunna, however, provide elements on which the structure of constitutionalism may be built, including *shura* (consultation), *bay'ah* (allegiance), principles of justice and the accountability of rulers.[8] Other antecedents, including the Medina Charter (discussed below), are also cited in support of the historical beginnings of an Islamic constitutionalism. Despite a number of discernible trajectories within Muslim intellectual thought on the subject,[9] claiming an Islamic

---

'Contextualizing Constitutional Islam: The Malaysian Experience', *International Journal of Constitutional Law* 13 (2015), 407; T. Moustafa, *The Struggle for Political Power: Law, Politics and Economic Development in Egypt* (Cambridge: Cambridge University Press, 2009).

[2] Alongside the notion of constitutional democracy.

[3] R. Bellamy (ed.), *Constitutionalism and Democracy* (Farnham: Ashgate, 2006), back cover; N. Walker, 'Constitutionalism and the Incompleteness of Democracy: An Iterative Relationship', *Journal of Legal Philosophy* 3 (2010), 206–33.

[4] M. Loughlin and N. Walker (eds.), *The Paradox of Constitutionalism: Constituent Power and Constitutional Form* (Oxford: Oxford University Press, 2008) At p. 1, they state 'the two fundamental though antagonistic imperatives: that governmental power ultimately is generated from "consent of the people" and that, to be sustained and effective, such power must be divided, constrained, and exercised through distinctive institutional forms'.

[5] J. Klabbers, A. Peters and G. Ulfstein (eds.), *The Constitutionalization of International Law* (Oxford: Oxford University Press, 2009).

[6] N. Krisch, *Beyond Constitutionalism: The Pluralist Structure of Postnational Law* (Oxford: Oxford University Press, 2010).

[7] In comparison to family law and devotional matters: see Kamali, 'Constitutionalism in Islamic Countries', 19.

[8] Ibid.   [9] El Fadl, 'The Centrality of Shariah', p. 55.

constitutionalism as inherently a part of the Islamic traditions would in the opinion of some scholars be an exaggeration and 'falling prey to an anachronism'.[10]

A more nuanced view of Islamic constitutionalism has been advanced by Mohammad Hashim Kamali, Abdullahi Ahmed An-Na'im, Khalid Abou El Fadl, Saïd Amir Arjomand, Haider Ala Hamoudi, Anver Emon and Nadirsyah Hosen (discussed below). These scholars seek to extract contextual equivalents, principles and norms from the sources so as to develop a notion of modern Islamic constitutionalism, rather than pronounce that the phenomenon *in its present formulation* always existed. They also seek to distinguish between doctrinal and classical Islamic law and contemporary Muslim state practices of law – an approach that the present chapter (and indeed this book) attempts to highlight.

A parallel way of engaging with Islamic constitutionalism is to set historical antecedents aside and investigate actual Islamic constitutionalism in operation: how far do Islamic law and *sharia* inform the constitutional text, and what are the likely implications of these formulations on state, public law and governance in these jurisdictions? This line of enquiry throws up a different set of questions compared to a purely theoretical discussion, in that it highlights the wide gap between an idealized Islamic constitutionalism and its actual minimal implementation in Muslim jurisdictions. It also questions whether inserting 'Islamic' clauses in constitutional documents results in more 'Islamic' governance, and whether this is the best way forward.[11] A range of Muslim jurisdictions will be touched upon, including Egypt, Tunisia, Iraq, Iran and Pakistan. Of these, (Shia) Iran and (Sunni) Pakistan are particularly useful examples, being states that have experimented with Islamic constitutionalism intensely and self-consciously and for long enough to offer some lessons on the subject.[12]

Building on existing scholarship as well as on personal experiences of state and government, this chapter also bears in mind certain questions when thinking about Islamic constitutionalism: how may we understand the parameters and characteristics of constitutionalism in relation to Islamic law? What challenges emerge as a result of this exploration, and what are the likely future possibilities and directions for an 'Islamic' state and government as a result of widespread 'constitutional Islamization'?[13] It advances a fourfold argument:

(i) that Islamic constitutionalism is a modern, pluralist concept, albeit with some historical roots;

[10] Ibid., p. 35.
[11] See, for instance, Sultany's arguments against Islamic constitutionalism in 'Religion and Constitutionalism'.
[12] This chapter and indeed this book are mostly informed by discourses and narratives of Sunni Islam and any in-depth analysis of Shia perspectives on Constitutionalism are beyond the scope of this project.
[13] This phrase is borrowed from Ahmed *et al.*, 'Measuring Constitutional Islamization'.

(ii) that historical ruptures, including those resulting from Muslim authoritarian rule, colonialism and a lack of direct involvement by Muslim jurists, have stunted its potential growth;

(iii) that the parameters of constitutionalism within the Muslim world are characterized by the selective application of Islamic law and by a wide gap between the rhetoric of Islamic constitutionalism and the realities on the ground; and

(iv) that this gap exemplifies existing contestation of what constitutes Islamic constitutionalism, resulting in the fragmentation of the authority and legitimacy of state and government.

The substance of the chapter is presented in five sections:

the first section sets out the meaning and scope of constitutionalism, both from Western and Islamic perspectives;

the second section identifies the historical roots of modern Islamic constitutionalism, including the Medina Charter, highlighting some of the current debates;

the third section focuses on constitutional texts in contemporary Muslim nation states, offering insights into experimentations with Islamic constitutionalism;

the fourth section discusses the question whether Islamic constitutionalism can lead to the establishment of an Islamic state; and

the fifth section provides some concluding reflections.

2.2 The Meaning and Scope of 'Constitutionalism'

The emergence of Islamic constitutionalism in its contemporary manifestations came about in the late nineteenth and early twentieth centuries with the reception in the Muslim world of Western constitutionalism.[14] Understanding the contours of Western constitutionalism is therefore a prerequisite to any discussion on Islamic constitutionalism. And just as Islamic constitutionalism is evolving and contested terrain, so is its Western counterpart a subject of debate and contest. Whilst most scholars on the subject agree that the concept gained currency during the nineteenth century, some seek the roots of Western constitutionalism in ancient Athens, revived during the English Civil Wars.[15] Others trace its roots to natural law doctrines in Christianity and Judaism.[16]

As noted, at its most basic level Western constitutionalism implies the upholding of the rule of law, the enforcement of effective limitations on governmental

---

[14] Grote and Röder, *Constitutionalism in Islamic Countries.*

[15] F. D. Wormuth, *The Origins of Modern Constitutionalism* (New York: Harper and Brothers, 1949). See also G. Scott, *Controlling the State: Constitutionalism from Ancient Athens to Today* (Cambridge, MA: Harvard University Press, 1999).

[16] J. Esposito and J. Voll, *Islam and Democracy* (New York: Oxford University Press, 1996), p. 51.

powers, and the protection of fundamental rights. It has been defined as 'government channeled through and limited by a constitution'.[17] Distinguishing constitutions from constitutionalism, it may be described as 'auxiliary precautions' against governmental encroachment upon the rights of the people,[18] leading to the opinion that modern constitutionalism 'came first and foremost to be defined in functional opposition to absolutism as a guarantee of *limited* (by law) government'.[19]

An-Na'im offers a contemporary and comprehensive explanation:

> Constitutional governance refers to a set of principles that limit and control the powers of government in accordance with the fundamental rights of citizens and communities, as well as the rule of law to ensure that the relationship between individuals and the state is regulated by definite legal principles of general application rather than the despotic will of a ruling elite.[20]

Constitutionalism, however, has its detractors, and one critic has offered a more cryptic definition: 'Constitutionalism is the name given to the trust which men repose in the power of words engrossed on parchment to keep a government in order.'[21] Waldron offers what he describes as a 'democratic critique' of the main elements of constitutionalism. He believes that judicial review, an important element of constitutionalism, is fraught with difficulties, and he is concerned that judges thereby wield considerable power, which may be dangerous and not always in the best interests of the people, since judges are typically unelected and not directly accountable to a democratic community.[22] Elsewhere, he states that constitutionalism

> comprises a commitment to fundamental self-determination (in some versions a commitment to popular sovereignty) along with an ideology of restrained and limited government which in many ways is quite uneasy with or hostile to the

---

[17] Scruton, *A Dictionary of Political Thought* (London: Macmillan, 1982), p. 94.

[18] Wormuth, *Origins*, includes separation of powers and judicial review as elements of constitutionalism.

[19] Walker, 'Constitutionalism', 209, original emphasis.

[20] An-Na'im, *Islam and the Secular State*, includes general principles, such as representative government; transparency and accountability; the separation of legislative, executive and judicial powers; and independence of the judiciary as principles of constitutionalism (p. 104). Henkin in turn presents an expanded list of nine elements that in his view are constitutive of constitutionalism: constitutional government, the separation of powers, the sovereignty of the people and democratic government, constitutional review, an independent judiciary, government limited by a bill of rights, control over the police, civilian control of the military, and no (or limited) state power to suspend the constitution: L. Henkin, 'Elements of Constitutionalism', Occasional Paper Series (Center for the Study of Human Rights, 1994).

[21] W. Hamilton, 'Constitutionalism', in E. Seligman and A. Johnson (eds.), *Encyclopedia of the Social Sciences*, vol. 4 (Cambridge: Cambridge University Press, 1931), p. 255, cited in R. S. Kay, 'American Constitution', in L. Alexander (ed.), *Constitutionalism: Philosophical Foundations* 16 (1998).

[22] J. Waldron, 'Constitutionalism: A Skeptical View', in T. Christiano and J. Christman (eds.), *Contemporary Debates in Political Theory* (Oxford: Wiley–Blackwell, 2009), p. 279.

idea of popular government and quite willing to neglect or sideline important tasks such as democratic empowerment.[23]

Constitutionalism and democracy are now increasingly linked as 'constitutional democracy', and this is a term that Islamic constitutionalism has had to grapple with.

As a concept, therefore, Western constitutionalism is not limited to the 'three-pillars' definition, but is evolving and responding to scrutiny from supporters and critics alike.[24] For the purposes of the present inquiry, with its comparativist nature, it is useful to rehearse here some of the main arguments. In addition to the critique offered by Waldron, others, too, appear sceptical of constitutionalism as a panacea for the protection of human rights. They suggest that constitutionalism is not necessarily a bulwark against usurped rights and oppression by government and by others in positions of power and authority.[25] Women, minorities, the poor and other vulnerable groups within societies are often not conceived of as 'we, the people'; one element of constitutionalism, and one upon which a great deal of Western scholarly pride rests, is the sovereignty of the people enshrined in text. But a reality check of many jurisdictions casts doubt on this as we pose a simple question: do all the people have a voice? Are they truly sovereign and able to make their voices heard?[26] Massive protests on the streets of Western capitals did not prevent the invasions of Iraq or Afghanistan; Western governments are routinely put in power by a minority of their electorate;[27] referendums are uncommon, and their outcomes often manipulated toward a government's pre-existing goals.[28]

Tensions abound between what limited government entails in constitutional texts and how that translates into a 'tyranny of the majority' (or indeed minority), the 'voiceless' sovereignty of the people, and partisan judges. Furthermore, whilst Western constitutionalism appears secular and supposedly neutral towards all sections of society, the religious underpinnings of many Western states are apparent. The UK's monarch, for example, is the governor of the Church of England and is required at least to be in communion with it (though

---

[23] Ibid.

[24] W. Waluchow, 'Constitutionalism', *Stanford Encyclopedia of Philosophy* (Spring 2014); W. Waluchow, 'Constitutions as Living Trees: An Idiot Defends', *Canadian Journal of Law and Jurisprudence* 18(2) (2005), n.p.; W. Waluchow, 'Constitutional Interpretation', in A. Marmor (ed.), *The Routledge Companion to Philosophy of Law* (New York: Routledge, 2012), pp. 417–33; Waldron, 'Constitutionalism'; D. Strauss, *The Living Constitution* (New York: Oxford University Press, 2010).

[25] Strauss, *The Living Constitution*; Waluchow, 'Constitutions as Living Trees'; Waluchow, 'Constitutionalism'; Waldron, 'Constitutionalism: A Skeptical View'.

[26] Loughlin and Walker, 'Introduction', in Loughlin and Walker, *The Paradox of Constitutionalism*.

[27] For example, Labour's 1997 UK election victory was gained with the votes of less than one-third of the electorate.

[28] In 2008, contrary to the government's hope, Ireland voted against amending its Constitution to enable ratification of the Treaty of Lisbon; the electorate was again asked to vote in 2009, and supported the change.

not necessarily a practising Christian). The US, despite the Establishment Clause in the First Amendment, is a predominantly Christian country, and examples of case law, policy and practice bear this out. The US Supreme Court, for instance, has ruled in favour of religious practices by giving their decisions a secular guise. In *McGowan* v. *Maryland*, 'the Court held that while Sunday laws requiring the closure of business on Sundays have a religious origin aiming at promoting church attendance, it can be recast as secular as a uniform day of rest'.[29] Likewise, in *Marsh* v. *Chambers* the Court upheld the practice of opening legislative sessions with prayers,[30] describing this as a long-standing and widely accepted practice. The constitutional text, clearly, does not always reflect faithfully how constitutionalism operates in practice.

Cognizant of the gap between a constitutional text and the complexities involved in interpreting and implementing it, An-Na'im's observation on broadening the contours of constitutionalism is particularly insightful. He would like to see constitutionalism to be inclusive of

> the network of institutions, processes, and the broader culture that is necessary for the effective and sustainable operation of this principle. In other words, I am more concerned with a comprehensive and dynamic set of values, and with social and political institutions and processes, than with formal application of abstract general principles and specific rules of constitutional law. Constitutional and legal principles are relevant and important, but the effective and sustainable implementation of these principles can be realized only through the broader and more dynamic concept of constitutionalism.[31]

So, constitutionalism is descriptive of a complex idea deeply embedded in the historical experiences of peoples asserting rights against arbitrary authority, subjecting those officials who exercise governmental powers to the limitations of a higher law. It upholds the desirability of the rule of law as opposed to arbitrary judgment or whim. The touchstone of constitutionalism is the concept of limited government under a higher law. In Islamic constitutionalism, this higher law is Islamic law and *sharia*, and it is to this that we now turn our attention.

2.2.1 Islamic Constitutionalism

So what is Islamic constitutionalism, what are its characteristics and parameters, and how has it been defined by different writers and from different perspectives? To begin with, Islamic constitutionalism flows from the constitutional text wherein Islamic law and *sharia* have been instituted and which forms the basis of state and government. Islamic law and *sharia* are thus constitutive of the

---

[29] *McGowan* v. *Maryland*, 366 U.S. 420 (1961) at 434, cited in Sultany, 'Religion and Constitutionalism'.

[30] *Marsh* v. *Chambers*, 463 U.S. 783, 792 (1983).

[31] An Na'im, *Islam and the Secular State*, p. 102.

structure of governance and of the political system through which the contents
of constitutionalism are reviewed, critiqued and revitalized. At its most abstract
level, and in popular Muslim consciousness for the most part, the Qur'an,
Sunna and *sharia* are analogous to constitutional texts. It is not uncommon to
hear it said that 'we do not need a constitution: the Qur'an and Sunna are our
constitution.' Believed by Muslims to be a supreme text of divine origin, few
would take issue with that statement, since the Qur'an in its many facets also
performs the role of constitutional guidance.[32] Abul A'la Maududi[33] describes
the Qur'an as the central pillar of Islamic constitutionalism, which in his opinion
means to establish 'the Divine Law and make Sharia the law of the land . . . And
if instead of God-given laws some other laws are adopted, it means nothing
short of rejection of the *din* [i.e. Islam and its way of life] as such'.[34]

But the Qur'an, like all constitutional documents, 'is replete with ambiguous
and general statements subject to varied interpretations'.[35] It is difficult to argue
that the *sharia* offers clear guidance on a specific form of government,[36] although
verses of the Qur'an and a number of incidents and practices from the Medina
period have been taken as indicators on how to construct the contours of Islamic
constitutionalism,[37] including *shura* (consultation), *bay'ah* (allegiance), and the
supremacy of *sharia*. Contrary to the way in which some Western writers have
invoked Christian and Judaic traditions to advance constitutionalism, 'Islam,
despite its strong legal orientation, provoked no [similar] interest [in developing
constitutional law].'[38]

The meaning of Islamic constitutionalism, like its Western counterpart, is
obviously open to debate. Different scholars place emphasis on those aspects
of constitutionalism which in their view constitute its most important features.

[32] The Government of the Kingdom of Saudi Arabia has long adopted this approach and only in
the past two decades adopted a Basic Law (1992) to regulate the governance structures of the
country.

[33] Founder of the religious political party Jamaat-e-Islami and pioneer of the call for an 'Islamic
State'. He was a prolific writer and his work influenced some of the religiously oriented
political parties in the Middle East, including the Muslim Brotherhood in Egypt.

[34] Maududi, *Political Theory of Islam*, pp. 158–9.

[35] M. H. A. Reisman, 'Islamic Fundamentalism and Its Impact on International Law and Politics',
in M. Janis (ed.), *The Influence of Religion on the Development of International Law* (The
Hague: Kluwer, 1991), p. 108.

[36] El Fadl, *Challenge of Democracy*.

[37] Kamali, 'Constitutionalism in Islamic Countries'; An-Na'im, *African Constitutionalism*.

[38] N. J. Brown, *Constitutions in a Non-constitutional World: Arab Basic Laws and the Prospects for
Accountable Government* (Albany: State University of New York Press, 2002) p. 108. Esposito
and Voll, *Islam and Democracy*, refer to early Western scholarship claiming roots of Western
constitutionalism in Christian and Judaic traditions. For a different viewpoint, however, see E.
Kedourie, *Democracy and Arab Political Culture* (London: Frank Cass, 1992), p. 5, where it is
argued that 'the idea of representation, elections, popular suffrage, political institutions being
regulated by laws laid down by a parliamentary assembly, laws being guarded and upheld by an
independent judiciary, and ideas of the secularity of state are all profoundly alien to the
Muslim political tradition'. Cited in Ahmed and Gouda, 'Measuring Constitutional
Islamization', note 48.

Rabb, for instance, defines it as 'at a minimum . . . a modern governing structure of limited powers in which a written constitution designates Islamic law as a source of law'.[39] Placing emphasis on judicial review as integral to the concept, Sultany offers a more detailed definition, thus: 'By Islamic constitutionalism, I mean the constitutionalization of religious law in a largely-liberal constitution through empowering constitutional court judges to review the validity of laws on the grounds of their compatibility with Islamic law.'[40] Arjomand, one of the most prolific writers on the subject, conceptualizes Islamic constitutionalism as an evolving phenomenon defined by various historical waves of constitutional and political ideas.[41] He identifies three main waves of Islamic constitutionalism: an early phase that gave rise to liberal constitutionalism in the Muslim world, followed by ideological constitution-making and the return to the rule of law, and lastly post-ideological constitutionalism.[42] In Arjomand's view, 'The conception of the place of sharia (Islamic law) in the constitutional order is crucial for the definition of Islamic constitutionalism, but it was not a constant and has in fact, varied considerably from one period to another.'[43]

So no single definition of Islamic constitutionalism is able to encapsulate the variety of constitutionalisms encountered in the Muslim world. As a modern concept heavily informed by Western constitutionalism, Islamic constitutionalism in its written formulation (though not necessarily in practice) may be understood as follows: it declares *sharia* as the (or a) principal source of the constitutional text; it subjects officials exercising governmental powers to the limitations of *sharia*; it includes repugnancy clauses in constitutional texts requiring all laws to be in consonance with *sharia*. By analogy to Western conceptions, it may therefore be said that the touchstone of Islamic constitutionalism is the concept of limited government under *sharia*. Similarly, and by analogy, Islamic constitutionalism describes and prescribes *sharia* as both the source and the limits of government power.[44]

From our understanding of the term 'constitutionalism' as meaning 'limited government by law', it would be fair to argue that the concept is embedded within established Islamic norms of governance: the exercise of power by those in positions of authority in an Islamic polity is (theoretically) limited, as it must remain within the confines of *sharia*; Islamic constitutionalism therefore describes and prescribes *sharia* as both the source of governmental power and the limitation imposed upon it. But Islamic constitutionalism, of course, comes in as many shades and hues as there are relationships between the constitutional text and constitutionalism: it would arguably be more appropriate and closer to reality to talk of Islamic *constitutionalism(s)* in the plural rather than as a single phenomenon.

---

[39] Rabb, 'We the Jurists', 527–8.   [40] Sultany, 'Religion and Constitutionalism', pp. 349–50.
[41] Arjomand, 'Islamic Constitutionalism', p. 116.   [42] Ibid.   [43] Ibid.
[44] I am grateful to Arjumand Kazmi for her input on developing this argument.

Western and Islamic constitutionalism(s) demonstrate the fluidity, plurality and dynamic nature of the debates surrounding those concepts. Both continue as works in progress, impacting on and being impacted upon by global developments, including webs of governance at sub-national, national and supra-national levels. Insofar as Islamic constitutionalism is concerned, world events of the past few decades have brought into prominence the subject of Islamic law, constitutionalism, and what it means to be defined as an 'Islamic' state.[45] The slogans that emanated from across the Muslim world during the Arab Spring were those demanding Islam *and* democracy, calling for 'constitutional democracy' in the Muslim world.[46] This link between democracy and constitutionalism may be seen as the latest stage in the evolution of Islamic constitutionalism.

2.3 The Historical Roots of Modern Islamic Constitutionalism(s)

Muslim nation states today are governed (mostly) through constitutional documents and act within a mutually recognized and reciprocal framework of international norms.[47] That the nation state as we understand and experience it today did not exist in seventh-century Arabia (and for a long time thereafter), and that modern nation states, including Muslim jurisdictions, have visibly different governance structures to that of the first seventh-century Muslim state of Medina, are both simple matters of fact. It is fair to say that for Islamic rules of constitutionalism, to be relevant and operative today, contextual and not literal equivalents must be extracted, using what we might call a 'historical lens'. Why is it important to go down this path, rather than accept constitutionalism as a purely modern concept and move on?

To begin with, Western constitutionalism and its Islamic counterparts are products of their respective historical pasts, wherein proponents seek the roots of this modern debate. Whilst Western political developments played a pivotal role, the constitutive role of intellectual and academic discourse in the evolution of Western constitutionalism cannot be underplayed. But the same is not quite true of Islamic constitutional history, where numerous ruptures in the form of colonial as well as post-colonial authoritarian rule have broken its conceptual thread. There appear to be a number of reasons for engaging with premodern Muslim history in debates on contemporary Islamic constitutionalism. Although not a consensus position, arguably the reiteration of a

---

[45] For an authoritative study on the impossibility of an 'Islamic State', see An-Na'im, *Islam and the Secular State.*

[46] A burgeoning field of study, it is contributing to an ever-increasing scholarship in many disciplines, including law, politics and international studies, constitutional theory, religious studies and Islamic law and Islamic studies. What is offered above and in the discussion below constitutes some selected highlights of this discourse.

[47] Depending upon the constitutional structure of the state, international treaties to which they are party become part of national law applicable in national courts.

Muslim identity and 'Islamic-ness' of state, law and governance holds value for most Muslims – and always has done – and it gives legitimacy and validation to Islamic constitutionalism today if it can be shown that there are contextual equivalents in Islamic history.[48]

Simultaneously, the historical approach also brings into relief those ruptures and disconnects between modern concepts and Islamic traditions; it challenges the Muslim consciousness at an individual and a community level to realize and to accept (or not) that not all modern concepts had their equivalents in early Muslim traditions. Finally, it also reminds us of certain 'uncomfortable' aspects of premodern Islamic legal traditions, such as the institution of slavery: despite its categorical presence in the Muslim past, it is one to which few Muslims today would subscribe.

2.3.1 The Medina Charter

In exploring and evaluating the historical roots of Islamic constitutionalism, we might reasonably argue that the first line of enquiry rests with the 'master' document of Islamic constitutionalism – the Medina Charter,[49] a set of deeds drawn up by the Prophet Muhammad upon his migration from Mecca to Medina in the year 622. (The two Arabic texts on which scholars mainly rely are those recorded by the eighth-century historian Ibn Ishaq[50] and by the medieval theologian Abu 'Ubayd.[51]) In terms of its primacy as a foundational document for Islamic constitutionalism, it is the oldest existing Islamic text on the subject. Mere antiquity, however, is not its sole claim to fame: the importance and authenticity of the Medina Charter has been acknowledged by, among others, the 'source-critical' scholar Patricia Crone, who has said that it 'sticks out like a piece of solid rock in an accumulation of rubble'.[52] Also known as the Constitution of Medina, the Charter has been variously described as a 'municipal

---

[48] This view has been challenged by, among others, Sultany, who argues that there is scant empirical evidence as to what 'demanding Islamic law and Shari'a as part of the constitution' in actual fact means to the popular Muslim consciousness; see Sultany, 'Religion and Constitutionalism'. Similarly, An-Na'im points to the complex nature of the influence of Islamic norms of individuals and state and government and the difficulty of ascertaining this in policy and legislation as well as in social life. See A. A. An-Na'im, 'Islam, Islamic Law and the Dilemma of Cultural Legitimacy for Universal Human Rights', in C. Welch and V. Leary (eds.), *Asian Perspectives on Human Rights* (Boulder, CO: Westview Press, 1990), pp. 31–2.

[49] A number of English translations of the Medina Charter are available, some using a slightly different numbering of its articles according to the preferences of the translators.

[50] M. Ibn Ishaq, *Sirat Rasul Allah*, translated from Guillaume's *The Life of Muhammad: A Translation of Ishaq's Sirat Rasul Allah* (Karachi: Oxford University Press, 1955), pp. 231–3 (numbering added).

[51] Abu 'Ubayd al-Qasim bin Sallam, *Kitab al-Amwal*, cited in Arjomand, 'The Constitution of Medina'.

[52] P. Crone, *Slaves on Horses: The Evolution of the Islamic Polity* (Cambridge: Cambridge University Press, 1980), p. 7, cited in Arjomand, 'The Constitution of Medina', p. 555. See also P. L. Rose, 'Muhammad, the Jews and the Constitution of Medina: Retrieving the Historical Kernel', *Der Islam* 86 (2011), 1–29.

charter' (by the earliest modern scholar, Julius Wellhausen,[53] who studied it in 1889), and as the 'so-called Constitution of Medina' (by R.B. Serjeant).[54] Abou El Fadl believes that 'the document does not read like a modern constitutional document – rather, it reads more like a contract or as a corporate organizational document.'[55] On the other hand, Hamidullah, translating and analysing the document in the 1960s through the lens of twentieth-century constitutionalism, called it 'the earliest written constitution in the world'.[56] We need, then, to see whether general principles of governance and constitutionalism may be extracted from the *Sahifah al-Madinah*, or whether it is simply a 'municipal charter' of limited utility and application.

Arjomand, in developing a socio-legal interpretation of the Medina Charter, divides the document into three parts: the Covenant of Unity, the Pact with the Jews of Medina, and the Supplement to the Pact with the Jews on Defence of the City. It established rights and obligations among the various groups of people residing in Medina, including the *Ansar* ('helpers') of Medina, the *Muhajirun* ('emigrés') who had left Mecca with the Prophet Muhammad, and the Jewish tribes of Medina, 'as they embarked upon a new journey of co-existence and cooperation in the nascent Muslim polity'.[57] The Covenant of Unity 'is simultaneously an act of foundation of a community of faithful covenanters (*mu'minin*), which defines the relation among them, and an act of confederation between them and the Muslims of Quraysh and Yathrib'.[58] The Pact with the Jews of Medina affirmed Jews as members of a unified *umma* and envisaged the establishment of one pluralist nation – the *umma* – formed from 'believers and non-believers' alike. It recognized diverse communities, as is evident from the fact that it did not treat any group 'as one monolithic population; instead it recognized their diverse ethnic, cultural, or linguistic characteristics, just as it acknowledges similar diversity within the Muslim population'.[59]

A model of freedom of religion and non-interference in religious matters was also envisaged in the Charter, which clarified that 'the Jews have their

---

[53] J. Wellhausen, 'Muhammads Gemeindeordnung von Medina', *in* Skizzen und Vorarbeiten, vol. 4 (Berlin: Reimer, 1889), 65–83, cited in Arjomand, 'The Constitution of Medina', note 2.

[54] By and large, Western scholars are less enthusiastic about the Medina Charter: see R. B. Serjeant, 'The Constitution of Medina', *Islamic Law Quarterly* 8 (1964), 3–16; and 'The Sunnah Jami'a Pacts with the Yathrib Jews, and the Tahrim of Yathrib: Analysis and Translation of the Documents Comprised in the So-called "Constitution of Medina"', *Bulletin of the School of Oriental and African Studies* 41 (1978), 1–41; M. Lecker, *The 'Constitution of Medina': Muhammad's First Legal Document* (Princeton: Darwin, 2004).

[55] El Fadl, 'The Centrality of Shariah', p. 48.

[56] M. Hamidullah, *The First Written Constitution in the World*, 2nd edition (Lahore: Sheikh Muhammad Ashraf, 1968). Arjumand does not agree with this sweeping statement but instead, agreeing with Wellhausen, believes that at the time the object of the charter was to create not a state but a political community.

[57] Ahmed *et al.*, 'Measuring Constitutional Islamization', citing A. Emon, 'Comment: Reflections on the "Constitution of Medina": An Essay on Methodology and Ideology in Islamic Legal History', *UCLA Journal of Islamic & Near Eastern Law* 1 (2002), 103.

[58] Arjomand, 'The Constitution of Medina', p. 561.

[59] Ibid.; Ahmed *et al.*, 'Measuring Constitutional Islamization'.

religion and the Muslims have theirs';[60] the lasting effect of this constitutional recognition of the Jewish religion was the institution of religious pluralism in Islam. Having made this point, though, and in view of evolving notions of Islamic constitutionalism, this religious pluralism did not last long. As Islam and Muslim rule over neighbouring lands expanded, tolerance for religious pluralism appears to have shrunk proportionately. Likewise, Muslim-majority jurisdictions today have failed to emulate this early religious pluralism of the Medina Charter, as is evident from their constitutional texts.[61]

Another issue dealt with constitutionally was the declaration of a sacred and protected enclave in Medina.[62] For the sake of stability in governance, the Medina Charter was used to ringfence a physical space where armed conflict was outlawed. This principle of a 'safe haven' was enshrined in the Charter as a legally enforceable rule. Arjomand also notes that the 'rite of bonding men into brotherhood through Muhammad's mixing their blood is a particular instance of group fraternization between the emigrants and their Yathribite hosts'.[63] He argues that this be considered a constitutional act, especially since it had legal implications, including mutual inheritance rights.[64] This clause in the Charter broke new ground, moving away as it did from lineage-based to religion-based relationships. Analysed through a constitutional lens, it may also be understood as the beginnings of the 'equality clause' in a modern constitutional text. The purpose of this fraternization was to demonstrate ways in which communities and nations could rise above discrete tribal and parochial loyalties. Herein too lie lessons for modern Islamic constitutionalism.

Though the Medina Charter may be read from a variety of perspectives other than the constitutionalist (e.g. the socio-legal, the political and the politico-military), it is the constitutionalist reading of the document that 'accounts for its designation in modern scholarship as the Constitution of Medina [and] acquires new immediacy with the current widespread preoccupation of Muslims throughout the world with Islamic constitutionalism'.[65] Serjeant, for example, is of the view that, from the perspective of Islamic constitutionalism, the Charter essentially framed the conceptual model of future political leadership, or Caliphate, in an Islamic state.[66] Ahmed and Gouda for their part argue that, while not being what Hamidullah describes as the world's first constitution, the Medina Charter nevertheless forms the roots of what is today described as Islamic constitutionalism.

---

[60] Arjomand, 'The Constitution of Medina'; Ahmed *et al.*, 'Measuring Constitutional Islamization', p. 32.

[61] For instance, the 1973 Constitution of the Islamic Republic of Pakistan, where a distinction between Muslim and non-Muslim is made, and the Malaysian Constitution, where the Malay population, mostly Muslim, have a privileged status in the hierarchy of citizenship. Similarly the laws of Middle Eastern Arab states make a distinction between Arabs and non-Arabs. Citizenship and nationality rights are not extended to non-Arabs in most of these jurisdictions.

[62] Arjomand, 'The Constitution of Medina', p. 560.   [63] Ibid., p. 559.

[64] Ibid. This rule of inheritance was later abrogated by vv. 8:75, 4:33, and 33:6 of the Qur'an.

[65] Arjomand, 'The Constitution of Medina', p. 555.   [66] Serjeant, 'The Sunnah Jami'a Pacts'.

As theorized by Maududi, the pioneer of the idea of the 'Islamic state' and 'Islamic democracy', the Medina Charter reflects the three cardinal principles of the Islamic political system – *tawhid* (the oneness of God), *risala* (God's message to mankind) and *khilafa* (caliphate).[67] It has also been described as 'a series of agreements drafted by the Prophet to regulate peaceful co-existence and relationships among all of the significant tribes of Medina (Yathrib) including Muslims, Jews, Christians and pagans'.[68] Kamali notes that it is the 'earliest constitutional document of authoritative standing on record', and that it laid the foundations of a new community in Medina by establishing a basis for the relationships between religious groups: 'Issues of leadership and subjugation of the powerful tribes to the authority of the new government, principles of equality and justice, freedom of religion, right of ownership, freedom of movement and travel, and combating crime were among the major preoccupations of this document.'[69] In view of the range of themes addressed, the Charter could arguably be described as the first written constitution to incorporate both religion and politics.[70]

No matter how the Medina Charter has variously been perceived by successive generations of scholars, they all agree that it represents a milestone in Islamic historical jurisprudence. So the lack of attention to a document of such seminal importance when seeking the roots of Islamic constitutionalism is puzzling. Arjomand puts it rather curtly: 'That so little attention is paid to this important document in the massive ideological literature on the Islamic state is surely proof of the poverty of Muslims' current historical understanding.'[71] An-Na'im, too, echoes this dissatisfaction at the lack of historical mention and indeed inspirational utilization of the Medina Charter by subsequent generations of Muslims:

> I am not suggesting that these documents collectively known as the Charter of Medina were a 'constitution' or that they provided 'citizenship' in the modern sense of these concepts. Still, I believe that the terms of those agreements were the historically contextual equivalents of a constitution and citizenship in the modern context. Consider that the Magna Carta (1215) and the English Bill

[67] Maududi, 'Political Theory of Islam', in K. Ahmad (ed.), *Islam: Its Meaning and Message* (1976), pp. 159–61.

[68] A. A. An-Na'im, *What Is an American Muslim? Embracing Faith and Citizenship* (Oxford: Oxford University Press, 2014), Chapter 1, note 1, citing Serjeant, 'The Sunnah Jami'a Pacts'; and Y. Yildirim, 'Peace and Conflict Resolution in the Medina Charter', *Peace Review* 18(1) (2006), 109–17.

[69] Kamali, 'Constitutionalism in Islamic Countries', p. 20.

[70] Yildirim, 'Peace and Conflict Resolution'.

[71] Arjomand, 'The Constitution of Medina', p. 557. In accompanying note 14, Arjomand refers to a notable exception, the Indonesian reformer Nurcholish Madjid, who found in the Charter the source of inspiration for his Paramadina Foundation and advocacy of religious pluralism and democracy. See A. F. Baki, 'Islam and Modernity: Nurcholish Madjid's Interpretation of Civil Society, Pluralism, Secularization and Democracy', *Asian Journal of Social Sciences* 33 (2005), 492–5.

of Rights (1689) are the basis of the unwritten conventions that constitute the constitution of the United Kingdom today.[72]

Kamali follows a similar line of argument: formal constitutions, and hence constitutionalism, have but a short history in Muslim jurisdictions, and the Medina Charter – a contextual equivalent of a constitutional framework, with elements of the main pillars of constitutionalism – is not highlighted. That there would be exact similarities is not to be expected; neither should we be looking for them: a gulf of some fourteen centuries in sociopolitical ideas and governance lies between the Charter and contemporary constitutional articulations. But a constitutionalist reading is certainly plausible and useful. As Arjomand remarks, we should attribute the absence of the Charter's significance in debates on Islamic constitutionalism to the absence of a constitutional history of the Muslim world:

> The historical jurisprudence of von Savigny, Gierke, and Maitland in the nineteenth century was not just a recording of objective facts but also *constitutive* of the idea of public and constitutional law in Western Europe. It constructed the historical–political reality of modern constitutionalism that endowed such medieval legal documents as Magna Carta with the significance they now possess.[73]

Looked at this way, the Charter has the potential to become the basis of Islamic constitutionalism by being constructed as such.

The Prophet Muhammad responded to a need and developed a foundational document as a starting point, and his Charter contains elements of the rule of law, limitations upon government, fundamental rights and religious pluralism. Such an interpretation of the principles found in the Medina Charter differs, unsurprisingly, from those in constitutional frameworks fourteen centuries on. Yet contextual equivalents are to be found, and these may be usefully employed despite the apologetic renderings and selective readings of some scholars. The puzzle of why the Charter has not been used as a template by successive generations of Muslims does not lend itself to an easy answer; but, bearing in mind the historical trajectories of Muslim states, a few inferences may be drawn. To begin with, those in positions of power and authority would have felt challenged by the pragmatism of the Charter. Its accommodation of non-Muslims as equals would have gone against the grain of unequal citizenship rights on the basis of religion, ethnicity and so on present in some constitutions of Muslim jurisdictions today. The Charter also prescribed a structure for the governance of multi-faith and multi-tribal communities. By implication, therefore, the rule of law implied accountability for those in positions of power and authority, a situation not necessarily palatable to monarchs and rulers.

[72] An-Na'im, *What Is an American Muslim?*, Chapter 1, note 1.
[73] Arjomand, 'The Constitution of Medina', 557, original emphasis.

At an Islamic state and governmental level, the Charter has not been accorded great importance, and very little is known of it in the general consciousness[74] – indeed, it would be quite telling were one able to count the number of times the Charter had received mention during the constitution-making deliberations of Muslim jurisdictions in recent years. Though the Charter's dynamic and inclusionary nature could be understood as one of the key principles of any theory of Islamic constitutionalism and governance, Islamic historical jurisprudence has not maintained an intellectual inquisitiveness in interrogating and interpreting for posterity what might have been developed as a pivotal document.

2.3.2 Current Debates on Islamic Constitutionalism

Islamic constitutionalism as a modern concept in its present articulations, and as informed by Western constitutionalist debates and understandings, is neither a homogeneous nor a static concept. In order to engage with the practice of Islamic constitutionalism, it is useful first to analyse some of the main theoretical perspectives on the subject. We shall turn, then, to an oft-repeated question in the existing literature: what are the contours of Islamic constitutionalism, and how compatible is it with Western conceptions of constitutionalism?[75]

A number of scholars, including Kamali, Al-Hibri and Brown, assert that it is indeed compatible with Western conceptions. They do so on the premise that there exist in their view significant parallels between the two traditions. Kamali, to begin with, notes common elements – 'commitment to the rule of law, consultative government of civilian characteristics, a substantive separation of powers, and limited government' – that make the substance of an elected and accountable constitutional government 'agreeable to Islam'.[76] He remains, however, aware of differences. Whereas constitutionalism in the West is entrenched in the secularist legacy of an Enlightenment that separated religion from politics, for example, many Islamic nations have enshrined Islam in their constitutions: 'Islam provides a set of general principles on justice, governance, accountability and rules of law that are not postulated in the Western nation state model.'[77] It is observed that Western constitutionalism is grounded in the

---

[74] For example, Pakistan is the only Muslim state in the world created in the name of Islam (cf. the popular slogan of pro-Pakistan Muslims of India: *Pakistan ka matlab kya? La ilaha illalah*, meaning 'What is the meaning of Pakistan? There is no God but Allah'). This view is not uncontested and reference is made to the speeches of Muhammad Ali Jinnah, the founder of Pakistan, who took great pains to reject any essentially religious character to the state. See F. Devji, *Muslim Zion: Pakistan as a Political Idea* (London: Hurst, 2013). Very few Pakistanis, though, are aware of the Medina Charter. It is only in recent months (since August of 2014), during public protests led by Imran Khan and Allama Tahir-ul-Qadri, that there has been popular awareness of the Charter through televised speeches made by such personages.

[75] Bearing in mind that various scholars may be comparing dissimilar conceptions of constitutionalism both Western and Islamic.

[76] Kamali, 'Constitutionalism in Islamic Countries', p. 20.

[77] Ibid., but see also the observation above, where, citing US case law, I argue that Western constitutional practice is not always secular.

view that there exists a fundamental duality of interests, wherein an individual's rights and liberties must be constitutionally protected against the power of the state; Islam's assertion of the underlying oneness within God's creation, on the other hand, 'provides a set of principles oriented toward an essential unity of basic interests between the individual and the state'.[78] Al-Hibri, too, supports the view that *sharia* is compatible with constitutionalism, citing *bay'ah*, *shura*, and broad consultation as indicative parallels.[79] She also suggests that, whether directly or indirectly, America's Founding Fathers were influenced by Islamic precedent, claiming that the library of Thomas Jefferson had at least one copy of the Qur'an.[80] Her apologetic argument evokes, however, a strong rebuttal from El Fadl, whom it is worth quoting at length to demonstrate the distance between their standpoints:

> A number of contemporary commentators have argued that Islam is fundamentally compatible with a constitutional system of government. In a style that has become all too common in the contemporary Muslim world, commentators will generate a laundry list of concepts such as *shura*, the contract of the caliphate, the ideas of *bay'ah*, and the supremacy of *Sharia*, and then conclude that Islam is compatible with constitutionalism. Some proclaim that the Qur'an is the constitution of Muslims and then rest in the comfort of the same assertion. These types of arguments, however, are for the most part vacuous. They are the product of an intellectual restlessness induced by the rather abysmal fortunes of the Islamic heritage in the modern age.[81]

Again, Brown argues that *sharia* does indeed provide a basis for constitutionalism. To his mind, the fact that the ideas of constitutionalism have not taken root in Muslim jurisdictions lies in the scant attention devoted to structures of political accountability rather than in any inherent flaws in the concept.[82] However, following Kamali and others, he points toward differences between Western and Islamic forms of constitutionalism: first, while Western constitutionalism is based upon the idea of popular sovereignty, *sharia* is based upon the will of God;[83] second, while Western constitutionalism focuses on the idea of limiting government, *sharia* provides the very principles of governance.[84]

---

[78] Kamali, 'Constitutionalism in Islamic Countries', pp. 20–1.

[79] A. Al-Hibri, 'Islamic Constitutionalism and the Concept of Democracy', *Case Western Reserve Journal of International Law* 24(1) (1992), 3–10; and 'Islamic Constitutionalism and the Concept of Democracy', in F. Dallmayr (ed.), *Border Crossings: Toward a Comparative Political Theory* (Lanham, MD: Lexington Books, 1999), pp. 61–88.

[80] A. Al-Hibri, 'Islamic and American Constitutional Law: Borrowing Possibilities or a History of Borrowing?', *University of Pennsylvania Journal of Constitutional Law* 1 (1999), 497. In note 19, Al-Hibri also cites supporting evidence that reference was made to Islam and Muslim cultures, albeit mostly in a negative vein, during the US constitutional debates (1787–8).

[81] El Fadl, 'The Centrality of Shariah', pp. 54–5.

[82] Brown, *Constitutions in a Non-constitutional World*, p. 162.

[83] Note here how the Objectives Resolution in successive Pakistani Constitutions has declared that whereas sovereignty belongs to Allah, it is expressed through the representatives of the people of Pakistan.

[84] N. J. Brown, 'Islamic Constitutionalism in Theory and Practice', in E. Cotran and A. O. Sherif (eds.), *Democracy, the Rule of Law and Islam* (London: Kluwer, 1999), p. 492.

Nadirsyah Hosen offers an interesting thesis that justifies the compatibility of the Islamic legal traditions with constitutionalism. 'Is *Sharia* compatible with the principle and procedural form of constitutionalism?' he asks.[85] In response, he argues that the Qur'an and *hadith* 'cannot be seen as the Islamic constitution but perhaps as its code of high constitutional principles': the Qur'an and *hadith* do not prefer a definite political system, yet 'both primary sources have laid down a set of principles, or ethical values and political morals, to be followed by Muslims in developing life within a state'.[86] Hosen then proceeds from this point to develop a list of what he terms 'principles of Islamic Constitutional law', framed as counterarguments to those who believe that 'Islamic constitutionalism' is an oxymoron.

Citing the renowned scholar Al-Mawardi in his support, Hosen argues that the caliph's powers are not unlimited. To this end, the institution of *wilayah al-mazalim* (redress of wrongs) may be reconceived as an administrative tribunal or constitutional court;[87] broadening the classic understanding of *ijma* (consensus of opinion among jurists on a point of law) to include the public's role in decision-making is another potential principle;[88] *shura* (consultation) and *ijma* are closely connected and may be developed as legislative power in an Islamic constitutional democracy.[89] As regards the protection of fundamental rights as a constitutional principle, Hosen proposes the redeployment of *maqasid-al-sharia* (the 'objectives of Islamic law', the core values of which include religion, life, intellect, honour and lineage) as an important principle of Islamic constitutionalism:[90] 'A new *ijtihad* could be performed by considering the theory of the *maqasid-al-Sharia* and examining the *Sharia* as a unity in which detailed rules are to be read in light of their broader premises and objectives.'[91] His final principle is to deploy the freedom of religion enunciated in the Medina Charter.[92]

But whilst Hosen's efforts at bringing Islamic law and historical antecedents to bear upon a modern phenomenon are in principle agreeable, the main challenge would be to achieve legitimacy and acceptance for such a novel proposition. Such principles mean going beyond historical articulations and applications of *sharia*, no doubt evoking opposition. A drastically different perspective considers Islamic constitutionalism from the conviction that the only constitution for an Islamic state is the divine revelations of the Qur'an and the Sunna, being fundamentally incompatible with Western-style constitutionalism or democracy (indeed, the 1992 Basic Law of Saudi Arabia is based upon this conviction).[93] Backed by Wahabi scholars, this school of thought is against adopting *any*

---

[85] Hosen, *Shari'a and Constitutional Reform in Indonesia*, p. 30, and 'In Search of Islamic Constitutionalism'.
[86] Hosen, 'In Search of Islamic Constitutionalism', 13–14.
[87] Ibid., 14–15, citing *Al-Ahkam al-Sultaniyah*, in which Mawardi produces a list of ten areas where the public may seek redress against the excesses of public officials.
[88] Ibid., 15.   [89] Ibid.   [90] Ibid., 17.   [91] Ibid., 18.   [92] Ibid.
[93] Grote and Röder, *Constitutionalism in Islamic Countries*.

human-made constitution; most modern Islamist movements, including Abul
A'la Maududi's highly influential Jamaat-e-Islami in South Asia, and Sayyid
Qutb in Egypt, are and always have been openly suspicious of Western-style
democracy and secularism, viewing these as against the will of God.

Quite different, then, from Hosen's, Maududi's concept of the Islamic
state is based on the ideology of 'theo-democracy', which repudiates national
sovereignty or the sovereignty of the people and replaces it with the sovereignty
of God and the vice-regency (*Khilafat* or Caliphate) of men. Theo-democracy
is inherently limited democracy, as not even the entire Muslim *umma* has the
authority to change an explicit command of God. In such a system, the ruler is
answerable on the one hand to God and on the other to his fellow men, who
have delegated authority to him. Maududi and Sayyid Qutb (himself inspired
by Maududi's writings),[94] base their political theory on the claim that Islamic
law and human nature (*fitra*) are in perfect harmony. By adopting Islamic conceptions of state and politics, 'modern humans can be both free and governed'.[95]

The dilemma for Muslims today is that they continue to hold the original
community established at Medina in 622 as the Islamic ideal, losing sight of
present-day realities.[96] For instance, for Muslims who believe Muhammad to
be God's final prophet, the model of the state he established in Medina cannot
be replicated after his death. After all, those who govern will always be ordinary
human beings who do not have the exclusively divine authority that the Prophet
had.[97]

There is today no universal consensus among Muslims about what the Medina model means, or how it can be applied. Sunni Muslims (who form the
majority of Muslims in the world) believe that the reign of the Prophet in
Medina, and, for three decades after his death in 632, that of the four 'rightly
guided caliphs', represent the most authoritative model of Islamic constitutional
theory.[98] Shia Muslims, meanwhile, have their own ideal models of the rightful
imamate after the rule of Ali, the last of the Medina caliphs, depending on their
respective doctrine and history (Ja'fari, Isma'ili, Zaydi and so forth).[99] Sunni
and Shia uphold their respective models as the ideal while constantly decrying
deviations by subsequent generations, often justified as coerced by compelling
circumstances, such as internal strife or external invasion.

---

[94] The works of Sayyid Qutb have received closer attention in recent years as he is seen as the
inspiration for the *salafi* ideology and for other Islamists, including leaders of Al-Qaeda. See S.
Qutb, *Social Justice in Islam* (ed. H. Algar, trans. J. R. Hardie and H. Algar) (Oneonta, NY:
Islamic Publications International, 2000) and *Milestones* (trans. A. Z. Hammad) (Indianapolis:
American Trust, 1990).

[95] A. F. March, 'Taking People as They Are: Islam as a "Realistic Utopia" in the Political Theory of
Sayyid Qutb', *American Political Science Review* 104(1) (2000), 189.

[96] An-Na'im, *Islam and the Secular State*, pp. 106–7, and *African Constitutionalism*, pp. 8–9.

[97] An-Na'im, *Islam and the Secular State.*   [98] Ibid., pp. 106–7.

[99] Ibid., citing S. A. Arjomand, *The Shadow of God and the Hidden Imam: Religion, Political
Organization and Societal Change in Shi'ite Iran from the Beginning to 1890* (Chicago: The
University of Chicago Press, 1984).

In 'Islamic Constitutionalism', Arjomand shows that there has been significant variation over time in the role of *sharia* in an Islamic constitution.[100] Though the journey can be traced back to the late nineteenth century with the drafting of the Tunisian Constitution of 1861 and the Ottoman Constitution of 1876, he argues, it was during the Iranian constitutional revolution of 1906–11 that serious debates took place among Shi'ite jurists about the role of Islam in *limiting* the autocratic powers of the Iranian state.[101] Though in that initial phase Islam and *sharia* were considered as *limitations* to government and law-making, a subsequent (and arguably more influential) phase of ideological development saw Islam and *sharia* as the 'basis' of a constitution. Finally, an incipient third phase of post-ideological constitutionalism is witnessing the return of Islam and *sharia* as a *limitation* to power.[102]

Islam and *sharia* as limitations upon law-making and governance came about as a result of robust intellectual and political scholarship by Shi'ite jurists in post-constitutional-revolution Iran. The key principle of this *mashruta mashru'a* or '*sharia*-permissible' constitutionalism was to set firm limits on the government and legislation of the autocratic shah. Its scholars were alarmed by the secular implications of constitutional government as advanced in the West, and they argued for the creation of a committee of jurists – the *Majles* – to perform a supervisory role to ensure legislation was consistent with *sharia*, thus giving themselves a prominent role in law-making and in making the government accountable.

Islamic constitutionalism's subsequent 'ideological' phase began with the creation of the Islamic Republic of Pakistan. There, state sovereignty was declared to reside in God, with the Qur'an and Sunna considered the basis of the constitution.[103] This premise underpinned the legitimacy of governments only insofar as they fulfilled the requirements of *sharia*, with Islam placed over and above people's freedom to legislate for themselves. A Federal Shariat Court was established in the 1980s to determine the conformity of laws with the Qur'an and Sunna, its judges nominated by the then army general turned president, Muhammad Zia-ul-Haq.[104] These 'ideological underpinnings' of constitutional governance also influenced the constitutions of Syria (1950), Kuwait (1962) and Egypt (1978), and culminated in the Iranian Constitution of 1979. This declared that all laws, including the constitution itself, found inconsistent with *sharia* were null and void. It also appointed a *vali-ye faqih* ('guardian jurist') as the

---

[100] Arjomand, 'Islamic Constitutionalism'.   [101] Ibid.   [102] Ibid.

[103] The Objective Resolution adopted by the Constituent Assembly of Pakistan in 1949 stated that 'sovereignty over the entire universe belongs to God Almighty alone' and that 'Muslims shall be enabled to order their lives in the individual and collective spheres in accord with the Holy Quran and the Sunna.' See L. Binder, *Religion and Politics in Pakistan* (Berkeley and Los Angeles: University of California Press, 1963), pp. 142–3.

[104] In practice, though, the jurisdiction of the Federal Shariat Court in Pakistan is fettered by limitations on which areas of law cannot be ruled upon as un-Islamic. For a detailed discussion see Chapter 4 below.

supreme authority over religious and political matters and gave him the right to call an end to interpretative debate on any subject of religious and political concern. This right has been consistently used to silence 'reformist' seminarians critical of the state's treatment of issues such as democracy and gender.

An important development within debates on Islamic constitutionalism is the increasingly robust slogan to be heard within the Muslim world (and incessantly during the Arab Spring): 'We want Islam *and* democracy'. Whilst neither the slogan nor the concept of Islamic constitutional democracy is new, the manner in which the two were articulated as complementary by the 'Muslim street' is a recent phenomenon. As in other aspects of Islamic constitutionalism, democracy as one of its integral components is interpreted varyingly. Maududi advances the concept of what he terms 'theo-democracy', wherein the state is governed by Islamic law and *sharia*. But this perception of democracy under the umbrella of *sharia* raises the questions which *sharia*, and whose interpretation of *sharia*? Most countries in the Muslim world today accord through their constitutional texts equal rights to men and women, including the right to vote and to be voted into public office, including being judges and heads of state. Yet there is an equally vocal constituency of Muslims (both scholars and laity) who contest this understanding, except when it suits their political interests. (By way of an example, Jamaat-e-Islami, the right-wing political party founded by Maududi, an advocate of theo-democracy and of limited rights for women, supported the sister of Pakistan's founder Muhammad Ali Jinnah in a presidential election in 1966; a decade or so later, they challenged Benazir Bhutto's right to run for prime minister on the basis that 'Islamic law' prohibits women from holding public office.)

Adopting a more positive position, in *Islam and the Challenge of Democracy*, Abou El Fadl discusses the challenge of understanding Islam and democracy as concepts and practices and asserts that there are both interpretative and practical possibilities in the tradition of Islamic political thought that might be developed into a democratic system. For example, the Qur'an itself does not specify a particular form of government, but it does outline a set of sociopolitical values that must be practised in any Muslim polity: 'pursuing justice through social cooperation and mutual assistance . . . establishing a non-autocratic, consultative method of governance; and institutionalizing mercy and compassion in social interactions'.[105] Democracy, then – especially a constitutional democracy – possesses the 'greatest potential' for Muslim polities to pursue justice and safeguard human dignity by ascribing to the 'democratic' values of equality of free speech, free association and universal suffrage, 'without making God responsible for injustice or the degradation of human beings'.[106]

The reality, however, is that states in the Muslim world *do* appear to make God responsible, by adopting 'Islamic' constitutional texts but leaving it to people to sort out the problems. On this basis, constitutional Islamization has been

---

[105] El Fadl, *Challenge of Democracy*, p. 5.   [106] Ibid., p. 6.

questioned and critiqued, arguing that there should be no place for religious law in constitutionalism;[107] neither Iran nor Pakistan as pioneers of 'Islamization' or of the 'shariatization' of constitutionalism could be termed success stories. Even ardent proponents have expressed deep disappointment at half-hearted Islamization and at the lack of social justice that the introduction of Islamic law was expected to usher in. The failures of the shariatization of Islamic constitutionalism in producing compelling constitutional jurisprudence both in Iran and in Pakistan have resulted in its being critiqued by post-ideological Islamic constitutionalism. In linking Islamic constitutionalism to social-contract theory, with *sharia* as a 'natural law', proponents argue in favour of Islamic constitutionalism guided by the principles of *sharia*, but also by the principles of democracy, human rights and pluralism: witness Iraq's 2005 Constitution by way of an example.[108]

2.4 Constitutional Texts in Contemporary Muslim States

As indicated in the introduction to this chapter, Islamic constitutionalism is a complex phenomenon demanding multiple levels of analysis. These include (i) the theoretical debates, (ii) the putting into operation of Islamic constitutionalism through the constitutional text and (iii) Islamic constitutionalism in practice. Having analysed the main threads of the theoretical perspectives, we now turn to how Islamic constitutionalism is manifested in constitutional texts.[109]

Beginning with Tunisia in 1861, a number of Muslim jurisdictions adopted the form of Western constitutions. When they did so, in order to indigenize and legitimize this foreign concept they inserted 'Islamic clauses' into the constitution.[110] The Tunisian Constitution, for example, opened with reference to God and to *sharia*, and the king had to take an oath in the name of God. Other jurisdictions declared their Islamic credentials by inserting similar provisions in their own constitutional texts:[111] Turkey followed suit in 1876,

---

[107] Sultany, 'Religion and Constitutionalism', focuses on four assumptions that underlie religious constitutionalism: that popular acceptance requires Islamic constitutionalism, that people's identity includes religious law and should be reflected in Islamic constitutionalism, that Islamic law's indeterminacy belittles the possible risks of its constitutionalization, and that the legal order's transparency requires an acknowledgement of the religious aspect. Using persuasive arguments supported by factual examples, Sultany rebuts all four assumptions, proposing instead an inclusionary constitution that excludes reference to religion.

[108] This is also the general train of thought in the writings of An-Na'im.

[109] General snapshots of the 'Islamicity' of constitutional texts will be provided as it is outside the scope of this chapter to offer any detailed study of such a wide spread of jurisdictions.

[110] Brown, *Constitutions in a Non-constitutional World*, p. 20. Article 4 appointed His Majesty the Sultan, under the title of Supreme Caliph, as the protector of the Muslim religion. Article 7 required the Sultan to carry out the provisions of Islamic law, and Article 11 proclaimed Islam as the state religion.

[111] P. Marshall, *Radical Islam's Rules: The Worldwide Spread of Extreme Shari'a Law* (Lanham, MD: Rowman and Littlefield, 2005); Ahmed and Gouda, 'Measuring Constitutional Islamization', p. 1.

with references to Islam and *sharia* a recurring feature. In 1882, Egypt became the third Muslim country to draft a Western-style constitution with Islamic provisions. Iran too wrote its formal constitution in 1906, followed by a supplementary one containing a Bill of Rights in 1907. Whilst all four had Islamic law as a common textual feature, another similarity was that all four were written as a tool for reform and an instrument for accountable government. All four were written in response to, and under pressure from, Western powers (Great Britain and France in particular).

From constitutional developments in the late nineteenth and the early twentieth centuries, critical shifts took place during the twentieth century which continue into the present. The arrival of the modern nation state clashed with the traditional law-makers in the Muslim world, i.e. the jurists who believed they had the authority to determine *sharia* and Islamic law. As Muslim states became independent from colonial regimes, they were keen to institute Islam into their constitutional texts as a sign of their sovereignty as well as religious identity; simultaneously they appropriated law-making into their hands. The result has been an ongoing struggle for legitimacy and authority. Iran's constitutional revolution of 1906–7, for instance, was the result of resistance against an absolutist monarchy and in support of the installing of *sharia* as a limitation on government. The 1979 revolution had as a key slogan the setting up of an 'Islamic government', and Ayatullah Khomeini ordered *sharia* to be translated into the constitutional documents.[112]

Modern Islamic constitutionalism from its very inception, then, was driven by political expediency rather than a genuine desire for Islamic governance. This approach, aptly described as 'constitutional Islamization',[113] is evidenced by the insertion of an 'Islamic supremacy' clause (declaring *sharia* to be a, or the, principal source of legislation), and/or a repugnancy clause stating that no legislation may be adopted in contravention of *sharia*, and requirements for the head of state to be a Muslim, for persons holding public office to take an Islamic oath, and so on. The usual diversity among Muslim jurisdictions is evident in the number and nature of Islamic clauses inserted.

There are significant differences in the way in which Islam is treated in the constitutions of Muslim countries,[114] 'especially in terms of its relationship to the state and public life',[115] and there is little uniformity in the number and substance of Islamic clauses inserted. For instance, it might be assumed that *all* Muslim jurisdictions would declare themselves to be an Islamic state, or declare

---

[112] Said Amir Arjomand, 'Islamic Constitutionalism', *Annual Review of Law and Social Science* 3 (2007), 125.

[113] Ahmed and Gouda, 'Measuring Constitutional Islamization'.

[114] N. Abiad, *Sharia, Muslim States and International Human Rights Treaty Obligations: A Comparative Study* (London: BIICL, 2008), p. 34; also T. Stahnke and R. Blitt, *The Religion–State Relationship and the Right to Freedom of Religion or Belief: A Comparative Textual Analysis of the Constitutions of Predominantly Muslim Countries* (USCIRF, 2005).

[115] A. A. An-Na'im, 'Human Rights in the Arab World: A Regional Perspective', *Human Rights Quarterly* 23 (2001), 707.

Islam to be the state religion, or insert a repugnancy clause. Yet this assumption is incorrect, and does not in fact represent the norm in the constitutions of predominantly Muslim countries.[116] In an empirical study of forty-five Muslim-majority countries, Ahmed and Gouda analysed Islamic constitutional clauses so as to inform some important questions:[117] how prevalent was constitutional Islamization? What were the main Islamic clauses? And which countries had the most and least Islamized constitutions?[118]

Their data shows that Islamization is to be found in the constitutions of many Muslim-majority nations. A small number describe themselves as 'secular' (notably Central Asian republics and Turkey, but also Mali), and some, including Uzbekistan and Sierra Leone, are completely silent on the treatment of religion, declaring neither Islam nor secularism as a principle. Although almost 60 per cent express some relationship to Islam in their constitutions, there is a tremendous variation in the degree and mode of constitutional Islamization: in terms of the number of Islamic clauses and their formulation, Iran appears to have the most 'Islamic' constitution in the world, followed by Saudi Arabia, the Maldives, Pakistan, Somalia, Afghanistan, Yemen, Bahrain, Iraq and Algeria. This categorization in no way reflects higher degrees of adherence to Islam or Islamic law; simply that numerically these countries' constitutional documents carry the highest number of references to it.

One popular clause is the 'state religion' clause: ten countries explicitly declare themselves to be Islamic states, along with a further fifteen which declare Islam to be the state religion (in the Maldives, for example, one must profess Islam in order to be a citizen). The constitutions of eighteen state that Islam will be a source of law, and six contain a repugnancy clause. The constitution of Iran states that judges should refrain from laws that violate Islam. The Saudi Arabian Basic Law of 1992 states, 'Judges bow to no authority' other than *sharia*. Fifteen constitutions require the head of state to be a Muslim, and some, including Iran and Yemen, also require this of the head of government. The Constitution of Pakistan requires members of Parliament not to 'violate Islamic injunctions'. Pakistan, Mauritania, Morocco, Egypt and Algeria provide for an advisory religious body (e.g. Pakistan's Council of Islamic Ideology), though in Iran this is not merely advisory but wields significant powers, including that of reviewing legislation to assess whether laws violate Islamic principles. The Pakistani Constitution also provides for a Federal Shariat Court that can 'examine and decide the question whether or not any law or provision of law is repugnant to the injunctions of Islam', as laid down in the Qur'an and Sunna.[119]

In terms of rights, while the Afghan and Bahraini constitutions limit some constitutional rights to what is permitted by Islam, Iran, Saudi Arabia and the Maldives make *all* rights subject to Islam. In terms of analogizing Islam and

---

[116] Abiad, *Sharia*, p. 34.   [117] Ahmed *et al.*, 'Measuring Constitutional Islamization'.
[118] Ibid., p. 2.
[119] But see the application of this constitutional provision in Pakistan in Chapter 4 below.

sharia as a limit upon the earthly authority of rulers, only the Saudi constitution explicitly provides that the king 'shall undertake to rule according to the rulings of Islam', while in the Maldives the president can be removed from office if he is 'in direct violation of a tenet of Islam'. Rarely, though, do we find clauses regarding other aspects of Islamic practice, for example *jihad*, giving to charity, or religious education.

A number of Muslim jurisdictions have inserted a repugnancy clause into their constitutions in efforts to 'Islamize' the legal system and afford it authority and legitimacy. In turn, these clauses in particular have been invoked in judicial review to challenge 'un-Islamic' legislation. It is useful to cite some of these by way of illustration.

Article 2 of the 1907 Constitution of Iran became the first Islamic constitutional 'repugnancy' clause: laws passed by the National Assembly 'must never to all ages be contrary to the sacred precepts of Islam and the laws laid down by the Prophet'. That language would subsequently be emulated by other Muslim states. Article 72 of the Iranian Constitution now provides, 'The Islamic Consultative Assembly cannot enact laws contrary to the usual and ahkam [*sic*] of the official religion of the country or to the Constitution'. The Constitution of Pakistan states, '(i) All existing laws shall be brought in conformity with the injunctions of Islam as laid down in the Holy Quran and Sunnah, in this Part referred to as the Injunctions of Islam, and no law shall be enacted which is repugnant to such Injunctions.'[120] In 1980, Article 2 of the Egyptian Constitution was amended to make *sharia the* principal source of legislation rather than *a* principal source. Since then, various revisions of the constitution of Egypt have held 'Islamic' provisions: 'Islam is the state religion ... The principles of Islamic Sharia are the principal source of legislation.'[121] In Iraq, 'Islam is the official religion of the State and it is a fundamental source of legislation ... No law that contradicts the Islamic provisions of Islam may be established.'[122] And in Afghanistan 'no law can be contrary to the beliefs and provisions of the sacred religion of Islam'.[123]

So on the face of it, Islamic supremacy and repugnancy clauses would appear to be overarching principles of Islamic constitutionalism, ensuring compliance of all national legislation with Islamic law. Yet the reality is different, and the limited and arguably political nature of these repugnancy clauses lies in the temporal limitations placed upon them.[124] The notion of repugnancy existed in the 1973 Constitution of Pakistan, whose courts have, since the establishment in 1980 of the Shariat Court, engaged in judicial review of

[120] Article 227 of the Constitution of the Islamic Republic of Pakistan, 1973.
[121] The latest revision was in 2013, with earlier revisions including the Constitution of the Arab Republic of Egypt (11 September 1971), Article 2, and the Provisional Constitution of the Arab Republic of Egypt (March 2011), Article 2.
[122] Constitution of Iraq (October 2005), Article 2.
[123] Article 3 of the Constitution of the Islamic Republic of Afghanistan (January 2004).
[124] H. A. Hamoudi, 'Repugnancy in the Arab World', *Williamette Law Review* 48 (2012), 427.

legislation to ensure *sharia* compliance.[125] The outcome of cases, however, has highlighted the limits of the repugnancy clause. For example, the Muslim Family Laws Ordinance 1961 is protected from scrutiny under the repugnancy clause. This has been demonstrated a number of times, in particular in the case of *Farishta*.[126] Likewise, in the widely publicized *riba* (interest on loans) case, the repugnancy clause was invoked to challenge the interest-based economy of the country. For over two decades the case has dragged on in various courts, but despite a ruling prohibiting *riba*, implementation is nowhere in sight.[127] In 1985, the Supreme Constitutional Court of Egypt exempted existing legislation from the repugnancy clause by upholding a provision of the Egyptian Civil Code that permitted *riba*.[128] Indeed, there appears to be a rising trend in the Arab world that repugnancy should not apply to legislation enacted prior to the date that the repugnancy clause was inserted into the constitution.[129] This is, of course, a rather incoherent position; as Hamoudi puts it, 'Either Islamicity of legislation is a cornerstone of a Muslim state or it is not. If it is then the date of the legislation *vis-à-vis* the date of repugnancy amendment is surely beside the point for advocates of conformity with Sharia.'[130]

It is no surprise, then, that commentators have dismissed the *sharia* provision in Muslim constitutions as 'chiefly symbolic'[131] and unlikely to meaningfully constrain legislative activity. Some, however, are of the opinion that even simply privileging Islam as 'a' source of law, albeit the weakest formulation, makes it possible to argue that Islam forms the 'fundamental legal framework' of such constitutions.[132] This line of argument has been advanced at an international level by 'objecting states' in the face of 'blanket' reservations by some Muslim states to the UN Convention on the Elimination of All Forms of Discrimination against Women (CEDAW), the UN Convention on Rights of the Child (CRC), and others.[133]

---

[125] See J. A. Redding, 'Constitutionalizing Islam: Theory and Practice', *Virginia Journal of International Law* 44 (2004), 773–97.

[126] For a detailed discussion, see the analysis of the *Farishta* case in Chapter 3 below.

[127] See K. A. Stilt, 'Islam Is the Solution: Constitutional Visions of the Egyptian Muslim Brotherhood', *Texas International Law Journal* 46 (2010), 73, 88. Despite the fairly long history of the repugnancy clause in the constitution of Pakistan and its application in the courts, there is not much cross-fertilization between Pakistani case law regarding repugnancy and developments in the Arab world. Unlike the Arab Middle East, Pakistan is a common law jurisdiction, a possible reason for this lack of cross-fertilization.

[128] This will be discussed in further detail in Chapter 4. An English translation of the decision is available as Supreme Constitutional Court (Egypt) Sharia and Riba: Decision No. 20 of 1985, *Arab Law Quarterly* 1 (1985), 100.

[129] Hamoudi, 'Repugnancy', 428.   [130] Ibid.

[131] Ibid., 431, citing N. Feldman and R. Martinez, 'Constitutional Politics and Texts in the New Iraq: An Experiment in Islamic Democracy', *Fordham Law Review* 75 (2006), 903.

[132] Brown and Sherif, 'Inscribing the Islamic Shari'a', p. 63.

[133] For example, upon accession to CEDAW Libya stated that accession 'is subject to the general reservation that such accession cannot conflict with the laws on personal status derived from the Islamic Shariah'; Iran, upon ratification of the UNCRC, entered the following reservation: 'The Government of the Islamic Republic of Iran reserves the right not to apply any

If the provision for *sharia* to be a/the source of law is a weak expression of Islamic supremacy, then the repugnancy clause is more robust. These clauses, it has been argued, originated in British colonial law, and indeed all forms of Islamic supremacy clause are more prevalent in former British colonies than in other Muslim states. In many cases, these clauses are the result of a popular demand acceded to by ruling elites to safeguard political interests,[134] and in some cases – for example Tunisia, Egypt, Turkey and Iran – were in fact first introduced during moments of liberalization and modernization.

Unsurprisingly, given the broad range of Islamic traditions across global cultures and societies, there is little uniformity of expression and implementation of repugnancy or supremacy clauses among the constitutions of Muslim-majority jurisdictions, and neither is there a predictable and consistent application discernible in the jurisprudence of states that possess such clauses (see Table 2.1).

Nisrine Abiad has made the important point that what is significant is the status accorded to Islamic law in *legislation*, not simply in the constitution.[135] She cites slavery as an example where Muslim states have demonstrated that they are able to 'take steps to limit the implementation of older Sharia-based norms which conflict with modern legal, social and political practice'.[136] But though the institution of slavery, which can be understood from the Qur'an as permitted in Islam, is now almost universally not allowed, the practice of charging interest abounds in the Muslim world, despite attempts through judicial review to outlaw what the Qur'an clearly prohibits.

So the plurality of approach regarding which aspects of Islamic law ought to be codified and made into legally enforceable rules varies from state to state in an apparently arbitrary manner. It is important to note that there is a great difference between writing Islam into a constitution and writing it into legally enforceable substantive laws.

The wide diversity of constitutional provisions among Muslim-majority jurisdictions on the one hand brings to the fore the plurality of the Islamic legal traditions, but on the other it also partially provides an answer to the question of why there is increasing militancy to be seen in attempts to install 'Islamic caliphates' in Muslim countries (and indeed beyond): such Islamist militants are able to declare existing Muslim jurisdictions, despite their degree of Islamization, to be universally 'un-Islamic'.

2.5 Can Islamic Constitutionalism Lead to an Islamic State?

Having explored constitutional Islamization and its implications for governance in Muslim-majority jurisdictions, the question to broach now is: does

provisions or articles of the Convention that are incompatible with Islamic Laws and the international legislation in effect.'

[134] D. Ahmed and T. Ginsburg, 'Constitutional Islamization and Human Rights: The Surprising Origin and Spread of Islamic Supremacy in Constitutions', *Virginia Journal of International Law* 54(3) (2014), 615–95.

[135] Abiad, *Sharia*, p. 32.   [136] Ibid., p. 33.

Table 2.1 The diversity of constitutional Islamization among Muslim-majority jurisdictions (adapted from T. Stahnke and R. Blitt, *The Religion–State Relationship and the Right to Freedom of Religion or Belief: A Comparative Textual Analysis of the Constitutions of Predominantly Muslim Countries* (Washington, DC: USCIRF, 2005); and D. Ahmed and M. Gouda, 'Measuring Constitutional Islamization: The Islamic Constitutions Index', *Hastings International & Comparative Law Review* 38(1) (2015), 1–76)

Declared to be Islamic states	Islam declared to be the state religion	No constitutional declaration of Islamicity	Declared to be secular states
Afghanistan	All 10 Islamic	Albania	Azerbaijan
Bahrain	states, plus	Gambia	Burkina Faso
Brunei	Algeria	Indonesia	Chad
Iran	Bangladesh	Lebanon	Guinea
Maldives	Comoros	Sierra Leone	Kyrgyzstan
Mauritania	Djibouti	Sudan	Mali
Oman	Egypt	Syria	Niger
Pakistan	Iraq	Uzbekistan	Senegal
Saudi Arabia	Jordan		Tajikistan
Yemen	Kuwait		Turkey
	Libya		Turkmenistan
	Malaysia		
	Morocco		
	Qatar		
	Somalia		
	Tunisia		
	UAE		

constitutional Islamization lead to the establishment of an 'Islamic state' (bearing in mind the controversial nature of the term)?

Abul A'la Maududi, one of the main architects of an 'Islamic state', linked enforcement of *sharia* to the need for an Islamic state and 'Islamic' democracy. In his view, the central pillar of Islamic constitutionalism is the Qur'an. In *The Islamic Law and Constitution*, he states that the Qur'an 'not only gives guidance in the political, social and economic fields. It prescribes punishments for certain crimes and enunciates principles of monetary and fiscal policy. These cannot be translated into practice unless there is a State to enforce them'.[137] And therein lay the necessity of an Islamic state. Islamic constitutionalism as elucidated by Maududi means establishing a state where Islamic law forms the law of the land, i.e. where there is no separation between state and religion, and there are three foundational pillars: *tawhid*, *risala* and *khilafa*.

---

[137] A. A. Maududi, *The Islamic Law and Constitution*, 4th edition (Lahore: Islamic Publications, 1969), p. 158.

Literal readings of the Qur'anic texts provide support to those who argue that there is no separation between religion and state in the Islamic traditions. Verse 4:59, especially, incorporates ideas which might be advanced as the basis for an Islamic state:

> O ye who believe! Obey Allah, and obey the messenger and those of you who are in authority; and if ye have a dispute concerning any matter, refer it to Allah and the messenger if ye are (in truth) believers in Allah and the Last Day. That is better and more seemly in the end.

Here, 'obey Allah' is understood to denote the *tawhid* principle of God's unity, and 'obey the messenger' to denote *risala* – the referring of all disputes to, and compliance with, the decisions of the Prophet. 'Those who are in authority' has been interpreted as authority vested in the *khilafa* (Allah's vice-regent, interpreted historically to include, for instance, the 'Four Rightly Guided Caliphs'[138] and the Ottoman sultans). But the fact that the interpretative universe of *tawhid*, *risala* and *khilafa* has to be broadened has been conceded even by Islamists.[139] The leader of Tunisia's moderate Islamist An-Nahdah Party, for example, is on record as stating that, in the interest of national stability, he would not call for changing the country's legal framework so long as its Islamic identity is highlighted and accepted. And even Maududi himself participated in electoral processes in Pakistan with the intention of promoting 'theo-democracy'.[140] More recently, Maududi's political party, the Jamaat-e-Islami (JI), has voted women members into Parliament: the JI is a coalition partner in the government of the Khyber Pakhtunkhwa.[141] Such contradictions have not gone unnoticed, and Maududi's canvassing for an Islamic state has been challenged by scholars and commentators.

Reisman makes this critical observation:

> As the [Muslim] Empire expanded, it also became more susceptible to a practical, if not theoretical, separation between the functions of Church and State. Admittedly, the influence of religion in government remained an important ingredient of political power, capable of conferring legitimacy on leadership. Political power without religious blessing was constantly threatened.[142]

Where the *ulema* (religious scholars) once commanded influence over the law-making process, increasingly the laws required to run day-to-day affairs became the prerogative of government. Rulers and dynasties legislated in accordance

---

138 The *Khulafa-i-Rashideen*: Abu Bakr Siddiq, Omar Ibn-al-Khitab, Usman bin Affan, and Ali ibn abi-Talib.

139 Ahmed *et al.*, 'Measuring Constitutional Islamization.   140 Ibid., p. 33.

141 In a television interview, the daughter of the late head of JI, Samia Raheel Qazi, stated that the preferred position of the JI was for women to be home-makers and not to venture into politics. However, they were constrained to adopt a 'pragmatic' approach and send women to Parliament if they wanted to influence policy and laws in order to achieve their objective of an 'Islamic' state.

142 Reisman, 'Islamic Fundamentalism', pp. 111–12.

with whichever school of juristic thought they subscribed to, this being a human articulation, varying from state to state and regime to regime, of the divine sources of law. Such states could be described as 'Muslim' merely by virtue of having Muslim-majority populations; but there could equally be as many shades of 'Muslim' state as there are schools of thought and perspectives. The notion that there might practically be a practicable 'Islamic state' to which all Muslims could or would subscribe is unsustainable.

An-Na'im has dedicated a lifetime of scholarship to developing what is arguably one of the most authoritative and historically embedded cases for the separation of religion and politics.[143] His view is that an 'Islamic state' is a contradiction in terms, as states cannot be 'religious' as humans can; to protect religious freedom, the state must be neutral and secular. The proposition of an 'Islamic state' is in his opinion the product of twentieth-century political developments spearheaded by Islamist groups and based upon the ideological views of men such as Abul A'la Maududi (1903–79) and Sayyidd Qutb (1906–66), and does not reflect the true history of Islamic society.[144]

Throughout post-Medina history through to the twentieth century, Muslims have organized themselves into states over which rulers have sought religious legitimacy, but none claimed to have established an 'Islamic state'.[145] Yet Saudi Arabia and Iran, the two *modern* states claiming to be such, represent different and opposing versions of Islam, each considering the other's doctrine and ideology to be 'heresy', and the extremes within each camp even calling the other *kafir* (infidel, non-believer). Which of these, if either, then, could be considered a 'true', 'Islamic' state? In An-Na'im's view, it is neither:

> The idea of an Islamic state to enforce *Sharia* as positive state law is incoherent because once principles of *Sharia* are enacted as positive law of a state, they cease to be the religious law of Islam and becomes the political will of that state.[146]

Given the undeniable diversity of opinions among Islam's various schools of juristic thought, any self-professed Islamic state and its elite would have the task of choosing *which* version of *sharia* to effect as state law. But this of itself would be a political and not a religious act. An-Na'im calls, therefore, for 'an institutional separation of religion and state while recognizing and subjecting the unavoidable connectedness of religion and politics to the limitations of fundamental constitutional rights'.[147]

The fundamental question at issue in constructing Islamic constitutionalism should be one of translating the essential justice and practical implications

---

[143] An-Na'im, *Islam and the Secular State.*   [144] Ibid., p. 45.

[145] A. A. An-Na'im, 'Islam, State and Politics', paper presented at the Human Rights and Renewing of Religious Discourse conference, 18–20 April 2006, at the Swedish Institute, Alexandria, p. 7.

[146] A. A. An-Na'im, 'An Inclusive Approach to the Mediation of Competing Human Rights Claims', *Constellations* 20(1) (2013), 11–12.

[147] Ibid., 12.

of historical models such as Medina, not of replicating these under radically different circumstances. If we take, for example, the notion of *shura*, the fruits of such consultation was neither binding nor practised in a systematic and inclusive manner: verse 3:159 of the Qur'an instructed the Prophet to consult with believers, but to implement his decision once he had made up his mind.[148] Verse 42:38 might describe believers as a community that decides matters through consultation, but the Qur'an does not describe in detail how such consultation might be done in practice and what happens when there is disagreement.[149] The simple point here is that there is a lack of detailed constitutional mechanisms set out in existing Islamic jurisprudence, where the dominant view remains that *shura* indicates a requirement to seek advice without necessarily being bound by it. The actual practice of the Prophet and of the caliphs of Medina confirmed this to be the 'correct' understanding, which became the norm for the Umayyad and Abbasid Caliphates and other states throughout the premodern history of Islamic societies.[150]

2.6 Concluding Reflections

This chapter set out to explore the characteristics and parameters of Islamic constitutionalism in relation to Islamic law and *sharia*. It highlighted the challenges emerging as a result of this exploration, suggesting likely future possibilities and directions for Islamic state and government. Here, then, are some concluding reflections.

Encouraged by the late Patrick Glenn's multivalent view, that all traditions contain elements of others and that everything is a matter of degree, the present chapter set out to investigate Islamic constitutionalism by adopting a comparative approach (i.e. between Western and Islamic perspectives).[151] The characteristics and parameters of constitutionalism, both Islamic and Western, are not static; neither are they homogeneous or monolithic. Each contains elements of the other; both are dynamic and evolving concepts responding to changing political, social and economic developments; yet both remain embedded in their respective heritages and histories and evolve therefrom. Historical ruptures, continuities and discontinuities have played a critical role in how both Western and Islamic constitutionalisms have developed.

An analysis of Islamic and Western constitutionalism(s) reveals that the lines between the religious and the secular remain blurred in both traditions. The West's (secular) jurisdictions declare secularity in their constitutional texts yet continue to be influenced by religious norms; conversely, Islamic constitutionalism has imbibed secular traditions from Western liberalism as well as from

---

[148] An-Na'im, 'Islam, State and Politics', p. 12.
[149] N. J. Coulson, 'The State and the Individual in Islamic Law', *International and Comparative Law Quarterly* 6 (1957), 55–6.
[150] An-Na'im, 'Islam, State and Politics', p. 12.   [151] Glenn, *Legal Traditions*, p. 35.

colonial rulers. Neither is there an effective cut-and-dried formula for keeping religion and politics separate. Secularity hides in its innermost recesses sparks of religiosity (witness those examples of American constitutionalist practices where the constitutional text is secular, yet, under judicial review, religious values and practices are upheld). On the other hand, in Muslim jurisdictions, despite religiously attributed constitutional texts, courts do not always uphold these, often siding instead with non-religious legislation. The repugnancy clauses in the constitutions of many Muslim-majority jurisdictions are a prime example of text that sets out to defend Islamic rules yet places limits upon the circumstances in which they apply.

Whilst Western constitutionalism emanates from a liberal heritage, Islamic constitutionalism is a hybrid concept, where Islamic law clauses have been grafted onto a Western, liberal framework of governance. A Western form has been required to incorporate the Islamic substance, which is itself then restrained by limiting clauses, an idea again emanating from the West. Yet it would not be true to say that this hybridity is alien to the Islamic societies to which it is applied. The constant pressure of applying Western modes of governance, principles and practices of democracy or accountability may be partly responsible for this fragmentation of form and substance.

Widespread ignorance of historical accounts of Islamic constitutionalism and their misinterpretation for political gain (such as in Pakistan or Iran) does not help the case, and the parameters and characteristics of Islamic constitutionalism and ways of governing Muslim nations are likely to remain contested: constitutionalism is a deeply politicized concept, both in its Western forms and in its Islamic articulations. There is a long way to go in constructing a historical reality that could supply badly needed *facts* for the debate. The Medina Charter is a prime example of how a significant and potentially foundational early document has systematically been undermined, and of how attempts have been made to erase from popular memory a possible constitutional template. The Charter could have been seen as laying down the foundations of a modern state as we understand it, with a defined territory, a diverse population bound by a common interest in peace and prosperity, mutually agreed rules, and a clear mode of governance. Or it could be nothing of the kind.

The main pillars of Islamic constitutionalism as demonstrated by the constitutional texts and practices of Muslim-majority jurisdictions comprise the declaration of Islamic identity, the insertion of Islamic-supremacy text, repugnancy clauses and aspirations towards an Islamic constitutional democracy. Simultaneously, a plurality of positions regarding the 'Islamic' nature of the constitutional text, as well as politically motivated Islamic pronouncements, are a characteristic of Islamic constitutionalism. Finally, geographical location and the history of colonialism have also influenced the Islamic-ness or otherwise of the particular shade of Islamic constitutionalism on offer. Thus Saudi Arabia, Iran and Pakistan take the lead in rankings of constitutional Islamization, whereas the Central Asian Republics of the former Soviet Union present its secular face.

Weighing up the range of views on Western and Islamic conceptions of constitutionalism, its various elements, and the extent to which it fulfils promised precautions against oppression, it is clearly still a work in progress.[152] Broadly speaking, constitutionalism is a particular response to a basic paradox in the practical experience of every human society: constitutional governance requires respect for and protection of collective as well as individual rights, with the state acting as protector and arbiter in both cases.

The present investigation of Islamic constitutionalism has thrown up some challenges and also offered ideas for the way forward. From the outset, the pluralist nature of the Islamic legal traditions, both in theory and in practice, provides a rich spectrum of ideas and of aspects of Islamic constitutionalism. This pluralism in turn results in an intense and ongoing contestation and a struggle for the appropriating of authority and legitimacy that presents itself as the greatest challenge to Islamic constitutionalism. But pluralism also opens up space for multiple ways forward, provided that a spirit of tolerance and mutual respect for others' perspectives prevails.

Most Islamic law scholars concede that Islamic constitutionalism is an underdeveloped aspect of study. At a positive level, this might open up new vistas for innovation regarding the basic elements of Islamic constitutionalism and its development as a modern and indigenous concept. But rather than engage seriously in a historically grounded and forward-looking debate, Muslim jurisdictions have taken an easy route, grafting Islamic clauses onto a Western framework, creating a mongrel that does not resolve deep-rooted issues of legitimacy and authenticity.

At present, Islamic constitutionalism is thus caught between these two systems, but it is possible to draw upon both to arrive at an indigenized constitutionalism. What is lacking is acceptance of where we are at and where we are heading. In order to retain a Muslim identity, one might make the Constitution of Medina our reference point but cast it in a liberal, Western framework. But between the two we lose touch with our own realities as well as the strong moral and ethical principles accompanying Islamic conceptions of governance, accountability and social justice.

Given the fragmented and contested notions and practices of Islamic constitutionalism, extremist movements such as ISIS and the Muslim Brotherhood pose a grave challenge to Muslim jurisdictions such as Saudi Arabia and Pakistan over how to settle the question of governance and constitutionalism. The fragmentation of authority and challenge to states and governments, including those that declare their Islamicity through constitutional clauses, is not likely to recede. This is a challenge that will hit liberal Muslim jurisdictions as well as conservative ones really hard. It is now time to engage with this debate and settle or agree on some key principles of Islamic constitutionalism and ways of governance to face this challenge. The challenge, this time, is not coming from the West, as much as it is emerging from within the Islamic world.

---

[152] An-Na'im, *Islam and the Secular State*, p. 103.

At the international level, the events of 9/11 changed perceptions of Muslims, Islam and *sharia* irrevocably and for the worse. The 'Muslim world', comprising people with such a variety of world views, nevertheless answers to a stereotypical identity of 'Muslim', with all the negativities now firmly entrenched in Western mindsets. The plurality within the Muslim world, as well as parallel political developments challenging undemocratic, non-accountable governments, appears lost on the wider world. Instead of heralding these as positive, popular demands for 'Islamic constitutional democracy', those monitoring constitutional developments in Muslim jurisdictions view it with concern. Western governments are fixated upon 'Islamic clauses', regardless of the fact that more and more people in the Muslim world are consciously placing demands and making claims on their governments to promote and protect their rights.[153]

A challenge confronting Islamic constitutionalism is that through constitutional Islamization it runs the risk of privileging the Muslim majority over and above non-Muslim minorities. This situation now arises in Egypt, Pakistan and Malaysia, to name just a few, where Muslim citizens have more rights than non-Muslims. This approach is likely to generate alienation and internal discord, resulting in instability, political division and violence (for example, the situation in Nigeria and Pakistan in recent years). The dominance of the debate over constitutionalization of religion can distract a citizenry from addressing socio-economic and political questions that are not necessarily reducible to concerns over religious law. Constitutionalization is worrisomely anti-participatory, empowering as it does just a few jurists to make decisions rather than demanding collective decision-making.

What, then, is the possible way forward towards achieving a coherent conception of Islamic constitutionalism? The first and arguably the most difficult step is self-analysis and self-reflection among individual Muslims, then collectively, and at the level of state and government in the Muslim world. This should hopefully result in a reality check and the recognition of some unsavoury home truths. Serious, difficult and courageous conversations are in order if Islamic constitutionalism is ever to take root and respond to the challenges thrown up by modernity.

Foremost is the challenge posed by the principles of what An-Na'im and Emon describe as 'historical' *sharia*, for instance the question of how to interpret a constitutional provision that protects freedom of religion and conscience yet simultaneously states that no law can violate *sharia* principles.[154] If historical *sharia* does not accord the right to change one's religion, and a Muslim does so, what are the implications for the constitutional protection of fundamental rights of incorporating historical *sharia* principles? Grafting rules of premodern *sharia* onto Western constitutional principles and/or modes of governance without

---

[153] Ahmed and Ginsburg, 'Constitutional Islamization'.
[154] A. M. Emon, 'The Limits of Constitutionalism in the Muslim World: History and Identity in Islamic Law', Islamic Law and Law of the Muslim World, paper no 08-09, 1–4.

undertaking a root-and-branch review of historical *sharia* is an inadequate response to modern challenges to Islamic law: 'The significance of a historicist jurisprudence of *sharia* is that it attempts to understand *sharia* holistically as a legal system of opposing views embedded in a context of governance structures and a shifting climate of, at times, competing codes of identity'.[155]

A historical account would also place in context the present-day reality that Muslim jurisdictions subscribe to the model of the modern nation state, and the clock simply cannot be turned back to seventh-century Arabia. The idea that a 'true' Islamic constitution can be arrived at by leaping 1,400 years back into a romanticized past poses a grave challenge to all Muslim states and societies, an escapist counternarrative for those disaffected by the social, political and technological realities of globalized twenty-first-century life. This stark reality thus requires acceptance before moving on.

An-Na'im, in *Islam and the Secular State*, argues that the prevalent view of Islamic constitutionalism as being in conflict with Western conceptions is based on the model of Medina as the perfect Islamic state. There, the Prophet Muhammad held a central authority that combined legislative, executive and judicial powers. But of course the idea of any kind of limitation or separation of powers was unknown not only in Medina but also anywhere else at the time. An-Na'im challenges calls for a revival of the Medina state, considering it inappropriate to seek to implement a historical model in today's context of governance with legitimacy:

> Whatever political or sociological justifications may have existed in the past for these aspects of *sharia* are no longer valid in the context of the modern Islamic societies . . . most Islamic states now provide for equality and prohibit discrimination on grounds of sex or religion. Many Islamic countries are also parties to international human rights treaties that require equality and non-discrimination. I find it significant that many Muslims around the world express commitment to the values of constitutionalism and civil rights. To assist these Muslims, I suggest the implementation of internal Islamic law reform in order to address the general constitutional concerns . . . Such reform, I suggest, will contribute to the process of legitimising and indigenizing the values of political participation, accountability, and equality before law, thereby enhancing the prospects of constitutionalism in Islamic societies.[156]

The plurality of the Islamic legal traditions and the distinctiveness of different Muslim jurisdictions must be acknowledged and turned into a positive attribute. Enabling Muslim communities as well as states and governments to focus on their own internal dynamics and processes will help to establish and consolidate constitutionalism, human rights and citizenship on their *own* terms, and not as a Western imposition.[157]

---

[155] Ibid., 34.   [156] An-Na'im, 'Islam, State and Politics', 14–15.
[157] An-Na'im, *Islam and the Secular State*, p. 138.

Constitutionalism ought best to be interpreted as a living concept, dynamic and evolving, and responsive to changing needs and circumstances; it ought not to be a monolith whose presence prevents it from effecting what it was created for. It entails limitations upon governments, so that they do not encroach upon people's rights, but it also obliges governments to protect others from having those rights encroached upon. Balancing the rights of people and the powers of governments has never been a static exercise. As a living concept, a constitution represents the individual and collective morality and ethics of a people, and these are subject to change. We do not today think of slavery, women's legal rights, primogeniture and illegitimacy in the way we once did, and one could go on. The constitutional text is of necessity vaguely phrased, as it must support and give space to a futuristic formulation of its principles.

The insertion by states of Islamic supremacy clauses and/or a repugnancy clause in their constitutional texts may be interpreted in a number of ways: an emphasis on Islam and *sharia* might simply be an honest declaration of Muslim identity; more often, though, it is an assertion of indigenous, cultural and national authenticity in a post-colonial world.[158] It might also be an act of political expediency to ward off political opponents demanding a return to an ideal 'Islamic state'. Finally, it might well be that, through constitutional Islamization, countries in the Muslim world are attempting to chart their own version of 'Islamic constitutional democracy' that may differ from the Western paradigm of democracy. Not inserting 'Islamic' clauses does not always translate into constitutional and democratic rule. Secularity is not a mark of representative government – a fact well illustrated by the Muslim-majority Central Asian Republics.

Islamization clauses are works in progress, and they must be accompanied by strong and effective implementing mechanisms. Delegating authority to a judiciary to determine the Islamic nature (or otherwise) of a law is a form of secular escapism. In particular, a pluralistic Islamic legal tradition cannot be adjudicated upon by what are largely judges who are not authorities in all the diverse legal traditions of Islamic law. The more robust use of *siyasa sharia* is one way forward. Islamic traditions have always granted legitimacy to government to legislate as required by the affairs of state. A law that does not invoke Islam and Islamic law is not in and of itself un-Islamic; where a constitutional text is silent regarding Islam, it might still be in accordance with the general principles of Islamic law and *sharia*. This is the critical acceptance that would facilitate a constitutionalism that is in consonance with the spirit of Islam as well as responsive to modern requirements of governance. Finally, it is a fact that many constitutional issues are political and not legal questions and ought to be dealt with as such. By bringing political issues into the legal–constitutional domain, those in positions of power and authority often deflect attention from more pressing and real issues of socio-economic and civil and political rights of citizens. There is a need to demystify Islamic constitutionalism by linking it

---

[158] Ahmed and Ginsburg, 'Constitutional Islamization'.

to the rights and obligations of states and citizens and to the accountability of those in positions of power and authority.

Very few scholars would deny the potential of using some of the basic existing concepts of governance in Islamic law to develop a modern, inclusionary Islamic constitutionalism. Thus *shura* consultation could be used as a basis for institutionalized constitutional principles that include the population at large, as advocated by some scholars since the mid-twentieth century.[159] Rahman has drawn upon *ijma* consensus to broaden the understanding of *shura* beyond just a few jurists and scholars.[160] Where this would raise controversies regarding who qualifies to participate in *shura* to reach *ijma*, An-Na'im's call for a religiously neutral secular state has a place. Issues relating to religion might be dealt with by jurists and scholars with particular expertise, but not all legislation is related to *sharia*.[161]

Advocates of Islamic constitutional law have sought to broaden the classic understanding of *ijma* consensus: in the past, only Muslim scholars had a role in reaching consensus, and the general public was of little significance. Rahman argues that the classical doctrine of consultation was in error, presented as it was as the process of one person (the ruler) asking subordinates for advice. In fact, the Qur'an asks for 'mutual advice through mutual discussions on an equal footing'.[162] In this context, *ijma* as a closely related concept to *shura* might therefore be implemented as a legislative power in the modern sense. Safi also notes that the 'legitimacy of the state . . . depends upon the extent to which state organization and power reflect the will of the *ummah*, for as classical jurists have insisted, legitimacy of state institutions is not derived from textual sources but is based primarily on the principle of *ijma*'.[163] According to this understanding, an Islamic constitution is a human product of legislation, based on the practice of *shura* consultation and *ijma* consensus, and thus, virtually, no longer the result of a divine act of revelation. It is set and approved by the people. In other words, *shura* and *ijma* offer a justification of Islamic constitutional law and need to be developed fully.[164]

In conclusion, I agree with An-Na'im when he says that we need to start from a position of accepting that neither constitutionalism as presently practised nor its suggested modification is the original position to be found within the Islamic legal traditions.[165] We must also accept that, historically, there was an absence of institutional arrangements for peaceful political dissent and for the orderly

---

[159] Asad, *Principles of State and Government*, pp. 51–8; An-Na'im, *Islam and the Secular State*, p. 108; Kamali, 'Constitutionalism in Islamic Countries'; Hosen, 'In Search of Islamic Constitutionalism'.

[160] Cited in Hosen, 'In Search of Islamic Constitutionalism'.

[161] This is the main thesis of An-Na'im, *Islam and the Secular State*.

[162] F. Rahman, *Islamic Methodology in History* (Karachi: Central Institute of Islamic Research, 1965), pp. 180–1.

[163] L. M. Safi, 'The Islamic State: A Conceptual Framework', *American Journal of Islamic Social Sciences* (Sept. 1999), 233.

[164] Hosen, 'In Search of Islamic Constitutionalism', 15–16.

[165] An-Na'im, *Islam and the Secular State*, p. 108.

transfer of power to freely elected leaders.[166] Likewise, issues that impact and reflect upon principles of Islamic constitutionalism, including equal rights for men, women and non-Muslims, and the issue of freedom of religion, must be addressed. The Muslim world individually and collectively must look inwards, as the cultural heritage of various Muslim communities might turn out to furnish examples of 'good practice' waiting to be emulated. By replenishing their ability and drawing upon appropriate examples, rationales and justifications for alternative interpretations that are more in keeping with contemporary realities of Muslim societies today are possible.[167]

[166] Ibid.
[167] See A. A. An Na'im, 'A New Islamic Politics: Faith and Human Rights in the Middle East', *Foreign Affairs* 75(3) (1996), 122–6; and An-Na'im, *Towards an Islamic Reformation*, pp. 97–100.

3

Contextualizing Family Law Reform and Plural Legalities in Post-colonial Pakistan

3.1 Introduction

Family law reforms in the Muslim world represent a fascinating yet challenging example of the ongoing contestations between contemporary notions of justice, equality and human rights on the one hand and established understandings of Islamic jurisprudence (*fiqh*) on the other.[1] They also represent a critical shift in Muslim thinking globally, in that family law is now being discussed as a multi-layered and complex subject straddling religion, politics, economics, gender equality and women's rights. New interlocutors in this discussion include Muslim women; NGOs; print and electronic media; national, regional and international human rights bodies; and national parliaments.[2]

Historically, family law reform projects in the Muslim world, including Pakistan, have been conceptualized within a framework of patriarchal norms and an understanding of a contractual nature of marriage and divorce supported by religious texts (mainly the Qur'an and the Sunna, or teachings and practices of the Prophet). Though religious texts ensured women a legal status and distinct (if not equal) rights in all spheres of life, Muslim women have continually confronted 'a moral and anthropological context that privileged male authority and the male voice'.[3] Family law reform in the Muslim world, often referred to as 'woman-friendly reform',[4] is an attempt at 'neutralizing' some of the unfettered male power within the institutions of marriage and divorce without displacing or challenging what are perceived as immutable religious texts.

---

[1] An-Na'im, *Islamic Family Law in a Changing World*, pp. xi–xii; Z. Mir-Husseini, 'Justice, Equality and Muslim Family Laws', in Mir-Husseini *et al.*, *Gender and Equality*, p. 7; L. Welchman (ed.), *Women's Rights and Islamic Family Law: Perspectives on Reform* (London: Zed, 2004); Mir-Husseini, *Marriage on Trial*; B. Stowasser, *Women in the Qur'an: Traditions and Interpretation* (Oxford: Oxford University Press, 1994).

[2] In the area of family law in particular, NGOs, women's groups and human rights groups have instigated family law reform using progressive interpretations of the religious text in Islam in most Muslim countries, including Pakistan, Bangladesh, Morocco and Egypt.

[3] J. Tucker, *Women, Family, and Gender in Islamic Law* (Cambridge: Cambridge University Press, 2008), p. 159 and note 1.

[4] For instance, prohibiting through statute the practice of 'triple *talaq*', where a woman is divorced immediately without any process or attempt at mediation or conciliation; restricting polygamy; requiring judicial process for divorce; and legalizing women's right to divorce.

Simultaneously, however, where 'Islamist' parties or individuals have come into power (for instance Nimeiri in Sudan, Imam Khomeini in Iran, and Zia-ul-Haq in Pakistan), they have engaged in law reform based on different readings of those same texts, leading to changes in the law adversely affecting women in these jurisdictions.[5]

The general premise underlying Islamic family law is that society consists of male-headed households where men hold authority and provide and protect vulnerable, weak and dependent females in their charge. In other words, family law reform implicitly assumes the supremacy of a *wilaya–qiwama* ('guardian–provider') nexus; that is, the connection between men's authority over women and their obligation to protect and maintain them. The main dynamic of law reform is the challenge mounted to this nexus by some societal constituencies. 'Complementarity' rather than 'equality' informs measures for law reform, in the belief that such distinctions between the positions of men and women (e.g. polygamy, unequal inheritance rights, males as guardians and females as wards) are defined by the Qur'an and Sunna and are therefore unquestionable. Although diversity in interpretation of the primary sources of Islamic law sallow for differing juristic opinions, resulting in laws that are woman-friendly, the opposite trend also continues, particularly at the societal level. This chapter advances the argument that the state and her people, government officials of various departments, judicial officers etc. all subscribe to this framework to a greater or lesser degree, and that law reform and family law development are constrained within these parameters.

A distinctive feature of family law reform in Pakistan is its embeddedness within the common law colonial legacy of 'Anglo-Muhammadan' as well as Islamic law. This legacy manifests itself in codification projects at state level, as well as through the case law of the high courts and Supreme Court. Whilst both arenas of legal development are informed by Islamic law, they do not always reinforce one another, resulting in less coherence and continuity between the two than is desirable. One of the hallmarks of *sharia* is its plurality of opinion, which is responsible for legal change as well as flexibility in the application of

---

[5] The most significant of these changes include an emphasis on controlling women's movements and dress code and undermining their equal rights, for instance the right to testify in court as a witness: in Sudan, for instance, the so-called 'September Laws' of 1983; in Iran post-1979; and in Pakistan, the 'Islamization of Laws' including criminal law and laws on evidence. The commonality between 'women-friendly' law reform and that of so-called 'Islamic' regimes is that they focus on women as markers of 'Islamization'. 'The different face of "Islamisation" is visible in Sudan where it is being promoted by an authoritarian regime with much more brutal effects . . . women's job and promotions opportunities in the government have been severely restricted, their mobility made dependent on male and state approval at various levels, their rights to land ownership curtailed and even their dress regulated . . . girls and women enrolled in educational institutions are formally subject to a dress code and may be expelled in the event of violation of this code . . . further various state-instituted bodies have been established to patrol streets to ensure appropriate behaviour'. A. Alrasheed, 'Sudanese Women in Exile: Islam, Politics and the State', conference proceedings: Thinking Gender – the NEXT Generation, 21–2 June 2006, e-paper no 1.

the law. Codification, on the other hand, removes the possibility of change and leaves little room for judicial flexibility. Contemporary codified law reform in the Muslim world is thus a double-edged sword, shutting down the flexible interpretative space of the Islamic legal traditions. In other words, the evolutionary potential and dynamic streak inherent within Islamic law has been and is being 'fossilized' by Western-inspired codification.

The historical development of 'modern' Pakistani family law and its reform is an intricate canvas which brings into relief features that are specific to the Pakistani legal landscape. These include the influence of her colonial legacy and common law, the powers and place of the courts, the 'myth' of the 'Islamic' character of the state, and the influence of all of these on the development and the dynamics of family law in Pakistan today.[6] The present chapter contextualizes family law reform within these plural legalities operating in post-colonial Pakistan.[7] It demonstrates that, in the zealously guarded domain of the 'Muslim' family, law reform is a 'subtle, almost imperceptible process of filtration through a maze of cultural norms and prevailing political . . . compulsions',[8] but one which ultimately has limited impact. The result has been half-hearted, piecemeal and incoherent reform in a top-down legislative process with minimal implementation on the ground.

The chapter is presented in six sections. Following this introduction, the second section contextualizes family law within the Islamic legal traditions. The third section presents a historical overview of Pakistan's colonial legacy and the influence of common law, with the fourth section analysing features of inherited 'Anglo-Muhammadan' law in post-colonial Pakistan. The fifth section then proceeds to analyse the dynamics of law reform engaging with the contestations arising out of the interpretative plurality of the Islamic legal traditions at the level of state, legislature, judiciary and society. The sixth section presents some concluding reflections.

3.2 The *Wilaya–Qiwama* Nexus and the 'Paradox of Equality'

There exists a complex body of literature framing the ongoing disputes over Muslim women's rights within the family, their wider linkages to women's status, and the interpretative space offered by Islamic legal traditions within which to analyse these plural legalities.[9] In attempting to understand the dynamics of

---

[6] Whilst the focus of the present chapter is on Pakistan, similar inferences will apply to other Muslim jurisdictions – in particular postcolonial countries.

[7] This chapter is essentially a case study of the Pakistan law reform landscape and not necessarily typical of other countries.

[8] S. S. Ali, 'Testing the Limits of Family Law Reform in Pakistan: A Critical Analysis of the Muslim Family Laws Ordinance 1961', in A. Bainham (ed.), *International Survey of Family Law* (Bristol: Jordan, 2002), p. 317.

[9] See, for instance, Mir-Husseini *et al.*, *Gender and Equality*; Y. Sikand, 'Reforming Muslim Personal Laws in India: The Fyzee Formula', *Women Living under Muslim Laws*, Dossier 27 (2005), available at www.wluml.org/node/499; L. Buskens, 'Recent Debates on Family Law

Muslim family law, writers have tended to use a theoretical framework that explains gender hierarchies and inequalities from an Islamic law as well as from an international human rights perspective.[10] Hevener's[11] classification of international human rights as evolving from the corrective to the protective and finally to the non-discriminatory legal state where women have equal rights in all spheres is one I have employed in earlier work.[12] An example of a 'corrective' right is the Muslim woman's right to inherit, albeit half the share assigned to a male relative in the same position. This 'correction' came in seventh-century Arabia, where women were not *sui juris* and capable of inheriting. That this half-share was a *minimum*, with potential for increasing as and when society evolved, was not taken forward; the minimum became the maximum, fixed and unchangeable. Examples of 'protective' rights in Islamic law are many, but include the right not to be forced into a contract of marriage, the right to initiate dissolution of marriage by *khul'* and the right to decide the time period for breastfeeding.[13] In the area of family law, most of the rights of women have been placed within the 'corrective' and 'protective' categories despite marriage in Islam being a civil contract between two consenting parties. The particular nature of Muslim marriage prevents the female party from acquiring equality, since the husband is conceptualized as the 'provider', and the wife as the one provided for (through *mahr* (dower) and maintenance).[14] This inherent contradiction of what may be termed 'the paradox of equality' drives the dynamics of family law and reform in the Muslim world.[15]

Reform in Morocco: Islamic Law as Politics in an Emerging Public Sphere', *Islamic Law & Society* 10 (2003), 70–131; D. El-Alami and D. Hinchcliffe, *Islamic Marriage and Divorce Laws in the Arab World* (The Hague: Kluwer, 1996); A. Quraishi and F. Vogel (eds.), *The Islamic Marriage Contract* (Cambridge, MA: Harvard University Press, 2008); L. Welchman, *Beyond the Code: Muslim Family Law and the Shari'a Judiciary in the Palestinian West Bank* (The Hague: Kluwer, 2000); Mir-Husseini, *Marriage on Trial*; A. El-Azhary Sonbol, *Women, the Family, and Divorce Laws in Islamic History* (Syracuse: Syracuse University Press, 1996); Stowasser, *Women in the Qur'an*; Tucker, *Women, Family, and Gender in Islamic Law*; I. Schneider, *Women in the Islamic World: From Earliest Times to the Arab Spring* (trans. S. Rendall) (Princeton: Markus Wiener, 2014); S. Mahmood, *The Politics of Piety: The Islamic Revival and the Feminist Subject* (Princeton: Princeton University Press, 2011); Barlas, *Believing Women*; A. Rab, *Exploring Islam in a New Light: A View from the Quranic Perspective* (Brainbow, 2010); A. Wadud, *Inside the Gender Jihad: Women's Reform in Islam* (Oxford: Oneworld, 2006); J. Esposito and N. J. DeLong-Bas, *Women in Muslim Family Law*, 2nd edition (Syracuse: Syracuse University Press, 2001).

[10] See in particular Ali, *Gender and Human Rights*, pp. 49–50 and generally Chapter 2.

[11] N. Hevener, *International Law and the Status of Women* (Boulder, CO: Westview Press, 1983), p. 4.

[12] Ali, 'Testing the Limits'.   [13] Ibid.

[14] *Mahr* (a sum of money or other property given to the wife by the husband at the time of marriage) has multiple connotations: it is described as a 'gift', but if this were so how can it be taken back if the wife initiates a divorce? For a discussion of the nature of *mahr* see A. Moors, *Women, Property and Islam* (Cambridge: Cambridge University Press, 1995); Ali, 'Is an Adult Muslim Woman *Sui Juris*?'; Pearl and Menski, *Muslim Family Law*, pp. 178–81.

[15] The phrase 'paradox of equality' is borrowed from A. Emon, 'The Paradox of Equality and the Politics of Difference: Gender Equality, Islamic Law and the Modern State', in Mir-Husseini *et al.*, *Gender and Equality*, pp. 237–58.

Esposito presents a compelling analysis of the unequal family law rights and responsibilities accorded to Muslim women and men, based on the distinction between *muamalat* (socio-economic relationships, necessarily evolving and mutable) and *ibadaat* (immutable religious duties to God).[16] Esposito believes that these categories result in a 'hierarchisation of Qur'anic values', with women and men being full equals in the spiritual and moral domain of *ibadaat* but unequal in the socio-economic and family law field of *muamalat*; but that, since such inequality in the sphere of socio-economics and the family is subject to change with changing societal perceptions, there remains the potential for complete equality between women and men.[17] A word of caution needs to be raised here. As I have stated elsewhere,

> Although Esposito's attempt at hierarchisation of rights within the Islamic tradition is an important step in his endeavour to develop a modern framework for achieving equality for the sexes and within family law, we must not lose sight of the fact that, in his attempt to realise the legislative value of Qur'anic verses, he places emphasis on exegesis (*tafsir*).[18]

This, Esposito argues, is due to the necessity of uncovering the motive, intent or purpose behind Qur'anic passages. This approach reasserts the original influence of Qur'anic values in the early development of law and, as such, seeks to renew the process by which Qur'anic values were applied to newly encountered social situations in the first centuries of Islamic legal history.[19] But it needs to be recognized that it was the very process of exegesis itself which resulted in restrictive interpretations of Qur'anic verses regarding the status of women; *tafsir* can work in both directions and is subjective.[20]

The principle of 'gradualism', too, offers a thoughtful approach to understanding the religious text in Islam, arguing that by sowing the seeds of (albeit unequal) rights in seventh-century Arabia, the ground was prepared for such rights to gradually evolve into complete equality between women and men in all spheres of life.[21] Proponents of equal inheritance rights for women use

---

[16]   Esposito and DeLong-Bas, *Women in Muslim Family Law*, pp. 106–8; F. Rahman, 'The Status of Women in Islam: A Modernist Interpretation', in H. Papanek and G. Minault (eds.), *Separate Worlds: Studies of Purdah in South Asia* (Delhi: Chanakya, 1982), pp. 285–310; Al-Hibri, 'Islamic Herstory'.

[17]   Esposito and DeLong-Bas, *Women in Muslim Family Law*; Rahman, 'The Status of Women in Islam'; Al-Hibri, 'Islamic Herstory'. See also F. Mernissi, *Women and Islam* (trans. M. J. Lakeland) (Oxford: Blackwell, 1991); An-Na'im, *Towards an Islamic Reformation*; Hassan, 'An Islamic Perspective'; M. M. Taha, *The Second Message of Islam* (trans. An-Na'im) (Syracuse: Syracuse University Press, 1987).

[18]   Ali, 'Testing the Limits', pp. 48–9.   [19]   Ibid.   [20]   Ibid., p. 49.

[21]   See Rahman, *Islam and Modernity*; L. P. Sayeh and A. M. Morse, 'Islam and the Treatment of Women: An Incomplete Understanding of Gradualism', *Texas International Law Journal* 30 (1995), 311–34; Ali, 'Testing the Limits', pp. 79–85; N. Salem, 'Islam and the Status of Women in Tunisia', in F. Hussain (ed.), *Muslim Women* (New York: St Martin's, 1984); Al-Tahir Al-Haddad, *Our Women in the Law and in Society* (ed. R. Husni and D. Newman) (Routledge, 2007).

this gradualist argument, suggesting that moving from no inheritance rights to rights which were half those of men was a promising departure point for women over thirteen hundred years ago. After all, no Qur'anic text or Sunna prohibits giving *more* than a half-share.[22]

Approaching the position of women within Islamic family law through an interpretative discourse over 'text and context' is also a well-trodden path, and one that offers hope to scholars arguing for equal rights within the Islamic legal traditions.[23] The practice of polygamy and the supposed right of a husband to beat his wife if she is disobedient[24] are often flagged up as examples of where a contextual analysis of the Qur'anic text can be advocated to present a woman-friendly interpretation.[25]

From a theoretical perspective, and in order to appreciate the dynamics of family law reform in Pakistan and other Muslim jurisdictions, I propose that a persuasive analysis can be arrived at by deconstructing how a Muslim woman as an autonomous legal person is transformed into an inherently *dependent* legal person under the perpetual guardianship (*wilaya*) of a male 'protector and provider' (*qawwam*). In classical *fiqh* (jurisprudence), the edifice of the patriarchal model of Muslim family law is wholly constructed upon the concept of *qiwama*, with the man as the woman's 'protector and provider' (whether fathers and daughters, husbands and wives, and so on). This '*qiwama* postulate', as Mir-Husseini terms it,[26] transformed what had been a sociocultural norm into a legal norm, and thereafter crept into both non-codified principles and codified family law in Muslim jurisdictions globally. Related to and serving to perpetuate gender hierarchies and the '*qiwama* postulate' is the concept of *tamkin* ('submission'/'obedience'). Making *qiwama* contingent upon *tamkin* means that wifely obedience becomes a material fact in family law cases, the

---

22   Ali, 'Testing the Limits', pp. 72–3.
23   *Asbab al-nuzul* or 'context of revelation' of Qur'anic verses is often employed to support the 'text and context' argument. Proponents of this approach argue that the context of the revelation informs application of a particular Qur'anic verse(s).
24   Verse 4:34 of the Qur'an is most frequently cited when justifying wife-beating. For a challenging feminist perspective of this verse, see R. Hassan, paper presented at a Qur'anic interpretation meeting held under the auspices of Women Living under Muslim Laws, Karachi, 8–13 July 1990 (paper on file with the author). For a detailed and incisive discussion see L. Hajjar, 'Domestic Violence and Shari'a: A Comparative Study of Muslim Societies in the Middle East, Africa and Asia', in Welchman, *Women's Rights*, pp. 233–68.
25   The works of Muslim scholars including A. A. An-Na'im, R. Hassan, A. Barlas, A. Al-Hibri, Z. Mir-Husseini, S. Mahmoud, A. A. Engineer and S. S. Ali (to name just a few) have provided alternative interpretations, arguing that a contextual reading of the Qur'anic text displaces gender hierarchies as the only reading. Reading the Qur'anic verses on polygamy through a contextual and feminist lens, these writers question polygamy as a general, unconditional right of the husband. Law reform in some Muslim jurisdictions, too, reflects this by restricting polygamy. See Pakistan's MFLO 1961, Morocco's Mudawwana 2004 and the Tunisian Family Code. Regarding verses permitting the beating of a disobedient wife, this contradicts other verses as well as clearly remaining contingent upon the economic superiority of the husband.
26   Mir-Husseini *et al.*, *Gender and Equality*.

husband being able to refuse maintenance if his wife has disobeyed him (in this context we find the word *nushuz* or 'rebellious disobedience' being used). The relationship between *qiwama* and *tamkin* has far-reaching consequences, as the absence of *tamkin* justifies the denial of maintenance and protection.[27]

'Guardianship' (*wilaya*) is another important concept within the Islamic legal traditions which is subject to a diverse range of scholarly interpretations regarding its meaning, scope and application. Generally, Islamic legal conceptions (informed by classical *fiqh* and social perceptions) understand *wilaya* to be the blanket rights of a male over (i) a minor, incapacitated or disabled ward in all major decisions relating to person and property, and over (ii) a female relative regarding consent to marriage.[28] A major focus of discussion over *wilaya* has been the right of an *adult* woman to conclude a marriage without the consent of her guardian (her *wali*). Schools of juristic thought differ as to the reach and remit of this right, i.e. whether the consent and presence of the *wali* is mandatory to the point that his absence would make a marriage void (we see this in the term *wilayat al-ijbar*, 'marriage guardianship with power of coercion') or whether consent is simply recommended as desirable and important to protect the female's interests. Views on the subject over the centuries suggest that every school of juristic thought has held its own unique position but has faithfully reported those of other schools.[29] This classical doctrine, known as *ikhtilaf al-fuqaha* ('diversity of opinions'), offered interpretative plurality as and when circumstances required. The colonial thrust toward codification and a black-letter approach to law weakened this egalitarian approach within the classical Islamic legal traditions. Masud has suggested that every rule of law within the Islamic traditions has gone through a three-stage process: (i) interpretation (of the source text), (ii) construction (of a rule) and (iii) reconstruction (as and when required due to changing situations and demands).[30] Using examples from the writings of classical jurists, he illustrates 'the shifting framework of reasoning' employed to arrive at rulings based upon *maqasid al-sharia* ('objectives of the law') rather than upon a specific text.[31] Applying this process to the doctrine of *wilaya*, Masud concludes that the concept of *wilaya* guardianship is one of social preference and not one of basic legal requirement.[32] For implementation within a pluralistic Muslim society, social preferences trump any law reform *even if* it finds legitimation in religious texts.

[27]   The concept of 'restitution of conjugal rights' incorporated into family law in colonial codes continues to this day.

[28]   Masud defines *wilaya/walaya* as 'the legal authority to manage the affairs of another person who lacks the required capacity'. M. Masud, 'Gender Equality and the Doctrine of Wilaya', in Mir-Husseini *et al.*, *Gender and Equality*, p. 128.

[29]   For a detailed exposition of the various Sunni juristic schools of thought, see ibid.; Mannan, *D. F. Mulla's Principles*; Pearl and Menski, *Muslim Family Law*; A. A. A. Fyzee, *Outlines of Muhammadan Law*, 4th edition (Oxford: Oxford University Press, 1974).

[30]   Masud, 'Gender Equality and the Doctrine of Wilaya', pp. 132–44.

[31]   Ibid., p. 140.   [32]   Ibid., p. 143.

I would like to propose some further development in this framework, by suggesting that the *wilaya–qiwama* nexus was thus interpreted, constructed and reconstructed by jurists, and informed by prevalent social norms, in an attempt to control the resources, and the distribution thereof, that underpin the institution of marriage and its dissolution. Deconstruction of the linkage between *wilaya* and *qiwama* requires an ends-oriented analysis of resource allocation and control within the institution of marriage, rather than a framework of 'gender and equal rights'. The paradox of equality is seen at play in the dynamics of family law reform where two conflicting norms are pulling reform in opposing directions: if the contractual element of the Muslim marriage is taken as a basis, then two consenting parties who have capacity ought to be entering into an equal partnership of marriage. But this is not possible looking at the marriage from the opposing position, where the husband assumes the role of protector and provider.

3.3 From 'Islamic' to 'Anglo-Muhammadan' Family Law? A Historical Overview of Pakistan's Colonial Legacy and the Influence of Common Law

Haider A'la Hamoudi's 'The Death of Islamic Law' presents us with a challenging idea:[33] the presence of a comprehensive 'Islamic law' is a myth, exemplified by the selectivity of Muslim states in choosing which aspects of *sharia* to incorporate into their state law. Hamoudi is of the view that 'law-making in many modern Muslim states gives rather short shrift to *sharia*, seemingly ignoring it in all areas save the law of the family and replacing it elsewhere with European-transplanted law'.[34] Even 'Islamists', he points out, engage in this selectivity:

> The Islamist does not want God's law to reign supreme in areas such as corporate law and the law of business entities where economic consequences may be dire ... On the other hand lies the law of the family, where God's law is deemed a vital necessity, and any development, any evolution, any alteration of the rules established centuries ago ... will not be countenanced.[35]

Hamoudi's analysis flags up the contested and porous nature of Islamic law and its receptivity to extrinsic influences, including local customary norms and European legal systems. It also lends support to the argument advanced in this chapter, that successive regimes have,[36] as a socio-economic and political strategy, colluded to ring-fence a certain form of 'Islamic' family law as *the* signifier of Muslim identity to be preserved at all costs.

---

[33] H. A. Hamoudi, 'The Death of Islamic Law', *Georgia Journal of International and Comparative Law* 38 (2010), 293.
[34] Ibid.   [35] Ibid.   [36] Pre-colonial, colonial and post-colonial regimes.

Centuries of Muslim rule and of legal institutions applying Islamic law preceded the British colonization of the Indian subcontinent.[37] In their pursuit of a colonial system of legal dispensation, the British shed aspects of (Indian and Mughal) legal governance but retained the 'family laws' of native communities, including Muslims. Siddique reiterates the generally held view that the colonial policy of retaining Islamic family law resulted from a convergence of economic interests between colonial legal systems (whose aim was to extract economic surplus) and the indigenous Muslim elite (whose aim was to reinforce their economic and socio-political dominance).[38] Anderson notes,

> Where the landed gentry and certain merchant groups were organized according to the dynastic principles of family and clan, the administration of family law played a role in broking wealth and power at the local level, ultimately underpinning the very intermediaries whose cooperation was essential to effective colonial rule.[39]

In other words, the political economy inherently at play due to the contractual nature of Muslim marriage, whilst lending support to existing patriarchal structures, also favoured colonial policies of governance.

The British colonial state initially adjusted existing structural features into new institutional forums, including the establishment of the colonial court. A hierarchy of civil and criminal courts was established by the Hastings Plan of 1772 tasked with applying indigenous legal norms. This meant, in respect of Muslims, 'the laws of the Koran . . . in all suits regarding inheritance, marriage, caste, and other religious usages or institutions'.[40] The birth of 'Anglo-Muhammadan law' thus came about by the application of British models of procedure and adjudication to a literalist, scripturalist 'Islamic law' explained by *maulvis*, religious scholars who acted as advisers to the courts. Derrett states that,[41] starting with the 1772 doctrine (the Hastings Plan), the idea that in cases where indigenous laws seemed to provide no rule the matter should be decided according to the Roman law formula of 'justice, equity and good conscience', by 1887 was held 'to mean the rules of English law if found applicable to society

---

[37] See M. U. ibn S. Jung, *The Administration of Justice in Islam* (Lahore: Law Publishing, 1980), pp. 57–88, for details regarding the administration of justice in India during early Muslim and Mughal rule.

[38] For this line of argument see O. Siddique, *Pakistan's Experience with Formal Law: An Alien Justice* (Cambridge: Cambridge University Press, 2013); D. Washbrook, 'Law, State, and Agrarian Society in Colonial India', *Modern Asian Studies* 15 (1981), 649, cited in M. R. Anderson, 'Islamic Law and the Colonial Encounter in British India', in C. Mallat and J. Connors (eds.), *Islamic Family Law* (London: Graham & Trotman, 1990), p. 206.

[39] Anderson, 'Islamic Law and the Colonial Encounter in British India', p. 208 and accompanying footnotes.

[40] Ibid., p. 209.

[41] See J. Derrett, 'Justice, Equity and Good Conscience', in J. Anderson (ed.), *Changing Laws in Developing Countries* (Allen & Unwin, 1963), pp. 114–53, cited in Anderson, 'Islamic Law and the Colonial Encounter in British India', p. 209, note 38.

and circumstances'.[42] By 1875, 'Anglo-Muhammadan law' had been displaced by new colonial codes in all subjects except family law and certain property transactions.[43]

Alongside this procedural anglicization of Islamic law, its substantive content, too, became coloured by the British rulers' insistence on a black-letter approach to law.[44] The interpretative plurality within Islamic law that had allowed it to remain cognitively open to changing societal needs and contexts was now frozen in its tracks by colonial judges' demands for simplistic responses that constituted 'the' law. Two contemporaneous developments fed into this process: because of the need for knowledge of indigenous legal arrangements, the translation of works on *sharia* and *fiqh* from Arabic and Persian into English and the collection of local customary 'laws' was undertaken, leading to an impressive body of scholarship. But in trying to pin down 'Islamic law' its flexibility was lost; some texts and perspectives became privileged, while others were ignored. In this regard, Charles Hamilton's 1791 translation of *Hedaya*,[45] Baillie's rendering of *Fatawa Alamgiri*,[46] Sir William Jones's 1792 translation of *Al-Sirajiyya*, and the translation of *Mishkat-ul-Masabith* (extracts from *Fatawa Kazee Khan*) and of *Principles and Precedents of Muhammadan Law* by Macnaghten became the textual bases of Anglo-Muhammadan law. Local Muslim elites also contributed to the development of Anglo-Muhammadan law through their writings, including the Tagore Law Lectures of 1891–2, Abdur Rahim's *Muhammadan Jurisprudence*, and Mulla's *Principles of Muhammadan Law*. These 'textbooks' of Anglo-Muhammadan law became part of a definitive, textual Islamic law as inherited by post-colonial Pakistan. As Kugle notes, 'The effects of British rewriting have created a lens of texts, terms and experiences which continue to distort the view of Shariah today.'[47] Siddique has stated that it merits further probing whether or not Muslims themselves, for instance, played a prominent subsequent role in the political contestations around, and eventual definition and development of, what came to be called Anglo-Muhammadan law.[48]

Confronted with (often inadequately) translated legal information and with native *maulvis* whose inputs reflected the complexity of pluralist legal traditions,

---

[42]   *Waghela v. Sheikh Musludin* [1887] 14 IA 89, 96, as cited in Anderson, 'Islamic Law and the Colonial Encounter in British India', p. 209, note 38.

[43]   For example, Code of Civil Procedure (Act VIII of 1859); Indian Penal Code (Act XLV of 1860); Criminal Procedure Code (Act XXV of 1861); Indian Evidence Act (Act I of 1872).

[44]   This is a puzzling contradiction in terms. Historically, the common law legacy is celebrated for its responsiveness to society; hence the difficulty in understanding why this undue emphasis was placed on the 'written law'. It may well be that imperial and colonial imperatives drove this approach.

[45]   A twelfth-century text of Central Asian origin that relied mainly on Abu Yusuf and Al-Shaybani.

[46]   A collection of *fatawa* (legal opinions) in the *fiqh* tradition commissioned by the Mughal Emperor Aurangzeb was translated as N. Baillie, *Baillie's Digest of Moohammudan Law* (1865).

[47]   S. A. Kugle, 'Framed, Blamed and Renamed: The Recasting of Islamic Jurisprudence in Colonial South Asia', *Modern Asian Studies* 35 (2001), 304.

[48]   Siddique, *Pakistan's Experience*.

a state of persistent distrust by colonial rulers of indigenous *maulvis* led to the collection and compilation of a corpus of local 'customary law'. In the late nineteenth century, following the adoption of the Punjab Laws Act of 1872, revenue collectors were tasked with ascertaining customary practices in every village. Yet this project was initiated with a preconceived notion that 'custom' was stable within a fairly static society and that, once ascertained, 'customary law' could be codified and dispensed within a British-inspired, colonial legal system. I have elsewhere challenged this perception by suggesting that

> culture is an evolutionary process of our 'beings' and 'doings'. It is an intricate tapestry that both reflects and detracts from collusions and resistances (individual/collective), to dominant behavioural norms in society at various points in our histories . . . it is important to remind ourselves of the highly political nature of this project: Who has the power to define culture determines whose voices are being heard and represented in this undertaking.[49]

Certain examples of the codification of custom arrived at by a 'useful' collusion of the colonial power and landed Muslim gentry, such as the exclusion of Muslim women as heirs in respect of land and other immovable property, were subsequently contested politically. Whilst such colonial understandings of the nature of 'customary law' were not strictly *inaccurate*, they nevertheless 'were arrested, frozen forms of representation'. The dynamics of family law reform in post-colonial Pakistan reflect the struggle between these frozen forms of representation at the formal, official and elitist levels of state and society and at the grass roots.

3.4 Features of Inherited 'Anglo-Muhammadan' Family Law in Post-colonial Pakistan

What, then, were the features of this 'Anglo-Muhammadan' law that was inherited in 1947, and which Pakistan took forward as a state established in the name of the Islamic religion? How painlessly did this colonial, socio-legal construct find acceptability in the newly independent Pakistan? To what extent did Anglo-Muhammadan law form the basis for law reform and subsequent legal developments? These questions go to the heart of the dynamics of family law reform in Pakistan and will be addressed in the sections below.

The most prominent feature of Anglo-Muhammadan law was the hybridity and plurality of norms informing it. Ironically, it was through the very effort of achieving a necessarily artificial uniformity that the reverse effect came about. Principles of Islamic law, English secular legal principles, and customary norms interacted to provide an 'amoebic, boundary-less set of regulatory norms'.[50]

---

[49] S. S. Ali, 'Overlapping Discursive Terrains of Culture, Law and Women's Rights: An Exploratory Study on Legal Pluralism at Play in Pakistan', in J. Bennett (ed.), *Scratching the Surface: Democracy, Traditions, Gender* (Lahore: Heinrich Böll, 2007), pp. 77–8.

[50] Ali, 'Testing the Limits', p. 92.

Anglo-Muhammadan law also accorded continued privilege to autonomous legal orderings away from the capital in peripheral regions where *panchayats* (village councils), *jirgas* (decision-making assemblies) and other local dispute-resolution forums were left untouched; hence the continued and thriving position of local customary law and 'cultural Islam' well into post-Independence Pakistan with her pluralist legal and judicial system.[51]

Whilst the pluralist legal system passed on to Pakistan was substantively fraught with contradictions, duality and (colonial) compromise, it was the rules of procedure that created what was for the vast majority of the population an alien legal system. The widespread and mandatory use of documentation in matters of law and evidence, together with the amplified role of the scribe, led to the alienation of a largely non-literate people, making legal institutions inaccessible to most of the population. But the most unforeseen consequence of Anglo-Muhammadan law and legal scholarship was perhaps its contribution to an environment in which a new politics of Muslim identity could flourish; a number of Islamicized laws were adopted in the area of family law between the eighteenth and twentieth centuries. The administration of Muslim law by a non-Muslim colonial power transformed personal law into grounds for organized political struggle, and in the late nineteenth and early twentieth centuries the Islamic identity thus engendered became a basis for colonial resistance.[52] Colonial vocabularies of identity such as 'Hindu' and 'Muslim', accompanied by artificial and monolithic concepts of 'Hindu personal law' and 'Muslim personal law', became part of the popular imagination of the post-colonial state and the dynamics of law reform. Ironically, it was Anglo-Muhammadan law, this inflexible, scripturalist and colonially generated version of Islamic law, that became the enduring legacy Pakistan inherited at the time of partition in 1947.

3.4.1 Muslim Personal Law (Shariat) Application Act 1937

The culmination of this influence of religious identity on law came with the Muslim Personal Law (Shariat) Application Act 1937 (the MPL),[53] as prior to its adoption Islamic personal law in India varied by region and community, often informed by customary practices.[54] The act originated in efforts, primarily among some religious scholars (*ulama*), to secure statutory enforcement of

---

[51] For a detailed overview and analysis of local dispute-resolution forums, see S. S. Ali and J. Rehman, *Indigenous Peoples and Ethnic Minorities of Pakistan: Constitutional and Legal Perspectives* (Richmond: Curzon, 2001).

[52] The assault against *wakf* became a rallying point for Muslims, and the Wakf Validating Act 1913 simultaneously affirmed a scripturalist version of Islam as it protected the economic interests of certain propertied classes.

[53] Act No 26/1937 of 7 October 1937, Indian Official Gazette (Part 4) of 9 October 1937, 50–1.

[54] An-Na'im, *Islamic Family Law in a Changing World*, p. 204.

sharia. Their successful lobbying resulted in the 1937 Act, which abrogated what were seen as 'non-Islamic' customs. Anderson sums this up thus:

> The Act affirmed, in the political arena, the equivalence of Muslim identity and a certain form of *sharia.* It was a statute of indigenous instigation, but its form and purpose reflected a view of *sharia* that had been reshaped under the British administration.[55]

It also highlighted the limits of law reform in the sphere of Islamic family law, especially where the empowerment of women was concerned. Its preamble, acknowledging Muslim women's organizations as new interlocutors in family law reform alongside religious scholars, is self-explanatory:

> For several years past it has been the cherished desire of the Muslims of British India that Customary Law should in no case take the place of Muslim Personal Law. The matter has been repeatedly agitated in the press as well as on the platform. The Jamiat-ul-Ulema-i-Hind, the greatest Moslem religious body has supported the demand and invited the attention of all concerned to the urgent necessity of introducing a measure to this effect. Customary Law is a misnomer in as much as it has not any sound basis to stand upon and is very much liable to frequent changes and cannot be expected to attain at any time in the future that certainty and definiteness which must be the characteristic of all laws. *The status of Muslim women under the so-called Customary Law is simply disgraceful. All the Muslim Women Organisations have therefore condemned the Customary Law as it adversely affects their rights.*[56] They demand that the Muslim Personal Law (*Shariat*) should be made applicable to them. The introduction of Muslim Personal Law will automatically raise them to the position to which they are naturally entitled. In addition to this [the] present measure, if enacted, would have very salutary effect on society because it would ensure certainty and definiteness in the mutual rights and obligations of the public. Muslim Personal Law (*Shariat*) exists in the form of a veritable code and is too well known to admit of any doubt or to entail any great labour in the shape of research, which is the chief feature of Customary Law.[57]

Having expressed dissatisfaction with customary laws and their adverse impact on Muslim women, Section 2 of the Act, however, rolls back on what it aspired to in the preamble by stating, 'Notwithstanding any customs or usage to the contrary, in all questions (save questions relating to agricultural land)...the rule of decision in cases where the parties are Muslims shall be the Muslim Personal Law (*Shariat*).'[58] The 'collusion' of colonial rulers with India's Muslim

---

[55] M. R. Anderson, 'Islamic Law and the Colonial Encounter in British India', in C. Mallat and J. Connors (eds.), *Islamic Family Law* (London: Graham & Trotman, 1990), p. 222.

[56] (Emphasis added.) Muslim women's groups have consistently held that it is customary practices and cultural perspectives of Islam that affect women adversely, whereas Islamic law is empowering and gives them rights; family law reform in postcolonial Pakistan continued this trend.

[57] Indian Official Gazette (Part 4), 9 October 1937, 50.   [58] Ibid.

landed gentry is evident here when 'questions relating to agricultural land' are excluded from the remit of the 1937 Act. This trend of excluding women from inheritance continued well into the post-Independence era, and it was only in 1962 that amendments to the 1937 Act conceded this right to women.[59] Also, in the interest of political expediency, un-Islamic customary practices denying Muslim women their rights were ignored when 'Islamizing' other laws.[60]

3.4.2 The Dissolution of Muslim Marriages Act 1939

Another response to the rising demands of Indian Muslims for Islamic family law during the colonial era was the Dissolution of Muslim Marriages Act 1939 (DMMA).[61] The Act's preamble states that its purpose was to 'consolidate and clarify the provisions of Muslim law relating to suits for dissolution of marriage by women married under Muslim law and to remove doubts as to the effect of the renunciation of Islam by a married Muslim woman on her marriage tie'.

The 1939 Act codifies and regulates the grounds on which a woman married under Muslim law may obtain a judicial decree of dissolution of marriage from the courts. Section 2 of the Act enumerates these grounds, which include, inter alia, the husband's whereabouts being unknown for four years, failure by a husband to maintain his wife for two years, the husband's failure to perform marital obligations for three years, the husband's impotence, husband's insanity, or his suffering from leprosy or VD. Cruelty and abuse, whether physical or mental, and emotional distress inflicted by the husband are also grounds for dissolution. The wife may also seek divorce if the husband interferes in how she manages her property or obstructs her in the performance of her religious profession or practice. One subsection extends the 'option of puberty' (*khyar-ul-bulugh*), by which a girl can repudiate a marriage entered into while she was a minor (including a marriage contracted on her behalf by her father or grandfather). Another important provision is Section 5, which states that dissolution of the marriage contract under the Act will not affect the wife's right to dower.[62]

---

[59] In the Punjab, the Muslim Personal Law (Shariat) Application Act 1948 was only passed by the Punjab Assembly when women demonstrated outside the Assembly building urging members to vote in favour of the bill. Their reluctance stemmed from the fact that the majority belonged to the landed class and were not prepared to give away immovable property to female heirs.

[60] For example, see s. 26 of Regulation IV, 1827: 'the law to be observed in the trial of suits shall be Acts of Parliament and Regulations of Government applicable to the case: in the absence of such Acts and Regulations, the usages of the country in which the suit arose; if none such appears, the law of the defendant, and in the absence of specific law and usage, justice, equity and good conscience alone.'

[61] Act VIII of 1939 of 17 March 1939, Indian Official Gazette (Part 4), 25 March 1939, 131–3.

[62] The DMMA was amended twice by the Muslim Family Laws Ordinance 1961 (MFLO). These amendments provided the added ground for dissolution where the husband took an additional wife in contravention of the procedure laid down in the MFLO. It also allowed women to repudiate marriages contracted by their guardians before they attained the age of sixteen (as opposed to fifteen as set out originally in the Act).

3.5 The Dynamics of Family Law Reform in Post-colonial Pakistan

In its present formulation, modern Pakistani family law is by and large a colonial construct derived from the Qur'an, Sunna, *ijma*, and *qiyas*, all of which are seen through the prism of Anglo-Muhammadan law.[63] Simultaneously, this law has, over the centuries, been influenced by the writings of scholars, *ulama*, *muftis* and *maulvis*. Customary practices, too, have significantly informed and influenced popular as well as 'formal' understandings and applications of family law by the courts and population. Family law has found expression and articulation in reports and recommendations of various law commissions[64] and codified laws.[65] The socio-economic and political environment of the post-colonial state, too, has played a tangible role in family law developments, as we will see later. A complex and intricately interwoven canvas of regulatory norms has thus evolved under the overarching umbrella of Islam and *sharia*. Pearl and Menski make the apt observation that 'Islamic law has always been a matter of religion as much as law, so that formal legal changes through state law were never quite able to override the sphere of *shari'a*, even if it may appear so.'[66] The existence of contesting narratives in family law implied by Pearl and Menski finds support in a number of Islamic law scholars, including An-Na'im, who is of the view that family law remains 'a highly symbolic location of the struggle between the forces of traditionalism and modernism'.[67] The conflict is at multiple levels: within Islamic law itself there is the contest between 'traditionalist' and 'modern' interpretations; another contest exists between 'Islamic law as an entity and the secularists of Western liberal thought'.[68] It is to this unrelenting and ongoing tension underpinning family law reform that we now turn our attention.

---

[63] Thus the MPL and DMMA were considered a victory for Indian Muslims in their quest for Islamic law. The laws regulating family issues in Pakistan include the Majority Act 1875, the Guardians & Wards Act 1890, the Child Marriages Restraint Act 1929, and the Muslim Personal Law (Shariat) Application Act 1937.

[64] The Commission on Marriage and Family Laws was appointed by the government of Pakistan under Ministry of Law Resolution No F17(24)/55-Leg, 4 August 1955. Its report was published on 20 June 1956 in the Gazette of Pakistan Extraordinary under notification No F9(4)/56-Leg. Other reports on family law and women's rights include that of the Pakistan Women's Rights Committee 1976, the Status of Women (Zari Sarfraz) Commission 1985, and the Commission of Inquiry for Women 1997.

[65] Muslim Personal Law (Shariat) Application Act 1962, Muslim Personal Law (Shariat) Application (Removal of Difficulties) Act 1975, Muslim Personal Law (Shariat) Application (Removal of Doubt) Ordinance 1972, Dissolution of Muslim Marriages Act 1939, Muslim Family Laws Ordinance 1961, West Pakistan Rules under the Muslim Family Laws Ordinance 1961, West Pakistan Family Courts Act 1964 (amended 2002), West Pakistan Family Court Rules 1965, Dowry and Bridal Gifts (Restriction) Act 1976, Dowry and Bridal Gifts (Restriction) Rules 1981.

[66] Pearl and Menski, *Muslim Family Law*, p. 29.

[67] An-Na'im, *Islamic Family Law in a Changing World*, p. 18.

[68] A. Black, H. Esmaeili and N. Hosen, *Modern Perspectives on Islamic Law* (Cheltenham: Edward Elgar, 2013), p. 108.

3.5.1 The Past's Simultaneous Absence and Presence in Family Law Reform

Family law reform in Pakistan adopts as a given starting point the 'received' versions of Anglo-Muhammadan laws and legal institutions left behind by the colonial rulers. To this extent, the past is present in the family law dispensation of Pakistan in that it is common law-based, precedent-bound, adversarial, structured and hierarchical.[69] Simultaneously, however, survivals from the pre-colonial Islamic law model of governance are also discernible in such local dispute-resolution forums as *jirgas, panchayats* and courts led by *qadis* (judges), drawing upon an 'eclectic body of rulings' of Islamic law,[70] inquisitorial and responsive to their immediate social context. This duality has led to contested narratives of what constitutes 'Islamic' family law both at the formal and informal levels. Which aspects of this 'received' family law reflect 'authentic' Islamic law, it might be asked, and from where did non-Muslim colonial law-makers derive the legitimacy to legislate on Islamic law? As the successor state to colonial Britain, what are the 'Islamic' or 'Muslim' credentials of Pakistan's law-makers? Who are the controllers and custodians of family law reform in Pakistan? Which school(s) of juristic thought do they represent, if at all, and on what basis are *reforms* within family law 'Islamic' and applicable to all Pakistani Muslims?[71]

Minimal discussion on these difficult questions has set the trend for an uncritical, ahistorical, and decontextualized discourse of family law reform.[72] Rather than undertaking a critical review of the inherited, colonial legal system in order to establish a dispensation of justice representative of the post-partition population, the elitist colonial project continued. This approach towards law reform encouraged a piecemeal 'fix-what-appears-wrong-and-everything-will-be-fine' strategy.[73] Siddique argues that there is an 'absence of the past in

---

[69] This is present in the form of various law codes, both substantive and procedural, promulgated during the colonial era (including the Code of Civil Procedure (Act VIII of 1859); the Indian Penal Code (Act XLV of 1860); the Criminal Procedure Code (Act XXV of 1861); the Indian Evidence Act (Act I of 1872)), as well as in the structures of courts.

[70] B. Turner, *Weber and Islam: A Critical Study* (London and Boston: Routledge and Kegan Paul, 1974), p. 119.

[71] The prolific writer and scholar Maududi challenged what he termed 'Western-inspired' law reforms in the political, social and economic spheres. As founder of Jamaat-e-Islami, a right-wing political party, and initially opposed to the idea of Pakistan as an independent Islamic state, he and his colleagues immediately engaged with post-independence lawmaking and the political scene. He criticized family law reform on the basis that Islam had created a dichotomy between the public and private spheres, with women belonging to the private sphere, with the male as head of the household, and with women as protected persons. See Maududi's relevant works: *Haquq uz Zojjain* (Lahore: Idara Tarjumanul Quran, 1943); *Khawateen aur Deeni Masayl* (Lahore: Islamic Publications, 2000); *Purdah* (Lahore: Islamic Publications, 2003); *Purdah and the Status of Woman in Islam* (ed. trans. Al-Ashari) (Lahore: Islamic Publications, 1975).

[72] Siddique, *Pakistan's Experience*, p. 41.

[73] 'A well rounded analysis of the weaknesses of this approach requires a contextual approach to the issue exploring legal, sociological, historical, political and economic aspects. History from below, living law, subaltern studies and some recent literature in the field is beginning to make an impact on how we approach this area of research', ibid.

Pakistan's reform narratives',[74] and a reluctance to probe into the pre-colonial period to draw comparisons and lessons and to ascertain the extent to which the colonial legal system was an 'alien' imposition.

The central 'official' narrative in 1947, at the birth of the state of Pakistan, was that of a cohesive polity of Muslims who had struggled for an independent state in order to live in accordance with Islamic principles and laws. Beneath the surface, though, existed the parallel narratives of the multiple identities of the various communities inhabiting the new state of Pakistan. Imbued with rich and deeply entrenched cultures, customs and traditions, these communities paid little deference to formal laws legislated by the state. Law reform within the sphere of the family only served to highlight opposing perceptions of what Islamic law stated and of how it might apply to various communities on the ground. Here the dynamics of family law reform in Pakistan entered contested terrain, with both the past and present being mapped in different ways to provide different signposts to the future. No narrative of the past is immutable, and the narrator often reads from a self-interested script. In the colonial past, it had been impossible for the British to approach Islamic law on its own terms due to their ignorance of *fiqh* as well as the imperative to undermine the legitimacy of Mughal rule and Islamic jurisprudence.[75] The British attempted to appropriate Islamic law through translation and codification, but both proved to be flawed processes.[76] In post-colonial Pakistan, too, law reform which was acceptable to all sections of the population – to all those different narrators of the past and present and signposters to the future – was virtually impossible to achieve. The outcome has proved to be similar to the colonial past, in that law and its reform remain only partially acceptable as 'Islamic'. Proponents of 'Islamized' law reform post-1947 continued with the same fundamental misconception as the colonial rulers: that 'Islamic' law could be completely codified and located in an authoritative text that could be readily implemented, and that one comprehensive text would apply to all Pakistani Muslims as a single, homogeneous community.[77] But rather than recognize the need to pass legislation informed by principles of Islamic law, reform was instead undertaken in a cautious and half-hearted manner. Fearful of being castigated for *not* passing legislation that was in consonance with Islamic law, those charged with reforming family law tried to please all constituencies but ended up pleasing none. Conservatives denounced reforms as too liberal and un-Islamic, while women's rights activists and NGOs felt that they had not gone far enough. There remains today a disconnect between, on the one hand, family law reform that has the potential to alleviate social, economic and political disempowerments and alienations and, on the other, Pakistan's official law reform discourse.[78]

---

[74] Ibid. p. 41.   [75] Kugle, 'Framed, Blamed and Renamed', 283.

[76] As Kugle states, 'The effects of British rewriting have created a lens of texts, terms and experiences which continue to distort the view of Shariah today'. Ibid., 304.

[77] Compare British policy on the subject: ibid., 270, 272.

[78] See M. Yasin and T. Banuri (eds.), *Dispensation of Justice in Pakistan* (Oxford: Oxford University Press, 2003); T. Banuri and M. Mahmood, 'Learning from Failure: Institutional Reform for

3.5.2 The Muslim Family Laws Ordinance, 1961: 'Western' Liberal Imposition or Return to 'Original' Islamic Law?

Another dynamic of Islamic family law reform in Pakistan is the polarization of perspectives and subsequent lack of unanimity on the form and content of Islamic family law. There is a continual state of tension between those who wish to hark back to a 'pristine' and 'just' Islamic legal system implemented in seventh-century Arabia and those who believe that modernization through codification and formalization of the judicial system is the only way forward. A further dynamic within this is the selective use within that 'pristine' Islamic law of forms by which women's rights to property, education, marrying a person of their choice and so on are absent. When challenged, this denial of women's rights is either skirted around or justified in the name of 'cultural Islam'.[79] The legal system of Pakistan and its reform processes do not engage with communities on the ground in an attempt to seek their inclusion and allay fears regarding the 'Islamic' legitimacy of laws adopted. Neither do they capture practices on the ground, thus failing to reflect peoples' understandings of which legal norms ought to apply to them. This disconnect leads one to pose the question: who sets the agenda for family law reform? Are they representative of the common Pakistani, or are they simply voicing the interests of elites? To what extent do people share ownership of the law reform project, and how can it be made more inclusive?

After Independence, consistent pressure from women's groups led to the setting up of a Commission on Marriage and Family Laws (the 'Rashid Commission') in 1955,[80] briefed with exploring ways of restricting polygamy and giving women more rights of divorce than had been granted under the Dissolution of Muslim Marriages Act 1939. The Rashid Commission reported in 1958, and three years later some of its recommendations were enacted in the form of the Muslim Family Laws Ordinance (Ordinance VIII of 1961).

As an example of the 'Islamization' of laws, Pearl and Menski hailed the provisions of the 1961 Ordinance as being 'as impressive as the reforms for instance introduced by Atatürk in Turkey in the opposite direction so many years ago. It may well be that Pakistan's "Islamisation" will provide the inspiration for other Muslim countries over the next 20 years.'[81] Ironically, although it was

---

Human Resource Development', in T. Banuri, S. R. Khan and M. Mahmood (eds.), *Just Development: Beyond Adjustment with a Human Face* (Oxford: Oxford University Press, 1998).

[79] For instance, girls' rights to education are undermined by the argument that their exposure to the outside world might lead to untoward 'Western' influences; also, a wife's right to include a clause whereby she may exercise a right of divorce is discouraged as being against the spirit of Islam (recalling a *hadith* of the Prophet Muhammad that divorce is the most abhorrent permissible act).

[80] The Commission on Marriage and Family Laws (the Rashid Commission) was appointed by the Government of Pakistan under Ministry of Law Resolution No F17(24)/55-Leg, 4 August 1955. Its report was published 20 June 1956 in the Gazette of Pakistan Extraordinary under notification No F9(4)/56-Leg.

[81] Pearl and Menski, *Muslim Family Law*, p. 27.

undertaken in a spirit of 'Islamization' with a view to codify hitherto uncodified principles of Hanafi Sunni Islamic law, some provisions of the 1961 Ordinance have been contested within communities and before the courts, which have handed down varying pronouncements as to precisely how 'Islamic' or 'un-Islamic' it is.[82]

The commission's major recommendations had included the abolition of polygamy, but, as has consistently been the case in Pakistan, elected governments find themselves unable to legislate and to implement meaningful reforms because of popular pressure. It took an army general, Mohammad Ayub Khan, to promulgate the Muslim Family Laws Ordinance 1961(MFLO), but even then polygamy was only limited (and even that half-heartedly) rather than abolished outright.

Yet the 1961 ordinance did contain some very important provisions advantageous to women. Under the Sunni Hanafi understanding of Islamic law the unilateral right to terminate the marriage contract belongs to the husband, and he must pay the wife dower on his third pronouncement of the word *talaq*, 'I divorce you'.[83] In 1961, for the first time in the history of the subcontinent, the right to this instantaneous and irrevocable triple *talaq* was curtailed,[84] and the principles of two other forms of divorce (*talaq-i-ahsan* and *talaq-i-hasan*) which offer time and scope for reconciliation were incorporated into statute, thus regulating and formalizing the divorce process.[85] For women, the right to divorce by *khul*[86] and a right to divorce that has been delegated to her by the husband (*talaq-i-tafwid*), recognized under traditional Islamic law, were also recognized in statute, the latter being incorporated as an option in the standard marriage contract (the *nikah-nama*). Polygamy was restricted, in that a husband desirous of a subsequent marriage had to submit an application to the Arbitration Council besides seeking the permission of his existing wives.[87] The chairman of the Arbitration Council would then need to satisfy himself that the proposed marriage was 'necessary'.[88] However, these provisions

---

[82] See, for instance, *Mst Farishta* v. *Federation of Pakistan* PLD 1981 SC 120; *Mst Zarina Jan* v. *Mst Akbar Jan* PLD 1975 Pesh 252; *Farid* v. *Mst Manzooran* PLD 1990 SC 511; also A. Huq, 'Section 4 of the Muslim Family Laws Ordinance 1961: A Critic', *Northern University Journal of Law* 1 (2010), 7–13; R. Gilani, 'A Note on Islamic Family Law and Islamization in Pakistan', in Mallat and Connors, *Islamic Family Law*, pp. 339–46.

[83] Under Shiite understandings of Islamic law, the 'triple *talaq*' is not permitted and three pronouncements of *talaq* at one sitting are considered as one.

[84] In Sunni Hanafi Islamic law, there are three modes of pronouncing *talaq*: *talaq al-ahsan, talaq al-hasan* and *talaq al-bida*. The first two offer some scope for reconciliation as the divorce does not become irrevocable for some time. *Talaq al-bida* is an irrevocable divorce, and as soon as it is pronounced there is no chance of reconciliation. This mode is not the one sanctioned by the Prophet Muhammad, and hence it is rejected by some Muslims.

[85] MFLO 1961, s. 7.

[86] The concept of the wife being able to 'buy' her freedom by returning her dower is technically known as *khul*' and affords a woman the right to get out of an undesirable union.

[87] MFLO 1961, s. 6.

[88] The wife's infertility, insanity or incapacity to perform marital obligations have been considered 'acceptable' reasons for remarriage (MFLO 1961, WP Rules, s. 14).

were neutered by the fact that an existing wife's refusal to grant consent would not prevent the husband from remarrying, while failure to obtain permission from the Arbitration Council would not invalidate a subsequent marriage. The only reprisal for non-compliance is that, in the event of failure to obtain permission, the husband is liable to

> pay immediately the entire amount of the dower, whether prompt or deferred, due to the existing wife/wives, which amount, if not so paid, shall be recoverable as arrears of land revenue; and on conviction upon complaint be punishable with simple imprisonment which may extend to one year, or with fine which may extend to Rs. 5000, or with both.[89]

A review of post-1961 cases, however, reveals that very few cases have been filed invoking failure to seek prior permission or to register a marriage. In the few reported cases, a plea was advanced to declare the subsequent marriage void and illegal,[90] but courts held these marriages valid as provided by the MFLO.

The ordinance also provided security for children of any predeceased issue of a deceased person under Section 4 of the MFLO by providing that the child steps into the shoes of their deceased parent as regards inheritance.[91] An-Na'im describes Section 4 of the MFLO as 'a significant reform to the classical law of inheritance by allowing for orphaned grandchildren by predeceased sons or daughters, to inherit.'[92] This provision of the law presents a departure from traditional Hanafi understandings and interpretation of Qur'anic injunctions on the subject which is informed by the principle that 'the nearer excludes the further'. The table of heirs in Hanafi Sunni law of inheritance is divided into 'sharers', 'residuaries' and 'distant kindred'. This implies that where sons and daughters (sharers) predecease their parent(s), their children slip from the category of sharers and are liable to be excluded from inheritance.[93]

Proponents of Section 4 of the MFLO allowing children of predeceased children to step into the shoes of their deceased parents to receive their share of inheritance argue that nowhere in the Qur'an are grandchildren prohibited from inheriting from their grandparents. This change in traditional Hanafi law of inheritance was justified on the basis that the ordinance

> aims at alleviating the sufferings of the children whose unfortunate lot it is to lose their father or mother during the lifetime of their grandfather, or grandmother as the case may be. The construction of such statutes should be just, sensible and liberal, so as to give effect to the purpose for which they are passed.[94]

---

[89] MFLO 1961, s. 6.

[90] *Abdul Basit* v. *Union Council, Ward No. 3, Peshawar Cantt* 1970 SCMR 753; *Inayat Khan* v. *District Magistrate, Sialkot* 1986 PCrLJ 2023; *Mst Ghulam Fatima* v. *Mst Anwar* 1981 CLC 1651.

[91] MFLO 1961, s. 4. This also amended the Child Marriages Restraint Act 1929 by raising the legal age of marriage for females from fourteen to sixteen, and from eighteen to twenty-one for males – see MFLO 1961, ss. 10 and 12, though s. 12 was revoked by the Federal Laws (Revision and Declaration) Ordinance (XXVII of 1981).

[92] An-Na'im, *Islamic Family Law in a Changing World*, p. 234.

[93] For a detailed exposition see Mannan, *D. F. Mulla's Principles*, pp. 84–150.

[94] *Yusuf Abbas* v. *Mst Ismat Mustafa* PLD 1968 Kar 480, 508.

To date, the most consistent attack on family law reform has been mounted against Section 4 of the MFLO (i.e. placing sons and daughters of predeceased children in the shoes of their parents as regards inheritance rights). One of the earliest cases was *Mst Farishta* v. *The Federation of Pakistan*,[95] where the Shariat Bench of the High Court of Peshawar accepted the argument that Section 4 of the MFLO was contrary to the injunctions of Islam and therefore invalid. The government appealed the decision[96] and the Shariat Bench of the Supreme Court reversed the earlier decision holding that

> Section 4 of the Muslim Family Laws Ordinance VIII of 1961 is a special statutory provision which is intended to be applied only to Muslims of Pakistan as a class by itself, and from that point of view, constitutes a personal law for the Muslims . . . with the result, that its scrutiny was outside the jurisdiction of the High Court . . . [97]

Likewise, in the case of *Allah Rakha* v. *Federation of Pakistan*, the Federal Shariat Court declared,

> The inclusion of the grandchildren in the inheritance from the grandfather in the presence of the sons and daughters at the time the succession opens and to have per stripes a share equivalent to the share which such predeceased son or daughter would have received if alive is, therefore, nugatory to the scheme of inheritance envisaged by Qur'an.[98]

The swing of the judicial pendulum continues from Section 4 MFLO being declared a positive development in accordance with the spirit of Islam,[99] to being contrary to the injunctions of Islam.

3.5.3 The 'Text and Context' Discourse and Its Implications for the Development of Islamic Family Law

A major dynamic of family law reform in Pakistan is the ongoing 'text and context' debate in Islamic law which is evident at all levels of state, government and society. The diversity in interpretation of Islamic legal texts vis-à-vis the contexts in which these have been received, understood and applied has resulted in piecemeal reform that has not received universal acceptance on the ground. This is evident from reports of all law commissions constituted to date, as well as from the judgments of the Pakistani courts.[100] Recommendations relating

---

[95] PLD 1980 Pesh 47.

[96] Upon appeal, cited as *Federation of Pakistan* v. *Mst Farishta* PLD 1981 SC 120.

[97] Ibid., 127.   [98] *Allah Rakha* v. *Federation of Pakistan* PLD 2000 FSC 1, 7.

[99] In *Mst Fazeelat Jan* v. *Sikandar* PLD 2003 SC 475, 476, where the court ruled, 'The trial Court was wrong in holding that the grandson, under the traditional Muslim Law of Inheritance, was excluded from the inheritance of his grandfather due to the absence of his own father'.

[100] In 1975, the Pakistan Women's Rights Committee was set up, chaired by Yahya Bakhtiar, then Attorney General of Pakistan, and it reported in 1976. Nothing came out of this exercise, as the report came when the government of the day was caught up in a political crisis that eventually brought it down. A third report, the Report of the Commission on the Status of

to laws on polygamy highlight this conundrum. All law reform commissions and committees so tasked have devoted much time and attention to the subject but have never recommended its complete prohibition, simply because the debate has resulted in multiple interpretations of the Qur'anic text relating to polygamy. Expressing dissatisfaction with the recommendations of the Family Law Commission 1956, the report of the 1997 Commission of Inquiry on the Status of Women stated,

> In Pakistan, polygamy escaped decisive censure of the Muslim Family Laws Ordinance, 1961. The Ordinance neither banned polygamy nor did it effectively restrict the practice. Even though the law requires the husband to secure permission from the Arbitration Council prior to entering into a second marriage, the valid grounds for such a permission are wide enough to give the Arbitration Council total discretion.[101]

Islamic family law permits a man to be lawfully married to up to four wives at the same time. Polygamy thus stands permitted in Islam, although the Qur'anic verse on the subject includes clear provisos:

> And if you fear that you cannot act equitably towards orphans, then marry such women as seem good to you, two, three or four, but if you fear that you shall not be able to deal justly [with them] then only one.[102]

This raises a number of questions. Does, for instance, the Qur'an create an *obligation* to be polygamous, or is it a qualified option to be exercised under those circumstances set out in that verse?[103] Al-Hibri is of the opinion that the mere fact that the Prophet Muhammad was polygamous in his later life is no evidence of a 'right' of all men to be polygamous. She argues that Qur'anic verses

Women 1985, chaired by Begum Zari Sarfaraz, also made some useful recommendations, but the government declared it a classified document and it was only when a new government came into power in 1988 that it was made public. The latest in the series of reports is that of the Commission of Inquiry for Women submitted in 1997. See also case law on s. 5 MFLO 1961 on registration of marriages, *Habib* v. *The State* PLD 1980 Lah 97; *Abdul Kalam* v. *The State* 1987 MLD 1637; *Muhammad Akram* v. *Mst Farman Bi* PLD 1989 Lah 200; on the failure to seek permission of an existing wife for a subsequent marriage, see *Abdul Basit* v. *Union Council, Ward No. 3, Peshawar Cantt* 1970 SCMR 753; *Inayat Khan* v. *District Magistrate, Sialkot* 1986 PCrLJ 2023; *Mst Ghulam Fatima* v. *Mst Anwar* 1981 CLC 1651.

101 Shirkat Gah Women's Resource Centre, 'Women's Rights in Muslim Family Law in Pakistan: 45 Years of Recommendations vs. the FSC Judgement', January 2000 special bulletin, February 2000, p. 26.

102 Verse 4:3.

103 A. R. I. Doi, *Shariah: The Islamic Law* (London: Ta-Ha, 1984), p. 146, outlines the various circumstances for which he considers polygamy to be the 'best solution'. These include the wife suffering from a serious disease, being barren, being of unsound mind, being old and infirm, being of irreparable 'bad character', moving away from her husband's place of residence, being disobedient and difficult to live with, and the fact of many men dying during war leaving behind a large number of widows. The final circumstance that Doi advances as justifiable is where a husband feels he cannot do without another wife and is capable of providing equal support to all. Doi in effect gives *carte blanche* to a man to marry if he feels like it, but this is hardly consonant with the contextual rationale behind the Quranic verse.

state clearly that neither the Prophet nor his wives are like other men and women, and employing it as a pretext for polygamy is not appropriate.[104] Second, the verse which has been used to justify polygamy also attaches a condition for such action, i.e. a requirement to deal justly with all one's wives. Reinforcing this is the Qur'anic statement (verse 4:129) that 'Ye are never able to be fair and just among women even if you tried hard', and 'modernist' Muslim scholars are of the opinion that for evolving a rule of law relating to polygamy these two verses must be read and interpreted together.[105] In response to the above argument, some Muslim thinkers assert that the word *tadilu* has a different meaning in verse 4:129 (to 'deal justly') to that in verse 4:3 (to 'do justice'); hence the view that these verses *cannot* be combined to draw an inference.[106] Abdur Rahman Doi also challenges the view of modernists who consider verse 4:129 as a legal condition attached to polygamous unions.[107] Citing Shaikh Mohammed bin Sirin and Shaikh Abubakr bin al-Arabi, he makes the point that the inability of a man to do justice between women referred to in the Qur'an is in respect of love and sexual intercourse only. The justice required of a man is, in the opinion of these scholars, confined to matters of providing equality in residence, food and clothes to his wives. By this argument, so long as a man can provide these he is seen as being 'just' between women.[108]

So, given such contestation over the Qur'anic basis for polygamy, how had the Rashid Commission reached its recommendations? The Commission had drawn on 'reformist' textual interpretations and sought inspiration from other Muslim states where polygamy had been abolished.[109] But the strong dissenting note of Maulana Ihtesham-ul-haq Thanvi, a member of the Commission, and a fear of adverse public opinion, had led to a 'watered-down' version which regulated rather than abolished polygamy altogether.

3.5.4 Judicial *Ijtihad*: The 'Silent Islamization' of the Pakistani Judiciary as a Vehicle for Law Reform

In his book *The Role of Islam in the Legal System of Pakistan*,[110] Martin Lau emphasizes the role of the judges in 'appropriating' Islam and Islamic law and

---

[104] Verse 33:32, 50. For example, while the Prophet encouraged widows and divorcees to remarry, his own wives were not to be remarried after his death. They were considered 'the mothers of all believers', and no believer may marry his mother. However, as the Prophet grew older he gave his wives the choice to leave and marry another male more fulfilling, perhaps, of husbandly duties. All but one wife refused to leave him. See Al-Hibri, 'Islamic Herstory', p. 216, citing S. Al-Afghani, *Al-Islam wal Mar'ah* (Damascus: Tarakki Press, 1945), p. 79.

[105] See Al-Hibri, 'Islamic Herstory', p. 216, for this line of argument; F. Rahman, 'The Status of Women in Islam: A Modernist Interpretation', in G. Nashat (ed.), *Women and Revolution in Iran* (Boulder, CO: Westview Press, 1983), pp. 45–9. Law reform in Muslim jurisdictions in the twentieth century has relied upon these interpretations.

[106] Al-Hibri, 'Islamic Herstory', p. 216 and accompanying footnotes.

[107] Doi, *Shariah*, Chapter 8, especially pp. 147–50.   [108] Ibid.

[109] Tunisia is an example. Turkey has a secular legal system that prohibits polygamy.

[110] M. Lau, *The Role of Islam in the Legal System of Pakistan* (Leiden: Nijhoff, 2006).

'its integration into the vocabulary of the courts'.[111] This has been a 'conscious process aimed at fulfilment of the general desire to indigenise and Islamise the legal system at the end of colonisation'.[112] This judge-led process used the language of Islamic law to enhance the powers of the judiciary and widen the scope of constitutional guarantees of rights. At the same time, judicial attitudes are inevitably reflective of societal perceptions as well as wider cultural perceptions, and are not always in consonance with 'official' law. As demonstrated in *Farishta* and other cases, judges have not been shy in declaring a statute 'un-Islamic' and therefore invalid, laying bare the fragility of any law reform process, even if undertaken in the name of Islam.[113]

Post-colonial Pakistan inherited a common law system, including her court system, which continues to date. During the 1980s, Zia-ul-Haq amended the Constitution to create Shariat Courts with the remit to entertain cases in the realm of Islamic law. Even he, however, was conscious of the limits of his 'Islamization' process, and hence a 'saving' clause was inserted declaring personal laws to be outside the remit of these Shariat Courts, and it was this that became the basis for the appellate judgment in *Farishta*.

Despite attempts at 'Islamization' of the legal and judicial system through case law and law reform, it is obvious that within the judiciary itself there are opposing perspectives at play. Even the Federal Shariat Court had to reconcile the common law legacy with the Islamic legacy by stating,

> The court maintains a balance between the judges trained in the common law tradition and the *ulama* judges who are experts in the Islamic legal traditions with the result that each issue presented before the court is shaped and refined in a unique way by the two traditions before a final decision is rendered. Silently, swiftly but surely *ijtihad* is being undertaken in a new way.[114]

The 'Islamization' of law and law reform by the judiciary is being undertaken within the framework of the Constitution of Pakistan and is reminiscent of the judicial *ijtihad* of the colonial period, where Muslim judges took on the role of using Islamic law in its context rather than in its classical renderings. By '(judicial) *ijtihad*' is meant the deduction of legal principle through a priori reasoning, without recourse to the teachings of a school of jurisprudence. An example of judicial *ijtihad* is the interpretation of *khul'* developed by the Pakistani judiciary and the meaning placed upon the concept in their decisions as described below.

In Islamic family law, the dissolution of marriage may take any one of the following routes: (i) at the instance and initiative of the husband (*talaq*), (ii) at

---

[111] Ibid., p. 1.   [112] Ibid.

[113] For an incisive analysis of *Farishta*, see L. Carroll, 'The Pakistan Federal Shariat Court, Section 4 of the Muslim Family Laws Ordinance, and the Orphaned Grandchild', *Islamic Law and Society* 9 (2002), 70–82; for case law see *Mst Farishta* v. *The Federation of Pakistan*; *Mst Zarina Jan* v. *Mst Akbar Jan* PLD 1975 Pesh 252; *Farid* v. *Manzooran* PLD 1990 SC 511.

[114] Federal Shariat Court: 2003, 1.

the instance and initiative of the wife (*khul'*), (iii) by mutual consent (*mubara't*). Contrary to popular perceptions, the Qur'anic injunctions on the subject, outlined in Sura 4, 'Women' (*Al-Nisa*), fall short of according men a unilateral right to dissolve the marriage tie without assigning any cause. In a landmark Pakistani case, *Mst Khurshid Bibi* v. *Mohammed Amin*,[115] their Lordships were of the view that *talaq* is not an unfettered right, as verse 4:35 of the Qur'an provides for the appointment of arbiters to curtail its unbridled exercise. These fetters, however, also have their limits, and if the husband is determined to go ahead with the pronouncement of divorce then no court is competent to stop him from doing so (the 1961 ordinance has, however, attempted to regulate and provide a role for judicial forums to restrain the husband).

But Islamic law also confers on a woman the right to seek dissolution of the marriage tie. In cases cited from the time of the Prophet Muhammad, the only question asked of the woman would be whether she was willing to forgo her dower. If she agreed, the marriage stood dissolved.[116] It was only later that this right became qualified, the woman having to convince a court of her fixed aversion and of the irretrievable breakdown of the marriage in order to obtain *khul'*.[117] Although some leading judgments from Pakistan's superior courts have tried to equate a man's right to pronounce *talaq* with the woman's right of *khul'*,[118] there are major differences between these two modes: no matter what obstacles one places in the way of a husband's right to *talaq*, at the end of the day *talaq* may be pronounced with or without the intervention of a court; but if a woman fails to convince a judge of the genuineness of her case, she cannot unilaterally terminate the marriage.[119] Social construction of the content of a woman's right to *khul'* overrides her rights under Islamic law.

Under a 2002 amendment to the Family Court Act 1964, where the wife seeks dissolution on the basis of *khul'* the court is simply required to pass an order to that effect on return of the dower to the husband without going into their previously held position that full repayment of dower is not automatic in all *khul'* cases. In *M Saqlain Zaheer* v. *Zaibun Nisa*,[120] for instance, the court refined and clarified the concept of *zar-i-khula* (the sum which needs to be repaid by the wife) in a manner that has benefited women by insisting that reciprocal benefits received by the husband should be taken into account: continuously living together, bearing and rearing children, housekeeping and so on can be counted as benefits offsetting the sum that the wife has to repay.

[115] PLD 1967 SC 97.

[116] The oft-quoted case of *Jamila*, who sought dissolution of marriage on the basis that she did not like her husband's looks and considered him ugly.

[117] PLD 1967 SC 97.

[118] For example in *Safia Begum* v. *Khadim Hussain* 1985 CLC 1869; and *Syed Mohammed Rizwan* v. *Mst Samina Khatoon* 1989 SMCR 25.

[119] See, for example, *Aali* v. *Additional District Judge I, Quetta* 1987 CLC 27; *Raisa Begum* v. *Mohammed Hussain* 1986 MLD 1418.

[120] 1988 MLD 427.

This particular amendment has been criticized due to the fact that it does not require the court to go into the details of whether the wife should repay *mahr* to the husband in lieu of *khul'* or whether is she entitled to keep some of it (as stated in *M Saqlain Zaheer* v. *Zaibun Nisa*). Under the 2002 amendments, courts simply have to rubber-stamp the *khul'* so long as the dower is returned, without developing the argument that taking back from the wife what the husband gave at the time of the marriage is against the spirit of Islam and an injustice to the wife. Amendment of the law relating to *khul'* appears to have overturned gains obtained through case law, in what amounts to a situation of 'two steps forward, one step back'.

3.5.5 Conflicting 'Islamization(s)' or Plural Islam? The Incoherence Of Law Reform

That Islamic law is plural in its interpretation, adoption and practice is an oft-repeated position for most writers on Islamic law and one that has been advanced in the present chapter. Competing interest groups play out their preferred understandings of Islamic law, and family law is the most common battleground for the opinions reflecting this plurality. As outlined in preceding sections, family law in Pakistan is based on principles of Islamic law; the judiciary has consistently developed its jurisprudence within an Islamic legal framework. However, some constituencies within Pakistan have always challenged the 'Islamic-ness' of the legal and judicial system, demanding 'wholesale replacement of the inherited colonial system'.[121] Whilst the judiciary has discretely led the 'Islamization' process through judicial decisions by invoking Islamic law as central to its decisions, this has not always been perceived as sufficient or, in some cases, the 'right type' of 'Islamization'. The late 1970s and the 1980s saw an aggressive form of overt 'Islamization' as government policy, when Zia-ul-Haq declared this to be his legitimating factor for overthrowing a democratically elected government. A number of laws were adopted in the name of Islam, the most controversial and damaging of these being collectively known as the 'Hudood Ordinances'[122] (from Arabic *hudud* meaning 'the bounds of acceptable behaviour').

Two parallel approaches to 'Islamization' thus emerged in Pakistan, coexisting in an uneasy relationship and with unintended adverse effects on women in

---

[121] Lau, *Role of Islam*, p. 5.

[122] The most virulent and most often used was the Prohibition of Zina (Enforcement of Hudood) Ordinance 1979. Some changes were also made in existing laws, including the Evidence Act, in 1984, where evidence of a woman in financial matters was given half the evidentiary weight to that provided by a man. It is beyond the scope of the present work to engage in detailed discussion on this law, so suffice it to say that it undermined women's position in society, albeit at a formal level because, insofar as evidence in court was concerned, judges continued as before and accepted women's evidence as equal to men. In other words, the lower evidentiary value of women's testimony, as required by the modified law of evidence, was simply ignored.

particular. The Muslim Family Law Ordinance exemplified a progressive interpretation by casting traditional Islamic law into a modern legal framework; the
Hudood Ordinances, on the other hand, represented a version of Islam and
Islamic law that was based upon a literal and often misplaced interpretation of
the sources.[123] For example, Section 7 of the MFLO attempted to institute a
divorce procedure by requiring the husband to send a written notice of divorce
to the chairman of the Arbitration Council set up under the Act. The purpose
of this provision was to ensure that the authorities were aware of the change of
marital status and that both parties were free to remarry should they choose
to do so, and it was therefore an attempt to protect women from being the
subject of ex-husbands who, having pronounced divorce, could later question
their own divorce were their ex-wives to remarry.

The most explosive provision of the MFLO, however, is Section 7(1), which
seeks to ensure that a copy of the written notice of *talaq* provided to the
chairman of the Arbitration Council is also given to the wife, making the fact
of the divorce clear and unequivocal. Contravention of this procedure makes
the husband liable to simple imprisonment of one year and/or a fine. This
seemingly straightforward procedural requirement since 1979 (until the passage
of the Women Protection Act 2006) became the cause of grave miscarriages of
justice as the MFLO interacted dynamically with the provisions regarding *zina*
(fornication and adultery) in the Hudood Ordinances and has given rise to a
large body of case law.

Prior to the Prohibition of Zina (Enforcement of Hudood) Ordinance 1979,
in most legal cases relating to non-registration of *talaq* a court would hold
that the woman was still married, since her husband had not gone through
the complete statutory procedure for obtaining a valid divorce. Courts acted
on the belief that the objective of the MFLO was to protect women from the
ill-effects of arbitrary divorce, and the subsequent waiting period of ninety days
was held to place some limitation and restraint upon the husband's unilateral
and arbitrary right to divorce. This safety net had been set out with an eye to
the social structure of Pakistan, where a divorced woman is akin to a pariah,
with little support or respect both within her family and in the wider social
circle. However, with the promulgation of the Prohibition of Zina Ordinance,
the insistence upon the provision of the MFLO that only a *talaq* duly written
and notified would be effective became a *dis*advantage to women. Vindictive
former husbands who had failed to send a written notice to the Arbitration
Council could now allege that a former wife who, after being divorced, had
remarried was in fact not married, was guilty of adultery and was liable to be
accused of *zina*, an offence punishable with lashes and/or stoning to death.[124]

---

[123] For instance, the Zina Ordinance failed to distinguish between rape and consensual sex,
requiring four adult male Muslim witnesses to the actual act of penetration!

[124] Leading cases include *Shera* v. *The State* PLD 1982 FSC 229; *Muhammad Siddique* v. *The State*
PLD 1983 FSC 173; *Mirza Qamar Raza* v. *Mst Tahira Begum* PLD 1988 Kar 169; *Muhammad
Sarwar* v. *The State* PLD 1988 FSC 42.

The courts finally declared that failure to notify the authorities of a *talaq* did not invalidate the *talaq*. In a landmark judgment, Naseem Hassan Shah CJ held that

> where a wife bona fide believing that her previous marriage with her former husband stands dissolved on the basis of a talaqnama although the husband has not got it registered with the Union Council enters into a second marriage, neither the second marriage nor the fact of her living with the second husband will amount to Zina because of her bona fide belief that her first marriage stood dissolved.[125]

Such judgments were 'damage-containment' responses by courts to the interaction of the MFLO and the Hudood laws. While these have saved women from the disastrous consequences of being found guilty of *zina*, they have in effect nevertheless nullified those provisions of the MFLO that offered some relief to women against arbitrary and unregistered *talaq*. An important point to note for our purposes is that the dynamics in this area of law reside in the differing interpretations of 'Islamic' law which gave rise to the MFLO and the Prohibition of Zina Ordinance, and in the judiciary's changing response to the cases before them under pressure from both conservative and modernizing constituencies. Legal pluralism has also played a decisive role by playing provisions of the codified family law (primarily the MFLO) against literalist, inflexible interpretations of Islamic law and rival versions of 'Islamic' laws including the Hudood Ordinances. The outcome is case law consisting of contradictory rulings, some declaring the MFLO un-Islamic; others upholding the Islamic nature of the statute. Section 7, requiring registration of *talaq*, has alternately been found both 'Islamic'[126] *and* 'un-Islamic'.[127]

Alongside the dynamic of plural Islamic law visible in the formal law-making and judicial system, a further layer of complexity has become more visible in recent years. In most post-colonial Muslim jurisdictions, governance issues are often mixed up and confused with Islamic law issues, and this has led to a nostalgia for a supposed 'Islamic' past that was radically displaced by colonial laws. Customary practices and dispute-resolution forums such as *jirgas* and *panchayats* have been a source of frustration and injustice. A combined assault on laws resulting from reform processes (both colonial and post-colonial) and customary practices has been mounted by 'Islamists' in a number of jurisdictions, including Pakistan. Demands for a return to 'Islam' and 'Islamic law' (*sharia*, as they term it) have become the basis of militancy. The militancy in Pakistan's Swat Valley is a good example. There, the Taliban initially built a constituency for themselves upon precisely this basis: a demand for 'Islamic law'. A

---

[125] *Mst Bashiran* v. *Muhammad Hussain* PLD 1988 SC 186.
[126] *Mst Kaniz Fatima* v. *Wali Muhammad* PLD 1989 Lah 490; *Ayaz Aslam* v. *Chairman Arbitration Council* 1990 ALD 702.
[127] *Mirza Qamar Raza* v. *Mst Tahira Begum* PLD 1988 Kar 169; *Allah Dad* v. *Mukhtar* 1992 SCMR 1273; *Allah Rakha* v. *Federation of Pakistan* PLD 2000 FSC 1.

relentless campaign for women's rights and justice within the family, broadcast on an FM radio channel, created sympathy among people who were frustrated by a lack of action by governmental institutions. By way of example, a widow had been denied her inheritance by her in-laws, and the local government had not acted to help her. Upon complaining to the militant Taliban leader Maulana Fazlullah through her mosque's *imam*, she was assured of her inheritance and her in-laws were threatened with 'dire consequences' if she was not reinstated in the family home. Irrespective of the turnaround in the stance of the Taliban and how women became the prime targets of their version of Islam and Islamic law, the fact remains that in the early days of the militancy, the gap left by formal governance structures, including the judicial system, was filled by the 'rough-and-ready' justice of the Taliban. They spoke the language of the people, delivered on their promise, and responded to the demands for justice by women and other vulnerable sections of society. The state and government, even after these incidents, failed to respond and rise to the occasion by ensuring rights and effective dispensation of justice. Unsavoury as it may appear to Western, liberal society, the Taliban, at least in their initial days, offered a bottom-up approach to access to justice, including women's rights in the family. Women did not have to pay fees to lawyers, travel to courts or suffer the inordinate delays that are a hallmark of the Pakistani and other judicial systems. And they were also assured that what was being given to them was a form of divine justice.

3.5.6 Present by Their Absence: The Thorny Issues of Family Law

Competing perspectives in family law reform have informed debates on the subject, reflecting an ongoing struggle between forces of literalist and conservative Islam and proponents of progressive, interpretative expressions of that same religious tradition. That various constituencies pull the law in different directions is also apparent from case law as well as from law reforms instigated by these individuals and groups. What is bemusing in these varying narratives is the eerie silence over certain thorny issues within Islamic family law that have failed to find champions on any side of the ideological divide, and in particular at the grass roots. These include Islamic conceptions of *halala* marriage, the triple *talaq*, post-divorce maintenance and the adoption of children. Since it can be argued that any meaningful developments in family law have in a sense transpired through judicial decisions, it is disappointing to note an absence of any serious engagement of courts in these important and challenging, yet little discussed, matters. A good example of such thorny issues is the concept of *halala.*

Halala (Urdu, in Arabic *tahlil*) is a short, intervening marriage to a third party which an ex-wife must go through before remarrying her ex-husband in order to make their remarriage *halal.* It supposedly emanates from a Qur'anic verse, the aim of which was to demonstrate the seriousness with which divorce should be treated in a Muslim marriage. In a patriarchal society, the need for *halala* has always been a hugely inhibiting factor on otherwise easily available *talaq* divorce, it being a serious reprimand for a man to have his ex-wife marry another man as a precondition for remarrying him. The Qur'an, in verse 2:230, states,

> And if he divorces her finally, she shall thereafter not be lawful unto him unless she marries another man. If [by chance this marriage also breaks] and the present husband divorces her, there shall be no sin upon either of them [i.e. the first husband and the divorced wife] to remarry – provided that both of them think that they will be able to be within the bounds set by Allah: and these are the bounds of Allah which He makes clear unto people of innate knowledge.

In Muslim societies including Pakistan, *halala* follows on from the (in)famous practice of the triple *talaq*. More often than not, men who have pronounced the triple *talaq* in haste tend to repent but are told that their wife will have to undergo a *halala* marriage if they are to remarry. Thus the least woman-friendly interpretation of the religious text is employed, to first make a woman lose her husband and home and *then* demand that she go through a marriage with another man only to be divorced promptly in order to marry her first husband. Whilst there is a feeling of unease among ordinary Pakistani Muslims at the injustice of these supposedly Islamic laws, they find themselves unable to accept an alternative interpretation challenging this practice.

The Muslim Family Law Ordinance attempted to address the situation by 'Islamizing' the statutory procedure for dissolution of marriage. As indicated earlier, the most common mode of *talaq* is for the husband to pronounce the triple *talaq*, resulting in immediate termination of the marriage and eviction of the wife from the marital home. The basic protection that Section 7 of the MFLO provided is the requirement that the husband follow a procedure for *talaq* by notifying the local authorities. This procedure, without stating so explicitly, incorporates a form of divorce called *talaq-i-ahsan* ('the most laudable *talaq*') in Section 7(3) that reads thus: 'Save as provided in sub-section (5), *talaq* unless revoked earlier, expressly or otherwise, shall not be effective until the expiration of 90 days from the day on which notice under sub-section (1) is delivered to the Chairman.' That ninety-day period is conterminous with a compulsory waiting period (*iddat*) during which the marriage is suspended but not terminated. By holding the husband to this period, after which the divorce becomes irrevocable, a man's unilateral right to divorce is toned down and chances for reconciliation are kept alive until the waiting period has expired. Section 7(4) requires the parties to appear before an Arbitration Council during the ninety days to attempt reconciliation. Section 7(6) minimizes the requirement for an intervening *halala* marriage by the woman in cases where former spouses wish to remarry. It states, 'Nothing shall debar a wife whose marriage has been terminated by *talaq* effective under this section from remarrying the same husband, without an intervening marriage with a third person, unless such termination is for the third time effective.' In other words, lack of a *halala* marriage is no bar to a remarriage to the same husband if *talaq* has not been pronounced three times. Muslim women through the centuries have borne the brunt of the need for *halala* (which involved having sex with the intervening husband) resulting from a hasty pronouncement of the triple *talaq*. The MFLO, by providing a breathing space, resulted in respite for women from the humiliation of marrying another man simply to remarry the husband who had so summarily divorced her.

So here we have a seemingly woman-friendly article of family law legislation. Yet a review of reported case law from the Pakistani courts reveals just a few scattered cases on *halala* marriages and the triple *talaq* but very little learned discussion or challenges to the negative interpretations and meanings placed on these terms. By and large, courts engage in damage limitation to save the marriage as best they can. In *Attiq Ahmed Khan* v. *Noor-ul-Saba*,[128] the Quetta Baluchistan High Court declared that a single pronouncement of *khul'* (upon declaration by a judge) does not constitute an irrevocable divorce and that the wife did not require a *halala* marriage in order to remarry her husband. This ruling, it may be noted, went beyond the position of classical Islamic law on *khul'* (where a pronouncement by a judge makes it final and irrevocable).[129] In *Ghulam Muhammad* v. *The State*,[130] a man who had divorced his wife became repentant and wanted to resume marital relations with her and revive their marriage. However, since he had not revoked the divorce within the stipulated period but had resumed sexual relations with her, they were accused of *zina*. The court decided that the divorce pronounced by the man had become effective, and could not be withdrawn by him. Thus the accused had not 'remarried' the female co-accused and no *halala* had taken place, and cohabitation between the two after their divorce therefore amounted to *zina*. Their conviction for *zina* was maintained, but in light of their not being aware of the legal consequences of living together after non-withdrawal of the divorce, their sentences were substantially reduced.

3.6 Concluding Reflections

Family law reform in post-colonial Pakistan (and in other Muslim jurisdictions) is firmly placed within the *wilaya–qiwama* nexus, resulting in a paradox of equality. Women are perceived as perpetual (legal) minors in need of lifelong guardianship such that no law reform is truly able to break free from this conceptualization. The law reform project in Pakistan is one of a fractured modernity, oscillating between modernity and tradition. In fact, nowhere in the Muslim world has there been observed a radical departure from the religious text

---

[128]   2011 CLC 1211.
[129]   A similar question was raised before the court in *Ghulam Abbas* v. *Station House Officer* (2009) YLR 201 Lahore High Court, leading to a similar outcome.
[130]   1994 PCRLJ 1856.

in the law reform project; neither is there sustained reform based on the principle of equality and non-discrimination. Except for Tunisia and Turkey, polygamy has, at best, been restricted or regulated; inheritance rights have remained untouched and women's rights to guardianship of children are dependent upon the outcome of court decisions and the precise circumstances of each case.

Islamic 'revivalist' initiatives and movements, too, are endangering law reform, as is evident from the increasingly robust challenges mounted to it within the judiciary as well as at a societal level. This chapter has used Pakistan as a case study, but its broader observations may resonate with law reforms in other parts of the Muslim world.[131] There is a conscious as well as a subconscious affinity and legitimacy, albeit to a greater or lesser degree, for varying strands of the Islamic legal traditions as drivers of family law reform.

In the case of Pakistan, there is a misconception that 'Islamization' as a law reform project was initiated by Zia-ul-Haq through his version of Islamic laws. Perhaps at a less overt level, but more consistently it is the Pakistani judiciary that has slowly but surely placed Islamic law at the centre of their decisions. It may safely be argued that the distinctive feature of Islamic family law in Pakistan is the development of case law. The 'brand' of Islamic law reflected in judgments oscillates between a conservative, literal application of the sources and a progressive, liberal interpretation in the manner of 'judicial *ijtihad*'. These disparate interventions toward 'Islamizing' laws have led to an incoherent law reform outcome. It is also suggested that despite attempts at the 'Islamization' of Islamic family law, family law and its reform processes maintain a distinct common law legacy, remaining reliant on Mulla's *Muhammadan Law* as a definitive, classical text. As a member of the judiciary has put it, 'Mulla is the definitive text and it would take a lot to dislodge it in court!'[132] Lack of clear Islamic law injunctions and multiple interpretations by various juristic schools and scholars, too, compel courts to turn to principles of common law, justice, equity and good conscience. These common law principles stand 'Islamized' and appropriated by Pakistani judges not simply as common law principles but as *universal* concepts of justice commensurate with Islamic legal principles.

The substantive content of 'Islamic' family law in Pakistan remains contested and pulled in different directions. Almost five decades of recommendations from four law reform commissions and as many decades of court judgments later, the Federal Sharia Court has struck down provisions of one of the few pieces of progressive legislations in Pakistan, i.e. the MFLO. The Council of Islamic Ideology (CII), a constitutional body tasked with determining the

---

[131] For instance, those common law post-colonial jurisdictions that have legislated in the area of family law, describing them as 'personal status laws'. For an overview see An-Na'im, *Islamic Family Law in a Changing World*.

[132] Personal communication, the identity of the informant to remain confidential at their request.

'Islamic' nature of laws in Pakistan, has also put its weight behind those who believe some provisions of the MFLO to be 'un-Islamic'. This leaves law reform initiatives such as the MFLO on shaky ground and in a state of flux.

Islamic family law advocates, whether at the level of society, the courts or legislature, maintain a tangible silence in areas that affect women at their greatest vulnerability, most prominently those relating to post-divorce maintenance, the triple *talaq* and *halala* marriage. An increasingly patriarchal, inflexible manifestation of Islamic law is in conflict with egalitarian, progressive, and arguably 'Western-inspired' liberal conceptions of Islam, leading to an ongoing tension between different articulations of an inherently plural legal tradition. Until the reform process is embedded within gender-equal and woman-friendly social change that internalizes and accepts this reform, law reform remains a matter of 'two steps forward, one step back'. Fazlur Rahman is of the firm view that legal reform can only be effective in changing the status of women in Muslim contexts when there is adequate basis for social change. It is only then that the Qur'anic objective of social justice in general, and for women in particular, can be fulfilled; otherwise its success will be limited, transitory and confined to certain social groups.[133]

Increasingly, there appears to be sympathy for a kind of law reform instigated in a number of Muslim jurisdictions through what are termed 'repugnancy clauses', meaning that where a legal norm is not *prohibited* in Islamic law, it must by default be *permitted*. These changes, however, are confined to matters of state and government, as well as commercial and financial transactions, where a wider berth for discretion is countenanced. The principle of 'repugnancy' and this broad discretion are not observed in the area of family law, in view of an obsessively protective attitude towards this as the last bastion of Muslim identity. For example, questions of post-divorce maintenance do not have to be prohibited because these are not repugnant to Islamic law principles, yet opposition to extending the period of alimony has been very fierce in Egypt; neither have they been accepted in family law reforms in Pakistan, or by the courts.[134]

To what extent is family law reform informed and driven by people on the ground? Although the constituencies, interlocutors and intermediaries have expanded beyond government, Parliament and the courts and now include women's rights and other pressure groups, law reform remains an elusive, inadequate process. More inclusivity is required of people whose voices are not likely to be heard in decision-making forums where reform is initiated, discussed and decided.

[133] Rahman, *Islam and Modernity*, p. 308.
[134] Hamoudi, 'Death of Islamic Law', 6–7. For a very detailed discussion of post-divorce maintenance in Pakistan and its case law, see A. Shahid, 'Post-divorce Maintenance for Muslim Women in Pakistan and Bangladesh: A Comparative Perspective', *International Journal of Law, Policy & the Family* 27 (2013), 197–215; Shirkat Gah, *Women's Rights*.

Is there a consistent vision for the politics of family law and its reform among the governments of Islamic countries? It seems far more likely that there are only piecemeal legislative attempts to calm acute social problems by reactionary law-making that is itself, in turn, tugged back and forth between conservative and liberal understandings of Islamic law, and between disputed versions within those traditions, without a clear vision of where society is to go or what it is to be.

4

In Search of Legitimacy: The Dilemma of Islamic Finance

4.1 Introduction

As highlighted in Chapters 1 and 3, Islamic law in its colonial and post-colonial variants is a modern phenomenon – at best a hybrid of its classical form and substance. The inevitable outcome of historical, socio-economic and political processes, Islamic law as generally experienced today exemplifies continuities, discontinuities and ruptures. Modernity, globalization and the nation state increasingly interact with religion, diverse cultures and official and unofficial legal orders, resulting in synthetic phenomena such as modern Islamic finance and banking.

Islamic finance law consists of rules (and institutions) that base their objectives and operations on Islamic law and *sharia*. A variant of Islamic commercial law, Islamic finance law 'is based on certain parts of classical Islamic law concerning commercial transactions.'[1] In popular Muslim consciousness, though, Islamic finance is equated with 'interest-free' banking the prohibition of (i) *riba* (exorbitant or excessive interest, or usury), (ii) *gharar* (uncertainty, risk or speculation), and (iii) *maysir* (gambling and games of chance).[2] In theory, engaging in religiously permissible, non-exploitative, equitable and ethical financial activities forms the cornerstone of Islamic finance; in practice, for many centuries the reality has been otherwise, and the vast majority of the Muslim world has engaged with conventional (interest-based) financial regimes in one form or another.

Classical Islamic finance has two arms: first, there is the 'profit-and-loss-sharing' paradigm, where lender *and* borrower share the risk of making or losing money, rather than the lender alone being guaranteed a fixed, predetermined return. Islamic finance, being equity-based, treats the financier and

---

[1] N. Foster and S. Archer (forthcoming), 'Islamic Financial Law: Law without a Legal System', conference paper, Business Inbetween Cultures: The Development of Islamic Finance, European Association for Banking and Financial History e.V., Sarajevo, 15–16 November 2012, p. 1.

[2] In migrant communities in the UK and US, and still to some extent in the Middle East, the focus remains prohibition of *riba*, whereas in Malaysia (discussed below) risk-sharing is currently the dominant construction of Islamic finance. I am grateful to Lena Rethal for alerting me to this distinction.

the entrepreneur as joint partners, co-joined in risk-taking and profit-sharing.[3] Capital is unsecured, unguaranteed, and not entitled to predetermined or fixed interest, and may appreciate or depreciate depending on the market. Second, there is the entrenched requirement of promoting social justice through mandatory almsgiving (*zakat*), voluntary almsgiving (*sadaqa*), and 'benevolent loans' (*qard hasan*). Modern Islamic finance has prioritized the profitable over the charitable arm, largely ignoring the moral economy that was an integral component of its classical antecedent. Furthermore, contemporary Islamic finance law is a law operating without a fully supporting legal system,[4] and the emergent picture is one that combines Islamic *form* with conventional (Western) *substance*, leading some commentators to observe that, in practice, Islamic finance appears to mimic the conventional financial regime.[5]

A 'need' for Islamic finance was identified by Muslim nations around the world in the late colonial period and upon their gaining independence, with a number of contributory factors lending their impetus to the process. During the colonial period, religious, ethnic and national identities became conflated. The idea of returning to one's roots and living life according to one's faith and indigenous norms became popular, with impoverished multitudes living under alien socio-economic and political regimes finding this a compelling narrative. Muslim leaders promoted Islam as an alternative that would usher in social justice and alleviate the existential problems of a population oppressed by both indigenous elites and foreign rulers. Religiously inspired political leaders and intellectuals set about developing models of Islamic finance in a bid to replace conventional models.[6]

At an institutional and an intellectual level, the widely held view has been that the knowledge and evolution of Islamic finance remained stagnant for many centuries;[7] it was only in the twentieth century that it saw a revival. In the 1970s, 'modern' Islamic finance began as a reaction to colonial domination of the Muslim world and with a desire for the re-Islamization of Islamic finance. Purporting to offer an alternative to conventional financial regimes, two main strategies were set out: in one, relevant Islamic norms were (and are)

---

[3]   Vogel and Hayes, *Islamic Law and Finance*, p. 194.

[4]   Foster and Archer, 'Islamic Financial Law'; N. D. Foster, 'Islamic Finance Law as an Emergent Legal System', *Arab Law Quarterly* 21(2) 2007, pp. 170–88.

[5]   M. A. El-Gamal, *Islamic Finance: Law, Economics, and Practice* (Cambridge: Cambridge University Press, 2006); I. Warde, *Islamic Finance in the Global Economy*, 2nd edition (Edinburgh: Edinburgh University Press, 2010).

[6]   A. Saeed, 'Sharia and Finance', in Peters and Bearman, *The Ashgate Research Companion to Islamic Law*, pp. 249–50.

[7]   Question marks are now being raised over this perspective by researchers including those at the International Centre for Education in Islamic Finance in Malaysia. They are presently trying to 'recover' Islamic financial innovations such as *esham* (apparently pioneered by the Ottomans in 1775). A counternarrative is possibly being generated on the basis of this research, leading to the inference that the 'stagnation' theory may be attributed to a Eurocentric politics of knowledge. See M. Cizakca, 'Can There Be Innovation in Islamic Finance? Case Study: Esham', paper presented at the 11th IFSB Summit, 20 May 2014, Mauritius.

reinterpreted in light of both their ethical values and modern financial under-standings; in the other, a strictly formal approach is adopted (partly by employ-ing *hiyal* or legal fiction), adhering closely to the wording of traditional inter-pretations. Both these strategies remain contested and open to negotiation.

By virtue of its multifaceted nature, Islamic finance has been approached from a variety of perspectives – legal, social, economic, political and religious. Addressing multiple audiences and constituencies (ranging from lawyers to bankers, economists, political scientists, policy-makers, socio-legal scholars and political economists), a broad spectrum of scholarship has emerged.[8] In view of this spectrum, it is important to clarify the ambition and focus of the present chapter: in keeping with the general themes addressed in this book, it offers a socio-legal and contextual perspective, highlighting Islamic finance's complex-ity, diversity and interpretative plurality within the legal traditions. To this end, this chapter brings to the fore the ongoing struggle by proponents of Islamic finance to achieve a two-way legitimacy and authenticity: on the one hand, Islamic finance attempts to reach out and legitimize itself to a Muslim con-stituency; on the other, it seeks to convince the wider world of its ability to present a viable alternative to conventional financial regimes.[9]

In a similar vein, there is the gap between rhetoric and reality when it comes to adopting Islamic finance within Muslim-majority jurisdictions. Despite calls from some quarters for wholesale Islamization of finance, at a practical level the picture is more problematic and divergent. Most jurisdictions (e.g. Malaysia and Pakistan) have adopted a dual system, allowing conventional and Islamic financial regimes to operate in parallel.[10] A similarly diverse approach was ini-tially evident in the Islamic finance standard-setting bodies in the Gulf region.

---

[8] See, for example, A. W. Dusuki, 'Corporate Social Responsibility of Islamic Banking in Malaysia: A Synthesis of Islamic and Stakeholders' Perspectives' (PhD thesis, Loughborough, 2005); H. Visser, *Islamic Finance: Principles and Practice* (Cheltenham: Edward Elgar, 2009); K. Ahmad, 'Islamic Finance and Banking: The Challenge and Prospects', *Review of Islamic Economics* 9 (2000), 57–82; L. Rethal, 'Whose Legitimacy? Islamic Finance and the Global Financial Order', *Review of International Political Economy* 18(1) (2010), 75–98; M. Asutay, 'Political Economy Approach to Islamic Economics: Systemic Understanding for an Alternative Economic System', *Kyoto Bulletin of Islamic Area Studies* 1(2) (2007), 3–18; M. U. Chapra, *The Future of Economics: An Islamic Perspective* (Leicester: Islamic Foundation, 2000); M. Umar Farooq, 'Exploitation, Profit and the Riba-Interest Reductionism', paper presented at the Annual Conference of the Eastern Economic Association, New York, 23–6 February 2007; N. A. Saleh, *Unlawful Gain and Legitimate Profit in Islamic Law: Riba, Gharar and Islamic Banking* (Cambridge: Cambridge University Press, 1986); N. Siddiqui, *Partnership in Islamic Banking* (Leicester: Islamic Foundation, 1985); S. Zaman, *Economic Functions of an Islamic State: The Early Experience* (Leicester: Islamic Foundation, 1991); S. Naqvi, *Ethics and Economics: An Islamic Synthesis* (Leicester: Islamic Foundation, 1981); T. Philipp, 'The Idea of Islamic Economics', *Die Welt des Islams* 30 (1990), 117–39; T. Al-Diwany, *Islamic Finance: What It Is and What It Could Be* (Bolton: 1st Ethical Trust, 2010); Z. Iqbal and A. Mirakhor, *An Introduction to Islamic Finance: Theory and Practice* (Singapore: Wiley Finance, 2007).

[9] For a similar discussion, see Rethal, 'Whose Legitimacy?'.

[10] Others (for example Saudi Arabia) did not wish to describe institutions as 'Islamic' as they feared that it would create a category that was not Islamic.

This divergence appears to be disappearing, and an agreement between the institutions to consult each other in matters of governance and regulatory standards appears to be more apparent.[11] Despite the fact that Islamic finance refers itself back to the self-same religious sources, it operates differently in different countries depending on their colonial legacies: the common law tradition, for example, seems to be more easily compatible with Islamic finance and with contemporary institutions, regulatory competence and so on. Islamic finance is also an area where traditionally trained religious scholars – the *ulema* – can compete with other constituencies to defend their authority to interpret Islamic law. Since the rise of the nation state and the appropriation of law-making by the state and her institutions, the *ulema* have been historically sidelined. But, sitting on the powerful Shariah Advisory Boards, they have made a strong comeback and found for themselves a new role.

This chapter offers snapshots of various aspects of Islamic finance and advances three main arguments: (i) that for Islamic financial regimes to succeed as viable alternatives to conventional regimes, aspects of profitability *and* of charity require equal attention and development – an important first step would be a root-and-branch review, delinking commercial profit-making from social and distributive justice – charitable aspects (*zakat*, *sadaqa* and *qard hasan*) and other concepts of social justice may be harnessed to advance human development projects within Muslim-majority jurisdictions (and indeed others);[12] (ii) that grafting Islamic financial forms onto conventional ones by way of a 'short cut' has led to critical compromises that need to be addressed; and (iii) that inter-disciplinary approaches to Islamic finance must be developed with a view to informing policy and practice.

The chapter begins by contextualizing Islamic finance within the legal discourse and traditions. It then presents an overview of the various principles and techniques of Islamic finance and of how these impact upon the contours of contemporary Islamic financial regimes. The next section offers a historical overview of modern Islamic finance with examples from Muslim jurisdictions, followed by a critical appraisal of Islamic finance as practised. Then a final section offers some concluding reflections, including those arising from the 'absences' in Islamic finance and how more realistic and ethical alternative (Islamic) financial regimes may yet be offered.

---

[11] For example, the Islamic Financial Services Board and the Audit and Accounting Organization for Islamic Financial Institutions.

[12] On this point, Rethal reports that some Malaysian *sharia* scholars take the opposite view, arguing that they have to be further integrated and that, more generally, Islamic finance should very explicitly embrace or be subordinated to *maqasid al-sharia*: instead of socially responsible investing, for example, which screens out prohibited activities, there should be 'social-impact' investing, focused on socially desirable projects such as immunization programmes. It is not clear how financialization and social justice can be easily reconciled. I am indebted to Lena for sharing these thoughts from her fieldwork.

4.2 Contextualizing Islamic Finance within the Islamic Legal Traditions

Islamic finance both classical and modern derives its inspiration, guidance and legitimacy from the primary and secondary sources, supplemented by the rich and varied rules of interpretation developed by jurists of the different schools over a span of fourteen centuries. The complex and multi-tiered edifice that is Islamic law draws upon a range of sources to arrive at usable legal formulations. Relevant verses of the Qur'an, supplemented by the Sunna, are the starting points of any rules, with secondary sources and juristic techniques (e.g. *ijma, qiyas, ijtihad, taqlid, ikhtilaf, takhayyur, talfiq, maslaha, maqasid-al-sharia, fatawa, darura,* and *'urf*) also employed, albeit with varying degrees of consensus. Of these, four allow for departures from existing norms: *'urf* (local custom), *maslaha* (public interest), *maqasid* (purposes), and *darura* (necessity).[13]

The challenge, as always, arises from the interpretative plurality of the Islamic legal traditions. Legal methodology (*usul-ul-fiqh*) has developed highly complex processes for extrapolating meanings and rules from the primary and secondary sources of Islamic law. But despite the presence of a sophisticated rule-making methodology, the outcome of applying a rule to a given situation is rarely certain. In particular, modern Islamic finance practice remains reliant on the institution of *ifta* (where, in the absence of set rules, *muftis* offer opinions on *specific* questions posed to them). But this juristic technique is not a purely jurisprudential exercise, as the *mufti* has one eye on the rules and the other on popular practice and custom.[14] So whilst Muslims generally subscribe to what can be argued to be the strict principles of Islamic finance, in reality there is also a quiet acquiescence to conventional, interest-based arrangements, a practice reflected in how *muftis* sometimes skirt around classical prohibitions on the barest of technical grounds. *Fatawa* played a central role in the birth of modern Islamic finance,[15] and individual *muftis* in their contemporary incarnations as members of Sharia Advisory Boards now facilitate financial products by issuing advisory opinions on *sharia* compliance.[16]

Classical Islamic jurisprudence does not perceive *fatawa* as binding,[17] and they are thus open to either acceptance or rejection by the parties seeking them and by the wider community. Their place in contemporary Islamic finance, however, is different. The Islamic Financial Services Board uses binding *fatawa* to lend credence and validity to its standards. The Islamic banking division of the State Bank of Pakistan employs a similar strategy, and *fatawa* sought by

---

[13] Warde, *Islamic Finance*, p. 49.
[14] See the discussions in Masud, Messick and Powers, *Islamic Legal Interpretation.*
[15] El-Gamal reports that contemporary Islamic banking was born as a consequence of a *fatwa* handed down at the First Conference of Islamic banks in 1979. El-Gamal, *Islamic Finance*, p. 33.
[16] Ibid., pp. 32–5.
[17] For a more detailed discussion on *fatawa* and the institution of *ifta*, see Chapter 8 below.

Islamic financial institutions are binding on them. Likewise in Malaysia, *fatawa* of the Shariah Advisory Councils of the central bank and securities commission are also binding. The irony here is that it is the modern nation state in some of its institutions that is departing from classical jurisprudence and established practice by making *fatawa* hard law rather than juristic opinion.

By way of example of the use of *fatawa* as facilitative of Islamic finance, as far back as 1904 the reformer Muhammad Abduh issued a *fatwa* at the request of the Egyptian government regarding the Postal Administration's Egyptian Savings Fund,[18] in which depositors received a fixed, predetermined rate of return. Abduh's *fatwa* adopted a cautious, carefully worded, and tolerant position on the fund.[19] As Mallat has observed,

> Egyptian muftis writing in the twentieth century acknowledge that they are tread-ing a delicate path and are dealing with powerful economic actors and institutions that have strong supporters in new, as well as in the established, commercial sec-tors. Because a fatwa that condemned interest-bearing transactions would be totally ineffective, most muftis have taken care to formulate their opinions in language that is either cautious or ambiguous.[20]

More recently, in 1989, the good offices of Grand Mufti Muhammad Sayyid Tantawi were employed to issue a *fatwa* legitimizing 'capitalization certificates' (interest-bearing government bonds underwritten by Egyptian banks). Despite the high esteem in which Sunnis hold the Grand Mufti of Egypt, Tantawi's *fatwa* did not go down well in, amongst other places, Pakistan: in a judgment of the Federal Shariat Court there, Tantawi's *fatwa* was dismissed as his 'solitary opinion' and disregarded.[21]

In addition to employing *fatawa* to disentangle complex issues in Islamic finance, the legal traditions have historically resorted to a range of legal stratagems and legal fiction (*hiyal*) to permit what would normally have been prohibited – again with ample scope for disagreement. Two examples of such legal fictions will suffice here, both employing varying interpretations of the sources of law to circumvent rules on technical grounds.

In order to circumvent the prohibition on *riba* and *gharar*, *murabaha* – a form of short-term financing – is permitted by proponents of Islamic finance. A *murabaha* transaction can encompass multiple transactions, with mark-ups that to all intents and purposes are actually interest. There also exists the *tawarruq* contract (a variety of *murabaha*), involving 'buy-back' of a commodity. For instance, a financial institution agrees to purchase an item for £1,000 on behalf of a client and sell it to him with an agreed mark-up (an extra £100, say), with

[18] Warde, *Islamic Finance*, p. 54.
[19] Ibid., citing C. Mallat, 'The Debate on Riba and Interest in Twentieth Century Egypt', in C. Mallat (ed.), *Islamic Law and Finance* (London: Graham & Trotman, 1998), pp. 69–88.
[20] C. Mallat, 'Tantawi on Banking Operations in Egypt', in Masud, Messick and Powers, *Islamic Legal Interpretation*, pp. 286–96, 294.
[21] Ibid.

payment to be made at a later date. Meanwhile, the client has sold the product, or the financial institution has arranged on his behalf to sell it back into the market, for £1,000. These transactions in all probability took place without the nominal product ever having been taken possession of by any party: the real purpose was to make available to the client the requisite finance of £1,000, albeit with a mark-up of £100. The *tawarruq* contract is highly contested as being non-compliant with many of the *sharia* rules regarding trade and sale of goods.

Another *hiyal* (fiction) generated through the use of classical jurisprudence is *takaful*, or 'Islamic insurance'. For a long time, scholars were unwilling to accept insurance as Islamically valid due to its perceived violation of *gharar* (i.e. the uncertainty built into the concept). But by using the exemption from *gharar* granted to gratuitous contracts, under *takaful* a group of Muslims can agree to pool their resources through payment of premiums that are in turn invested in Islamically permissible commercial products. Any member of the group suffering a loss is given premiums and profits as 'gifts'. Such compensation is similar to an insurance payout but uses a different terminology.[22]

In addition to varying juristic techniques, the main characteristics of the four Sunni schools of juristic thought – Hanafi, Maliki, Shafi'i and Hanbali – and their diverse positions on various aspects of law assume due prominence and further accentuate the plurality of perspectives and their implications for Islamic finance. Rahim is of the view that the four schools 'are substantially the same, and they differ from each other merely in matters of detail'.[23] These 'details' include differences of opinion on the authenticity of certain *ahadith* and on the weight given to analogy or reason (*qiyas*) in arriving at decisions not clearly covered by the Qur'an and *hadith*. In response, it is submitted that 'detail' is hugely significant in areas such as Islamic finance where clarity and certainty of outcome are critical. And the complexity does not only arise from the varying views of the different schools: there are also differences *within* each school.

'Detail' can often overshadow the underlying principle when it comes to establishing regulatory norms in finance and banking. It is not surprising that the rules governing finance during the Ottoman Empire (Hanafi) differed from those operating in South East Asia (Shafi'i), North Africa (Maliki) and Saudi Arabia (Hanbali). For example, *salam* is a form of sale using advance payment for goods to be delivered on a fixed future date (though the goods need not be in existence at the time of payment). Classical Islamic law principles state

---

[22] H. A. Hamoudi, 'On Form and Function in Islamic Finance', *Chicago Journal of International Law* 7(2) (2007), 613. See also Vogel and Hayes, *Islamic Law and Finance*, pp. 151–2; Warde, *Islamic Finance*, pp. 153–4; M. B. Mohd, *Principles and Practice of Takaful and Insurance Compared* (Malaysia: International Islamic University, 2001), cited in H. A. Hamoudi, 'Jurisprudential Schizophrenia: On Form and Function in Islamic Finance', *Chicago Journal of International Law* 7(2) (2007), 605–22.

[23] A. Rahim, *Muhammadan Jurisprudence* (Lahore: Mansoor, 1995), p. 20.

that *salam* may extend to all articles sold by weight or capacity, except gold and silver; Hanafis take the position that animals cannot be sold by *salam*, whereas Shafi'is hold that they can. Again, regarding *'urf* (custom) as a source of law: one *hadith* clearly prohibits conditional sale (e.g. *A* agrees to sell his car to *B* on condition that *B* sells his house to *A*), yet the majority of Hanafi and Maliki jurists nevertheless allow such sales where a custom exists.

In contextualizing finance within the Islamic legal traditions, it is evident that the interpretative plurality and absence of a single authoritative voice in Sunni Islam is a challenge in the modern commercial and financial environment. In a globalized landscape where harmonization of laws (especially in the field of finance) is necessary for efficient operation, a unique Islamic finance law acceptable to all segments of the Muslim world is well-nigh impossible. The difficulty of reaching a universal consensus can be further highlighted by an exploration of the principles and techniques of Islamic finance and their application in the Muslim and non-Muslim world, and it is to this that we now turn our attention.

4.3 Principles of Islamic Finance

The classical system of Islamic finance is distinguishable from its Western-style counterpart by its religious orientation, being entirely premised on the application of principles of *sharia* formulated over fourteen centuries ago. The Qur'an and Sunna institute general principles as prerequisites of financial transactions and enjoin mutuality and freedom such that neither party is made worse off. Anything below this threshold is likened to suicide.[24] Another cardinal principle is the importance of fulfilling contractual obligations.[25]

Islamic finance has two main trajectories: rules for permissible profitable trading, and the equitable, just and charitable distribution of wealth and resources. Though it is mostly the first that has caught the attention of the financial world, it is arguably the second that promises a genuine alternative to its conventional counterpart. Restrictions are placed on contractual freedom, in particular the strong prohibitions against *riba* and *gharar*,[26] and in this sense Islamic finance can be said to be 'prohibition-driven', and hence the novel techniques used to facilitate '*sharia*-compliant' financial products.[27] (In addition to these prohibitions, Islamic finance also has a number of other principles and characteristics that will be discussed later.) A further principle of Islamic finance is its perception of money as a medium of exchange rather than a commodity capable of being sold. Making money from money is deemed unacceptable, and money only becomes capital when it is invested in business and through human effort.[28]

---

[24]　Qur'an, 4:29.　　[25]　Qur'an, 5:1.
[26]　El-Gamal, *Islamic Finance*, p. 46; Ercanbrack, *Transformation*, p. 50.
[27]　El-Gamal, *Islamic Finance*, p. 46.
[28]　A. M. Venardos, *Islamic Banking and Finance in Southeast Asia: Its Development and Future* (Singapore: World Scientific, 2006), p. 57.

4.3.1 Prohibition of *Riba*

God has permitted sale and prohibited usury.   (Qur'an, 2:275)

You who believe, do not consume usurious interest, doubled and redoubled. Be mindful of God so that you may prosper.   (Qur'an, 3:130)

Whatever you lend out in usury to gain value through other people's wealth will not increase in God's eyes, but whatever you give in charity, in your desire for God's approval, will earn multiple rewards.   (Qur'an, 30:39)

Gold for gold, silver for silver, wheat for wheat, barley for barley, dates for dates and salt for salt, like for like, hand to hand and any increase is *riba*.   (*hadith*)

Every loan that attracts a benefit is *riba*.   (*hadith*)

The prohibition of exorbitant interest is the most important feature of Islamic finance and exemplifies the Qur'an's general rejection of exploitative practices. In particular, commerce in Islam is based on the moral responsibility of the wealthier in society to provide for those with fewer resources; prohibiting a practice that would place an excessive burden on a vulnerable debtor is one logical outcome of the Qur'anic ethos of social justice. Yet, as Ercanbrack so aptly observes, despite this clear aversion to *riba*, 'scarcely is there a principle the meaning of which has been so vehemently contested over centuries of commercial practice and jurisprudential thought'.[29]

There is a great deal of scholarship and debate on the meaning and interpretation of *riba*, and these do not need to be set out in any detail here.[30] In broad terms, then, controversy and contestation over *riba* arose out of the jurisprudence on the relevant Qur'anic verses and *ahadith*. In its most general usage, *riba* (literally 'increase' or 'growth') denotes interest to be paid by a debtor to the lender, but the term has come to be linked with excessive or exploitative rates of interest (irrespective of how the debtor has emerged from the transaction). Questions arise regarding the scope of *riba*, bearing in mind the commercial practices of seventh-century Arabia and whether an expansive or restricted meaning is ascribed to the term.

In pre-Islamic times, *riba* consisted of the doubling and redoubling of the principal sum. The Qur'an did not accept this as a fair transaction and so, while permitting commercial profit, encouraged co-operation but rejected profiteering. It is important therefore to distinguish between usury and the lending of

---

[29] Ercanbrack, *Transformation*, p. 70. The topic has also been discussed in detail by many other academics: see for example M. U. Farooq, 'Riba, Interest and Six Hadiths: Do We Have a Definition or a Conundrum?', *Review of Islamic Economics* 13(1) (2009), 105–41.

[30] F. Rahman, 'Riba and Interest', *Islamic Studies* 3 (1964), 1–43; Vogel and Hayes, *Islamic Law and Finance*; Warde, *Islamic Finance*; Mallat, 'Debate on Riba and Interest'; M. A. El-Gamal, 'An Economic Explication of the Prohibition of Riba in Classical Islamic Jurisprudence', Proceedings of the Third Harvard University Forum on Islamic Finance, 2000; M. A. El-Gamal, 'A Basic Guide to Contemporary Islamic Banking and Finance' (2000), available at www.lariba.com/dev/knowledge-center/islamic-banking-guide.pdf, p. 9; M. A. El-Gamal, *Islamic Finance: Law, Economics, and Practice* (New York: Cambridge University Press, 2006).

money to enable engaging in commercial activity, with the principal returned plus an additional sum as profit: 'Not all interest is the prohibited Riba ... [and] Not all Riba is interest.'[31] Present-day *murabaha* transactions, sidestepping *riba* and returning the principal with a mark-up, can be seen as a practical distinction between *riba* and acceptable profit.

But understandings of *riba* are not limited to Qur'anic verses: two *ahadith* (above) are also cited.[32] Again, there are differences of scholastic opinion over the scope and application of rules on *riba* stemming from the *hadith* prohibiting trade in goods of the same species and kind in different quantities: Hanafis extend the prohibition to all perishable goods capable of being measured by weight or volume; Shafi'is and Malikis restrict the prohibition to monetary commodities and storable foodstuffs.

Historical differences of opinion in interpreting the verses and *ahadith* continue in modern case law. In a string of much-publicized cases on *riba*, Pakistan's Federal Shariat Court interpreted the Qur'an's message as prohibitive:

> In the case of usury, the eater stays away from all labour and toil and from the security of his home, he continues to receive all gains and interests. In this way, he is not a participant in the trade or business. These and several other differences between sale and usury underline the emphatic Quranic injunction of considering one of them as totally prohibited and the others as pure and permissible.[33]

4.3.2 Prohibition of *Gharar*

Alongside the prohibition of *riba*, a major principle of Islamic finance today is the prohibition of transactions involving *gharar*: 'the sale of probable items whose existence or characteristics are not certain, due to the risky nature which makes the trade similar to gambling'.[34] But of course risk, just like credit, is essential to any financial system and needs to be addressed, hence the Qur'anic injunctions. In Islamic finance, El-Gamal argues, *riba* is essentially 'trading in credit', while *gharar* is 'trading in risk':[35] 'In other words, Islamic jurisprudence uses two prohibitions to allow only for the appropriate measure of permissibility of transferring credit and risk to achieve economic ends.'[36]

---

[31] El-Gamal, 'Economic Explication', pp. 31–44.

[32] 'Every loan that attracts a benefit is *riba*' is not found in the six authentic collections of *ahadith* but is narrated on the authority of the Companions of the Prophet rather than the Prophet himself: its authenticity being suspect, it is not accepted by most Islamic legal scholars.

[33] See p. 14 of the judgment of the Federal Shariat Court of Pakistan per Khalil-ur-Rehman J. Wajihuddin Ahmed J. described *riba* in relation to its impact on society: 'Manifestly, such transactions, where idle money, attracts and generates more idle money leads to inequities in society, making the rich richer and the poor poorer. That which applies to individuals applies equally to their institutions, big and small, local, national and international. It is thus that the inequities and injustices so generated have transcended geographical frontiers and engulfed nations, states and communities alike.'

[34] El-Gamal, *Basic Guide*, p. 7.   [35] El-Gamal, *Islamic Finance*, p. 47.

[36] Ibid., p. 48. This is why, as touched upon earlier, combining the two as risk-sharing and avoidance of one party profiting to the detriment of the other would work more effectively.

4.3.3 Prohibition of *Maysir*

> O you who have believed, indeed, intoxicants, gambling, sacrificing on stone altars, and divining arrows are but defilement from the work of Satan, so avoid it that you may be successful. (Qur'an 5:90)

Maysir is seen by some legal scholars as similar to or part of a continuum with *gharar*, with risk and uncertainty possibly surrounding and prohibiting both. Again, though, a *gharar* transaction might have an underlying gambling element or might be innocent of such intention. Where some minimum threshold of certainty is reached (e.g. the specifics of the objects of sale and the parties' control over them), some schools permit the transaction. The Shafi'is prohibit the sale of absent specific objects altogether, whereas the Hanafis permit their sale by description but with the proviso that the buyer can reject the object on seeing it even if the description was accurate.[37] The Hanbalis and Malikis, on the other hand, consider as binding the sale of absent objects by description as long as these answer to the agreed description and do not affect the market price.[38]

4.4 The Charitable Arm of Islamic Finance: *Zakat* and *Qard Hasan* as Alternative Regimes for Social Justice

Of the two arms of Islamic finance, the commercial and profitable has attracted closer attention than the charitable. This section looks at the main concepts and institutions of this charitable arm and its potential as a vehicle of social justice.[39]

4.4.1 *Zakat* as Obligatory Payments to the Needy

> *Zakat* is only for the poor and needy, and those employed to administer it, and those whose hearts are made to incline to truth, and to free captives, and those in debt, and in the way of Allah and for the wayfarer – an ordinance from Allah. And Allah is knowing, wise. (Qur'an 9:60)

Almsgiving, one of the five pillars, is a fundamental principle of Islam and Islamic finance. In addition to its other benefits, it has as objectives the circulation of resources, monetary and otherwise, and the lessening of the gap between rich and poor for 'social benefit' or 'public welfare' (*al-maslaha al-ijtima'yya* and *al-maslaha al-'amma*). It has been called 'a key component of the moral economy'.[40] Every Muslim is obliged to pay two types of *zakat*: *zakat al-fitr*

---

37 Vogel and Hayes, *Islamic Law and Finance*, pp. 91–2.   38 Ibid.

39 *Wakf* is another institution for advancing social justice: it is the '[permanent] transfer of a corpus of valuable property to ownership of God with declaration of dedicating its usufruct perpetually for religious, charitable or pious purposes as recognized by Shariah'. Mannan, *D. F. Mulla's Principles*, p. 270. Discussion of *wakf* has not been included here for reasons of space.

40 H. Latief, 'Islamic Charities and Social Activism: Welfare, Dakwah and Politics in Indonesia' (PhD thesis, Utrecht University, 2012), p. 310.

is given to the poor during Ramadan; under *zakat al-amwal,* Muslims whose wealth reaches a minimum level are generally obliged to pay a small percentage, the rate varying depending upon the type of wealth.[41]

Zakat is open to varying interpretation because of the limited guidance in the Qur'an. On the one hand, the categories of beneficiary set out in Verse 9:60 can be interpreted differently; on the other, the Qur'an does not elaborate on how *zakat* ought to be administered, leaving it to Muslim communities to develop parameters for collection and disbursement. Issues arose quite early on as a result of this ambiguity, including whether *zakat* ought to be institutionalized or remain personal; and whether the state ought to collect *zakat* and, if so, centrally or otherwise. But most important is the question whether Muslims are obliged to pay it voluntarily or as an obligatory and legally enforceable tax to a state agency.[42]

The practice of *zakat* in Muslim jurisdictions is far from uniform,[43] most likely a result of the multifaceted functions – spiritual, political and economic – that *zakat* is meant to perform: it is a personal act of worship to purify one's soul and one's wealth, a means of state revenue-raising, and a way of reducing poverty and inequality.[44] *Zakat,* in addition to its spiritual value, acted as support for 'certain socioeconomic and sociopolitical structures necessary in early Islam'.[45]

Today, *zakat* ranges from complete state incorporation as a regular tax (Saudi Arabia, Libya, Yemen, Malaysia, Pakistan, Sudan),[46] to institutions receiving voluntary payments (Jordan, Egypt, Bahrain, Kuwait), to an act of private conscience and personal piety (Morocco, Oman).[47] Indonesia, the country with the largest Muslim population in the world today, has also joined the ranks of Muslim states where *zakat* has been incorporated as a regular tax. The various regional and provincial governments have enacted regulations

---

[41] Generally 2.5 per cent. Farmers may be levied 5–10 per cent of their harvest, depending on the type of irrigation. Even wealth originating from buried treasure can be taxed, at up to 20 per cent.

[42] A. Salim, *Challenging the Secular State: The Islamization of Law in Modern Indonesia* (Honolulu: University of Hawaii, 2008), p. 116. See also Latief, *Islamic Charities,* fn. 23. Latief mentions the time when the first Caliph waged war against *zakat* refuters, citing M. H. Haikal, *Abu Bakr al-Siddiq* (Cairo: Matba's Masdar Shirka Musahim Misriyya, 1958) especially Chapter 5, pp. 111–20.

[43] As in other areas of the legal traditions, the four main juristic schools are not always in agreement in determining the type of wealth subject to *zakat,* who should pay and receive *zakat,* and the types of mechanism for *zakat* distribution. Brought up as a Hanafi Sunni in the South Asian understanding of *zakat,* I personally was surprised to learn that there was more than one interpretation relating to this act of worship: a Sudanese student explained to me how only that part of her jewellery which was not worn throughout the year for which *zakat* was due was subject to *zakat.* My South Asian version dictates that every item of jewellery must be subject to *zakat,* whether worn or not.

[44] Salim, *Challenging the Secular State,* p. 116.   [45] Ibid.

[46] Sudan, Yemen and Pakistan include implementation of *zakat* as a state function in their constitutions.

[47] Salim, *Challenging the Secular State,* p. 117.

where mandatory *zakat* of 2.5 per cent is deducted from the salary of civil servants.[48]

Of state-led *zakat*, Pakistan's example has attracted the closest attention, not least due to the ambitious Islamization agenda of General Zia. In 1980, the first Zakat and Ushr Ordinance set out structure, collection and disbursement mechanisms for *zakat* and the Ministries and Departments of Religious Affairs now included in their title Zakat and Ushr. While Pakistan was perceived as a pioneer in instituting Islamic finance, including a structured system of implementing *zakat*, it cannot be described as a success story for others to emulate. Pitfalls of the system were many, leading one to agree with An-Na'im and others who argue that religion cannot be 'enforced' by state institutions and must remain within the private domain.[49] While the state may, and ought to, facilitate respectful and tolerant practice of religion and belief, it is not her function to impose and Islamize peoples' personal practice. There is no evidence that state-implemented *zakat* collection has had any salutary effect on improving the economic situation of millions of Pakistanis living below the poverty line.[50]

A number of social, religious, economic and political problems emerged in the wake of state involvement in *zakat* administration.[51] By incorporating *zakat* into state structures, an 'official' Islam was established, privileging a particular understanding advanced by one juristic school to the exclusion of others. After fierce opposition from Shi'a Pakistanis, whose understanding of *zakat* did not allow for state intervention, in 1981 the Zakat and Ushr Ordinance was amended, granting them an exemption. In an atmosphere of contestation, conservative Sunni *ulema* were indignant that Sunni would convert to Shi'a to avoid paying *zakat*. Also, the formalization of *zakat* led to many people taking advantage of exemption clauses.

The institutionalization of *zakat* in Pakistan has led to a resistance to paying it into government hands. Practices on the ground are disparate and far from homogeneous. From my decades of personal experience there, I would say that most *zakat* payers prefer to give directly to the beneficiaries. Yet even here there is great variation depending upon individual preferences and ideas as to what *zakat* is meant to achieve. Two striking examples from my own community in the Swat Valley will make the point. Mr A believed in converting *zakat* beneficiaries to *zakat* payers, and each year would hand one or two families a significant capital sum to set up a business or similar. A year later he would assess the situation and, if required, again give *zakat*. By year three most would be breaking even or in profit and in no further need of charity. Mr B, by contrast,

---

[48] M. Buehler, 'The Rise of Shari'a By-laws in Indonesian Districts: An Indication of Changing Patterns of Power Accumulation and Political Corruption', *South-East Asia Research* 16(2) (2008), 260–2.

[49] See generally An-Na'im, *Islam and the Secular State*.

[50] In fact, it is feared that the number of those living below the poverty line has increased over the past decades: see the *Human Development Report* for Pakistan.

[51] Salim, *Challenging the Secular State*, pp. 118–19.

announced his 'zakat payment day' in mosques and in the community, and people would file up to receive one rupee's zakat each. This was barely enough to buy a family a meal, yet Mr B felt he was doing good work by handing out zakat to hundreds of people rather than just a few.

Such variation, of course, continues, but new practices have set in too. Trusted organizations such as the Eidhi Foundation, Muslim Aid, Islamic Relief and Muslim Hands are now recipients of zakat from professionals and communities in Pakistan and overseas; development and humanitarian agencies are now receiving zakat, lending some formality to what has historically been considered personal worship and private piety.[52]

4.4.2 *Qard Hasan*: The Charitable Loan

> If the debtor is in a difficulty, grant him time until it is easy for him to repay. But if ye remit it by way of charity, that is best for you if ye only knew. (Qur'an 2:280)

The techniques of Islamic finance bear a charitable component insofar as *sharia* treats certain loans as charitable acts: 'the attitude of Islamic financial institutions is that they should forsake some of their profits by, for instance, extending a *qard al hasan* to help the distressed borrower'.[53] Despite its express affirmation in the Qur'an and the potential for empowering entire communities, this element of Islamic finance is, sadly, practised only to a very limited extent in Muslim countries;[54] its implementation by Islamic banks, too, is not uniform, with some, for example, requiring service charges to be paid and others not.[55]

In classical jurisprudence, the only 'acceptable' loan is the *qard hasan*,[56] as it does not involve interest on the principal. A *qard* should be repaid with goods

---

[52] A similar trend has been reported from Indonesia. See Latief, *Islamic Charities*. Salim depicts a clear shift in *zakat* practice among Indonesians, from merely 'a [form of] financial worship' representing religious piety to becoming part of the Indonesian sociopolitical/-economic system. The efforts of *zakat* agencies to incorporate the state's role in optimizing *zakat* collection, for example by issuing *zakat* laws and urging Muslims to channel their *zakat* funds to officially recognized *zakat* agencies, have characterized this structural shift. A. Salim, *The Shift in Zakat Practice in Indonesia: From Piety to an Islamic Socio-Political-Economic System* (Chiang Mai: Asian Muslim Action Network and Silkworm Books, 2008), pp. 1–5.

[53] R. Wilson, 'Why Islamic Banking Is Successful? Islamic Banks Are Unscathed Despite of Financial Crisis' (sic), *onislam.net*, 15 February 2009, cited in Warde, *Islamic Finance*, p. 148.

[54] For further discussion on this point, see A. Abdul Gafoor, *Interest-Free Commercial Banking* (Groningen: APPTEC, 1995); J. W. Wright, 'Islamic Banking in Practice: Problems in Jordan and Saudi Arabia', Occasional Paper No. 48, Centre for Middle Eastern and Islamic Studies, University of Durham, 1995, p. 5.

[55] *Qard hasan* is the basis for a few Islamic microfinance schemes, such as Amanah Ikhtiar Malaysia (which charges a services fee for training, advice etc.). Islamic Relief has also extended some *qard hasan* loans.

[56] The term is spelt variously in different jurisdictions with different languages and dialects. In Iran it is known as *qard al-hasanah*, in Malaysia *al-qardhul hasan*, in Pakistan *qarz-e-hasna*, Bangladesh *qard-e-hasan* and in Jordan *al-qird al-hasan*: H. Timm, 'The Cultural and Demographic Aspects of the Islamic Financial System and the Potential for Islamic Products in the German Market' (PhD thesis, Stralsund University, 2005).

of an identical description rather than with the very same goods originally borrowed. There is, as we might expect, contestation: Hanafis take the view that, where identical goods cannot be repaid, then their value at the time they were loaned is to be repaid; Hanbalis adopt the position that the value of the goods as of the date they became unavailable is to be repaid.

Although *qard hasan* forms an important nominal pillar of Islamic finance, its impact on the lives of needy individuals and communities is minimal. To begin with, the capital available to Islamic financial institutions is a very small fraction of the entire sector's capital, both nationally and internationally. From this small fraction, that dedicated to *qard hasan* is even smaller. Second, lacking stringent mechanisms for identifying and monitoring deserving cases (for example, a student needing a college registration fee, a farmer needing farm implements, or a villager needing to repair a damaged roof), projects aimed at empowering the poor have been misused. Pakistan's government-sponsored Yellow Cab Scheme of the 1990s, in which, by means of *qard hasan*, the unemployed were sold cars to use as taxis, is a case in point: the scheme failed when it was discovered that a great many undeserving persons had used their connections to obtain these *qard hasan* loans. By all accounts, few borrowers returned the loan, repaid capital was not available to reloan, and the scheme was discontinued.[57]

4.5 Techniques of Islamic Finance: An Overview

The techniques of Islamic finance are constructed in line with *sharia* precepts as embodied in the Qur'an and Sunna and in secondary sources such as *ijma* (consensus), *qiyas* (reasoning by analogy) and *ijtihad* (independent reasoning). They include *musharaka* (joint partnership), *mudaraba* (profit sharing), *murabaha* (sale with mark-up), *salam* (advance purchase), *istisna* (commissioned manufacture), *bay' mu'ajjal* (credit sale), and *ijara* (lease). The existence of classical discourse on the construction of financing has proved useful to scholars of Islamic economics, since it serves as a ready reservoir of concepts and practices to be tapped for contemporary application. There is already a great deal of scholarship on these techniques, and rather than go into detail on their workings this section will instead look at some of the juristic aspects of just a representative few of them.

There is consensus among Sunni juristic schools (Hanafi, Maliki, Shafi'i and Hanbali) that partnership financing – *musharaka* and *mudaraba* – is permissible since such methods date to the Prophet's lifetime.[58] Some contemporary scholars such as Usmani view these as 'the ideal financing techniques', with

---

[57] Some Islamic banks also use *amanah* (secured deposits) to facilitate current accounts for their clients.

[58] T. Usmani, *An Introduction to Islamic Finance*, available at https://archive.org/details/AnIntroductionToIslamicFinanceByShaykhMuftiTaqiUsmani_772, p. 25, last visited 28 October 2015.

others are to be employed only where partnership is unsuitable.[59] El-Gamal, by contrast, sees no justification in creating a hierarchy in techniques since all are based in the religious sources: any appropriate technique may be employed so long as the actors do not derogate from the teachings of Islam.[60]

4.5.1 The *Musharaka* Partnership

Classical jurists categorized *musharaka* under two broad headings: *shirk al-mulk* (partnership by operation of law) and *shirk al-aqd* (joint commercial enterprise), the former being where parties jointly acquire property through, for example, inheritance, the latter created by agreement between parties. *Shirk al-aqd* is conceptually subdivided into *shirk al-amwal* (a general partnership, where all partners contribute capital) and other forms of partnership – *shirk al-mufawadah* (universal), *shirk al-wujooh* (goodwill), *shirk al-amal* (labour and skills). Of all these, only the *shirk al-amwal* 'general partnership' enjoys an overwhelming consensus among classical jurists,[61] and indeed in the context of Islamic banking *musharaka* is understood to mean *shirk al-amwal*. The other subdivisions are mostly accepted as valid by Hanafis but do not enjoy the support of the other Sunni schools, perhaps due to the likelihood of one party taking undue advantage of the other.[62]

Jurists are agreed on the *sharia* legality of the *musharaka* partnership but do not agree on certain details, for example how profit is to be shared. The Malikis, Shafi'is and Hanafis agree that partners are entitled to profit proportionately to their investment;[63] by contrast, the Hanbali school holds that shares are reached by mutual agreement and need not reflect relative contributions.[64] Abu Hanifa, founder of the Hanafi school, harmonized the two positions by holding that shares should be commensurate with capital contributions if both partners are active in the enterprise, an arrangement that may be altered where one is an inactive sleeping partner. (As for loss-sharing, all schools agree with the maxim attributed to Ali ibn Abi Talib: 'Profit is based on the agreement of the parties, but loss is always subject to the ratio of investment.'[65])

4.5.2 The *Mudaraba* Partnership

In *mudaraba*, one party provides the capital and the other manages its investment in a lawful enterprise. The juristic schools agree on the legality of *mudaraba* but disagree on details,[66] one important issue of contestation being whether

---

[59] Ibid., p. 12.   [60] El-Gamal, 'Economic Explication', p. 23.

[61] M. Ayub, *Understanding Islamic Finance* (Chichester: John Wiley and Sons Limited, 2007), p. 310.

[62] Ibid., pp. 310–11.   [63] Usmani, *An Introduction to Islamic Finance*, p. 24.

[64] Ibid.; Ayub, *Understanding Islamic Finance*, p. 316.

[65] Ayub, *Understanding Islamic Finance*, p. 317; Usmani, *An Introduction to Islamic Finance*, p. 25.

[66] Usmani, *An Introduction to Islamic Finance*, p. 31.

either party can claim benefits (such as a salary) outside an agreed sharing formula. Hanbalis argue that the entrepreneur can claim a daily food allowance from the capital regardless of whether the food was eaten when at home or not;[67] Hanafis argue that shelter, travel and food must relate to a business trip.[68]

How did Islamic banking grow out of such debates? As noted earlier, the principles of partnership financing form the basis of modern Islamic banking. Starting in the 1940s, scholars including Qureshi, Siddiqui, Ahmad, Maududi and Hamidullah opened up a discussion of profit- and loss-sharing banking based on *mudaraba*.[69] Maududi in particular suggested that if a deed of partnership could be executed between a bank and its depositors, the bank could then take the role of the active partner in an enterprise, allowing it to invest depositors' money in any *sharia*-lawful venture.[70] This was further developed in the 1950s through the notion of the 'two-tier' *mudaraba*, in which the bank would enter into *mudaraba* partnerships with a further tier of entrepreneurs: 'Such a practice is possible since classical law permits a *mudarib* to choose not to perform the productive work himself but to invest the partnership capital with other *mudaribs*. The institution's profits then come not from interest income but from a percentage of the profits from the second-tier *mudarabas*'.[71] This approach created a chain of relationships between a bank and its customers. In relation to its depositors, a bank is a *mudarib*, investing the capital in a gainful venture; in relation to its borrowers, a bank is a financier, expecting them to invest wisely.

During the 1970s, institutions such as the Islamic Development Bank, the Dubai Islamic Bank and the Faisal Islamic Bank began to emerge, based on this juristic framework, offering current, savings and investment accounts using different techniques to cater to depositors' different requirements. Services such as loans, credit investigations, guarantees, import/export financing etc. are also offered on the basis of other techniques.

4.5.3 *Murabaha*

As a form of sale, *murabaha* pre-dates Islam. The term derives from *ribh* (profit), and refers to the sale of something for the price the seller paid, plus a sum by way of profit. Trust is, of course, placed in the seller, who must truthfully disclose the price he has already paid, and some jurists have been critical of *murabaha* on the grounds that humans are fallible:[72] a person is susceptible to being defrauded where he relies solely on trusting a business associate. Such concern does not, however, rid *murabaha* of its legality.

---

[67] Ibid., p. 34.   [68] Ibid.   [69] Abdul Gafoor, *Interest-Free Commercial Banking*.
[70] A. A. Maududi, *The Economic System of Islam* (Lahore: Islamic Publications, 1970), p. 217.
[71] Vogel and Hayes, *Islamic Law and Finance*, pp. 130–1.
[72] Ayub, *Understanding Islamic Finance*, p. 216.

To what degree, then, is the modern practice of *murabaha* compliant with the theories of the classical jurists? There are several points where scholars of the four Sunni schools do not agree. These include the questions of what in fact constitutes the price already paid; whether payment must be prompt or can be deferred; whether non-disclosure, fraud or defect can negate the contract; and whether a seller can profit twice with respect to one object. The differences of opinion and their practical effects are often complex and subtle.

In calculating the price already paid, the Hanafis allow the addition of costs which must necessarily be met with respect to an object (e.g. transport and duty):[73] A asks B to buy him a motorbike using *murabaha*; if it is bought for £1,000, and £100 is paid for transport and assembly, then B may claim £1,100 plus the agreed mark-up. Personal expenses such as food and accommodation cannot be added to the original price, as these should be covered under the mark-up.[74] A more liberal approach is taken by the Hanbalis: parties are free to determine which expenses are included in the original price and which in the seller's mark-up, so long as the purchaser has given his pre-informed consent.[75] The Malikis and Shafi'is ask whether expenses are directly linked to the object: services that the seller could undertake himself may not be added to the original price.

Regarding deceit and defect, both Hanafis and Malikis allow the purchaser to rescind a *murabaha* contract if he discovers such problems,[76] though Abu Yusuf of the Hanafi school also allows the purchaser simply to deduct the sum by which he has been defrauded.[77]

It is common in *murabaha* transactions for B, who has purchased an object on behalf of A and made a profit, to later repurchase the same object from A at a discount, and this is something to which most scholars do not object. Yet scholars do disagree over whether B may make a profit if he resells the object. For Abu Hanifa, a seller cannot profit twice on the same object and must deduct his original mark-up from the second sale; but other scholars (such as Abu Yusuf) consider the second sale an independent *murabaha* contract and allow B to make a subsequent profit.

As to deferred payment, Shafi'is have no difficulty with the idea while other schools (including the Malikis) require prompt payment upon receipt.[78]

4.5.4 *Murabaha* in Contemporary Context

Under classical formulations, then, *murabaha* is simply a form of sale. But modern requirements have necessitated innovations that allow its use as a

---

[73] Ibid., p. 217.   [74] Usmani, *An Introduction to Islamic Finance*, p. 71.
[75] Ayub, *Understanding Islamic Finance*, p. 218.
[76] Al-Qurtubi, *Al-Kafi fi Fiqh Ahl-al-Madinah* vol. 2, p. 705; Hamilton, p. 472.
[77] C. Hamilton, *The Hedaya: Commentary on the Islamic Laws*, vol. 2 (Karachi: Dar-ul-Ishrat, 1989), p. 473.
[78] Ayub, *Understanding Islamic Finance*, p. 216.

financial instrument. A customer wanting certain goods may approach a bank and ask it to purchase them on the basis of *murabaha*. The bank, with a strict reading of classical *murabaha*, may order the goods and charge their original cost plus a mark-up. However, as the customer will not necessarily have payment to hand, payment for the goods is not likely to be instantaneous and the purchaser's business is invariably financed by the bank in credit installments. The active participation in the buying of the goods entitles the bank to earn profit legitimately while running the risk of losing out should anything go amiss.[79]

As noted above, to respond to complex legalities a number of juristic techniques not normally ascribed to any particular school of thought need to be applied alongside the primary sources of law. For instance *maslaha* (public interest), though not universally acknowledged by all schools, is especially used in the field of finance. For *murabaha* to become a technique of finance, a jurisprudential journey had to be undertaken by Shafi'i scholars, notwithstanding that Shafi'i is not the most widespread or otherwise influential of the juristic schools. But had the Maliki view been applied, no bank would finance such *murabaha* transactions.[80]

So strict adherence to classical jurisprudence is not without pitfalls. A purchaser's unilateral rescinding of a transaction because an object does not tally with his specifications, for example, will affect the smooth running of a bank. To this end, jurisprudence was flexible enough to develop the '*murabaha* to purchase order', a device mixing Maliki and Shafi'i principles, whereby a purchaser is bound to accept the goods by making a prior promise.[81] However, the practical application of the '*murabaha* by purchase order' has been criticized as not in accordance with *sharia*, since risks are stealthily shifted to the customer.[82]

4.6 Launching Islamic Finance in a Globalized World: An Overview

The evolution of the modern Islamic finance sector has been traced by Warde through three phases: early years (1975–91); globalization (1991–2001); and post-9/11,[83] while a prior phase comprising theoretical developments from the 1930s to the 1960s may also be added. Islamic finance has its genesis there, in the post-colonial discourse of Islamization of state and society in the writings of Abul A'la Maududi (founder of the Jamaat-e-Islami), Hasan al-Banna (founder of the Muslim Brotherhood), and the Salafi jurist Muhammad Abduh, who raised Islamization as a requisite for Muslim states and governments and argued that Muslims must develop 'Islamic' institutions rather than accept

---

[79] Vogel and Hayes, *Islamic Law and Finance*, p. 140.
[80] On the arguments justifying this marriage of convenience see Ayub, *Understanding Islamic Finance*, p. 220.
[81] Ibid., p. 224; El-Gamal, *Islamic Finance*, p. 67.
[82] Vogel and Hayes, *Islamic Law and Finance*, pp. 140–3.   [83] Warde, *Islamic Finance*, p. 2.

Western impositions.[84] Indian scholars such as Maududi, Uzair and Ahmed started writing on Islamic finance in the 1940s with a view to its implementation after future independence, though the debate remained mainly at a theoretical level. From the mid-1970s, the quadrupling of oil prices led to an assertiveness and mood for experimenting with Islamic finance with a view to establishing an alternative banking system. Instead of functioning on the basis of interest, they would form partnerships based on profit and loss sharing with both depositors and would-be borrowers, through the traditional Islamic practice of *mudaraba*.[85]

The decade before 11 September 2001 marked a departure, with institutions moving more towards pragmatically replicating conventional finance with *sharia*-compliant contracts. Another significant factor was the rise of the Malaysian model of Islamic finance; despite being religiously controversial, this was more innovative and forward-looking.[86] And hence a paradox emerged: Islam is said to be incompatible with the new order emerging after the end of the Cold War, yet it is in the age of globalization that Islamic finance was able to thrive well beyond the Muslim world.[87] After the 9/11 attacks, in an atmosphere of Islamophobia and the global 'war on terror', a paradoxical impetus was lent to the Islamic finance industry and to bringing the Arab and Malaysian models closer.[88]

The development and operation of Islamic finance has not met with uniform success globally; an ambivalence towards it is reflected in the relatively few nations codifying its tenets, thereby restricting its operation to the domain of private institutions. In Pakistan, Iran and Sudan – singled out as 'pioneers' in Islamization[89] – the introduction of Islamic finance was done half-heartedly, or, as Berger says, 'with enough loopholes to remain functioning within the international financial market'.[90] All three have introduced Islamic finance within different religious, political, economic and cultural circumstances, and without a systematic root-and-branch replacement of the conventional regime.[91] In Pakistan, the government introduced partial financial Islamization through profit- and loss-sharing banking, but dragged its feet over Islamizing the economy and financial institutions, despite an activist judiciary forcing its hand (see the case law below). In Malaysia, on the other hand, Islamic finance has been the project of a political elite that decided to link it to the nation's economic development. Iran operates an Islamic finance system.

In terms of the concrete appearance of Islamic finance institutions, the first Islamic bank, Egypt's Mit Ghamr Savings Bank, was well received by farmers and working-class communities and operated between 1963 and 1967, after

---

[84] Saeed, 'Sharia and Finance', p. 249.   [85] Warde, *Islamic Finance*, p. 2.
[86] Ibid., p. 3.   [87] Ibid.   [88] Ibid., p. 4.
[89] M. S. Berger, 'Sharia and the Nation State', in Peters and Bearman, *The Ashgate Research Companion to Islamic Law*, p. 227; also A. Saeed, 'Sharia and Finance', in ibid., p. 255.
[90] Berger, 'Sharia and the Nation State', p. 227.   [91] Warde, *Islamic Finance*, p. 115.

which its operations were taken over by the Bank of Egypt.[92] In Malaysia, the *sharia*-compliant Pilgrims Savings Corporation was set up in 1963 to help people save towards performing *haj*.

Spurred on by oil money and a motivation to develop Islamic finance for Muslims worldwide, various initiatives were brought together under the banner of the Organisation of Islamic Cooperation (OIC), parallel to which, scholarship was lent impetus by a proliferation of research institutes and organizations: at the 1974 OIC summit, the intergovernmental Islamic Development Bank was created, followed over the next six years by the Dubai Islamic Bank, the Kuwait Finance House, the Faisal Islamic Bank of Egypt, the Islamic Bank of Sudan, the Jordan Islamic Bank for Finance and Investment, the Bahrain Islamic Bank, and the Islamic International Bank for Investment and Development.[93] During this period the International Association of Islamic Banks was set up to help refine and develop practices and concepts.[94]

It was assumed that initial profit- and loss-sharing schemes would primarily be replacing conventional interest-based operations; with time and experience, however, this arrangement presented challenges and posed numerous questions. In subsequent years, Islamic finance was impacted by economic transformations that led to a slow crumbling of the underlying principles of the *ijtihad* of the 1970s that had led to the Islamic financial institutions of that era. Profit- and loss-sharing schemes proved unsuccessful, leading people to ask whether, in keeping to the letter of Islamic requirements, their spirit had been lost. A near-obsessive insistence that *riba* equated to interest was finally confronted, and a 1989 *fatwa* (albeit controversial) by Tantawi challenged this 'dogmatic fixation' and set the stage for a growing convergence between Islamic and conventional finance.[95]

As Islamic finance matures, a number of developments are now in evidence. Monitoring and regulatory mechanisms and a harmonization of rules are becoming clearer and firmer. Standard-setting and co-ordination are being increased through bodies such as the Islamic Finance Services Board,[96] the International Islamic Financial Market,[97] the Liquidity Management

---

92 Ibid., p. 71.
93 Some international investment banks were also created, including the Islamic Investment Company in Nassau (1977), the Islamic Investment Company of the Gulf in Sharjah (1978); the Shariah Investment Services in Geneva (1980), and the Bahrain Islamic Investment in Manama (1980). See T. Wohlers-Scharf, *Arab and Islamic Banks: New Business Partners for Developing Countries* (Paris: OECD, 1983), p. 80, cited in Warde, *Islamic Finance*, p. 90, note 13.
94 One of the first initiatives of the IAIB was the publication of *A Handbook of Islamic Banking* (Cairo: IAIB, 1977–86) as a reference work. A compact English-language publication is Al-Nagar *et al.*'s *One Hundred Questions & One Hundred Answers Concerning Islamic Banks* (Cairo: IAIB, 1980).
95 Warde, *Islamic Finance*, p. 90.
96 Based in Kuala Lumpur, the IFSB started operations in 2003.
97 The IIFM was founded in 2002 by the collective efforts of the Islamic Development Bank, Autoriti Monetari Brunei Darussalam, Bank Indonesia, the Central Bank of Bahrain, the

Center,[98] the Islamic International Rating Agency,[99] the Accounting and Auditing Organization for Islamic Financial Institutions,[100] and the International Islamic Liquidity Management Corporation.[101] In 2005, the International Islamic Center for Reconciliation and Commercial Arbitration for Islamic Finance Industry was launched in Dubai.

What are the issues and the challenges, then, that have arisen on the ground from the introduction of Islamic finance in some of these jurisdictions?

4.7 Between the Government's Eloquent Silence and Judicial Activism: The Story of Islamic Finance in Pakistan

On 2 March 2014, Pakistan's press reported, 'Shariat court to take up 22-year-old riba case on March 24',[102] which announcement was followed by an eloquent silence. A similar news item had appeared five months earlier declaring that the Federal Shariat Court would take up hearing of this case on 21 October 2013.[103] Such periodic stories, informing the public of an impending court hearing on *riba*, and the government's resistance to implementing a prohibition, highlight the paradox of Islamic finance in a country hailed as the pioneer of wholesale Islamization.

As I said above, the Islamization project is a modern one, full of paradoxes and contradictions, and the case of Islamic finance in Pakistan is exemplary – in particular the manner in which aggressive judicial activism has clashed with state and governmental institutions in pushing for implementation of Islamic finance.

The Islamization of laws in Pakistan has arguably been a judge-led process, initiated to enhance the power of the judiciary and expand the scope of constitutionally guaranteed fundamental rights:[104]

Central Bank of Sudan, and the Bank Negara Malaysia (delegated to Labuan Financial Services Authority) as a neutral and non-profit organization. It is a key standard-setting organization for Islamic finance and banking.

[98] The LMC is an Islamic investment bank incorporated in 2002 and regulated by the Central Bank of Bahrain, its aim being to provide Islamic financing and investment to help grow the Islamic capital market.

[99] Based in Bahrain, the IIRA started operations in 2005 to facilitate development of national and regional financial markets by delineating the relative investment or credit risk of entities and instruments.

[100] The AAOIFI was established in Algiers in 1990 and registered in Bahrain in 1991.

[101] Based in Kuala Lumpur, the IILMC was founded in 2010. It is an international institution established by central banks, monetary authorities and multilateral organizations to create and issue short-term *sharia*-compliant financial instruments to facilitate cross-border Islamic liquidity management.

[102] *The Tribune* (online), 2 March 2014.

[103] 'Shariat Court to Hear Riba Case Again', www.thenews.com.pk, 20 October 2013.

[104] Lau contends, with justification, that more visible manifestations of the Islamization of the legal system, including the Hudood Ordinances, obscured the role of judges in this regard. Lau, *Role of Islam*, p. 1.

The judicial appropriation of Islam and its integration into the vocabulary of the courts was a conscious process aimed not only at the fulfillment of a general desire to indigenize and Islamise the legal system after the end of colonial rule but it was also a way of enhancing judicial power and independence.

Islamization is not confined to a few distinct areas of law but has become an integral part of the legal discourse, being relied on in a wide range of issues.[105]

Although established in the name of Islam, Pakistan's experiments with the Islamization of law and state have been marred with controversy since its creation in 1947; despite calls, the wholesale replacement of the inherited colonial system was never achieved because of a lack of sufficient and robust support.[106] The Islamization of the legal system was assigned to Parliament rather than to the judiciary, but with the creation of the Federal Shariat Court (FSC) in 1980[107] this separate body was tasked with examining parts of the legal system on the basis of Islam. Selectivity and caution in institutionalizing Islamic law was evident even under its apparently most ardent supporter, General Zia: true to the paradoxical nature of the Islamization project, he too kept personal status and fiscal laws out of the jurisdictional purview of the FSC.[108]

Initially, the FSC adopted a pragmatic approach regarding the limits imposed upon it with regard to fiscal laws,[109] skirting around the issue of *riba* by declaring it a fiscal matter and outside its jurisdiction. This was evident in a number of cases, including *Essa EH Jafar* v. *Federation of Pakistan*,[110] where the FSC held that it did not have the jurisdiction to declare un-Islamic those parts of the Pakistan Refugee Rehabilitation Finance Corporation Ordinance 1960 which provided for payment of interest on loans. In *Khalid Abdur Raoof* v. *Federation of Pakistan*, the FSC refused to invalidate an amendment to the Zakat and Ushr Ordinance 1980, on the grounds that it 'fell into the spheres of both fiscal and Muslim personal law'.[111] That a court established to judge the Islamicity

---

[105] Ibid.

[106] Ibid., p. 5. See also Siddique, *Pakistan's Experience*; A. Haydar, 'From the Anglo-Muhammadan Law to the Shariah: The Pakistan Experiment', *Journal of South Asian and Middle Eastern Studies* 10(4) (1987), 33–50; R. Mehdi, *Islamisation of the Law in Pakistan* (Richmond: Curzon, 1994); Binder, *Religion and Politics*; B. Metcalf, 'Islamic Arguments in Contemporary Pakistan', in W. Roff (ed.), *Islam and the Political Economy of Meaning* (London: Routledge, 1987), pp. 132–59.

[107] Established under President's Order No. 1 of 1980 as incorporated in the Constitution of the Islamic Republic of Pakistan 1973 under Chapter 3A.

[108] A second constitutional mechanism to assist in the Islamization of laws came in the form of an advisory body, known as the Council of Islamic Ideology.

[109] Under Article 203-B of the Constitution of Pakistan 1973, Muslim personal law and fiscal laws stood excluded from the jurisdiction of the Federal Shariat Court. This exclusion was initially limited to three years but was extended to four in 1983, to five in 1984, and then to ten years in 1985.

[110] PLD 1982 FSC 212.

[111] Lau, *Role of Islam*, p. 160. *Khurshid Alam* v. *Muslim Commercial Bank* PLD 1983 FSC 20 also met with the same fate, the court holding that it did not have jurisdiction to deal with banking matters. The petitioner had sought to have declared un-Islamic the payment of interest on a loan.

or otherwise of laws was excluded from certain areas, including fiscal matters, became an embarrassment – not to the government, but to the judges of the Shariat Court. The Islamization project required champions, and the FSC had within its ranks some ardent supporters who took the debate over Islamic finance to the next level.

The limits of what constituted 'fiscal laws' beyond the purview of the FSC again came under discussion in *Muhammad Sadiq Khan* v. *Federation of Pakistan*.[112] The case highlighted the deep ideological differences within the FSC, with some judges taking issue with the restrictions imposed on their prerogative to declare laws un-Islamic. Justice Taqi Usmani voiced the strongest dissent: by retaining an expansive definition of 'fiscal', the court was 'denuded of all meaningful powers and was rendered to almost a nullity'.[113]

After the expiry in 1990 of the ten-year period during which the FSC's jurisdiction had been restrained, the issue of fiscal laws emerged again. In what became a legal landmark known simply as 'the *riba* case', the FSC in *Mahmood-ur-Rehman Faisal* v. *Secretary, Ministry of Law*[114] explicitly determined the legality of interest. In a 189-page judgment, Justice Tanzil-ur-Rehman, an ardent supporter of Islamization, declared all laws providing for the payment of interest un-Islamic. The FSC set a date – 1 July 1992 – on which such laws would cease to have effect.[115] The government appealed to the Shariat Appellate Bench of the Supreme Court, where the case lay pending for eight years before the decision was finally arrived at in the year 2000,[116] upholding the FSC's judgment. The government requested a review, and in 2002 the case was sent back to the FSC, where it remains. To date, all the laws which the FSC declared repugnant to Islam remain in force and it is very much business as usual. Every now and then a date is set for a hearing, but 'the *riba* case' remains undecided, as does the fate of *riba* in Pakistan.

An impressive number of cases before the FSC have held that laws providing for payment of interest are repugnant to Islam. As Lau puts it, judicial self-assertion 'has been able to threaten the foundations of the country's financial system through the invalidation of all laws providing for payment of interest'.[117] The government and relevant institutions have been slow to eradicate interest from its banking system and economy. Despite its independent stance and its clear desire to eliminate interest payments, the judiciary restrains itself

---

[112] PLD 1983 FSC 43.

[113] PLD 1983 FSC 50. Another judge, Zahoorul-haq J., argued that 'it should be left open to the FSC to decide on the vires of stipulations for the payment of interest in areas of law where interest was incidental to these laws and which could therefore not be regarded as fiscal laws'. Lau, *Role of Islam*, p. 161.

[114] PLD 1992 FSC 1.

[115] The government of Pakistan had requested an extension but this was turned down. Rahman J. observed that he himself as former chair of the Council of Islamic Ideology had submitted a report on elimination of interest from the economy in the country as far back as 1980.

[116] *Federation of Pakistan* v. *Mahmood-ur-Rehman Faisal* PLD 2000 SC 770.

[117] Lau, *Role of Islam*, p. 165.

from a headlong confrontation with the government.[118] So Islamic finance in Pakistan proves to be something of a contradiction, reflecting the wider paradoxes and contradictions within state and society. Pragmatism appears to rule from the three branches of government down to the man on the street. The government's rhetoric and reality do not match, and apart from a small percentage of subscribers to Islamic banks most continue to use conventional banks that operate Islamically permissible 'profit-and-loss' accounts.[119] The Islamic finance project has few ardent supporters outside the manifestos of religious parties and judges who now and then demand that the government Islamize the economy. An eloquent silence of acquiescence towards conventional finance continues, with few indications of change in the foreseeable future.

4.8 Malaysia: An Aspiring and Innovative Dual Financial Regime

In sharp contrast to Pakistan, Malaysia's socio-economic and political history has led to a different shade of pragmatism informing the question of Islamic finance. Overwhelmingly Muslim Pakistan was established in the name of Islam and is committed, at least in its rhetoric, to Islamization. Malaysia's Muslims – mostly ethnic Malay – on the other hand make up just over 60 per cent of the population, 30 per cent being Chinese and the rest non-Muslims of Indian origin.[120] After Independence, the urge to Islamize was not much in evidence. Malaysia's financial resources lay largely in the hands of the minority Chinese and Indian populations, and a necessary prerequisite for Islamic finance was the economic empowerment of the majority ethnic Malays.

As mentioned above, Malaysia's earliest experience with Islamic finance dates back to 1963, when the Pilgrims Savings Corporation was established.[121] But what really set Malaysia apart from Pakistan was the creation in the 1980s of an Islamic banking sector alongside its conventional financial regime and the subsequent development of Islamic capital markets.[122] Moreover, the Malaysian Islamic finance project was clearly driven by a government using Islam as a vehicle for advancing economic development. Islamic finance emerged as an elite project within a culture of patronage and consumerism, and with a government aspiring to become a regional and global hub.[123]

---

[118] Lau, *Role of Islam*, has an analysis of the *riba* cases in the Pakistani courts.
[119] The profit-and-loss accounts attract returns that appear very much on the scale of interest but with a different name: 'mark-up', 'profit' and so on.
[120] Warde, *Islamic Finance*, p. 125; L. Rethal, 'Global Ambitions, Local Realities: The Everyday Political Economy of Islamic Finance in Malaysia', in J. Elias and L. Rethal (eds.), *The Everyday Political Economy of Southeast Asia* (Cambridge: Cambridge University Press, forthcoming 2016), p. 1.
[121] Rethal, 'Global Ambitions', p. 1; Warde, *Islamic Finance*, p. 70.
[122] Rethal, 'Global Ambitions', p. 1.
[123] Writing from a political-economy perspective, Rethal makes a persuasive argument to advance this viewpoint: see Rethal, 'Global Ambitions'.

For Malaysia, Islamic finance was made an ambitious project and not, as in Pakistan, an obstacle to change. It was to be used as a tool to promote financial innovation.[124] Warde makes the important observation that an 'Islamic financial system that could offer a growing array of sophisticated financial services was part and parcel of the effort to turn Kuala Lumpur into a leading regional, if not international, financial centre'.[125] Unlike Pakistan's, where even the most ardent proponent of Islamic finance, General Zia, was uncomfortable with a complete overhaul of the economy to meet the demands of Islamization, Malaysia's government was completely behind the project. The desire was to acquire legitimacy and authenticity for innovative financial products whilst remaining within the framework of Islamic jurisprudence. Such a pragmatic approach led the deputy prime minister, Anwar Ibrahim, to remark, 'In implementing Islamic principles in banking and finance, we must address the substantive issues rather than be always preoccupied with terminology and semantics.'[126]

Mahathir Mohamad, upon taking office as prime minister in 1981, led a range of supporting initiatives to pave the way for Islamic finance, albeit alongside the existing financial regime. A number of Islamic research centres and universities were set up to legitimate the Islamic finance project generally and to design interest-free products such as bonds, securities and Islamic insurance.[127] In 1983, the Islamic Banking Act created the innovative Bank Islam Malaysia Berhad, the first fully fledged Islamic bank. In 1985 came the Syarikat Takaful Malaysia, an Islamic insurance company, and in 1994 the Islamic Interbank Money Market was introduced. Islamic unit trusts, Islamic debt securities and the RHB Islamic Index were instituted to promote credible capital markets.[128] And as Islamic finance was pursued as an integral component of Malaysia's development strategy, Islamic banks were encouraged to 'think globally' to transform Malaysia into a world leader in the sector. To this end, compliant mortgages, credit cards and a range of financial services were offered to consumers.

An important step in this direction was the collaboration between the Arab and Malaysian Islamic financial regimes. After initial criticism of how the Malaysian finance industry was 'cutting corners' in Islamic products, common ground was increasingly found. From 2002, sovereign Malaysian 'Islamic bonds' (*sukuk*) targeted Arab investors, leading to similar products in the Arab financial markets.[129] Malaysia also enacted the Islamic Financial Services Act

---

[124] Warde, *Islamic Finance*, p. 126.   [125] Ibid.   [126] Ibid., p. 127.

[127] Ibid. The International Islamic University was set up in 1983. The Malaysian Institute of Islamic Understanding (IKIM) held seminars on all aspects of religion and finance.

[128] Warde, *Islamic Finance*, pp. 128–9; Rethal, 'Global Ambitions'. The RHB Islamic Index tracks the performance of listed companies that do not contravene Islamic principles.

[129] A number of initiatives have followed, and Malaysian and Arab regulators started working more closely: the Dubai Financial Services Authority entered into a memorandum of understanding with Bank Negara Malaysia. Since 2006, three Arab banks have been allowed to

2013 as a comprehensive legal, regulatory and supervisory framework, while simultaneously maintaining a conventional financial system. Abroad, Malaysian policy-makers have played crucial roles in international initiatives to promote and regulate Islamic finance. Setting up such organizations gave the requisite Islamic legitimacy to Mahathir's development initiatives. Conscious of the plurality within juristic interpretation, a national Syariah Board was established to harmonize financial practices and to review the compatibility of new products with Islamic law.

The political dimension to, and rhetoric behind, Malaysia's Islamic finance industry is readily apparent: it is the means by which ethnic Malays can achieve economic empowerment, and by which Malaysia can become *the* global leader in Islamic finance. However, despite some grass-roots initiatives amongst the rural poor, the fruits are being reaped by the political elite at two levels: first, they are able to use the services available for their own advancement; simultaneously, that elite is connecting with the poorer sections of society through patronage, offering those services and winning votes.[130] Despite the negative aspects, at a regional and international level Malaysia has succeeded in becoming a leader in the sector, opening up collaborative spaces to her Arab counterparts. Not surprisingly, common financial interests have proved a sobering influence and the gap between varying juristic interpretations has been narrowed in a very pragmatic manner.

The manner in which the threads of Islamic finance were woven into the Islamization projects of Pakistan and Malaysia bears testimony both to its disparate nature and to competing visions of states and societies as to its aims. The ideal scenario is for high profitability alongside 'genuine' Islamic substance; hence the attraction of even tenuously *halal sharia*-compliant products. But the inevitable periodic scams in the name of *sharia*-compliant investments have jolted investors out of their complacency, cast doubt over 'pristine' initiatives, and dented trust in Islamic finance.[131]

4.9 Islamic Finance: A Critical Appraisal

Despite its operational presence since 1973 and the degree of maturity within its concepts and practices, Islamic finance remains contested terrain, with proponents as well as critics. Resurrecting classical *sharia* roots, pioneers set out

operate in Malaysia – Kuwait Finance House, Saudi Arabia's Al-Rajhi, and the Asian Finance House. Rethal reports that corporate *sukuk* now have a share of around half of the domestic bond market while *sukuk* issued in Malaysia account for more than 70 per cent of the global *sukuk* market. Rethal, 'Global Ambitions'.

130 Islamization of the economy was shaped by increasing electoral competition between two political parties in Malaysia: UMNO and PAS.

131 The 'Taj Company scandal' continues to haunt. When the Taj Company sought public investment in the Islamically permissible business of printing the Qur'an, people rushed to buy their *halal* shares. When the investments and the frontline management of the company vanished, it became one of the biggest financial scandals in Pakistan's history.

to assert a Muslim identity and to address the poor economic situation of the vast majority of the Muslim population by establishing an Islamic economy. In a collaborative relationship between scholars, economists, bankers and political elites, a conscious effort was made to link classical formulations with contemporary forms of finance and banking.

A number of factors – still ongoing – impacted on the evolution and reception of Islamic finance among different constituencies. First and foremost remains the plurality of the Islamic legal traditions, which has led to varying understandings of the principles and techniques of Islamic finance. This has impacted on its contours, and on the various products considered *sharia*-compliant. The prime example of this plurality, as discussed above, is the controversy over the meaning and scope of *riba*, as the entire edifice of Islamic finance is built upon its prohibition. Again, as discussed above, the contestation over *riba* has led to the issue of technical adherence to the form of classical *sharia* at the cost of substance. In order to avoid *riba*, financial experts and scholars engage in convoluted and complex arguments to arrive at the kind of *sharia*-compliant products and transactions we saw earlier in the chapter. In reality, though, these products resemble conventional financial products but with an Arabic name tag and a *sharia*-compliance certificate from a Shariah Supervisory Board. (It is worth mentioning here the inherent conflict of interests in the position of such boards: their rulings are paid for by banks but they are expected to curtail the ability to innovate. The fact that some *sharia* advisers sit on the supervisory boards of more than one bank creates obvious conflicts.) This question over the form and substance of *sharia*-compliance is by far the strongest criticism of Islamic finance and banking techniques, and one that is also trickling down slowly to the lay Muslim population.

The complex nature of present-day global economic challenges was never remotely envisaged during the classical age of Islamic civilization, and it would be fair to assume that the classical *fuqaha* have not necessarily provided answers to all the questions posed by novel practices in our own age. Creativity and innovation, therefore, are essential requisites if contemporary Islamic scholarship is to keep pace with financial activities and institutions. And yes, at present, classical Islamic financial techniques and contracts are being used as templates in remodelling almost any contemporary financial transaction along *sharia*-compliant lines. Carefully crafted contracts judiciously avoid *riba* and *gharar*, building instead upon the permissible principles of equitable financial transaction such as the *mudaraba, musharakah, murabaha, salam* and others discussed above. Conventional financial institutions, meanwhile, now have what are called 'Islamic windows' which offer products to suit a Muslim clientele. Whether or not these non-Islamic institutions ringfence their *sharia*-compliant investments is another matter entirely, since the commingling of capital in conventional funds which might have elements of non-*sharia*-compliant investments – in alcohol, tobacco, gambling etc. – might make their outward window-dressing highly dubious. Yet this is nevertheless a remarkable position, going against the grain of the infamous 'clash of civilizations' mantra of Samuel P. Huntington and numerous others who insist that Islamic norms are completely at odds with the West's.

4.10 Is Islamic Finance Failing?

The stated aims and objectives of Islamic finance were – and are – laudable. They are, to quote from *A Handbook of Islamic Banking*, 'The promotion of social justice and equality and the alleviation of poverty through the establishment of a *zakat* fund, for the collection and distribution of funds to the poor, and the provisions of interest-free loans (*qard hasan*) to deserving individuals.'[132] But from laudable beginnings focusing on the equitable and charitable aspects of finance, we soon slipped into a conventional regime aimed squarely at commercial profit-making. Whereas Islamic finance was meant to reach out to the rural areas, and to the impoverished populations of the Muslim world, its resources were mostly extended to elites rather than those in need. In practical terms, the use of due-diligence checks before handing out money to clients has meant that the need for stability and the avoidance of bad debt inevitably defeats what is arguably the prime social purpose of Islamic finance: what kind of bank, after all, will long survive if it lends to people who cannot repay?

The 'unique selling point' of Islamic finance is that Muslims, for religious reasons and/or a lack of trust in government-run institutions, can have an effective alternative. *Zakat* and *qard hasan* have real, transformative potential to improve the lives of millions of Muslims around the world, yet they appear to occupy very little space in the sector. Although financial inclusion discourses play an increasingly important role in Islamic banking and finance, this arm of Islamic finance has slipped below the radar of the Islamic finance industry, its regulatory bodies, and states and government. The rhetoric of empowering poor Muslims by employing the social justice inherent in Islamic finance belies the reality.[133] The disparate practices of *zakat* payment to be found amongst communities which perceive it through differing cultural lenses are witness to its fluid nature and its potential as a developmental catalyst. (Practices can be dispiriting as well as uplifting: some communities are more diligent in paying than others.[134]) As a form of worship it is also open to multiple interpretations, in terms of both 'zakat-able' items and beneficiaries. *Qard hasan* loans, meanwhile, could be usefully employed as grants for education, or

---

[132] *A Handbook of Islamic Banking* (note 94 above), cited in Warde, *Islamic Finance*, p. 182.
[133] Rethal sees a renewed focus on microfinance within Islamic banking. It is doubtful, though, whether the problems of social justice and inclusion will be resolved through this mechanism.
[134] According to a report in the *Saudi Gazette*, if rich citizens had paid their *zakat* regularly, there would not, argued a number of scholars, be a single poor family in the kingdom. Quoting statistical reports, the scholars said that if *zakat* was collected regularly it would lead to a turnover of more than SR60 billion a year. 'The Rich Fail to Pay Zakat, Scholars Claim', *Saudi Gazette* (online) 17 April 2014.

for necessary repairs to homes. Voluntary *sadaqa* giving could be reframed as an inter-faith, socially inclusive mechanism, since it does not require beneficiaries to be Muslim.

Advocates of Islamic finance have argued that it could 'bring about more efficient mobilization of savings, more equitable and just distribution of resources, more responsible and profitable lending as well as less volatile business cycles and more stable banking systems'.[135] Theoretically, perhaps, but its translation into practice has not been so. Others have observed that Islamic finance faces an existential problem, having 'failed to achieve its articulated, functional goal of an alternative system of commerce based on notions of fairness and social justice'.[136]

Within individual consciousness, interest in Islamic finance is neither uniform nor consistent, fluctuating between religious enthusiasm, ambivalence and simply evasion. Most Muslims continue to bank in the conventional model, and the intricacies of classical Islamic finance are beyond their knowledge and competence. At the same time, recent efforts to develop Islamic finance cannot be separated from global capital. The two are highly interconnected – take, for example, the importance in the sector of players such as HSBC or Citibank, or the fact that Islamic banks nevertheless use LIBOR as their benchmark even though its calculations take no account of *sharia*. And since Islamic finance is essentially constructed as a response to conventional finance with its fickle and footloose global flow of money, it struggles to move beyond that conventional system as its reference point. Nevertheless, Islamic finance as part of the globalization of economic activity has challenged territorially limited state authority.

One of the fastest-growing aspects of the global financial system, the receptiveness towards Islamic finance in Western circles – legal, financial and political – is remarkable. Since the 1970s, collaborative initiatives between Islamic and conventional institutions have multiplied at a rapid pace. The World Bank, in its 2014 Global Financial Development Report, includes 395 Islamic banks and financial institutions from fifty-eight countries. 'Islamic windows' and *sharia*-compliant products have taken root and are expanding exponentially. This is all the more astonishing bearing in mind the West's uneasy relationship with certain other aspects of Islamic legal traditions.[137]

---

[135] Warde, *Islamic Finance*, p. 177.   [136] Hamoudi, 'Jurisprudential Schizophrenia', p. 605.

[137] The Islamic financial services industry has a global reach, is the fastest growing aspect of the Islamic legal tradition, and has captured the interest of both Muslim states and Western financial institutions. The Middle East has 56 per cent of the total *sharia*-compliant market. There are approximately 450 such companies located in the region, with the UAE in the lead, followed by Bahrain, Kuwait, Iran and Saudi Arabia. Asian companies have 20 per cent of the *sharia*-compliant market, with Malaysia the key player. Europe has 114 companies, accounting for approximately 14 per cent, with the UK the lead player, boosted by the FSA's regulatory initiatives. The US and Canada have forty-four companies (5 per cent). Africa, Australasia and South America have negligible numbers (MENA Report 2009, in a presentation by Agil Natt on Islamic finance: 'Reality Check and Way Forward', Warwick Law School, 2010).

So why are influential constituencies – Muslim and non-Muslim, Western and non-Western alike – rallying around Islamic finance with minimal resistance? Two reasons stand out: first, the common financial interests of powerful individuals and states form sturdy collaborative bridges across religious and cultural divides to hold anti-Islamic and anti-Western sentiments at bay; second, unlike other areas of Islam, the Western mass media do not portray Islamic finance as a 'backward' idea which is in conflict with 'modern' conventional regimes. The result is a globalized and expanding international finance industry to which Muslim and non-Muslim clients can readily subscribe.

But a paradox has reared its head: on the one hand, Islamic financial institutions are growing at a phenomenally fast pace and enjoy the support of global finance as well as of Western states; simultaneously, apprehensions within *Muslim* communities regarding the 'Islamicity' of Islamic finance are growing as more and more people realize that there is more focus on form than on substance, and that the application of classical jurisprudence is ultimately simply mimicking conventional practices.[138] Nevertheless, formalistic adherents to Islamic law continue to support Islamic financial products, no matter how fragile the arguments for their legal basis. This very much exemplifies the interpretative plurality of the Islamic legal traditions and their attendant dilemmas of legitimacy, authority and authenticity.

For a financial system drawing its inspiration and validity from Islamic law to work effectively, rigorous scholarship needs to be developed. This scholarship must be sufficiently competent and courageous to ground itself in the primary and secondary sources of law while remaining aware of contemporary exigencies and the complexities of modern financial transactions. There is a dearth of economists with an adequate grasp of classical *fiqh* and contemporary concepts of finance, able to discern not only the letter of the Islamic law but also its spirit in validating any given transaction.[139] But how are such jurist–economists to transform a legal tradition comprising general principles and diverse interpretation into statutes and regulations with globally predictable effects? With no harmonized regulatory framework, the existing decentralized system means that Shariah Supervisory Boards can give *fatawa* on the permissibility or otherwise of a transaction or product depending on how their bank's management presents it.[140] This, of course, poses both legal and practical challenges to recognition in any jurisdiction where a contrary view has been taken.

So despite the largely successful initiatives of Islamic financial institutions, one cannot overlook the serious challenges that need to be addressed if those

[138]   Hamoudi, 'Jurisprudential Schizophrenia', p. 605. See M. El-Gamal, 'Limits and Dangers of Sharia Arbitrage', in N. Ali (ed.), *Islamic Finance: Current Legal and Regulatory Issues* (Cambridge, MA: Islamic Finance Project, Islamic Legal Studies Program, Harvard University, 2005), pp. 127–31.
[139]   N. Ryan, 'The Rise and Rise of Islamic Finance', *The Market*, 2 August 2008.
[140]   R. Wilson, *The Development of Islamic Finance in the GCC* (London: LSE, 2009), p. 11.

institutions are to be fully equipped to compete in a global environment.[141] In a series of working papers for the Centre for Islamic and Middle Eastern Law,[142] Foster argues for the need to develop expert knowledge in the area of Islamic finance law. As an emerging, expanding and maturing system,

> Not only does one need a broad and deep knowledge of the sharia, but also of the vehicular system, as well as of comparative law for the study of the interaction between them, legal history for the study of the Law of Islamic Finance as a legal system in development.[143]

Piecemeal legislation, regulation and dispute resolution have resulted in dual regimes and the 'grafting' of Islamic scions on to conventional rootstocks. Vastly complex court cases in both Muslim and non-Muslim jurisdictions have been the result.[144]

In support of Islamic finance, however, it has been observed that, at least in theory, it departs from practices largely developed in and promulgated by Western-based elite actors,[145] and that, while Islamic financial products often mirror conventional ones, there is a difference in their underlying reasoning, with Islamic finance presenting a greater inherent reflexivity.[146] Rice sees Islamic financial products as endowed with a 'moral filter' of what is deemed socially desirable, and thus not merely subject to the markets.[147] Yet it should by now be clear that such statements do not always receive confirmation from practice on the ground. In Asutay's study of profit- and loss-sharing methods in ten Islamic banks, only three allocated funds to *qard hasan*, and even then at

---

[141] For a discussion of the practical problems of this paradigm, see generally Abdul Gafoor, *Interest-Free Commercial Banking*; Vogel and Hayes, *Islamic Law and Finance*, p. 132; C. Wright, 'Innovations in Islamic Finance: Balancing Innovation and Integrity, May 2015' available at www.euromoney.com/Article/3448162/Innovations-in-Islamic-Finance-2015-Balancing-innovation-and-integrity.html.

[142] N. Foster (SOAS Working Papers): '"Lead Us Not into Temptation": The Formulation of the Present Orthodoxy and the Deficiencies of Regulation'; 'Making People Behave Properly in Islamic Finance: Some General Thoughts'; 'Some Thoughts from Legal Academia on "Reappraising the Islamic Financial Industry after the Downturn: Introspective Reflections"'; 'Islamic Financial Intermediation: Revisiting the Value Proposition – The Role of Law'; and 'Operating with a Truncated Legal System: Financial Law without Insolvency Law'.

[143] Foster, 'Some Thoughts from Legal Academia', p. 7. At p. 4 of the same paper, Foster observes, 'Indeed, the need for specialisation is arguably greater in IF than in other fields, because the skill base required is so much wider. The ideal specialist in the Law of Islamic Finance needs competence in the English and Arabic languages, a knowledge of the foundations of the sharia as well as its financial aspects, combined with expertise in English financial law and practice. This is a very tall order indeed.'

[144] For example *Beximco Pharmaceutical v. Shamil Bank of Bahrain* EC [2004] EWCA Civ 19.

[145] B. Maurer, 'The disunity of finance: alternative practices to western finance', in K. Knorr Cetina and A. Preda (eds.), *The Oxford Handbook of the Sociology of Finance* (Oxford: Oxford University Press, 2012), pp. 413–30, cited in Rethal, 'Global Ambitions'.

[146] For example B. Maurer, 'Re-socialising Finance? Or Dressing It in Mufti? Calculating Alternatives for Cultural Economies', *Journal of Cultural Economy* 1(1) (2008), 65–78, cited in Rethal, 'Global Ambitions'.

[147] G. Rice, 'Islamic Ethics and the Implications for Business', *Journal of Business Ethics* 18(4) (1999), 345–58, cited in Rethal, 'Global Ambitions'.

minimum levels.[148] The moral economy of Islam appears to have made a shift. While Islamic finance has been conceptualized as comprising two arms of equal importance – the profitable and the charitable – experience tells a different narrative. The commercial arm is construed as the arm of Islamic finance; the charitable that of social justice, falling within the realm of welfare and social activism. This is certainly not the purpose of the injunctions in the Qur'an, where both arms are meant to work in tandem.

[148] M. Asutay, 'Conceptualising and Locating the Social Failure of Islamic Finance: Aspirations of Islamic Moral Economy vs the Realities of Islamic Finance', *Asian and African Studies* 11(2) (2012), 93–113.

5

Muslim Women's Contributions to Drafting CEDAW: An Untold Narrative

5.1 Introduction

One of the most challenging encounters between Islamic and international human rights law comes in the shape of women's human rights. This can be clearly seen in the ratification process of the United Nations Convention on the Elimination of All Forms of Discrimination against Women (CEDAW). The treaty, adopted by the General Assembly of the United Nations on 18 December 1979,[1] has been hailed as an international bill of women's rights and is the most comprehensive treaty in the field,[2] with 188 ratifications.[3] But it is also the treaty that, upon signature and ratification, attracted the largest number of reservations from states.[4] Amongst those states entering reservations, some Muslim states specifically mentioned Islam and Islamic law as their reasons,[5] whilst others did not invoke religious grounds.[6] A third group of Muslim states ratified CEDAW without entering any reservations at all, or entered reservations to Article 29 alone,[7] whilst a fourth group (Iran and Somalia) have neither signed

---

[1] Adopted by UN General Assembly Resolution 34/180 (1979).

[2] E. Y. Krivenko, *Women, Islam and International Law: Within the Context of the Convention on the Elimination of All Forms of Discrimination against Women* (Leiden: Martinus Nijhoff, 2009), p. 43, describes CEDAW as 'the most progressive and comprehensive among existing international treaties dealing with women's human rights'. That is not to say that CEDAW has not been critiqued for its 'silences', including the omission of violence against women.

[3] As of April 2014, the latest state party being Palestine.

[4] A list of reservations is available at un.org/womenwatch/daw/cedaw/reservations-country.htm.

[5] Bahrain, Bangladesh, Brunei, Egypt, Iraq, Kuwait, Libya, Malaysia, the Maldives, Mauritania, Morocco, Oman, Pakistan, Saudi Arabia, Syria and the UAE have expressly mentioned Islamic law and *sharia* as reasons for entering reservations to substantive provisions. I have used membership of the OIC at the time of the drafting of CEDAW as the criterion for inclusion as a Muslim state. Israel, too, reserved on the basis of religion, specifically 'concerning the appointment of women to serve as judges of religious courts where this is prohibited by the laws of any of the religious communities in Israel', and 'to the extent that the laws on personal status which are binding on the various religious communities in Israel do not conform with the provisions' of one article.

[6] Algeria, Jordan, Niger, Tunisia and Turkey have entered reservations on the basis of national laws.

[7] Indonesia, Mauritius and Yemen have reserved on Article 29 (on dispute resolution), but not on any of the substantive provisions. Afghanistan, Albania, Azerbaijan, Benin, Bosnia–Herzegovina, Burkina Faso, Chad, the Comoros, Côte d'Ivoire, Djibouti, Gabon, Gambia, Guyana, Guinea, Guinea Bissau, Kyrgyzstan, Lebanon, Mozambique, Mali, Palestine,

nor ratified the treaty. In keeping with the interpretative plurality of the Islamic legal traditions, there is little uniformity in the positions adopted by Muslim states towards CEDAW, in the articles reserved, or indeed in the text of those reservations.

Literature on CEDAW in relation to Muslim states has focused almost entirely on their reservations,[8] with sparse critical engagement with the drafting processes of CEDAW and interventions made by representatives of Muslim states during the deliberations. Little is mentioned of the positive role played by delegates of Muslim states in including a developmental perspective on women's human rights in collaboration with other states from the developing South. This has led to the impression, as Waltz states with reference to the drafting processes of the Universal Declaration on Human Rights (UDHR), the International Covenant on Civil and Political Rights, and the International Covenant on Economic, Social and Cultural Rights, that, 'Frequently, it is supposed that Muslim states were either absent, fundamentally contested the process and project, or played no significant role. That is not the case.'[9]

The present chapter contributes to filling this gap in the literature by linking the inputs of delegates from Muslim states during the drafting process to the subsequent reservations entered by their governments. More specifically, it seeks to bring to the fore the active contribution of delegates of Muslim states who

---

Senegal, Sierra Leone, Sudan, Surinam, Tajikistan, Togo, Turkmenistan, Uzbekistan and Uganda have not entered reservations.

[8] B. Clark, 'The Vienna Convention Reservations Regime and the Convention on Discrimination against Women', *American Journal of International Law* 85 (1991), 281; A. E. Mayer, *Islam and Human Rights: Tradition and Politics*, 3rd edition (Boulder, CO: Westview Press, 1999); J. Resnik, 'Comparative Inequalities: CEDAW, the Jurisdiction of Gender, and the Heterogeneity of Transnational Law Production', *International Journal of Constitutional Law* 10(2) (2012), 531–50; L. R. Pruitt, 'Migration, Development, and the Promise of CEDAW for Rural Women', *Michigan Journal of International Law* 30 (2009), 707, does refer to discussions in the drafting process but without focussing on Muslim states; F. Raday, 'Gender and Democratic Citizenship: The Impact of CEDAW', *International Journal of Constitutional Law* 10(2) (2012), 512–30; M. A. Freeman, C. Chinkin and B. Rudolf (eds.), *The UN Convention on the Elimination of All Forms of Discrimination against Women: A Commentary* (Oxford: Oxford University Press, 2013); E. Sepper, 'Confronting the "Sacred and Unchangeable": The Obligation to Modify Cultural Patterns under the Women's Discrimination Treaty', in S. Kouvo and Z. Pearson (eds.), *Gender and International Law* (Abingdon: Routledge, 2014), pp. 169–212. My own doctoral research (and some subsequent work) too has focussed on CEDAW reservations by Muslim states: see Ali, *Gender and Human Rights*; S. S. Ali (ed.), *Conceptualising Islamic Law: CEDAW and Women's Human Rights in Plural Legal Settings: A Comparative Analysis of the Application of CEDAW in Bangladesh, India and Pakistan* (Delhi: UNIFEM Regional Office, 2006), p. 245.

[9] S. Waltz, 'Universal Human Rights: The Contribution of Muslim States', *Human Rights Quarterly* 6(4) (2004), 801. Waltz's is the most prominent contribution to the literature on Muslim states in the drafting of the Universal Declaration of Human Rights. There are synergies between Waltz's work and the present chapter, which takes forward her suggestion of looking into records of other human rights treaty-drafting processes. The exception to her statement is in the form of a book on the *travaux préparatoires* of CEDAW, which is not the same as an analytical account of Muslim states' interventions. See L. A. Rehof, *Guide to the* Travaux Préparatoires *of the United Nations Convention on the Elimination of All Forms of Discrimination against Women* (International Studies in Human Rights 29) (Dordrecht: Martinus Nijhoff, 1993); also Freeman, Chinkin and Rudolf, *The UN Convention*, whose commentary on each article refers to its *travaux*.

went beyond their assigned roles to advance women's rights. Muslim (women) delegates were present not simply as 'passive witnesses' but as active participants – negotiating, challenging and contributing. Despite their ideological, political, cultural and religious diversity, their role was part of a complex and multi-layered process of diplomacy, alliance-making and consensus-building.

The chapter is presented in four parts: the first problematizes the relationship between Islamic and international human rights law; the second provides an overview of the drafting processes of CEDAW, and Muslim delegates' interventions and contributions; the third links the reservations of Muslim states to their inputs during the drafting process; and the final part offers some concluding reflections.

5.2 Problematizing the Relationship between Islamic Law and International Human Rights Law

Much water has flowed under the bridge in terms of human rights discourse since the 1970s when CEDAW was drafted, and the entire spectrum of arguments need not be rehearsed here. Nevertheless, it is useful to engage with some of the questions and challenges surrounding Islamic and international human rights law by way of informing a discussion on the input of Muslim states' delegates to the drafting process.

In the opening lines of *Human Rights, Southern Voices*, William Twining expresses the need for an inclusive understanding and conceptualization of human rights:

> A just international order and a healthy cosmopolitan discipline of law need to include perspectives that take account of the standpoints, interests, concerns, and beliefs of non-Western people and traditions. The dominant Western scholarly and activist discourse on human rights has developed largely without reference to these other standpoints and traditions. Claims about universality sit uneasily with ignorance of other traditions and parochial or ethnocentric tendencies.[10]

Increasingly, international law is perceived as contested space where blurred boundaries between law and politics often result only in the watered-down, mediated formulations finally signed up to by states[11] – what Martti Koskenniemi describes as 'an aspect of hegemonic contestation, a technique of articulating political claims in terms of legal rights and duties'.[12] The *making* of international human rights law exemplifies this contestation both during the drafting process and upon ratification through reservations and objections. A

---

[10] W. Twining, *Human Rights, Southern Voices: Francis Deng, Abdullahi An-Na'im, Yash Ghai, and Upendra Baxi* (Cambridge: Cambridge University Press, 2009), p. 1.

[11] K. Kavanaugh, 'Narrating Law', in A. M. Emon, M. Ellis and B. Glahn (eds.), *Islamic Law and International Human Rights Law: Searching for Common Ground?* (Oxford: Oxford University Press, 2010), p. 17.

[12] M. Koskenniemi, 'International Law and Hegemony: A Reconfiguration', *Cambridge Review of International Affairs* 17(2) (2004), 197, cited in Kavanaugh, 'Narrating Law', p. 17.

persistent theme in the abundant literature is whether human rights treaties reflect norms that are universal, that are West-centric, or that are even out-right expressions of hegemonic imposition upon the post-colonial non-West.[13] Comparatively rare in the English-language literature are 'Southern voices' presenting non-Western perspectives on human rights.[14]

In the context of the present inquiry, the debate over divergence/convergence and compatibility/incompatibility between international human rights and other legal systems is of particular relevance. Although much is made of positions adopted by Muslim states regarding their resistance to some human rights treaties on the basis of an asserted incompatibility with Islamic law, little publicity is accorded to Western states that voice incompatibility on the basis of their own national laws and policies.[15] Yet the archival records reveal that, during the CEDAW drafting deliberations,[16] an unstated hierarchy of laws informed *all* delegates' preferences for which text of CEDAW to affirm or contest. Delegates evoked incompatibility with CEDAW on the basis not just of religious law but of secular law besides, with CEDAW ranking below a nation state's secular statutes if it conflicted with these. Against a backdrop of Cold War politics, too, the relationship between the capitalist and socialist blocs was pronounced. Yet both these aspects remain understated in the literature, leaving contestation on the basis of 'religion' (for which read 'Islam') as the main focus of attention, and apparently exculpating entrenched ideological and national constitutional positions. Reservations to CEDAW were anticipated by all states parties engaged in the drafting process. Whilst appreciating the process and the remarkableness of this document on women's rights, they were well aware that many of the provisions would attract reservations from their governments, and this view was not confined to delegates of Muslim states.

Although a rich human rights scholarship presents a wide range of perspectives and opinions, in terms of the discourse on Islamic and international human rights law they fall into two broad categories: those who adopt the compatibility/incompatibility approach, and those who find this distinction equally problematic and who argue for a shift in the way in which the debates are framed. Some scholars who advance the viewpoint that Islamic and international human rights law are incompatible offer historical, philosophical and institutional grounds for their position. Jack Donnelly describes human rights as a 'set of social practices'[17] born out of necessities in the emerging modern societies[18] and not 'a timeless system of essential moral

---

[13] Kavanaugh, 'Narrating Law'.

[14] A valuable contribution to this debate is Twining, *Human Rights, Southern Voices*.

[15] See the discussion below on the archival records of the CEDAW drafting process.

[16] These deliberations took place mainly in New York between 1973 and 1979, when CEDAW was finally adopted.

[17] J. Donnelly, *Universal Human Rights in Theory and Practice* (Ithaca: Cornell University Press, 1989), p. 17.

[18] J. Donnelly, 'Western Perspectives', in E. A. Kolodziej (ed.), *A Force Profonde: The Power, Politics and Promise of Human Rights* (Philadelphia: University of Pennsylvania Press, 2003), p. 31, cited in R. Afshari, 'On Historiography of Human Rights: Reflections on Paul Gordon

principles'.[19] He advances the view that most non-Western cultural and political traditions, 'like the pre-modern west, lacked not only the practice of human
rights, but also the concept ... As for non-western societies, we cannot find
the notion of natural law in Islamic, Indian and Chinese cultural traditions'.[20]
Rhoda Howard, too, has similar views regarding the absence of equal human
rights for all irrespective of social status, these being alien in non-Western
societies and traditions.[21] Bernard Lewis[22] and Daniel Pipes[23] argue that Islam
contradicts modern human rights norms and conventions, reflecting as it does
the norms and conventions of seventh-century Arabia.[24] Ann Elizabeth Mayer
supports the view that Islamic and international human rights schemes have
important points of divergence, especially with regard to women and minority
communities. She is suspicious of Muslim scholars who 'put forward distinctive
Islamic schemes of human rights' and in some cases 'seek to accentuate the formal resemblance between their schemes and the international ones even where
that resemblance is misleading in terms of the actual protection they intend to
provide'.[25]

On the other hand, Lauren,[26] Morsink,[27] Weissbrodt,[28] Strawson, Vasak,[29]
Baderin,[30] and Laqueur and Rubin[31] hold that human rights is a universal
ideology that resonates with both Western and non-Western cultural and

Lauren's *The Evolution of International Human Rights: Visions Seen'*, *Human Rights Quarterly*
29(1) (2007), 1–67.

[19] Cited in Afshari, 'On Historiography of Human Rights', p. 6.   [20] Ibid.

[21] R. Howard, 'Human Rights and the Search for Community', *Journal of Peace Research* 32(1)
(1995), 1–8.

[22] B. Lewis, 'Freedom and Justice in the Modern Middle East', *Foreign Affairs* (May–June 2005),
36.

[23] D. Pipes, 'Cartoons and Islamic Imperialism' (2006), available at danielpipes.org/article/3360.

[24] This view was earlier advanced by A. Pollis and P. Schwab: 'Human Rights: A Western
Construct with Limited Applicability', in Pollis and Schwab (eds.), *Human Rights: Cultural and
Ideological Perspectives* (New York: Praeger, 1979), pp. 1–18.

[25] Mayer, *Islam and Human Rights*, p. 57.

[26] See in particular P. G. Lauren, *The Evolution of International Human Rights: Visions Seen*, 2nd
edition (Philadelphia: University of Pennsylvania Press, 2003); and Afshari's critique 'On
Historiography of Human Rights'.

[27] J. Morsink, *The Universal Declaration of Human Rights: Origins, Drafting and Intent*
(Philadelphia: University of Pennsylvania Press, 1999).

[28] D. Weissbrodt, 'Human Rights: An Historical Perspective', in P. Davies (ed.), *Human Rights*
(London: Routledge, 1988), p. 1.

[29] K. Vasak, 'Toward a Specific International Human Rights Law', in K. Vasak (ed.), *The
International Dimension of Human Rights*, vol. 2 (Westport, CT: Greenwood Press, 1982),
p. 672.

[30] M. A. Baderin, 'Human Rights and Islamic Law: The Myth of Discord', *European Human Rights
Law Review* 2 (2005), 165. For a more detailed exposition of Baderin's views on the subject see
his *International Human Rights and Islamic Law* (New York: Oxford University Press, 2003).

[31] W. Laqueur and B. Rubin (eds.), *The Human Rights Reader* (New York: New American Library,
1979), 1, argue, 'Nor is it true that the idea of human rights is an invention alien to most
non-western cultures and that it has been foisted on a more or less unwilling world. Even if
there were no explicit covenants to that effect in traditional societies in Asia, Africa and Latin
America, the idea of freedom was hardly alien to those civilisations.'

religious traditions. Strawson, for instance, challenges the oft-repeated notion of (human) rights as emanating from a purely Western philosophy and tradition on two grounds: first that the existence of a single, homogeneous, monolithic, 'Western' human rights tradition is highly questionable; and second that the historical and philosophical roots of rights are distinctly discernible in non-Western cultural and religious traditions.[32] Baderin has argued that 'the myth that the sharia is an antithesis to . . . rights has been sustained for so long mainly due to the generalized and confrontational approach often adopted in comparison between Islamic law and international human rights law'.[33]

There is also a category of scholars who believe in the existence of human rights within the Islamic traditions but who vary in the nuances with which their viewpoints are expressed. Abdul Aziz Said, for example, distinguishes between human rights as understood in Western traditions and the 'duty-related or duty-based' human rights understood within the Islamic traditions. He states that Islam is

> a belief system predicated fully upon *Haqq*, which is the Arabic word for [a] right. But *Haqq* is also truth. It is justice. It is duty. It is the word of the Divine. *Haqq* is God. The essential characteristic of human rights in Islam is that they constitute obligations connected with the Divine and derive their force from this connection.[34]

The distinguished Islamic scholar Mohammed Arkoun was of the view that

> Islamic thought always included a discourse on the rights of God and the rights of man (*huquq Allah/huquq adam*), with the former having primacy and priority over the latter . . . the respect of human rights is an aspect of, and a basic condition for, respecting the rights of God.[35]

Again, Abdul Aziz Sachedina in *Islam and the Challenge of Human Rights* presents his own views thus:[36] 'I do not believe that the Universal Declaration can be dismissed outright as merely a product of Western secular philosophy . . . liberal views about human individuality, dignity, and agency are

---

[32] J. Strawson, 'Reflections on the West's Question: "Is there a Human Rights Discourse in Islam?"', paper presented at the Critical Legal Conference, University of Edinburgh, September 8–10, 1995, p. 2.

[33] Baderin, *International Human Rights and Islamic Law*, p. 167.

[34] A. A. Said, 'Precept and Practice of Human Rights in Islam', *Universal Human Rights* 1 (April 1979), 63. As I have said elsewhere, within the Islamic tradition the term *huq* (a 'right'; plural *huqooq*) has always existed and is one that translates with relative ease into the English term 'rights'. Furthermore, that 'right' or 'rights' is the established meaning of the term in Arabic in the sense of a claim right (to use the Hohfeldian classification of rights) is also evident from the use of the term in languages that have drawn on Arabic, for instance Persian, Urdu and Pukhto (although in the Pukhto spoken in Afghanistan *huq* is used to denote 'law'): see Ali, *Gender and Human Rights*, pp. 15–16.

[35] M. Arkoun, *Rethinking Islam: Common Questions, Uncommon Answers* (Boulder, CO: Westview Press, 1994), p. 108.

[36] A. Sachedina, *Islam and the Challenge of Human Rights* (Oxford: Oxford University Press, 2009).

compatible with Islamic revelation.'[37] He believes that there is a need 'to shift the debate over compatibility to investigation of the possibility of seeking legitimacy for the declaration through theological–ethical doctrines that could dispel the sinister attitude that prevails among Muslim religious thinkers toward the document's European pedigree'.[38] He also believes that the 'Qur'an lays down the foundation of theological pluralism that takes the equivalence and equal rights of human beings as a divinely ordained system'.[39] However, adding an important caveat in the context of women's human rights, he acknowledges that

> even the most persuasive arguments against the moral relativism that afflicts human rights discourse at the international level, especially in the Muslim world, have failed to convince the traditionalist Muslim leadership to acknowledge the full citizenship of a woman as a bearer of rights equal to those of a man.[40]

But possibly the most thought-provoking and sophisticated contributions to Islamic and international human rights debates are those of the renowned Islamic scholar Abdullahi Ahmed An-Na'im.[41] Engaging in discourse on the (in)compatibility of Islamic and international human rights norms is in his view unfruitful. He argues that the very manner in which the question of this relationship is framed is flawed and problematic, as it immediately creates a confrontational environment for debate. He writes, 'however, I believe how one's understanding and practice of Islam influence and is influenced by one's commitment to upholding the universality of human rights is a necessary and productive inquiry'.[42] An-Na'im suggests that, whilst in their current formulations international human rights norms are heavily West-centric, this does not preclude a discussion of how they might be transformed into truly universal concepts. For this, he proposes debate and discussion at two levels: intra-community dialogue among Muslims, and inter-community dialogue between Muslims and others, leading to broader consensus. He is clear in his views relating to divergent norms within Islamic and international human rights norms as regards women's and minority rights as well as freedom of religion. However, he does not perceive these as insurmountable divergences incapable of resolution. More recently, An-Na'im has proposed the notion of the secular state enabling religious freedom and protecting human rights.[43]

Agreeing with An-Na'im's position regarding the potential for transforming West-centric human rights into truly universal ones, I suggest that CEDAW

---

[37] Ibid., p. 16.

[38] Ibid., p. 211, note 10. Sachedina goes on to state that this negative attitude has also served as a powerful weapon for Muslim political authorities to deny human rights to their own citizens, especially women and minorities.

[39] Ibid., p. 201.   [40] Ibid., pp. 115–16.

[41] A prolific writer on Islam and human rights, An-Na'im has published numerous monographs, articles and chapters, amongst which stand out *Towards an Islamic Reformation*, *African Constitutionalism*, and *Islam and the Secular State*.

[42] An-Na'im, 'An Inclusive Approach'.

[43] See An-Na'im, *Islam and the Secular State*; and 'The Compatibility Dialectic: Mediating the Legitimate Coexistence of Islamic Law and State Law', *Modern Law Review* 73(1) (2010), 1–29.

provides such an example: by, for instance, acknowledging and protecting the rights of rural women, the concerns of a truly universal constituency of women across the North–South and East–West divides is addressed.[44] Likewise, women's universally accepted right to access health facilities cuts across countries, regions and cultures. The existing literature on CEDAW remains focused on the post-ratification reservations entered by (mainly) Muslim states and the negative implications for women's rights in those jurisdictions.[45] Rehof, for example, remarks that the record of negotiations on the text of CEDAW reveals various geopolitical and philosophical tensions, including the role of religion in society. Many of these issues continue to affect the Convention.[46] Freeman's excellent commentary on CEDAW, drawing upon Rehof's work, describes the *travaux préparatoires* of each substantive article with reference to discussions in drafting committees.[47] However, the input of delegates from Muslim states is not the focus of this commentary, and engagement with archival records of the drafting process remains limited. Both texts provide important background material for the present chapter.

After decades of wrangling over the question whether or not Islam recognizes women's rights, it would perhaps be more pertinent to pose the question thus: do women's rights as enunciated in CEDAW resonate with comparable values within the Islamic legal traditions? This then opens the way to related questions: could a Muslim intra-community dialogue employing the moral and ethical framework of the Qur'an arrive at a notion of women's rights that reflects contemporary understandings of the concept? If there is resistance to women's rights emanating from CEDAW among some Muslim communities, who is articulating it and to what end? Who has the right to engage in this contestation of women's human rights? Is it the privilege of those in positions of power and authority, who are unaware of human suffering? Or, as Baxi proposes, is it those voices of human suffering – including, historically, women and other vulnerable members of communities – who can best create an inclusive discourse of human rights? It is not a matter of whether or not elites in certain societies and communities consider human rights applicable to them; the prior question is whether or not all traditions concede to people the right simply to be human before proceeding to say whether we have human rights, however conceptualized or defined within these traditions. In his essay 'From Human Rights to the Right to be Human: Some Heresies',[48] Baxi alerts us to the need to seek the human rights of all, as opposed to seeking some who are able to enjoy

---

[44] See Article 14 of CEDAW.

[45] No detailed study similar to (for instance) Waltz's analysis of Muslim states' roles in drafting the UDHR and the two covenants has come to light. There is, therefore, little analysis of the drafting processes per se and of what actually transpired in the many meetings.

[46] Cited in Rehof, *Guide to the* Travaux Préparatoires. Also cited in Freeman, Chinkin and Rudolf, *The UN Convention*, p. 413.

[47] Freeman, Chinkin and Rudolf, *The UN Convention*.

[48] U. Baxi, 'From Human Rights to the Right to Be Human: Some Heresies', *India International Centre Quarterly* 13(3–4) (1986), 185–200.

human rights. This, he believes, is a more useful distinction than where these rights come from. He writes of 'the endeavour to conceptualize the right to be human where the antinomy between "needs" and "rights" is dissolved',[49] and believes that 'there is an immeasurable distance between what we call "human rights" and the right of all to be human; that this distance can begin to be traversed only if we claim the audacity to look at human rights models from the standpoint of the historically oppressed groups'.[50] An emerging discourse on human rights, of which Baxi is one of the leading scholars, problematizes the very notion of human rights and argues that, in order for the concept to make sense and be helpful, it ought to be inclusive of, and explored from the perspective of, human suffering.

It is fair to state that the debate over Islamic and international human rights law remains inconclusive and as controversial as ever. So, if human rights in their present formulations are indeed a Western construct, should the non-Western world then simply renounce human rights and withdraw from any discussion on the issue? Or should there be a serious intra- and inter-cultural dialogue to search for what Pannikar terms 'the homeomorphic equivalent' of human rights in diverse cultural and religious traditions?[51] I would like here to submit that human rights concepts as they are currently formulated were not originally present in *any* legal or religious cultural tradition: the concepts of human rights as we see them expressed in covenants and conventions are, historically speaking, 'new' concepts both for the West *and* the non-West. True, they have antecedents in theology, philosophy, culture and religious traditions, but individual human rights as they have come to be conceptualized since the UDHR and other human rights instruments are a new development. Just as Islamic conceptions of human rights are plural, so are those espoused within Western human rights traditions; Western and non-Western legal traditions are both pluralistic in their formulations. How else could we understand the outright refusal of the USA to ascribe to international human rights instruments,[52] or the reservations to CEDAW by the governments of the United Kingdom and France?[53]

So a persuasive approach to truly universalizing human rights norms is to accept the fluidity and evolving nature of human rights, by identifying human suffering and violations and offering support and solidarity. Who would have considered, a couple of centuries ago, that slavery would be universally prohibited as an abominable violation of human rights, despite its (erstwhile) universal presence in all communities, cultures and religious traditions? Likewise, perceptions of women's and minority rights are very different today and continue to change (albeit very slowly): neither violence against women nor the rights of

---

[49]   Ibid., 192.   [50]   Ibid., 199.
[51]   R. Pannikar, 'Is Human Rights a Western Construct?', *Diogenes* 120 (1982), 77.
[52]   The USA has ratified neither CEDAW nor the CRC.
[53]   The UK entered amongst the highest numbers of reservations to CEDAW.

lesbians were raised as burning issues during the CEDAW deliberative process in the 1970s; today, no international women's human rights conference would omit them.

5.3 The CEDAW Drafting Process

CEDAW and the post-ratification position of Muslim states instigated the present enquiry into the intriguing story of the drafting stages of CEDAW. What was the nature of the deliberations, especially the inputs by delegates from Muslim states? And how were these linked up (or not) with subsequent reservations? Despite the overwhelming portrayal by commentators of the reservations process as being negative, static and undermining of the treaty, later developments demonstrate a more nuanced and complex picture. As a result of constructive dialogue and objections entered by other states, parties that had originally entered a wide range of reservations scrutinized them and often withdrew them completely, partially or with modifications.[54] Observation of this development in the jurisprudence of CEDAW raised a question: if the CEDAW reservations regime was dynamic and fluid, with states reconsidering their original positions, was this trend not simply a continuation of the deliberative process at the drafting stage? If so, it would imply that Islamic law as understood by Muslim states is also essentially evolving and responsive to changing contexts, be these national or (as in the case of CEDAW) international.[55]

Within the UN, the Commission on the Status of Women (CSW) is the body tasked with responding to women's rights issues, including taking the lead in drafting women's rights treaties. In 1972, a CSW resolution requested the Secretary General of the UN to call upon member states to transmit their views on or proposals for a possible international convention on women's rights.[56] A working paper on a new instrument was consequently developed, and included views and comments from governments. A working group based on 'equitable

---

[54] Krivenko develops this line of argument in a highly persuasive manner in *Women, Islam and International Law*.

[55] The motivating factors for engaging in archival research into the CEDAW drafting process were many and compelling. As a Muslim female academic and activist who has held public office and represented Pakistan at the UN, the WHO and the Organization of Islamic Cooperation (OIC), the processes and positions informing what might be called 'performances' on the international stage were familiar territory. I was a member of the Pakistani delegation to the Beijing Plus Five sessions at the UN in June 2000. In my capacity as cabinet minister for health, population and women's development in the North West Frontier Province (now Khyber Pukhtunkhwa), I represented Pakistan at the World Health Assembly along with the federal minister for health in May 2001. I led the Pakistani delegation to the OIC meeting on the role of women in Muslim societies held in Tehran in June 1995, and was a member of the Pakistani delegation in the OIC conference on Muslim women parliamentarians held in Islamabad in August 1995. With the insights of a participant in and observer of similar forums, I have been fascinated by the fluidity, the shifting positions and the flexibility (as well as rigidity) of processes and positions and wanted to explore CEDAW's drafting with these in mind.

[56] Resolution 5 (XXIV) of the Commission on the Status of Women.

geographical distribution' was set up to look at the draft treaty.[57] In all, four working groups were set up during the drafting process, starting in 1973 and ending with the adoption of CEDAW in December of 1979. In all these forums, delegates from Muslim states were active participants in the drafting process, as is obvious from the records. In 1976, the CSW presented its draft to the General Assembly. This draft was discussed article by article in the Third Committee of the General Assembly, after which it was adopted.

As to the physical records of the drafting process, these are located in the UN library in the Palais des nations in Geneva. Some of the materials were lost in transit from New York to Geneva – a limitation this research (and others) is subject to. The records of what was said are, sadly, not verbatim but instead concise and rather sanitized. Tone of voice, facial expression and body language are, of course, all lacking, yet some statements nevertheless spring to life on the page, offering insights into the atmosphere and environment within which the drafting took place.

Drafting treaties is a complex and time-consuming process, not least due to the effort and perseverance required to arrive at a consensus. Especially demanding is the effort needed to instil certain aspirational and standard-setting norms within human rights treaties beyond what delegates believe their respective governments will sign up to. Thus they consciously strive for a forward-looking model of human rights 'without prejudice to national positions', and this approach indeed comes across in the records of the various drafting meetings of CEDAW. It is perhaps due to this deliberately aspirational stance on the part of delegates that there appears to be a disjuncture between the text and the reservations later entered on the basis of national and religious interests. This perhaps also partially answers the oft-posed question: given that there was such an active participation by delegates of Muslim states throughout the drafting process, why did those same states enter such far-reaching reservations?

Law-making as a process speaks to its times and is born of multiple narratives, and the drafting of CEDAW was no exception. Socio-economic, religious, political and ideological posturing evidently contribute to a treaty during its drafting as well as after its adoption, and in the context of the present inquiry this was manifested through the wider capitalist/socialist polarity, since CEDAW was drafted at the height of the Cold War. Divisions were also visible in those developed and developing countries' concerns and priorities under the umbrella of the burgeoning 'non-aligned' movement, as well as in the positions adopted by Muslim states. Krivenko has noted that the process and circumstances of the adoption of CEDAW were characterized by two main tendencies:

---

[57] At its 1,856–1,875th meetings, the Economic and Social Council (ECOSOC) elected fifteen members: Canada, Chile, Colombia, the Dominican Republic, Egypt, Finland, Hungary, Indonesia, Liberia, Nigeria, the Philippines, the USSR, the USA, the UK and Zaire (E/CN. 6/573).

Firstly, when the idea about a convention on women appeared, there were many voices arguing that such a convention would be unnecessary and superfluous. When it nevertheless came to the negotiation of such a convention this tendency had been transformed into an ideological and religious confrontation and, therefore, a need to use 'constructive ambiguity' in formulating the terms of the future convention.[58]

The second tendency came to the fore when ECOSOC declared 1975 to be International Women's Year and the General Assembly declared a 'UN Decade for Women: Equality, Development and Peace 1976–1985', raising the pressure to draft and adopt CEDAW. As a consequence, some controversial questions were put aside or left ambiguous in the text, leading to reservations by some states parties.

As the evidence from the UN archives began to build up, a number of observations began to crystallize and a number of questions arose. For instance, it became apparent that certain conceptual disparities were arising from translation to and from the various languages of the delegates, leading to some confusion, debate and division during the drafting; was there, then, a common cultural/linguistic understanding of what constituted ideas such as 'equality' or 'non-discrimination'? And did delegates adopt radically different positions on equality, e.g. equity and diversity as opposed to equality and sameness? Was there a predetermined 'script' prescribing a predetermined path for the various provisions, or were there genuine discussions and attempts to understand varying perspectives and positions?[59] Most importantly, were the deliberations during the drafting process indicative of the struggle between 'universalist' and 'relativist' approaches to human rights? If so, did such relativity emanate only from Muslim delegates (in the name of 'Islamic' values), or was a universality of norms and rights also questioned on ideological and political grounds?

It is important to bear in mind that these divisions were not mutually exclusive but presented a complex tapestry of overlapping alignments as well as adversarial groupings. The drafting process as recorded evokes a picture of mixed and evolving norms rather than of fixed and static positions. While one session might be characterized by developing states aligning themselves against developed states, in another we see Muslim states disagreeing among themselves, and in yet another broader groupings coalesce across the capitalist/socialist or Muslim/non-Muslim divides.[60]

---

58 Krivenko, *Women, Islam and International Law*, p. 22. At note 77 she perceptively observes the 'two lines of confrontation at the time of elaboration of CEDAW: firstly between socialist and Western states and secondly between Islamic and Western and socialist states. Nowadays, the former line of confrontation has disappeared almost completely thereby reinforcing the latter line of confrontation'.

59 I am grateful to Elisabetta Grande for her comments on an initial version of this chapter, which was presented at the (Not) Outside My Culture: The paradoxes of Personal Autonomy in a Plural Society' conference, Max Planck Institute, May 2014, and for alerting me to these questions.

60 See the analysis of the discussions below.

5.3.1 The Muslim Delegates in the Drafting Process

A notable and possibly surprising aspect of the CEDAW drafting process is that (except for the occasional male delegate stepping in to cover a meeting) all the delegates to the UN Commission on the Status of Women, including all those hailing from Muslim states, were themselves women.[61] Had there been a strategic decision on the part of Muslim states to overturn stereotypical assumptions about Muslim women? Given that these were nations spread across several continents, it must be more than coincidental that their delegates were all female, yet it must be assumed that there was no formal prior agreement that this would be the case. Much more likely is that these were the most suitable candidates for the roles, chosen for their competence and with an expertise and passion for human rights and women's rights. There is little doubt that these were outstanding, well-informed, vocal and competent women, steeped in their own cultural and religious contexts as well as in issues of international law. They came across as astute professionals, realistic as well as aspirational in their inputs, prepared to defend their corner but also to leave doors open for future developments. They demonstrated an admirable rootedness in their local contexts and were prepared to voice their concerns regarding formulations of CEDAW that they believed would endanger ratification and acceptance within their communities. They sought to express the diverse positions and contexts of women as well as the constraints under which they operated in their respective societies.

Reading through records of the many meetings of the drafting committees and working groups, some Muslim women stand out in their interventions. These include Mrs Esfandiari of Iran, Begum Tazeen Faridi of Pakistan, Mrs Tallawy and Mrs Aziza Hussein of Egypt, Mrs Gueye of Senegal, and Ms Salyo of Indonesia. The contributions of Miss Kamila Tyabji of India were striking and counterintuitive on three counts: she was a Muslim representing a nation where Muslims only formed around 10 per cent of the population, her interventions did not evoke Islam or Islamic law, and she adopted a position based in secular women's rights activism. Her presence and interventions on such a public platform reflected such various possibilities of what it might mean to be 'a Muslim woman'. The same is true of Senegal's Mrs Gueye, who made some highly perceptive interventions during the drafting process, guided primarily by her desire to draft a strong treaty to advance women's rights yet without alluding to Islam or Islamic law.[62]

---

[61] Susan Waltz is quite right when she states that UN delegates hailing from Muslim states, including those assigned to the drafting processes of human rights treaties, were mostly women (Waltz, 'Universal Human Rights', p. 829). They were Mrs Shaista Ikramullah and Mrs Aziz Ahmed (Pakistan), Bedia Afnan (Iraq) and Halima Embarek Warzazi (Morocco), whose names appear in the summary records of drafting meetings of the Universal Declaration of Human Rights, the International Covenant on Civil and Political Rights, and the International Covenant on Economic, Social and Cultural Rights.

[62] A paper based on this chapter was presented as a keynote address of the Annual Conference of the British Association of Islamic Studies, London, April 2015, and I was asked why I was only

As mentioned earlier, the archival material is incomplete, and this leaves gaps when piecing together a complete story. More importantly, though, after forty years have passed, accessing complete biographical details for all the Muslim delegates proved an insuperable challenge. Sadly some of the delegates have passed away, but their obituaries do shed light on their lives and backgrounds.

Mrs Aziza Hussein of Egypt, for example, was born in 1919 in Zefta, Gharbia Governorate, and graduated from the American University of Cairo. She set up a centre for rural women and was the first Egyptian female member of the UN delegation to address the General Assembly. Her work in creating awareness of Egypt's population problem and the needs of women, and her establishment of women's clinics, were key to the establishment of a formal population policy in 1966, a Family Planning Association in 1967, and changes in family law in 1979. India's Miss Kamila Tyabji (1918–2004) was the daughter of India's chief justice and studied at St Xavier's College, Bombay, and St Hugh's College, Oxford, where she read law as a contemporary of Indira Gandhi. She is thought to have been the first Muslim woman to go to Oxford. Called to the Bar in London, she established a law practice and was the first woman to argue a case before the Privy Council. Rather than marrying ('All the men are too frightened of me', she once said), she formed a loose-knit commune of upper-class intellectuals. She returned to India in 1965 during the Bihar famine and was highly critical of inadequate bureaucracy, which she saw as the result of bumbling male planning. She turned her attention to the development of women's power and established the Women's India Trust to support underprivileged women in earning a living.[63] Mrs Tazeen Faridi (1920–2010) of the Pakistani delegation was from a similarly august political background, being the daughter of Begum Inam Habibullah (former president of the Women's League of the Muslim League, founder of the Taleemgah Niswan educational society for minority women, founder member of Delhi's Lady Irwin College, and general political activist). Mrs Faridi enjoyed a long and distinguished career (including the presidency of the All Pakistan Women's Association, vice presidency of the International Council of Women, and a ministry post in Sindh overseeing social welfare) and was awarded a number of prestigious honours by the government of Pakistan. It is clear, then, that these were not women who had been chosen on the strength of the likelihood of their being submissive to patriarchal political or religious norms.

5.3.2 Themes Arising from Muslim Delegates' Interventions and Contributions

Despite the acknowledged gaps in the records, a fairly detailed picture of the discussions nevertheless emerges. As touched upon above, to judge from the

referring to a few Muslim delegates: the working groups set up to draft CEDAW were composed of representatives of various regions and legal systems, and at any given time only around one-third of delegates were from Muslim countries.

[63] *The Guardian*, 15 June 2004, obituaries.

subsequent academic literature on the reservations entered by states, it would seem as if most of the discussions in the drafting sessions had been generated by Muslim delegates arguing against provisions on the basis of their incompatibility with Islamic laws.[64] Furthermore, if we were to judge solely from the objections of Western states to reservations entered by Muslim states, it would appear as if those Western states were a homogeneous entity, in complete agreement with CEDAW's substantive provisions and keen advocates of them. But the archival records tell a far more complex story and show that such a narrow focus fails to capture the true nature of the process. The drafting of CEDAW was certainly not a matter of secular, Western human rights values pitted against the entrenched religious traditions and laws of Muslim nations desperate to uphold patriarchal norms. In fact, the nations of the non-Muslim world were more than capable of bringing their own entrenched positions, legal hierarchies and global alliances to the table, while Muslim delegates were more than capable of pressing for women's rights.

5.3.3 The Minimal Discussion of Islamic Law

The most surprising finding from the archival records was the absolutely minimal discussion of Islamic law during the CEDAW drafting process. Contrary to the expectations raised by the existing literature on CEDAW, even mentions of Islamic law, *sharia* and religion were few and far between. Conscious that this observation goes against the existing narrative, I set about to collect and to reproduce below all interventions alluding to those ideas made during the drafting process according to the relevant accessible documents (some three dozen in total, including various draft texts of CEDAW, written interventions by states and UN specialized agencies, NGO submissions, and so on).[65]

Between 21 October and 2 December 1977, twelve meetings of the Third Committee were held to discuss the Report of the Working Group of the Whole on the Drafting of the UN Convention on the Elimination of Discrimination against Women.[66] This report presented an article-by-article account of the drafting process thus far, including interventions, objections and reservations made by various states. Records of these meetings show the active participation of delegates of Muslim states, yet not once were 'religion', 'Islam', 'Islamic law' or '*sharia*' invoked.[67] Of the numerous meetings of the CSW and discussions in

---

[64] Along with a mention of Cold War politics and the capitalist/socialist divide. Yet existing literature does not go into any great depth regarding the impact of the Cold War divisions on the drafting of CEDAW.

[65] Those records with no mention of Islamic law included A/C.3/32/L.59; E/CN.6/SR.632; E/CN.6/SR.638; E/CN.6/SR.640; E/CN.6/SR.642; E/CN.6/SR.649; E/CN.6/SR.651; E/CN.6/SR.652; E/CN.6/SR.658; E/CN.6/SR.672; E/CN.6/SR.673; E/CN.6/SR.674; and E/CN.6/SR.679.

[66] A/C.3/32/L.59, dated 6 December 1977.   [67] See ibid.

the General Assembly, six documents recorded mention of Islamic law and/or religion by delegates of Muslim states.[68]

The first reference to 'religion' (i.e. Islam) was in the summary records discussing a draft text of Article 2.[69] Mrs Esfandiari of Iran stated that

> in principle, she could accept the text of draft article 2. However, as Iran was not a secular state, some of the provisions of the new text were not consistent with certain Iranian laws dealing with religion. Were these provisions to be applied, it would first be necessary to amend Iran's civil legislation.[70]

Religion is cited as the reason for disagreement with the draft text, but within the context of national legislation based on Islamic law, rather than of Islamic law per se. No other Muslim delegate made an intervention in the debate on the basis of religion, a pattern followed throughout the drafting process, where Muslim states adopted varying positions on draft articles. This is quite contrary to the situation at the time of ratification, where a number of Muslim states entered reservations to Article 2 on the basis of Islamic law and *sharia* (see below).

The next reference came during discussions on Article 9, relating to the equal nationality rights of men and women and the equal rights of women to transmit nationality to their children. One came from the Pakistani delegate, who asserted a Muslim woman's right to 'custody of her children in accordance with her personal law' ('personal law' here indicating Islamic law) as supportive of the article.[71] A further reference to 'religion' came from the Iraqi delegate, who believed that Article 9 violated her religious teachings and the laws of Iraq prohibiting marriages between Iraqi officials and non-Arab foreigners.[72] It is pertinent to note that, in contrast to Iraq's opposition on the basis of religion, all other states participating in the protracted deliberations on Article 9 mentioned their national laws as reasons for not being able to support various proposed formulations; these included (in the various committees) the Netherlands, Japan, Italy, Barbados, Chad, Norway, Mali, Syria, Canada, France, Guinea, Greece, Afghanistan, Argentina, Ethiopia, the USSR (Byelorussian SSR), the UK and the US. Yet in the existing literature on CEDAW the fact that all Western and other non-Muslim states were privileging their national laws over international law is made invisible, leading to a very selective reading of history. What is represented as history is that one Muslim state mentioned 'religion' as well as its national laws, which single fact has become a generalized statement applicable to all Muslim states during the CEDAW drafting process.[73] A possible reason for this generalization from a selective fact might be the tendency of some Muslim delegates to conflate the concepts of Islamic law, *sharia* and the national

---

[68] A/32/218; E/CN.6/573; E/CN.6/591; E/CN.6/606; E/CN.6/SR.642; E/CN.6/SR.650.

[69] E/CN.6/SR.642, p. 10.   [70] Ibid.   [71] E/CN.6/606.   [72] E/CN.6/591.

[73] This assertion is supported by the drafting history presented in Rehof, *Guide to the* Travaux Préparatoires, pp. 103–9.

laws and constitutions of Muslim states (as in, for instance, the cases of Iraq and Iran cited above).

A third set of references came about during the drafting of Article 15, relating to the legal capacity of women. Mrs Hussein of Egypt said that she

> would accept the text of article 15 . . . but she wished to make a reservation with respect to the provisions in paragraph 4, which was inconsistent with her country's legislation. Egyptian law, being based on Islamic law, required a woman to follow her husband and to have the same domicile. The law, however, was being revised and she would therefore not oppose the provisions of that paragraph.[74]

In common with her Iranian counterpart's observations on an earlier article, Mrs Hussein, too, used her country's legislation 'based on Islamic law' as her reason for expressing her reservation. Yet it is important to note the ambivalence in her observation: she leaves the door open for accepting CEDAW by referring to future legal developments in her country that she anticipates as *consistent* with provisions of CEDAW. Further, she implicitly portrays the very nature of Islamic law as dynamic, and susceptible to change and development. How else could one explain the flexibility of a 'religious' law that is otherwise perceived as immutable and unchangeable? Mrs Salyo of Indonesia, meanwhile, stated that

> in her country, where the majority of the population was Muslim, the law similarly restricted a wife's freedom to choose her residence. But Indonesian legislation provided that the residence should be decided by joint agreement between husband and wife and not by the husband alone. She was therefore able to accept article 15.[75]

Her interpretation of Islamic law varied from that of her Egyptian colleague, in that whilst there are still restrictions on the wife choosing her residence unilaterally, joint agreement is required by Indonesian law, which is based on Islamic law. The Iranian delegate, however, aligned herself with Egypt: 'under Iranian civil law which was based on Islamic law, women did not have the right of free movement and choice of residence'.[76] There is an important distinction between 'Islamic law' and 'civil law . . . based on Islamic law', yet the statement is read as though the two ideas are the same or, at the very least, similar. Pakistan's Mrs Faridi, on the other hand, did not consider the text of this paragraph as being contrary either to her country's laws or to her understandings of Islamic law, making the simple intervention that 'her delegation accepted article 15'.[77] This discussion, too, betrays the dynamic and plural nature of Islamic law. How else could one explain the flexibility of a 'religious' law that is otherwise perceived as immutable and unchangeable? In the end, despite these reservations and nuanced differences, *all* the representatives of Muslim states present accepted the text of the draft article.

---

[74] E/CN.6/SR.650, p. 2.   [75] Ibid., p. 3.   [76] Ibid., p. 5.   [77] Ibid., p. 6.

A final set of references to Islamic law were made during deliberations on the text of Article 16. The Egyptian delegate felt that matters such as inheritance and dissolution of the marriage contract must give consideration to the family law of various states, which 'respect religious provisions which are closely connected with the faith and belief of nations'.[78] The Pakistani delegate, Mrs Faridi, stated that her agreement to the original wording of the article was 'subject to the Constitution of Pakistan, which was based on Islamic law'.[79] Bahrain expressed reservations regarding the equal responsibilities of parents towards their children, 'whether married or not', since this ran counter to 'Islamic law', which penalized relationships outside marriage.[80] At the CSW meeting held on 28 September 1976, nevertheless, when a draft of Article 16 was put to the vote it was adopted by twenty-one votes in favour and none against, with Egypt and the US abstaining. However, subsequent writing on Article 16 presents its drafting as witness to a 'West–Islam' divide. In actual fact, all Muslim states except Egypt voted in favour of adoption, as did all Western and non-Muslim states except the US.

5.3.4 Moving beyond Traditional Islamic Family Law and a Predetermined Script

The archival records show that there was not one sole, predetermined script with which delegates drafting CEDAW were engaged. Instead, a number of drafts were submitted by different states or groups of states: a draft presented by the Philippines,[81] followed by a second prepared by the USSR, stated themselves to be based mainly upon the Declaration on the Elimination of Discrimination against Women.[82] A third draft emerged, prepared in common by the Philippines and the USSR,[83] followed by a draft that became known as the 'alternative' text, based on amendments of that third draft. This alternative text was put together by representatives of Egypt, Finland, the UK and the US, and a representative of the International Labour Organization. There was also the working paper prepared by the UN Secretary General on the basis of inputs and replies received from states, NGOs and international organizations and specialized agencies of the UN.[84] Other drafts and working papers too were floated, reflective of various amendments suggested at various meetings. Delegates to the drafting process did not feel restrained by one single text, and proposed a variety of formulations. And so another fascinating fact that emerges from the materials, therefore, is that the delegates of Muslim states, true to their

[78] E/CN.6/573, para. 73.
[79] E/CN.6/591, para. 156. She also explained that Pakistan had abstained from the vote on Article 16 as a whole because 'the Pakistan Committee which was considering the rights of women had not yet submitted its report'.
[80] A/32/218, para. 127.   [81] UN Doc. E/CN.6/573/Annex 1 of 6 November 1973.
[82] UN Doc. E/CN.6/AC.1/L.2 of 7 January 1974.
[83] UN Doc. E/CN.6-/AC.1/L.4 of 8 January 1974.   [84] UN Doc. E.CN.6/591 of 21 July 1976.

backgrounds in feminist activism, moved well beyond any predetermined 'script' as initially placed on the negotiating table. This they did on two levels: first by challenging traditional conceptions of Islamic family law, and second by presenting counterproposals reflecting the particularities of their own cultural contexts. These included proposals regarding setting a minimum age for marriage, family planning and women's rights to education.

The first challenge came in the form of robust interventions to ensure that Article 16 expressly prohibited child marriages in the strongest possible terms. They proposed that states be required to set a minimum age for marriage and that, as a protective measure, registration of marriage be made compulsory. Within traditional conceptions of Islamic family law, as well as in Muslim cultural contexts, puberty has long been considered as the minimum age for marriage, and this has led to an acceptance of what can reasonably be considered the marriage of children. Spurred on by cultural practices in Asia, the Middle East and Africa, child marriages remain one of the most undermining for women's personal development and empowerment. Colonial rulers attempted to eliminate the practice through legislation, but with minimal success.[85] Local reformers and human rights activists later adopted a different perspective and raised it as a health issue, but popular perceptions of its permissibility on cultural and religious grounds meant that the practice continued.

Yet during the drafting of CEDAW, and especially in the CSW, all delegates of Muslim states adopted a unified stance against child marriages. Mrs Hussein stated forcefully that she 'should make clear that child marriages were prohibited' in Egypt.[86] Mrs Faridi of Pakistan, too, was firm in her position: 'in tropical countries where puberty often occurred at an early age, it was of the greatest importance to set a minimum legal age for marriage. Pakistan had had great difficulty in introducing such a minimum and now wished to raise it'.[87] Delegates who were not shy in using Islamic law to defend positions on certain formulations during the drafting process displayed a vigour and enthusiasm for moving beyond traditional understandings of the minimum age for marriage by seeking to raise it. Interestingly, the unanimity among the delegates of Muslim states on this point was not replicated in their respective national laws, where the minimum age of marriage varied with the ideological position of the regime in power.[88]

---

[85] For instance in India, where British colonial rule adopted the Child Marriages Restraint Act 1929.

[86] E/CN.6.SR.651, para. 50.   [87] Ibid., para. 55.

[88] Prior to the 1979 revolution, Article 1049 of the Civil Code of Iran prescribed the minimum age for marriage as fifteen for girls and eighteen for boys. This was amended in 1991 thus: 'Marriage before reaching the age of puberty is prohibited. Note: A contract of marriage before reaching puberty is valid if authorized by the natural guardian provided that the interest of the ward has been taken into consideration.' By an amendment to Article 1210 in 1991, the age of puberty was stated as nine full lunar years for girls and fifteen full lunar years for boys. By an amendment in the Civil Code, minimum age at marriage has been set at thirteen and fifteen respectively (*The Civil Code of Iran* (trans. Taleghany) (Littleton, CO: Fred B. Rothman & Co.,

The next challenge regarded family planning, which according to some inter-pretations is not permitted in Islam.[89] The delegates of Muslim states supported the proposal made by the Indian delegate. Ms Tyabji (herself a Muslim woman, though not speaking from an Islamic perspective) called for the 'equal rights of men and women to decide freely and responsibly on the number and spacing of their children and to have access to the information, education and means to enable them to exercise this right'.[90] Mrs Hussein (who, to judge from the record, made the highest number of interventions evoking Islamic law) gave her unequivocal support to Ms Tyabji's proposals on women's reproductive rights, stating that she 'approved the text proposed by the representative of India, which filled a gap in the Declaration on the Elimination of Discrimination Against Women'.[91] The records indicate similar support from delegates of all other Muslim states.[92]

5.3.5 Solidarity of Ideas across the Ideological Divides

The focus thus far has been on inputs to the 'script' by delegates of Muslim states as a challenge *to* or *from* a pluralist Islamic law tradition. But alongside this observation, it is also important to report those times where Islamic law was *not* invoked, in order to demonstrate the broader world view of Muslim state *practice* as evidenced in the contributions of their delegates. This is critical if we are to break the stereotypical perception that Muslim states always adopted positions by invoking 'Islamic' perspectives. The sheer weight of evidence from the drafting process provides a far more complex picture, testifying to active participation *without* reference to Islam.

One of the most pronounced themes to emerge during the CEDAW drafting process was the sense of solidarity amongst delegates across religious, cultural, ideological and political divides with the common aim of adopting a robust women's rights treaty. CEDAW's long preamble is one example,[93] distinctive in that it recalls the broad historical, economic, political and social factors contributing to discrimination against women, with mention of colonialism,

1995)). In Pakistan, the Child Marriages Restraint Act 1929 and the Muslim Family Laws Ordinance 1961 prescribe sixteen as the minimum age of marriage for girls, and the same is prescribed by Egyptian law. Saudi Arabian law sets seventeen as the minimum age for the marriage of girls.

[89] There is no clear Qur'anic injunction in this regard, and those arguing that Islam permits contraception as well as those who believe it prohibits it tease out meanings to support their stance. Those who argue in favour cite the permission of the Prophet Muhammad for *coitus interruptus*, while those against believe that the duty to increase the Muslim population and not to prevent a human being from coming into the world runs against family planning.

[90] E/CN.6/SR.650, para. 104.　　[91] Ibid., para. 106.

[92] Ibid. It is interesting that, this point having been agreed on, a reversal was sought at the 1994 International Conference on Population and Development through an alliance of self-proclaimed Muslim clergy and the Catholic Church! My thanks to Shirin Rai for highlighting this.

[93] It is fully twice the length of that to the UDHR.

apartheid, imperialism and other factors one would not necessarily expect to find in a women's rights treaty. For example, the preamble speaks eloquently to the alliances fostered among former colonized states, irrespective of the ideological, political or religious differences between and among them, since, despite the opposition of Western states to the inclusion of such references, the numerically advantaged non-Western states, supported by China, the USSR and others, were able to win out.[94] Another factor in making this contested preamble possible was the fact that, in addition to the Cold War's alignment of nations into capitalist and socialist camps, the developing South was during the 1970s positioning itself under the umbrella of the non-aligned movement and making claims to rights and resources. In numerical terms, a combination of socialist, developing and non-aligned states outnumbered the capitalist/Western bloc.

Women from diverse backgrounds rallied to ensure a wide range of rights in areas such as political and public life, and representation (Articles 7–8). In Part III of CEDAW, women's rights to education, employment, health, and economic and social benefits (Articles 10–13), and the application of these to rural women in particular (Article 14), met with significant support from most delegates. Records show that delegates from all geographical regions were enthusiastic about including such rights, some of which were clearly aspirational in nature. In deliberations on education, delegates from the Muslim states of Indonesia, Pakistan, Egypt, Guinea, Iran, Senegal and Morocco all supported a comprehensive article.[95] The Iranian delegate's suggestion went so far as to include 'the elimination of any stereotyped concept of masculine and feminine roles at all levels and in all forms of education, in particular by revising textbooks and school curricula accordingly and by encouraging co-education'.[96] Guinea and Indonesia were concerned about the knowledge gap between men and women and suggested a specific mention in the article to address this, whereas Egypt, Indonesia, Iran and Pakistan wanted reference to a guarantee giving rural women adequate 'family planning advice and services'. The Pakistani delegate also wanted the phrase 'all appropriate measures shall be taken to ensure women equal opportunity at all levels' to be included.[97]

The solidarity among women and their desire to share perceptions and experiences informing their interventions was clear from the manner in which both Western and non-Western delegates spoke. Thus Mrs Devaud of France observed that the Belgian intervention

> sought to ensure that girls had the same length of schooling as boys. Indeed, in countries like France, and particularly in the rural areas, girls often had to leave school if their mother died in order to bring up their brothers and sisters. In large families, the eldest girl was often obliged to discontinue her studies at an early age to help her mother at home. It was never the boy but always the girl, and in most cases, the eldest girl, who was sacrificed in that way.[98]

---

[94] T. Meron, *Human Rights Law-Making in the United Nations: A Critique of Instruments and Process* (Oxford: Clarendon Press, 1986).
[95] See UN Doc. E/CN.6/SR.642.   [96] Ibid.   [97] Ibid.   [98] Ibid., p. 2.

This statement resonated with Mrs Gueye from Senegal, who responded by saying that 'in her country too, particularly in the rural areas, girls left school at an earlier age than boys to help their mothers at home or to get married'.[99] France's intervention is quite revealing, as one might not have expected such an admission from a country at the heart of Europe, and it is a good example of the openness of the debating environment and of delegates' eagerness to share their experiences in order to draft a comprehensive text. The important point to be learned here is that the discussion was far from being a matter of Muslim nations holding patriarchal positions based in Islamic law, as against Western nations arguing from a position of pre-assumed equality.

Like all legal instruments, CEDAW reflected the dominant discourse and contemporary issues in human rights of the day. The 1970s was the era of the Women in Development (WID) model for women's inclusion into development processes worldwide.[100] CEDAW delegates from the non-Western states (including Muslim states) were well aware of the limitations on the ground in their own countries regarding women's access to basic needs, yet still they grasped the opportunity provided by CEDAW to lay claim to basic rights such as health, education and employment.[101] One example of this strategy was the proposal for a new paragraph to the preamble, as sponsored by three Muslim states – Bangladesh, Pakistan and Somalia – and Singapore:[102]

> Concerned also that in situations of abject poverty where basic needs of the majority of the population are not provided for, women have the least access to such basic needs of life such as food, education and training for employment.[103]

In a similar vein, Morocco proposed a formulation for Article 13 which was adopted by the working group at its thirty-third session:

> Each State Party shall take all appropriate measures to eliminate discrimination against women in the field of economic and social life and to ensure for women on the basis of equality the same rights as men, in particular . . .

Several states, including Pakistan, Benin and Syria, made interventions proposing an equal right to participate in politics and to have leadership roles. On women's voting rights, the Pakistani delegate supported taking all appropriate measures to ensure women the right to vote without discrimination, to be eligible for election to all publicly elected bodies, to hold public office, and to exercise public functions. It is particularly interesting to note that a number of

---

[99]   Ibid.

[100]   See S. Rai, *Gender and the Political Economy of Development* (Cambridge: Polity Press, 2002), in particular pp. 56–69.

[101]   Ibid.; see also generally M. Saward, *The Representative Claim* (Oxford: Oxford University Press, 2010).

[102]   Doc. A/C.3/32/WG.1/CRP.2.

[103]   After deliberations, the working group adopted this paragraph by consensus with minor amendments, and the text now reads, 'Concerned also that in situations of poverty, women have the least access to food, health, education, training, and opportunities for employment and other needs'.

Muslim countries did not at the time allow women to vote or run for office, yet there was no note of dissent from any of the Muslim delegates in affirming their support to the drafting of this article.

But one of the most groundbreaking articles related to the rights of rural women, a provision that is not included in any other human rights instrument.[104] In their commentary on CEDAW,[105] Freeman, Chinkin and Rudolf note,

> The drafting of article 14 was noncontroversial. Initially, rural women had only been considered in provisions on employment and education. It was at the 26th session of the Commission on the Status of Women (CSW) in 1976 that a representative of the FAO raised the plight of rural women. She suggested that the existing drafts of the Convention did not take adequate notice of the challenges faced by rural women. The FAO representative reminded delegates about the concerns expressed at the Mexico Conference and beyond. Following the Mexico Conference, States were keen to emphasise the importance of engaging rural women in development, exemplifying the WID analysis.[106]

The working group formed to draft Article 14 comprised Egypt, India, Indonesia, Iran, Pakistan, Thailand and the US (four of which being Muslim states).[107] Drafts were presented to the CSW by India, which noted that two-thirds of the world's women lived in rural areas and deserved specific focus. The aim of proposing a separate article was to enable rural women 'to participate, equally with men, in agricultural and rural development and to enjoy all benefits such as planning, health, training, community activities, credit, agricultural credit, agricultural reform, etc.'.

Reflecting upon the many instances of women's solidarity across ideological, religious, political and cultural divisions, a more holistic appreciation of the CEDAW drafting process emerges. Instead of the oft-mentioned linear understandings informed by binaries of West/non-West, Muslim/non-Muslim, summary records reflect the reality of the rich discourse generated through cross-fertilization of ideas. Shared experiences of women's issues resonate across the many divides leading to the developmental human rights, including education, health and employment.

5.3.6 The Unspoken Hierarchy of 'Religious', National, and Constitutional Laws

When it came to disagreements over draft texts, delegates primarily invoked national laws and constitutions, and only secondly religious laws, as their

---

[104] For a comprehensive analysis of the drafting process of Article 14, see Pruitt, 'Migration, Development, and the Promise of CEDAW', 707; and 'CEDAW and Rural Development: Empowering Women with Law from the Top Down, Activism from the Bottom Up', *Baltimore Law Review* 41 (2011), 263.

[105] Freeman, Chinkin and Rudolf, *The UN Convention*, p. 361.   [106] Ibid.

[107] The Byelorussian SSR, Kenya and France also participated in the general discussion of Article 14.

main reasons for disagreeing with a certain formulation. An unstated hierarchy informed the deliberations – national laws and constitutions were the key consideration in whether or not any given country accepted a given formulation, and so the language of various articles was debated at length to arrive at acceptable formulations. Delegates would at times invoke religious and national laws to support a particular text, but on other occasions would do precisely the opposite and invoke each by way of disagreement. During discussions on Article 1, for example, the Pakistani delegation issued a communiqué on its attitude toward CEDAW, with Mrs Faridi emphasizing that discrimination against women was 'contrary to the injunctions of Islam', 'violate[d] constitutional guarantees' and was 'an offence against human dignity', thereby clearly justifying her country's support of CEDAW by reference to religious *and* constitutional norms. On the other hand, during discussions on Article 2, she stated that a requirement to amend the Constitution of Pakistan in order to 'embody a principle of equality was too intrusive into the internal affairs of the state'.[108] She preferred a text that condemned discrimination in a general fashion to one providing for concrete measures to eliminate it: 'Her delegation's vote on the draft convention as a whole would take into account the constitution of the Islamic republic of Pakistan'.[109] It is clear that she found herself needing to face both ways at once, simultaneously voicing support for CEDAW as an aspirational text while in fact ceding primacy to the Pakistani Constitution. The relationship between national laws and religion was also apparent in the intervention by Iran noted above. Mrs Esfandiari is reported to have stated that

> in principle, she could accept the text of draft Article 2. However, as Iran was not a secular state, some of the provisions of the new text were not consistent with certain Iranian laws dealing with religion. Were these provisions to be applied, it would first be necessary to amend Iran's civil legislation.[110]

But these do not seem to have been simply matters of Muslim nations alone wishing to support the idea of women's rights in public while in fact minimizing their effect at home. In the discussions on Article 9 (nationality), Mrs Carlsson of Sweden adopted a similar approach, declaring that the question was currently under study in Sweden and in the Council of Europe, and that her delegation would be unable to reach a decision until the outcome of those deliberations was known.[111] Likewise, the French, Guinean and Greek delegates all evoked national legislation as reasons inhibiting their acceptance of certain paragraphs of the draft article. An interesting rejoinder was made here by the Belgian delegate, Mrs Coene, in response to delegates invoking national legislation:

> the elaboration of an international convention was precisely one of the means of achieving progress in law and national legislation, and . . . the work in which

---

[108] This statement was issued at the 26th Session of the Commission on the Status of Women, 15 September 1976.
[109] E/CN.6/SR.642, p. 10.   [110] Ibid.   [111] E/CN.6/SR.640, p. 3, pt. 9.

the Commission was engaged would have little meaning if the future convention had to be compatible in every respect with existing legislation – in other words, if the results of the Commission's efforts were to constitute the lowest common denominator.[112]

Contrary to popular perceptions, therefore, all delegates privileged religious and national laws and constitutions over formulations of CEDAW. Yet literature on CEDAW makes it appear as if it was only a religious (read Islam) versus CEDAW hierarchy at play – a fact amply contradicted from the archival evidence.

5.3.7 Ideological Differences as Highlighted by Divergent Positions on Gender

The debate was not simply a cut-and-dried matter of gaining agreement on equal rights for women vis-à-vis men; camps disagreed on whether or not this formulation implied a difference between the sexes that should in itself be done away with – whether the convention should have as its aim to 'eliminate discrimination against women' or whether its purpose should be 'the elimination of discrimination based on sex in general'. This conversation brought to the fore differences of opinion regarding the position, status and roles of women, in which the Muslim delegates did not all agree. The Swedish delegation (also on behalf of the Danish delegation and the observers for Norway and Finland) was in favour of including discrimination on the basis of sex:

> Indeed, the fact of assigning to each sex a very specific role in society, to which individuals should conform, limited the possibilities for the development of the personality. In that regard . . . women would be unable to play that role in the political and economic fields if men failed to play an increasing role in the education of children and in family life. The Nordic delegations would prefer a draft convention which sought to abolish discrimination based on sex in general.[113]

While the US delegation shared this view, their Cold War opponents in the USSR saw a distinct difference in the sexes:

> it was essential to bear in mind that women performed a two-fold function, of which procreation was the more important since it perpetuated the human species. Women therefore should be in the best possible position to perform their functions both as citizens and as mothers. It was therefore natural that women should enjoy a privileged position when they are pregnant or when their children were very young.[114]

When a number of Muslim states added their views to the pot, they did not do so by raising points of Islamic law. Senegal, for instance, pointed out that

---

[112] E/CN.6/SR.640, p. 3, pts 11, 12 13, p. 2, pt 3, respectively.   [113] E/CN.6/SR.632, p. 5.
[114] Ibid., pp. 5–6.

'discrimination based on sex was directed against women rather than men. If the question at issue was simply that of discrimination in general, the Commission should mention discrimination based on race or the discrimination practiced against countries of the third world'.[115] Egypt believed that this discussion mostly concerned drafting matters, and that delegations could consider deleting the terms causing controversy from the draft text. India, meanwhile,

> was not entirely in agreement with the views expressed by the representatives of the Soviet Union or the Nordic countries. The situation in those countries especially with regard to employment was not the same as in the developing countries, where the scarcity of jobs excluded women from the more responsible positions. The Commission should therefore refrain from going into too much detail and should leave governments sufficient leeway by not specifying rights that they would be unable to guarantee.[116]

For her part, Mrs Faridi of Pakistan failed to see why the members of the Commission were reluctant to retain the words 'against women', since they were part of the draft convention's title which they had just adopted.

A working group (including Egypt, Pakistan, Morocco, Senegal, Iran, Indonesia and Bahrain) deliberated on Article 16 in eight meetings held during November of 1978. During consideration of Section (1)(d), relating to the care and custody of children, the draft had indicated that women should have the 'same rights and responsibilities, whether married or not'. The UK proposed that this be amended to 'irrespective of their marital status', to which Egypt expressed reservations.[117] The delegate of Egypt commented that

> equality did not mean identity; it was more a question of ensuring the complementary role of the spouses in the interest of the family, the basic unit of all society as recognized in Article 6 on the declaration on the elimination of discrimination against women. Time would be needed to develop a system ensuring the equality of rights to men and women without undermining the unity and concord of the family and its legitimate interests from a legal point of view. She accordingly wished to enter reservations with respect to any future reference to unmarried mothers.[118]

The question of equal rights in the dissolution of marriage strongly divided the delegates. While the North viewed equality of rights in the dissolution of marriage as a *sine qua non* for the elimination of discrimination between spouses, non-secular states viewed the computation of equality between the spouses as a weighing of the whole set of rights and obligations of each spouse against that of the other. Records of the negotiations cite numerous comments from the Egyptian delegate, who felt that matters such as inheritance and the ending of a marriage contract must give consideration to the family laws of

---

[115] Ibid., p. 6.   [116] Ibid.
[117] However, 'irrespective of their marital status' was adopted in the final version.
[118] E/CN.6/SR.650, pt. 74, 29 September 1976.

states which 'respect religious provisions which are closely connected with the faith and belief of nations'. Pakistan's agreement to the original wording of the article was subject to the provisions of the Constitution of Pakistan, based on Islamic law. Mrs Faridi also explained that Pakistan had abstained from the vote on Article 16 as a whole 'because the Pakistan Committee which was considering the rights of women had not yet submitted its report'.[119] Egypt's Mrs Hussein reminded delegates that 'measures to improve the situation were under consideration [and] time would be needed to develop a system ensuring equality of rights to men and women without undermining the unity and concord of the family and its legitimate interests from the legal point of view'.[120]

Interestingly enough, even when employing Islamic law as a reason for disagreeing with equal rights in marriage and at its dissolution, the delegates from Muslim states (including Egypt and Pakistan) also cited impending law reforms as reasons for their inability to agree with this provision of CEDAW. Thus both religion and 'secular' rationale were simultaneously marshalled to advance their positions.

5.3.8 Reconciling Diverse Vocabularies

A significant aspect of the deliberations on CEDAW involved the making of terms and concepts acceptable to the widest possible number of states. By ensuring that terms employed in the CEDAW text were culturally sensitive to all societies, including Muslim ones, delegates persevered to find acceptable terminology that would retain the meaning as well as the context of diverse traditions.

The term 'unmarried mothers' attracted comments from delegates of a number of Muslim states, including Iran and Egypt, whose delegate said that her delegation was 'not opposed to the elimination of discrimination against unmarried mothers' but also noted that 'the issue was a very delicate one which fell within the cultural, educational and social domain rather than within the law. A provision of that nature would make many countries reluctant to ratify the convention, particularly if the word "mothers" was replaced by "parents"'.[121] A similar comment came from the Indonesian delegate, who observed that 'the question of unmarried mothers was a very sensitive issue in Indonesia, and hoped that the commission would not take a decision which would prejudice opinion in her country'.[122] The term 'parenthood' made the Pakistani delegate 'uncomfortable': 'the English concept of parenthood was difficult to translate. It would be better to speak of the roles of the father and the mother'.[123]

---

[119] This was the Women's Rights Committee set up by the Government of Mr Z. A. Bhutto in 1976.

[120] E/CN.6/SR.650, para. 74, p. 8.   [121] E/CN.6/SR.650, pt. 90, 29 September 1976.

[122] 651st meeting, 27 September 1976, on Article 16(3), pt. 92.

[123] 665th meeting, 10 December 1976.

During discussion of the right to education,[124] the Indonesian delegate expressed a similar national position with regard to the addition of the phrase 'psycho-sexual education' into Article 10: 'this form of education would be unacceptable'. The Pakistani delegate supported her position, while the Iranian delegate for his part found it difficult to accept the idea of the 'identical nature of family roles'.

During the same discussion, the Cuban proposal that 'maternity should be considered as a social function' attracted varied responses from Muslim states. While Syria and Mali saw maternity as a social function, Morocco did not. In response to the Cuban delegate's proposed wording – 'the recognition of common responsibility of both men and women in the upbringing and development of their children' – Morocco instead proposed 'it being understood that the interest of the children is the primordial consideration in all cases', which met with the approval of delegates and was adopted as the agreed text.

5.4 Linking Contributions of Muslim Delegates with Subsequent Reservations

Thirty-two of the fifty-eight member states of the Organisation of Islamic Cooperation have ratified CEDAW without entering any reservations: legally speaking, they have undertaken the obligation to respect all its substantive provisions. Twenty-four have entered reservations, of which sixteen have cited either Islamic law or *sharia* as reasons for doing so. Table 5.1 gives a detailed overview of articles reserved and whether or not this was done on the basis of Islamic law and *sharia*.[125]

As is clear from the table, Articles 2, 9, 15 and 16 emerge as the four most reserved articles by Muslim states, leading to a possible superficial inference that their contents run counter to *sharia*. However, a closer analysis presents a more complex picture. Sixteen of the twenty-four reserving states cite *sharia* as the basis for entering reservations to one or more articles. Others simply reserve their positions without giving a reason; yet others cite their national laws, customs and constitutions for entering particular reservations. Ten of the twenty-four reserving Muslim states have entered reservations to Article 2. Of these only five (Bahrain, Bangladesh, Libya, Morocco and the UAE) cite *sharia* as the basis for their reservations. Fourteen out of the twenty-four Muslim states have entered reservations to Article 9(2) (on equal nationality rights). Of these, none have mentioned *sharia* as their motivation. Nine out of the twenty-four Muslim states reserved Article 15(4) (on a wife's right to choose her domicile on a basis of equality with her husband). Of these, only the UAE specifically cites *sharia* as the reason. Finally, Article 16 (on equal rights entering, during and at the dissolution of marriage) attracted reservations from nineteen out of the

---

124   642nd meeting, 27 September 1976.
125   From un.org/womenwatch/daw/cedaw/reservations-country.htm.

Table 5.1 Reservations entered by Muslim states parties to CEDAW

Name of country	Articles reserved, and reasons
Algeria	9(2), 15(4), 16, 29: *sharia* not mentioned
Bahrain	9(2), 15(4), 29: *sharia* not mentioned
	2, 16: *sharia* mentioned as a reason for reserving
Bangladesh	2, 13(a), 16(1)(c)(f): *sharia* mentioned as a reason for reserving (reservations to 13(a) and 16(1)(c)(f) later withdrawn)
Brunei	General reservation mentioning *sharia*
	9(2), 29: *sharia* not mentioned
Egypt	29: *sharia* not mentioned
	2, 9(2), 16: *sharia* mentioned as a reason for reserving
Indonesia	29: *sharia* not mentioned
Iraq	2(f)(g), 9(1)(2), 29(1): *sharia* not mentioned
	16: *sharia* mentioned as a reason for reserving
Jordan	9(2), 15(4), 16(1)(c)(d)(g): *sharia* not mentioned
Kuwait	9(2), 29(1): *sharia* not mentioned (initially also reserved 7(a), later withdrawn)16: *sharia* mentioned as a reason for reserving
Lebanon	9(2), 16(1)(c)(d)(f)(g), 29(1): *sharia* not mentioned
Libya	Initial general reservation on the basis of *sharia*, later modified to just 2 and 16(c)(d) reserved
Malaysia	General reservation on the basis of *sharia*
	Initially reserved 2(f), 5(a), 7(b), 9, 11, 16, but later withdrew reservations to 2(f), 9(1), 16(b)(d)(e)(h)
Maldives	7(a): *sharia* not mentioned
	16: on the basis of *sharia*
Mauritania	General reservation on the basis of *sharia*
Mauritius	29(1): *sharia* not mentioned; initially also reserved 11(1)(b)(d), 16(1)(g), later withdrawn
Morocco	9(2), 15(4), 29(1): *sharia* not mentioned
	2, 16: *sharia* mentioned as a reason for reserving
Niger	2(d)(f), 5(a), 15(4), 16(1)(c)(e)(g), 29(1): mention of 'custom' as a reason for reserving
Oman	General reservation on the basis of *sharia*
	9(2), 15(4), 16(1)(a)(c)(f), 29(1): *sharia* not mentioned
Pakistan	General reservation on the basis of its constitution
Saudi Arabia	General reservation on the basis of *sharia*
	9(2), 29(1): *sharia* not mentioned
Syria	2, 9(2), 15(4), 16(1)(c)(d)(f)(g)(h), 29(1): *sharia* not mentioned
	16(2): *sharia* mentioned as a reason for reserving
Tunisia	9(2), 16(c)(d)(f)(g)(h), 29(1): *sharia* not mentioned
Turkey	Initially reserved 15(2)(4), 16(1)(c)(d)(f)(g), 29(1): *sharia* not mentioned; later withdrew all except 29(1)
United Arab Emirates	9, 29(1): *sharia* not mentioned
	2(f), 15(2), 16: *sharia* mentioned as a reason for reserving
Yemen	29(1): *sharia* not mentioned

twenty-four. Of these, only Bahrain, Bangladesh (later withdrawn), Egypt, Iraq, Kuwait, Libya, the Maldives, Morocco, Syria and the UAE specifically declared *sharia* as the basis. There are also a number of Muslim states (Brunei, Malaysia, Mauritania, Oman and Saudi Arabia) that have entered general reservations to CEDAW on the basis of *sharia*. These tend to be the most difficult to analyse in terms of the obligations undertaken by states entering such reservations. Finally, it is pertinent to mention that five Muslim states have, over the years, withdrawn reservations, including ones entered on the basis of *sharia*.

At first glance it might appear that, since Muslim states reserved similar articles, a homogeneous *sharia* must be the driving force. But this does not hold true on closer analysis. In fact, one definite finding of the above analysis is that it points towards (i) a plural understanding of what constitutes Islamic law and *sharia* and consequently which articles of CEDAW are perceived to conflict with it; (ii) a patriarchal mindset of governments informing reservations to a treaty focusing on women's rights; and (iii) compulsions of domestic/national politics, where predominantly conservative societal trends demand such reservations.

The strongest common denominator of all the reserved articles is the patriarchal lens through which women's position is perceived within the family. The idea of 'women's rights' is considered in most Muslim countries to be part of a 'Western' agenda to undermine cultural and religious values and therefore something to be resisted. Yet Muslim state practice is not at all consistent in its resistance. Thus Egypt, while entering reservations to CEDAW's Article 16, did not enter similar reservations to Article 23(4) of the 1966 International Covenant on Civil and Political Rights (ICCPR), which declares, 'states parties to the present Covenant shall take appropriate steps to ensure equality of rights and responsibilities of spouses as to marriage, during marriage and at its dissolution'. Precisely the same paradox occurs in relation to Morocco, which was reminded of this inconsistency in the Concluding Observations of the Human Rights Committee:[126] 'although several reservations have been made by Morocco in acceding to the Convention on the Elimination of All Forms of Discrimination Against Women, Morocco remains bound to the fullest extent by the provisions of Articles 2, 3, 23 and 26 of the Covenant'.[127] So it appears that such equality does not conflict with *sharia* when it appears in the ICCPR, and only does so when it appears in a convention on women's rights! Likewise, recognizing equal rights for children of both sexes under the UN's Convention on the Rights of the Child (CRC) is acceptable to all Muslim states, yet once those same girls become adult women and the subject of CEDAW articles, those same states are willing to enter reservations on their rights.

In an incisive analysis, Sonbol shows the 'contradictions between Islamic law as presented by the Qur'an and Sunna and the justifications used by Muslim countries to hold reservations against full implementation of the CEDAW

---

[126] CCPR/C/79/Add.44, at E/4, 23 November 1994.   [127] Ibid.

Convention'.[128] She illustrates the connection between historical contexts and laws during particular periods of Islamic history to show that *sharia* is in practice used today as a justification for entering reservations against CEDAW, when the actual reason lies elsewhere: 'This is in fact a product of contemporary gendered laws rather than God's eternal rules'.[129]

So, is there a link in Muslim state practice in international law at the ratification process to the inputs during the drafting stage of CEDAW? Is it simply *realpolitik* driving the varying positions of different states, or the plurality of the Islamic legal traditions, which is informing this heterogeneity of approaches? A clear convergence emerges between both trends, and there are definite linkages between the positions adopted by delegates of Muslim states at the drafting stage and those upon ratification. The content and formulation of Articles 9, 15 and 16 were the subjects of the most protracted debates in the various drafting meetings, as covered in the analysis above. In fact, of the sixteen substantive articles of CEDAW, these three were the very same (indeed the only) articles where Islamic law and *sharia* were mentioned. But still the positions were not uniform. There was a certain fluidity, ambivalence, and dynamism in the debates and positions adopted by the delegates of the various Muslim states, a fluidity that continued to be reflected in the text of the reservations entered by Muslim states at the time of ratification. This ambivalent trend, reflecting political expediency on the part of some Muslim states, is further in evidence when some decided to withdraw some of their reservations, including those entered on the basis of *sharia*. Nisrine Abiad sums up this trend well when she notes,

> The withdrawal of reservations formulated in the name of Islam invites an examination of the legitimacy of the grounds upon which the reservations were entered to begin with . . . [W]hen a Muslim state formulates a reservation and founds it on a sacred and immutable religious set of laws, and this same country subsequently withdraws that reservation, the extent to which the previous considerations were in fact authentically based on religious considerations may be legitimately questioned.[130]

In other words, the act of withdrawing a reservation raises the reasonable inference that some Muslim states might be citing *sharia* as the impeding factor in acceding to human rights treaties when it does not actually impede their accession.[131] Such reservations appear in fact not to be based on *sharia* but instead driven by political considerations. Krivenko, on the other hand, looks at these withdrawals in a positive light, as demonstrating a constructive and

---

[128] A. A. Sonbol, 'A Response to Muslim Countries' Reservations against Full Implementation of CEDAW', *Journal of Women of the Middle East & the Islamic World* 8 (2010), 348.

[129] Ibid., 350.   [130] Abiad, *Sharia*, p. 90.

[131] See also A. E. Mayer, 'The Convention on the Elimination of All Forms of Discrimination against Women: The Political Nature of "Religious" Reservations' (online paper), 9; J. Connors, 'The Women's Convention in the Muslim World', in J. P. Gardner (ed.), *Human Rights as General Norms and a State's Right to Opt Out* (London: BIICL, 1997), pp. 100–2.

interactive process among states. Might it also be that, conscious of the multiple interpretations available and possible within the Islamic legal traditions, states' withdrawals of religiously motivated reservations are recognition of a dynamic and evolving Islamic law?

The most compelling reason behind the reservations to Articles 2, 9, 15 and 16 (and in some cases Article 7, on women's right to vote) and their subsequent withdrawal by some states appears to be a combination of political and social expediency. Muslim societies, for various reasons beyond the scope of the present chapter, are divided in many ways, but most prominently along the fault line of those sections that adhere to 'traditional' ways of living Islam and those that believe in progressive interpretations. While this variety in thinking has always been present in all societies, in the Muslim world, broadly defined, it has achieved phenomenal proportions, resulting in dangerous divides that challenge state and society. In other words, varying responses to modernity, including CEDAW, reflect a state of what we have elsewhere referred to as 'fractured modernity'.

In this light, then, it is interesting to note that reservations entered on the grounds of Islamic law are perceived as being more undermining of the treaty than those entered on the basis of a supposed incompatibility with national laws and constitutions. In other words, it is assumed that the impacts and outcomes of reserving on the basis of national laws are different to those based on Islam. It might be argued that there exists an assumption that Muslim states were implicitly propounding a hierarchy of religious norms, human rights and national sovereignties, with Islam as the superior reference point to which deference must be paid. Of course, if that *were* the case, why did some Muslim states enter reservations in the name of Islam while others did not? Would it not make more sense that it was cultural articulations rather than religious doctrine which were behind the differences in approach to certain of the rights set out in CEDAW? One inference would be to say that entering 'Islamic' reservations did *not* indicate rejection of international human rights law, or indeed its incompatibility with Islamic law, but rather that it was a simple reiteration of the 'Islamic' normative base of women's rights.[132] But this is not the general understanding or indeed analysis of most writers on the subject:[133] they believe that by making Islam and Islamic law their reference point, Muslim states were making a very clear statement: that they embraced

---

[132] It is interesting to recall the remarks of the Iranian representative, who stated in the context of the UDHR, 'Divergence does not emerge from the context, it rises from the very initial phase. Islamic law is founded on the very original concept that divinity reigns supreme and divine law is pre-eminent to human law. The Declaration is genuinely secular in its theme and essence and, as such, differs from Islamic law in its origin. There may be similarities or even complete compatibility on some provisions, in particular those that meet the conditions of *jus cogens*, but the original perceptions remain widely apart.' Cited in T. Meron, 'Iran's Challenge to the International Law of Human Rights', *Human Rights Reporter* 13(8) (1989), 9.

[133] See generally Mayer, *Islam and Human Rights*.

Islamic human rights norms and rejected international human rights standards as an alien imposition.[134] Yet the evidence from the drafting process does not support such an understanding: barring some narrow points of divergence, a convergence towards a core common universal understanding of women's rights clearly emerged from the deliberations.

5.4.1 Anticipating Reservations while Acknowledging Common Ground

The records of the drafting process reveal that delegates were holding to two apparently conflicting positions. On the one hand, they declared that there was a strong possibility of reservations being entered by their states when it came to the ratification process; on the other, they were also accepting of the fact that a commonality of issues and concerns affecting women irrespective of culture, tradition and religion had been recognized.

The UK delegate, Mrs Cockcroft, comes across as being not overly enamoured of the outcome, perhaps indicating that her government was going to enter reservations (the UK did in fact enter one of the highest numbers of reservations): 'the text was the result of a compromise, and was not perfect. While many aspects met the concern of the United Kingdom Government, a few fell somewhat short of her wishes'.[135] Mrs Devaud of France was a shade more complimentary of the process:

> the Commission's work, although difficult, had been directed with dispatch and authority... [S]he feared, however, that governments might hesitate to ratify certain provisions which were worded in unduly complicated terms: she would have preferred a Convention that was easier to implement. Her delegation had nevertheless participated in the consensus subject to the reservations she had already explained.

Mrs Hutar of the US, too, had mixed reactions: 'She noted with satisfaction that there were broad areas of agreement... [H]er delegation had participated in the consensus but wished to enter reservations with regard to certain provisions.'[136] Subsequent paragraphs of her intervention went on to explain these reservations in quite some detail.[137]

When it came to the delegates of Muslim states, however, Mrs Faridi, the Pakistani delegate,

> welcomed the fact that the Commission had been able to work out the essential elements which would serve as a basis for amending the legislation of countries throughout the world in the area with which the draft Convention was concerned. Her delegation had entered a few reservations; however, they did not relate to the Convention as a whole but only some of its minor aspects. The draft was of course not perfect and could be improved, but the fact that many countries had

---

[134] Ibid.   [135] E/CN.6.SR.679, para. 19.   [136] Ibid., para. 25.   [137] Ibid., para. 26.

approved it indicated that *despite differences in their systems and ways of life, they had much in common.*[138]

And the view of the Egyptian delegate meanwhile was that

> owing to differences of views in the Commission, it had been difficult to reach agreement. The Commission should therefore take pride in the fact that the *draft Convention had been adopted by consensus which showed that women from different regions of the world had a great number of interests in common.*[139]

What strikes one when reading accounts of the speeches is the degree to which delegates from the Western hemisphere and the developed world come across as lukewarm towards what was undeniably a great achievement – the drafting of an international bill of women's rights – whereas the delegates from Muslim states took the opportunity to point out the core common universal values that had been agreed upon.[140] Yet the focus of academic literature on reservations,[141] and on objections entered by Western states to the reservations of Muslim states, suggests a different angle is being taken. Almost by default, and ignoring the drafting process, the literature makes it appear as if it was the delegates from *Western* states who were the most enthusiastic supporters of women's rights, with *Muslim* delegates holding them back.

5.5 The Contributions of Muslim Delegates: Some Concluding Remarks

My interest in analysing the inputs of Muslim delegates to the CEDAW drafting process is a practical one: existing narratives have tended to make their input either invisible, inconsequential or even oppositional to that of their Western counterparts. The archival records tell a more nuanced and complex story.

The most pronounced dislocation of the existing CEDAW narrative is the fact that there was minimal discussion of Islamic law and *sharia* during the drafting process. Furthermore, on most occasions when religion *was* mentioned, it was in the context of the national laws of the respective state. And this leads to a further important observation of the process: the conflation of the terms 'Islamic law', 'national law' and '*sharia*'. This is critical to an understanding of

---

[138] Ibid., para. 29, emphasis added.   [139] Ibid., para. 35, emphasis added.

[140] As mentioned earlier, one-sixth of the CEDAW Working Group consisted of representatives from Muslim states. The interventions of the Egyptian and Pakistani delegates are presented as examples of the viewpoint of the Muslim delegates in general.

[141] Beside the works cited above, the following have focused on Muslim states' reservations: J. Connors, 'The Women's Convention in the Muslim World', in M. Yamani (ed.), *Feminism and Islam: Legal and Literary Perspectives* (Reading: Ithaca Press, 1996), pp. 351–71; A. Haugestad, *Reservations to the United Nations Women's Convention, with Special Focus on Reservations Submitted by Muslim Countries*, Studies in Women's Law, 39 (Oslo, 1995); L. Lijznaad, *Reservations to UN Human Rights Treaties: Ratify and Ruin?* (Dordrecht: Martinus Nijhoff, 1995); C. Chinkin, 'Reservations and Objections to the Convention on the Elimination of All Forms of Discrimination against Women', in Gardner, *Human Rights as General Norms*, pp. 64–84.

the broader picture of the reservations entered subsequently by Muslim states, where a similar conflation is visible. *Sharia*, as we saw in the discussion in Chapter 1, is the overarching umbrella of norms and principles, based on the Qur'an and Sunna, informing all aspects of life for Muslims. Islamic law is but one element of *sharia*, and it has historically drawn upon more than just the religious text: factors extraneous to religion inform Islamic law. That national laws are 'based upon' Islamic law does not imply that national laws are sacrosanct or coterminous with either *sharia* or Islamic law, but simply that national laws may be inspired by both. The outcome of this conflation had led to confusion both within Muslim communities and in the wider world. The withdrawal of reservations initially based upon 'Islamic law' by some Muslim states is an example of this confusion. If Islamic law and *sharia* are immutable, how can these suddenly become open to change? How can a provision of CEDAW be un-Islamic today but Islamic tomorrow, as the withdrawal of reservations would suggest? To appreciate what is happening, we must remember always to look through the lens of the interpretative plurality of the Islamic legal traditions when reading the interventions of the delegates of Muslim states, and pay attention to how understandings of Islam vary with cultures, traditions and national laws and constitutions.

The present study also evidences Muslim delegates' multiple identities and autonomous participation in the drafting deliberations, something which clearly jars with the fact that the final text attracted reservations from Muslim states. But if representatives were truly autonomous, then state reservations were inevitable. The question of reservations does, however, illuminate the autonomy of Muslim women, who, despite the odds and the formal constraints upon their positions, managed to form alliances and contribute to a dynamic and progressive understanding of women's rights and contributions to global society. And this is, of course, an ongoing challenge for those who believe in progressive, dynamic and reflective understandings of Islamic law and who embrace the principles of universal human rights.

So how can we interpret the participation of Muslim delegates in the drafting processes of CEDAW? Did Muslim women's public contributions, framed and informed by their religious and national laws and political leanings, conflict with their 'backstage', unheard voices as women? How did these women deal with this challenge and balance the duality inherent in their performance? Depending upon the audience and the stage, these individuals of necessity performed varyingly, employing different aspects of their relational autonomy and multiple identities at different turns. The records reflect the necessary 'alliance-making' performances of Muslim women across the North/South and socialist/capitalist divides of the day. The process witnessed robust interventions from all the delegates of Muslim states, aimed at protecting their ideological, political and national interests, and their national constitutions and laws, in addition to their support for women's rights. Their performances as autonomous beings who were nevertheless unavoidably bound by their gender, culture, tradition and politics is a fascinating example of gendered discourse on an international stage. Thus an important paradox emerged: Muslim women were simultaneously supportive of women's rights and of their cultural and religious contexts; bound by their cultures, traditions and multiple identities, and yet expressive of their passion for women's rights, Muslim women proved to be adept performers on a world stage. Depending upon the specific audience and their co-performers, the varying shades of their multiple identities reflected their skills as sophisticated political actors.

Given that CEDAW was formulated with the active participation of delegates representing all regions of the world, a question remains pertinent: why the large numbers of reservations? Delegates were seeking common denominators with their respective national laws and constitutions as well as religious and cultural vocabularies. Yet nowhere did they preclude reservations by their states when the time came for ratification. But there is, of course, another possible reason for the number of reservations entered. In weaving together a counternarrative during the drafting process, were women delegates not coming together in solidarity to consciously subvert the status quo? They certainly accomplished this by raising the bar of women's rights, despite the knowledge that some provisions would be unacceptable to their respective states and governments.

The rich texture of the archival material may be read in different ways. Readings to date have suppressed the positive and robust contributions of Muslim women delegates by making them invisible. Their performance appears to have been measured only by the yardstick of the reservations entered to CEDAW by Muslim states, rather than on the basis of its wide-ranging provisions and their contributions to them. It is apparent from the records that, at their first incarnation, the positions adopted by delegates from Muslim states on Articles 9, 15 and 16 appear to be the same as those reflected in subsequent reservations. To this end, the most pronounced linkage is the plurality of interpretation of the Islamic legal tradition that was being employed both by the delegates and by their governments when entering subsequent reservations. But the nuances and complexity of the narrative are lost if we are unable to recall what the delegates actually said. For instance, during the discussion on Article 16 (equal rights regarding marriage), Mrs Hussein stated that

> under current Egyptian legislation women did not have equal rights let alone equal duties with men in the matter of marriage and the dissolution of marriage. But measures to improve the situation were under consideration ... [and] time would be needed to develop a system ensuring equality of rights to men and women without undermining the unity and concord of the family and its legitimate interests from the legal point of view.[142]

Mrs Hussein had exceeded her official position by expressing frustration at the unequal status of women and men in Egyptian society, but proceeded

---

[142] E/CN.6/SR.650, para. 74, p. 8.

on a more positive note to say that all was not lost: they were aware of this undesirable situation but needed time to improve matters. Others, too, went beyond their official position in expressing a personal viewpoint. Thus Mrs Faridi, an outspoken women's rights activist, in a moment of exasperation at some delegates regarding the role of the CSW, declared that

> she had been astonished to hear that the Commission was a political body. The Commission had been established as a result of the steady pressure exerted by women's organizations in the world in order to promote the cause of women. It was above any political considerations. It endeavoured to ascertain what was good or bad for women, and not for countries. It was composed of women experts who placed women's interests before everything else, and she expressed the hope that it would continue to work in that spirit.[143]

Similarly, the Moroccan delegate, explaining why a certain paragraph in Article 16 should be amended, stated that

> it failed to take into account a fact which *was a matter of common sense*, namely, that men and women, in order to be truly equal, did not need to be treated as being the same, which would be contrary to nature ... There was a danger that in the name of dedication to the principle of equality, the privileges accorded to women under the natural law by virtue of their femininity, might be lost.[144]

Interventions from Muslim delegates also displayed a sense of confidence in bringing to the table issues that their Western counterparts were not otherwise confronted with. When, for instance, the US delegate suggested a certain formulation of the right to education, the Indonesian delegate pointed out that the wording would restrict married women from entering education. In the US, where facilities for education were more readily available to all women, marriage was not a bar to re-entering education, but in resource-poor developing countries, on the other hand, married women were sometimes excluded from education and it was difficult for them to return. The Indonesian delegate 'drew the attention of the United States delegation to the fact that, in Indonesia, young married women were unable to attend secondary school'. The US delegate withdrew her proposed amendment to address the Indonesian delegate's concerns, as she had been unaware of the restrictions engendered by limited resources and a cultural mindset regarding the place of married women.[145]

Such examples also reflect the delegates' strong sense of rootedness in their national and local contexts, and their acute awareness of the issues facing women in their respective jurisdictions. And their inputs into the drafting process also chime with their profiles as autonomous activists. Mrs Faridi, while working on a health and education project in the most deprived areas of Karachi, often rode in a donkey cart, an act that 'horrified other company wives'. Miss

---

[143] E/CN.6/SR.667, pt. 6, p. 2.   [144] A/C.3/32/L.59, emphasis added.
[145] E/CN.6/SR.640, para. 41.

Tyabji, a daughter of India's elite (her grandfather was chief justice, her father a well-known lawyer) who had lived on London's Park Lane, left her comfortable life as an insurance lawyer and walked through rural India to support famine victims. She believed strongly in the economic empowerment of women, and set up the Women India Trust through which women could earn a livelihood close to their homes. Mrs Hussein set up Egypt's first women's rural health centre and worked with rural women in family planning and in campaigning against female genital mutilation. While on the one hand the records show Mrs Hussein as a delegate who did not appear to support the equality of men and women within the family, still her 'real' self came to light in one statement:

> The draft convention had good legal provisions and she generally accepted its broad lines, but could not agree to the provisions concerning measures to ensure protection for women in absolute and general terms. Although recognizing the need for protective measures, especially for working women, who had suffered the worst discrimination, any idea that women were the weaker sex, must be avoided.[146]

In deliberations on Article 11 (on employment), on the other hand, she expressed wariness of governments who might take advantage of the phrase 'equal treatment with men as regards working conditions' in order to deny women the special attention they deserved.[147]

Through their performance as participants and contributors on the international stage, the women delegates of Muslim states were laying claim to certain rights, well aware that some of these were futuristic in nature. By raising issues of concern in their local contexts, and often making statements that did not match with their official profiles, they were making claims of representativeness well beyond their official status as government delegates. What is most remarkable, though, is that women from such diverse backgrounds came together to develop a women's human rights treaty, and from their work the most amazing document emerged.

---

[146] E/CN.6/SR.615, para. 25.   [147] E/CN.6/SR.646, p. 7, para. 55.

CEDAW? What's That? 'Domesticating' 'International' Women's Human Rights in Muslim Jurisdictions: Reflections on Pakistan's Engagement with CEDAW

6.1 Introduction

Chapter 5 provided the untold narrative of a complex and nuanced process of Muslim women's contribution to the drafting of CEDAW. This chapter investigates the extent to which CEDAW finds a place in governmental and non-governmental policy documents, legislation, judicial decisions, governance structures and institutions in Pakistan. It poses the question whether CEDAW's pre- and post-ratification processes and attendant discourse have 'domesticated' it within state, government and society in that jurisdiction. The study suggests that in a country where pluralism is deeply embedded in legal culture as well as in religious and cultural norms, human rights instruments in general and CEDAW in particular receive an ambivalent and mixed reception as the newest layer of plural legalities.

This chapter draws upon a variety of governmental and non-governmental sources,[1] and upon surveys of judicial decisions of the high courts and the Supreme Court that have invoked CEDAW since Pakistan's ratification in 1996,[2] and is informed by academic literature on the approach of Pakistan and other Muslim states to CEDAW. I was a participant in the accession process and draw upon those personal experiences in developing the present study.[3] This

---

[1] Including Government of Pakistan (GOP) documents, discussions in the Prime Minister's National Consultative Committee for Women (1994–5), documents relating to the Senate Commission of Inquiry for Women (1995–7), working papers on the GOP's position regarding CEDAW, Pakistan's country reports to the CEDAW Committee, shadow reports to the CEDAW Committee from NGOs and civil society organizations, and the Concluding Comments of the CEDAW Committee upon consideration of Pakistan country reports.

[2] For a study of cases in the superior courts from 1980 to 2003 where human rights norms and instruments inform judgments, see S. S. Ali, 'Interpretative Strategies for Women's Human Rights in a Plural Legal Framework: Exploring Judicial and State Responses to Hudood Laws in Pakistan', in A. Hellum, J. Stewart, S. S. Ali and A. Tsanga (eds.), *Human Rights, Plural Legalities and Gendered Realities: Paths are Made by Walking* (Harare: Weaver Books, 2006), pp. 381–406.

[3] My study of CEDAW, Islamic law and the laws of Pakistan advances the case for ratification: Ali, *A Comparative Study*. As a member of the women's and human rights movement I campaigned for CEDAW in seminars and workshops. I was also a member of the Senate Commission of Inquiry for Women, which led to the commission's 1997 Report of the Commission of Inquiry

chapter has also benefited from discussions and personal communications with members of the Pakistani NGO communities, in particular those involved in the thirty-eighth session of the CEDAW Committee, in 2007, where Pakistan's country reports were under discussion.

As mentioned in Chapter 5, literature on CEDAW focuses on the post-ratification scene, especially in Muslim states due to the far-reaching reservations entered by them citing Islamic law and *sharia*. Hence there is a need to take a step back and explore the pre-ratifications debates and discourse and then link them to the post-ratification situation. The present chapter attempts to undertake this task using Pakistan as an example.

6.2 CEDAW within a Religious, Cultural and Socio-legal Context

Since its inception as an independent nation in 1947, Pakistan has struggled with multiple strands of its identity (religious, cultural, ethnic, linguistic)[4] and the manner in which these inform conceptions of state, government, law and society, as well as the status of women. Pakistan's Islamic identity (and its role in the Constitution and in law-making, as well as in the broader nation-building project) is the core element in debates on women's rights in that jurisdiction. As Mullally so aptly observes,

> Although the fundamental rights chapter of the Constitution guarantees equality before the law, the pursuit of gender equality has frequently been sacrificed to religious–cultural claims defining and limiting women's status. Yielding to such claims has served the interests of nation-building while at the same time guarding against any serious threat to the modernizing agendas of Pakistan's political élite. Lost within such compromises is the recognition of women as bearers of rights, with equal rights to participate in the definition of religious–cultural norms.[5]

It is pertinent, besides, to highlight the discursive nature of an Islamic legal tradition which is susceptible to multiple interpretations of the Qur'an and Sunna (the primary sources of Islamic law), resulting in a plurality of views regarding authoritative and legitimate formulations of 'Islamic' law:[6] General Zia-ul-Haq's 'islamization' of laws and society in Pakistan in the 1970s and 1980s, for example, used the slogan *chador aur chardewari* ('women veiled and

---

for Women in Pakistan. I was a member of the Prime Minister's National Consultative Committee, where I was privy to discussions leading to the Cabinet's decision to ratify, and I bring this privileged insight to this chapter. In the post-ratification period I held the post of Cabinet minister for health, population and women's development in the government of the North-West Frontier Province (now renamed Khyber Pukhtunkhwa province) (1999–2001) and was the first chair of the National Commission on the Status of Women (NCSW) (2000–1).

[4] Pakistan is home to some half a dozen major ethnic groups and a similar number of smaller ones, including Punjabi, Baluch, Sindhi, Pukhtun and others.

[5] S. Mullally, '"As Nearly as May Be": Debating Women's Human Rights in Pakistan', *Social and Legal Studies* 14 (2005), 341.

[6] See generally Ali, *Gender and Human Rights*.

within the confines of the home') despite its questionable basis in the Islamic tradition;[7] meanwhile, the established right within the Hanafi school of juristic thought (of which most Pakistanis are adherents) of an adult Muslim woman to enter into a contract of marriage without the intervention, presence or consent of her male guardian (*wali*) was challenged in the Saima Waheed case.[8]

The vast majority of Pakistanis are adherents of Sunni Islam, which does not subscribe to an official clergy. This simple but important observation provides a background in which to understand why individuals and groups vie for authority and legitimacy in the name of Islam and Islamic law. In the sphere of women's rights, this absence of an organized clergy leads to 'forum shopping' for opinions of religious scholars by government and people to advance their rights or undermine them as the case may be.[9] The potential for using Islam as a socio-economic and political tool in both the public and private spheres is significant and is employed by religious and secular parties as well as by the wider public. The founder of Pakistan did not envisage the nation as a theocracy, a position evident from his public expressions of Pakistan as a modern, democratic state where everyone was equal before, and afforded the protection of, the law.[10] Yet parallel to such sentiments have always existed religious and conservative forces demanding a clear expression and manifestation of an Islamic identity. Soon after the Independence of Pakistan the liberal, democratic element inside as well as outside government realized the importance of 'playing the Islamic card'.[11] Aware that multi-ethnic, multicultural and multi-lingual Pakistan needed a central theme to bind it together as a nation, religion became the obvious binding force. Consequently, Pakistan's Islamic identity has been highlighted in pronouncements from government, a trend that has found favour with the majority of the population, for whom 'cultural Islam' is an important part of their identity.[12]

---

[7] For a detailed discussion see K. Mumtaz and F. Shaheed, *Women of Pakistan: Two Steps Forward, One Step Back?* (Lahore: Vanguard, 1987), Chapter 7.

[8] *Abdul Waheed* v. *Asma Jehangir* PLD (1997) Lahore 301. In a similar case the father was convicted for murdering his daughter who had married of her own volition without the consent of the family: see *Muhammad Siddique* v. *The State* PLD 449 (2001). The Maliki and Shafai schools, however, hold that a woman's consent must be given through her *wali*: Mannan, *D. F. Mulla's Principles*, p. 390.

[9] For example, Maulana Fazlullah, a militant clergyman from the Swat Valley, has used FM radio to broadcast venomously misogynistic rhetoric exhorting men to keep women inside the house, declaring them the cause of all evils in society; while in 2010, Islamabad's Lal Masjid seminary led a vigilante campaign against women of 'loose morals' in the name of an Islamic duty to 'promote virtue and prevent vice'.

[10] See his presidential address of 11 August 1947 in J. Ahmed (ed.), *Speeches and Writings of Mr. Jinnah* (Lahore: Sh. Muhammad Ashraf, 1964).

[11] For a detailed discussion with reference to the Constitution, see G. W. Chaudhary, *Constitutional Development in Pakistan* (London: Lowe and Brydone, 1971) and 'Religious Minorities in Pakistan', *Muslim World* 46 (1956), 313–23.

[12] See generally Lau, *Role of Islam*; and 'Sharia and National Law in Pakistan', in J. M. Otto (ed.), *Sharia Incorporated: A Comparative Overview of the Legal Systems of Twelve Muslim Countries in the Past and Present* (Leiden: Leiden University Press, 2010), pp. 373–432; A. M. Weiss,

In the context of women's rights, Islam has been and continues to be used both for *and* against women's rights and equality, depending on who is deploying the argument and at what forum.[13] Since the inception of Pakistan, this plurality of views has been apparent in the pronouncements of various political and governmental actors, as well as the population in general. Muhammad Ali Jinnah, the founder of Pakistan, advocated women's rights, education and economic empowerment and was accompanied by his sister Fatima in public engagements to highlight women's presence in the public sphere. Likewise, Ra'ana Liaquat Ali Khan, the wife of Pakistan's first prime minister, founded the All Pakistan Women's Association (APWA) to empower women in the field of education and skills development. But it was during this period that the conservative politician Abul Ala Maududi wrote his famous book *Purdah and the Status of Women in Islam*, which argued for women's complete segregation and a role inside the home prohibiting engagement in the public sphere.[14] The gap between various ideological positions regarding the rights of women in Pakistan became fertile ground for disputes over women's rights in Islam and international law. Last but not least, customary practices, heavily influenced by patriarchal norms, inform perceptions of women's status and undermine or cancel out women's rights in Islam.[15]

Differing conclusions over women's (in)equality produced by diverse lines of argument based on Islam and Islamic law are evident from the debate on whether Pakistan should become party to CEDAW. The fifteen-year journey

'Interpreting Islam and Women's Rights: Implementing CEDAW in Pakistan', *International Sociology* 18(3) (2003), 581–601; A. M. Weiss (ed.), *Islamic Reassertion in Pakistan* (Syracuse: Syracuse University Press, 1986); F. Halliday and H. Alavi (eds.), *State and Ideology in the Middle East and Pakistan* (London: Macmillan Educational, 1988).

13 See the discussions in Rahman, 'The Status of Women in Islam'; Esposito and DeLong-Bas, *Women in Muslim Family Law*; A. Al-Hibri, 'Muslim Women's Rights in the Global Village: Opportunities and Challenges', *Journal of Law and Religion* 15 (2001), 37–66; Hassan, 'An Islamic Perspective'; Mernissi, *Women and Islam*; L. Ahmed, *Women and Gender in Islam: Historical Roots of a Modern Debate* (New Haven: Yale University Press, 1992); Barlas, *Believing Women*; Mir-Husseini, *Marriage on Trial*; S. Haeri, *Law of Desire: Temporary Marriage in Shi'i Iran* (Syracuse: Syracuse University Press, 1989); H. Afshar, *Islam and Feminisms: An Iranian Case Study*, Women's Studies in York (Basingstoke: Macmillan Press, 1998).

14 Maududi typifies the complexity of Pakistani understandings of 'Islamic' law: in various books he argued that women's empowerment through employment in the public sphere is the cause of societal evils and is prohibited in Islam, asking at one point in *Purdah*, 'Why should a woman who wins her own bread, supports herself economically and does not depend on anyone for security and maintenance, remain faithfully attached to one man only for the sake of her sexual desire?' In 1966, nevertheless, Maududi and his party turned a political somersault by supporting a female presidential candidate while the 'liberal' opposition parties (and that of the incumbent president) published pamphlets arguing *against* women as heads of state.

15 For instance, Islamic law accords women inheritance rights, yet cultural articulations negate this by denying daughters the right to inherit land; male child preference continues as a cultural norm but has no support in Islam, as the Prophet Muhammad himself had no male offspring to survive him and his preference for his daughter Fatima was exceptional in its explicitness; adult women have the right to marry of their own choice, but societal norms expect women to defer to the spouse chosen by the family.

toward final accession in 1996 was difficult and contested, both within official circles and within various social constituencies, and reflected the plurality of views regarding what constitutes 'Islamically' and culturally acceptable human rights and whether UN human rights instruments are compatible with human rights in the Islamic legal traditions.[16] The debates also reflected the different 'galleries' (national and international) to which government and society perform, and the various audiences observing these performances. Pakistan's history of participation in human rights treaties (including CEDAW) has also been influenced by a political history that has oscillated between elected governments and military regimes, both of which have used Islam as a tool of political expediency.

The debate, then, over women's rights and the place of CEDAW is driven by a range of divergent opinions and viewpoints.[17] In her analysis of plural legalities and their impact on women's rights in Pakistan, Shaheed notes that the intersection of culture with custom, law and politics has direct implications for women's rights.[18] It is the power elite who decide what constitutes 'valid' culture and custom and how these will be applied in the formal and informal realms.[19] Pakistan's discourse of women's rights and of CEDAW is influenced by the interpretations of those in positions of power (often mitigating *against* women's rights), who are not necessarily those in government.[20] While government may subscribe to the rhetoric of women's rights, and may desire to be *seen* to subscribe by the international community and by elements of Pakistani civil society, there exists a dissonance between formal laws and governmental policy on the one hand and practices and beliefs on the other.[21]

6.3 The Arduous Journey towards Accession

Demands for the ratification of CEDAW were made by women's NGOs and the human rights movement in Pakistan as soon as it was adopted at the UN in

---

[16] This approach is, of course, not confined to Muslim countries: there is a rich body of literature on universalism versus relativism in human rights debates, including 'Asian', 'African' and 'Western' concepts of human rights.

[17] See, for example, Y. Zaidi, 'The Interplay of CEDAW, National Laws and Customary Practices in Pakistan: A Literature Review', in Ali, *Conceptualising Islamic Law*, pp. 199–263.

[18] For this line of argument, see generally F. Shaheed, 'Engagements of Culture, Customs and Law: Women's Lives and Activism', in F. Shaheed, S. Warraich, C. Balchin and A. Guzdar (eds.), *Shaping Women's Lives* (Lahore: Shirkatgah, 1998), 61–80.

[19] F. Shaheed, 'Citizenship and the Nuanced Belonging of Women', in Bennett, *Scratching the Surface*, p. 33.

[20] For instance, in 2008, Baluch tribal senators in Parliament supported the burying alive of women who had acted against cultural norms. Similarly, at the height of the militancy in the Swat Valley in 2007–8, girls' schools were burned down and a 'call' to keep them at home was heeded by parents and families concerned about the safety of their daughters. Students of religious *madrasahs* have been known to harass women who do not cover their head when in public.

[21] Witness, for instance, the wide gap between enrolment of girls and boys in schools. At a formal level all children have access to schools but cultural practices hinder girls from going to school.

1979,[22] yet it took fifteen years of consistent lobbying to keep the issue alive until the decision to accede was finally made.[23] On a number of occasions during the mid- to late 1980s,[24] the government signalled its intention to sign the convention, but the issue remained unresolved. It is worthwhile discussing briefly one particular such initiative in 1987, as it reflects the thinking within many sections of state and society regarding the place and position of women and their stereotypical roles in religion, custom and tradition.

In 1987, it was recommended by a committee of federal ministries that Pakistan sign,[25] but only with a blanket reservation stating, 'The Government of the Islamic Republic of Pakistan agree[s] to ratify the convention to the extent that articles and sub-clauses are not repugnant to the teachings of the Holy Quran and the Government of Pakistan shall be the sole judge of the question whether such repugnancy exists.'[26] This proposal, an example of 'playing the Islamic card' before a conservative domestic audience, would have been unacceptable to the international community, since it would have given Pakistan the right to interpret CEDAW in accordance not with international norms but with domestic understandings of women's rights. Conversely, such a reservation would no doubt have met with the approval of those significant numbers of Pakistanis who consider Islam to be the overarching normative framework informing their legal and social system.

The Ministry of Foreign Affairs, however, conscious of how such a reservation would be received internationally, opposed this on the grounds that other states

---

[22] Pakistan has a robust women's rights and human rights movement dating back to before Independence. For an overview see Mumtaz and Shaheed, *Women of Pakistan*; S. S. Ali, 'Law, Islam and the Women's Movement in Pakistan', in S. M. Rai (ed.), *Gender and Democratisation: International Perspectives* (London: Routledge, 2000), pp. 41–63.

[23] Prominent among the groups and organizations lobbying for CEDAW were the Human Rights Commission of Pakistan, the Aurat Foundation, Shirkat Gah Women's Resource Centre, the All Pakistan Women's Association, the All Pakistan Women Lawyers Association, Simorgh Women's Resource & Publication Centre, the Applied Socio-economic Research Resource Centre and the Women's Action Forum.

[24] The government considered the issue in 1984 but no decision was made (see *Working Paper: The Convention on Elimination of All Forms of Discrimination against Women* (Islamabad: Government of Pakistan, Ministry of Foreign Affairs, 1994)). In 1985, the National Commission on the Status of Women, formed to assess the situation and make recommendations for improvement, repeated the demand for accession. However, no action was taken, and in response to the candid views presented in the report by its outspoken female chair, Zari Sarfaraz, the government withheld publication (see *Report of the Pakistan Commission on the Status of Women* (Islamabad: Government of Pakistan Printing Press, 1986)). The report was finally circulated when Benazir Bhutto assumed power in 1988. It is interesting that General Zia-ul-Haq's government, known for its oppressive policies toward women, found it necessary to create a Women's Division in the Cabinet Secretariat that was later formed into a fully fledged Ministry of Women Development and Youth Affairs in 1989. It was this ministry that led the consultation for signing CEDAW. In 1989, Benazir Bhutto issued a directive to look into CEDAW with a view to exploring accession. This was done to coincide with the 10th Anniversary of CEDAW and ahead of her attending a UN-sponsored symposium in New York. Again, no positive outcome came of this initiative. See *Working Paper*, p. 3.

[25] Including the Ministries of Law and Justice, Religious Affairs, Education, and Foreign Affairs, and the Cabinet Secretariat.

[26] See *Working Paper*, p. 2.

would enter objections, the reservation being conceived as contrary to the 'object and purpose of the Convention' under Article 28(2).[27] Despite this, the ministry's comments on the difficulties encountered by non-Western states in ratifying CEDAW resonated with the sentiments of the proposed reservation:

> [CEDAW] was the result of Western women's rights activists and does not take into account the varied socio-economic conditions as well as the diverse customs, values, and religious and ethical perspectives of different societies in various parts of the world . . . The Convention has been used by Western human rights activists as an instrument to criticise not only the situation in various Islamic countries but also the very fundamentals of the Islamic faith.[28]

The Ministry's statement also reflected the existence and power of popular ideas of gender stereotypes, in that 'diverse customs, values, and religious and ethical perspectives' and 'varied socio-economic conditions' were taken to inevitably imply a defensible gender *in*equality and a conflict with ideas of non-discrimination. If anything, of course, it can be argued that it is a government's duty to *remove* 'varied socio-economic conditions' insofar as they threaten access to basic human rights. Deeply entrenched in the Ministry's comments were popularly held convictions regarding the 'alien-ness' of women's rights emanating from 'Western' forums,[29] regardless of the fact that these rights were being demanded by Pakistani women themselves. A final reason for reluctance to ratify CEDAW in 1987 was that becoming a party would entail international scrutiny of the position of women in Pakistan, including the compilation of a country report and discussion thereof by the CEDAW Committee, a situation the Ministry of Foreign Affairs did not feel comfortable with. The matter did not progress much further.

During Benazir Bhutto's second tenure as prime minister (October 1993 to November 1996), serious efforts were initiated towards ratification. The government's renewed motivation is apparent from a letter written in August 1993 by the secretary of the Ministry of Women Development to the Foreign Secretary, recommending that 'the issue of Pakistan's ratification may be re-examined in view of the fact that women in Pakistan have made substantial progress in improving their status and also as citizens of this country and that *Pakistan's non-ratification was creating international embarrassment.*'[30]

A series of meetings was held in Islamabad, some of which I had the privilege to attend in my capacity as a member of the Prime Minister's Consultative

---

[27] Ibid.   [28] Ibid.

[29] Such popular rhetoric is evident in newspaper and journal articles, as well as in books authored by, amongst others, members of Jamaat-e-Islami (the Islamic Party), who frame the West as the morally corrupt 'other' conspiring to undermine a pristine Muslim populace through notions of human rights, liberalism and 'permissive' societal structures. For a detailed discussion see S. A. Cheema, 'Problematizing "Authenticity": A Critical Appraisal of the Jamaat-i-Islami Gender Discourse' (Warwick University PhD thesis, 2011).

[30] *Working Paper*, p. 3 (emphasis added).

Committee on Women. Four meetings are especially noteworthy,[31] at which representatives from the relevant ministries (including the Ministry for Religious Affairs, the Interior Ministry and the Council of Islamic Ideology) and NGOs[32] presented their views and comments on possible ratification.[33] The agreed outcome was that a case be prepared for the government to sign CEDAW, subject to one specific 'temporary' reservation to Article 2(f), which relates to requiring states parties to 'take all appropriate measures, including legislation, to modify or abolish existing laws, regulations, customs and practices which constitute discrimination against women.'

Unsurprisingly, the proposal to enter a specific reservation to Article 2(f) met with stiff opposition from the Ministry of Women Development, backed by legal academics working on the subject, women's groups and human rights activists,[34] who challenged the government's assertion that ratification without reservation was impossible. But, finding itself performing to different galleries, the government was obviously keen to emphasize its Islamic identity, both to the international community and in relation to its Muslim state counterparts. Reserving its position on Article 2(f), on the ground that it was inconsistent with Islamic law, would establish a point regarding the protection of Pakistan's Muslim identity. The fact that other Muslim countries had already entered substantial reservations was highlighted, and it was argued that this much was expected of Pakistan.[35] The hypocrisy of Western governments was also mentioned by the anti-CEDAW lobby, pointing as it did to their reticence to sign without reservations.[36]

Supporters of ratification without reservation (including NGOs, members of civil society, academics and activists, some of whom were represented on the Prime Minister's Consultative Committee) reacted strongly to this proposal, arguing that Iraq, Egypt, Libya and other reserving states did not form the entire spectrum of Muslim countries: Turkey, Tunisia, Senegal, Mali, Indonesia and Yemen were equally 'Islamic' jurisdictions yet had ratified CEDAW unreservedly.

---

[31] These meetings were held on 5 October 1994 and on 4 January, 31 January and 13 June 1995.

[32] The consensus among those NGOs in Pakistan whose views were solicited was that Pakistan should ratify CEDAW without reservation (I was personally present at this meeting, held in the Foreign Office on 5 October 1994). The NGOs present included the APWA, Aurat Foundation, Shirkat Gah, the Human Rights Commission of Pakistan, and Behbood.

[33] These views were sought by the Ministry of Foreign Affairs through O.M. No UN(II)-9/4/94, dated 19 May 1994.

[34] The prime minister had constituted a consultative committee of concerned individuals and organizations to assist in the ratification process. I was a member of the committee as an academic specializing in CEDAW and Islamic law. The APWA, the Human Rights Commission of Pakistan, the Aurat Foundation, Shirkat Gah, Simorgh, Applied Socio-economic Research, and Behbood (being among the best-known and reputable in the field of women's rights) were among the NGOs on the committee (see Ali, *A Comparative Study*, for a comprehensive list).

[35] *Working Paper*, p. 6.

[36] CEDAW is the most reserved human rights treaty in the catalogue, with national constitutions and domestic legislation the most cited reasons for entering reservations. More than a dozen European states have entered reservations on the basis of national laws and constitutions.

Pakistan, they argued, should come up with her own position regarding CEDAW and women's rights and not blindly follow other countries over the specific issue of whether reservations ought to be entered.[37]

It was to assess whether CEDAW did in fact conflict with 'Islamic' values that, in 1995, I undertook a comparative study of the provisions of CEDAW alongside the laws of Pakistan and of 'Islamic' law more widely.[38] The study, which was used as a campaign document in NGO seminars and workshops as well as by the government, noted that one-sixth of the CEDAW drafting committee comprised Muslim states, and that it was consequently hard to believe that an 'un-Islamic' document running counter to the spirit of Islamic law could have won their approval. Furthermore, although some Muslim states had entered reservations to certain articles on the basis of their being repugnant to Islamic law and *sharia*, even these countries were not uniform in their opposition.[39] The Consultative Committee ultimately proposed ratification without reservation.

6.4 Did CEDAW Conflict with Domestic Law?

The problem that then arose was how to address the fact that certain laws in force at the time were clearly discriminatory to women.[40] The question was raised in the Prime Minister's Consultative Committee on Women as to whether these laws would require modification or repeal prior to ratification, or whether the process of review of domestic laws could continue thereafter. The view prevailed that the existence of certain provisions of domestic law which were incompatible with the substantive provisions of CEDAW should not preclude Pakistan from becoming a state party:[41] it was argued that a number of European, African and Asian countries had found themselves in similar situations but were making an effort to overcome the problematic provisions in their respective domestic laws. What was required for the present moment

---

[37] Ali, *Comparative Study*, pp. 131–41.

[38] Ali, *Comparative Study*. The study demonstrated that, apart from a few laws informed by a literalist interpretation of the Qur'an and Sunna (including sections of the law of evidence, criminal law and inheritance laws), most laws did not conflict with CEDAW.

[39] For example, Algeria cited national laws, Indonesia has not entered reservations to CEDAW's substantive articles, Turkey's initial reservations (now partially withdrawn) cited the Turkish Civil Code and the Turkish Law of Nationality, Tunisia reserved on the basis of conflict with the Tunisian Nationality Code and Personal Status Code, Mali and Senegal ratified without reservations.

[40] Including the Child Marriages Restraint Act 1929, Offence against Property (Enforcement of Hudood Ordinance) 1979, Offence of Zina (Enforcement of Hudood Ordinance) 1979, Offence of Qazf (Enforcement of Hudood Ordinance) 1979, Qanoon-i-Shahdat Order 1984, Citizenship Act 1951, Punjab/Sindh/NWFP/Baluchistan Muslim Personal Law (Shariat Application Act) 1962, and the Pakistan Penal Code 1860.

[41] The late Shehla Zia, the director of the Aurat Foundation (a national women's resource and information centre), and myself both advocated this viewpoint in the 4 June 1995 meeting of the prime minister's Consultative Committee on Women held in Islamabad.

was for Pakistan to demonstrate goodwill and genuine concern for promoting gender equality by ratifying CEDAW.

It is uncertain what precise impact the lobbying of human rights groups and academics had on the government's final decision,[42] but one factor stands out clearly in its decision-making: the impending Fourth World Conference on Women, scheduled to be held in Beijing in September 1995, was an incentive to ratify, particularly as Prime Minister Benazir Bhutto was leading the delegation. The Cabinet's decision (less than two weeks before the Beijing Conference) to ratify CEDAW came at a politically opportune moment and placed Pakistan in a favourable light. Yet contrary to the impression given by government spokespersons that there would be no reservations or declarations, the subsequent instrument of March 1996 included the following declaration: 'The accession by [the] Government of the Islamic Republic of Pakistan to the [said Convention] is subject to the provisions of the Constitution of Pakistan.' A single reservation was also entered to Article 29(1) (dealing with dispute resolution), stating, 'The Government of the Islamic Republic of Pakistan declares that it does not consider itself bound by paragraph 1 of article 29 of the Convention.'[43]

The declaration led to a number of objections from states who argued that it undermined the convention.[44] Domestically, NGOs and civil societies, as well as some academics, were of the view that the declaration amounted to creating a hierarchy of laws, with CEDAW ranked below Islamic law and the Constitution of Pakistan.[45]

6.5 Domesticating CEDAW in Pakistan

While the pre-accession process presented an opportunity for a critical examination of formal and informal laws, customary practices and religious norms, accession brought its own challenges and highlighted tasks necessary for effective implementation and monitoring. Both the government and NGOs were required to develop a methodology for collaboration as part of the process

---

[42] In addition to lobbying the government, proponents of CEDAW also campaigned through seminars and workshops to generate support and raise awareness of the substantive provisions of the Convention. For instance, from April to June of 1995 the Women's Study Centre at the University of Peshawar, of which I was the director, held a series of seminars on the subject at Quaid-i-Azam University Islamabad; a similar one was held by the Sustainable Development Policy Institute, and a third, with the support of the APWA, was held in Lahore in the summer of 1995.

[43] Multilateral Treaties Deposited with the Secretary-General, UN Doc. ST/LEG/SER.E/15 (1997), 175.

[44] Including Austria, Germany, Portugal, the Netherlands, Norway, Denmark and Sweden.

[45] Shirkat Gah, the Human Rights Commission of Pakistan, the Aurat Foundation, the Women's Action Forum and others were critical of the declaration and continue to record their disagreement in shadow reports and presentations on the subject. See, for example, National Commission for Justice and Peace, *Discrimination Lingers on . . . A Report on the Compliance of CEDAW in Pakistan* (Lahore, 2007) and Shirkat Gah Women's Resource Centre, *Talibanisation and Poor Governance: Undermining CEDAW in Pakistan* (Lahore, 2007).

of monitoring and reporting to the CEDAW Committee. Unfortunately, given economic constraints and limited human resource capacity, the institutional structures which in an ideal world might help domesticate CEDAW into Pakistani law have not been put in place as part of governmental routine. In fact, since accession CEDAW has been viewed as a 'project' to be taken up subject to available funding (which is mostly expected to come from foreign donor agencies) without becoming part of mainstream, budgeted government functions. Time and again, and with support from international donors, 'project' proposals have been written and funding received, and consultants have been hired at governmental and NGO levels to write Pakistan's country report as well as shadow reports on behalf of the country's NGOs and civil society.

But this project-like approach towards CEDAW resulted in Pakistan missing the deadlines for submitting its initial, second and third periodic reports, which were finally entered in August 2005 and considered in May 2007.[46] The Fourth Periodic Report, too, was a late submission. As for NGOs and civil society, two shadow reports have been submitted thus far. The first (*Discrimination Lingers on . . . A Report on the Compliance of CEDAW in Pakistan*) was, according to its authors, endorsed by over 900 Pakistani human rights organizations.[47] A second shadow report (*Talibanisation and Poor Governance: Undermining CEDAW in Pakistan*),[48] expressing the views and concerns of twenty-three organizations, was submitted to augment *Discrimination Lingers on . . .* and reviewed questions posed by the CEDAW Committee and the government's responses.

At a most basic level, Pakistan's Constitution requires that an international treaty, on ratification, does not directly become part of the domestic legal system. One of the first steps necessary to domesticate CEDAW would therefore be to incorporate it into national legislation through an Act of Parliament, a step that the government has not so far taken. Following discussion of the government's Combined Initial, Second and Third Periodic Report,[49] and prompted by questions raised by NGOs in Pakistan's two shadow reports, the CEDAW Committee expressed its concern that the convention had not been incorporated into Pakistani law,[50] to which the government responded in its Fourth Periodic

---

[46] The Fourth Periodic Report (CEDAW Committee, 11 August 2011, UN Doc. CEDAW/C/PAK/4) was received and considered by the CEDAW Committee in 2013. The Ministry of Women Development holds the mandate to prepare Pakistan's country reports, including engaging with civil society and government departments and ministries in their preparation; this task is now undertaken by the NCSW.

[47] See note 45 above, this chapter. The lead organizations on this report were the National Commission for Justice and Peace and the Democratic Commission for Human Development.

[48] Shirkat Gah Women's Resource Centre, *Talibanisation and Poor Governance*. The report was produced by Shirkat Gah with input from a number of other NGOs, and responds succinctly to the government's reports and to the prevailing atmosphere of militancy and lack of security in Pakistan at the time.

[49] CEDAW Committee, 3 August 2005, UN Doc. CEDAW/C/PAK/1–3; CEDAW Committee, 5 October 2006, UN Doc. CEDAW/C/PAK/Q/3; CEDAW Committee, 1 March 2007, UN Doc. CEDAW/C/PAK/Q/3/Add.1.

[50] CEDAW Committee, 11 June 2007, UN Doc. CEDAW/C/PAK/CO/3, at p. 3.

Report by stating, 'An International Convention or Treaty is not directly applicable in Domestic Law on Ratification in Pakistan. However, the provisions of such Treaties and Conventions are taken into consideration in formulating legislation and by Courts when interpreting the law.'[51] Since this is the government's latest position on the matter, it does not appear that any steps are anticipated to domesticate CEDAW in the near future.

The government's position regarding its reservations to CEDAW, too, is under close scrutiny at home and abroad. The position is reiterated in its Combined Initial, Second and Third Periodic Report, as follows:

> The Declaration facilitated Pakistan's accession to the Convention and represents the legal position on the matter ... The objective was not to go against the object and purpose of the Convention while assuaging the concerns of those who had misgivings about the Convention. Subjecting the implementation of the Convention to the Constitution of Pakistan was a sensible course of action ... Its authors had the benefit of studying [the UDHR, CERD, ICCPR and ICESCR] – the major international human rights instruments then in existence. Many of the principles contained in these documents are reflected in the Constitution. It can therefore be argued that in substance the declaration did not have a negative effect in the implementation of the Convention while at the same time enabling Pakistan to accede to the Convention. In practice also there do not appear to be any legislative, policy or administrative actions taken by the Government, which contravene provisions of the Convention on basis of the declaration. The shortcomings in the implementation of the Convention, inevitable in any country, are not directly attributable to the declaration.[52]

In other words, by ratifying CEDAW but with a declaration and reservation, Pakistan was performing a difficult balancing act before international and domestic audiences demanding very different things of it.

Neither civil society in Pakistan nor the CEDAW Committee were convinced by this statement,[53] and Pakistan's delegation was queried on the subject and Pakistan was urged to withdraw its declaration.[54] The committee also sought clarification over which law would prevail in the event of a conflict of laws, to which the Pakistani delegate responded that

> the Constitution guaranteed the equality of rights of men and women and banned discrimination based on race, religion, caste or sex. It was also true that no law could stand if it were found to be inconsistent with the basic law in the Koran, which provided the basis for Pakistan's traditional respect for women and protection of their rights.[55]

Another member of the delegation also made the point that Pakistan had ratified the convention in 1996 but 'its basic law as stipulated in the Constitution

---

[51] CEDAW/C/PAK/, at p. 12.   [52] CEDAW/C/PAK/1–3, at p. 8.
[53] See shadow reports at note 45 above, this chapter.   [54] CEDAW/C/PAK/CO/3, at p. 3.
[55] CEDAW Committee, 19 July 2007, UN Doc. CEDAW/C/SR/781, at p. 4.

remained in force...There was no need to be concerned about any conflict between the Convention and Muslim principles, as Islamic law provided even more effective protection of women's rights than the Convention.'[56]

Such differing responses offered to the CEDAW Committee by the Pakistani delegates highlight yet again the varying perceptions between and among government circles over where CEDAW is placed in the legal pluralities of the country. One thing stands out clearly: the government has no intention of modifying its position, stating that the matter is still under review.[57] In the Fourth Periodic Report, it adopts a similar response by observing,

> 35. The matter of Conditional Accession is under review. The Ministry of Women Development has requested comments from all relevant Federal Ministries and the Provincial Women's Development Departments concerning the withdrawal of the Declaration. Of the total responses received, only 21% supported withdrawal of General Declaration, hence, the consensus could not be developed. However, it is worth mentioning that the General Declaration did not affect the legislation process for eliminating discrimination against women and State obligation towards CEDAW implementation as various amendments in the existing laws are being made and new acts/bills are also introduced to protect women's rights.[58]

Recalling the positions adopted by various delegates during the drafting process of CEDAW (in Chapter 5) regarding priority of their national constitutions and laws, it is not surprising that the government of Pakistan, too, does not intend to reorder the existing hierarchy of laws (Islamic, constitutional and national laws and international human rights law). That she can simultaneously 'domesticate' and implement CEDAW as well as Islamic law and the constitution of Pakistan brings to the fore the plural legalities at play in most post-colonial jurisdictions. As examples of this interplay, the Fourth Periodic Report to the CEDAW Committee provides a list of laws that arguably confirm the stance of the Government of Pakistan that despite the declaration, discrimination against women is being addressed through legislation. It has to be said that an impressive array of laws have been adopted for the protection of women.[59] Of these, perhaps the most significant of all recent legislations is the Prevention of Anti Women Practices Act 2011, which aims to banish harmful, age-old

---

[56] Ibid. at pp. 4–5.

[57] The delegation had indicated in its Combined Initial, Second and Third Periodic Report, as well as in the meeting to consider the country report, that the NCSW had been given the mandate to report back on whether Pakistan ought to withdraw the declaration. The Fourth Periodic Report does not share the outcome, if any, of the NCSW report.

[58] CEDAW/C/PAK/4, at p. 11.

[59] These include the Protection against Harassment at Workplace Act 2010; the Prevention of Anti Women Practices Act 2011, and the Criminal Law (Second Amendment) Act 2011, commonly known as the Acid Control and Acid Crime Prevention Law. Through the latter, legislation has been enacted whereby the act of mutilating women by the use of acids or other corrosive substance is punishable with death or life imprisonment.

customary practices such as giving a female in marriage or otherwise in *badla-e-sulha*,[60] *wanni* or *swara*, depriving a woman of inheriting property, forced marriage and marriage with the Holy Quran. Various provisions of CEDAW are addressed through this Act. The foremost significance of this law is the acknowledgement of discrimination through customary practices and their criminalization. This has come a long way from trying to justify discrimination on the basis of customary practice.[61]

6.6 Legal Obstacles to Full Domestication

Further obstacles in domesticating CEDAW, and a constant point of issue in country and shadow reports as well as in committee deliberations, are those laws which are explicitly discriminatory to women and in direct conflict with CEDAW. These include the Citizenship Act 1951, the Law of Evidence Act 1984 and the Hudood Ordinance of 1979.[62] The Pakistani delegation at a meeting to consider its reports to CEDAW in 2007 expressed the government's commitment to abolish 'not only the 1979 Hudood Ordinance but also all discriminatory legislation'.[63] The Fourth Periodic Report therefore dealt at length with developments in this area and described the various steps that had been taken to address discrimination. Yet although some progress was reported, the discriminatory laws remain in force.[64]

Finally, an indicator of domestication would be a level of awareness, discussion and use of CEDAW's substantive provisions among civil society, academics, communities and individuals, as well as the judiciary. In short, how far has its implementation percolated down through Pakistani society?

Although the personal skills and exertions of Salma Waheed, Secretary of the Ministry of Women Development from 1993 to 1996, were crucial to effective co-operation between the government and wider civil society in the pre-accession process, the relationship between the two regarding CEDAW is in general erratic at best and hostile at times. The first shadow report, *Discrimination Lingers on . . .*, complained of an absence of co-operation post-accession: 'Despite that NGOs were ignored in preparation of the government report, as

---

[60] Literally meaning 'exchange for peace', an old custom where a girl is given in marriage to a man of the family of a victim who has been murdered by a male member of the girl's family, in exchange for ending enmity and vendetta. Sometimes this may also occur with offences other than murder. Courts in Pakistan have taken note of these practices and declared them void and against the law and against Islam. The practice, however, continues, though with more chances of failure in the face of vibrant print and electronic media: courts and government institutions are thus constrained to take notice and legal action.

[61] Enacted on 22 December 2011 as the Criminal Law (Third Amendment) Act 2011.

[62] The Hudood Ordinance sets out punishments for, amongst other things, extramarital sex: see the discussion in CEDAW/C/PAK/CO/3, paras. 5, 16 and 17.

[63] CEDAW/C/SR/78, at p. 6. The Women Protection Act 2006 has to an extent 'disabled' the Hudood law on extramarital sex.

[64] See CEDAW/C/PAK/4, paras. 43–64, for details of discriminatory provisions.

civil society organisations we pledge ourselves for a meaningful collaboration in the implementation of the human rights standards and commitments in CEDAW'.[65] The government, nevertheless, reiterated its commitment to collaboration with civil organizations, and noted that it had followed the harmonized reporting guidelines and engaged in an inclusive process for preparing the country report.[66]

The processes leading to accession had provided an opportunity for individuals, groups and NGOs to raise the discussion of women's rights, and CEDAW became the subject of campaigns.[67] In the post-ratification period, CEDAW became part of training programmes run by governmental and non-governmental bodies; translations of CEDAW into national and minority languages made its contents more accessible at the grass roots. The treaty also became a tool for women's rights forming part of human rights education in NGO advocacy training sessions. Yet the fact remains that indigenizing CEDAW's substantive provisions and taking ownership of this 'bill of women's rights' remains at a superficial level.[68]

6.7 Using the CEDAW Model to Advance Women's Rights in Pakistan

From 1999 to 2001 I held the portfolio of Cabinet minister for health, population welfare and women development in the government of what was then the North-West Frontier Province. As an academic and activist whose training and interest was human rights and Islamic law, my policy initiatives were motivated and informed by the ideas within CEDAW. In the years after accession, there was a rare opportunity when I, as an academic activist, was able to put research findings into practice and test CEDAW as a supportive tool and strategy for women's rights in Pakistan. More importantly, as a Cabinet minister I considered it an obligation to implement Pakistan's CEDAW undertakings. Suffice it to say that I encountered stereotypical perceptions of what needs to be done to 'take care' of the 'women question' at play at every level of government, and beyond in civil society.

Yet it is noteworthy that a government then led by a military general (Pervez Musharraf) had a total of seven women ministers out of twenty-eight in its provincial and federal cabinets, while many a democratically elected government has far fewer. (This step in itself was in keeping with the spirit of CEDAW, although CEDAW was not the motivation behind these appointments.) Soon after taking office, all women ministers met in Islamabad to set up an informal Women Ministers Forum laying out an agenda, both legislative and at policy

---

[65] National Commission for Justice and Peace, *Discrimination Lingers on . . .*, p. 6.
[66] CEDAW/C/PAK/4, at pp. 10–11. The guidelines are set out in Annex I of the report.
[67] Including the 1993–5 campaign for CEDAW ratification.
[68] As one NGO activist remarked, 'CEDAW has been confined to a module in a human rights training programme; nothing more!' (personal communication).

and institutional levels, to take up women's issues and address problems confronted by women in the public and private spheres. The forum's first initiative was, having studied similar bodies in India, South Africa, the UK, Egypt and other countries, to establish a statutory National Commission on the Status of Women (NCSW), an autonomous watchdog for policies and actions insofar as they affected women, to monitor implementation of women's rights under national and international law, including CEDAW.[69] The process of setting up the NCSW (of which I was appointed first chair), provided a number of lessons in the manner in which the women's rights agenda might be advanced, and in how deep the conviction runs within government.

The first draft produced used CEDAW and its Optional Protocol as a template,[70] the idea being that there would be the NCSW at the national level and individual complaints mechanisms in the provinces. Women ombudspersons would entertain petitions and provide decisions that would be implemented through government departments and ministries. This draft met with stiff resistance from officials who felt that the NCSW replicated the role of the Ministry of Women Development.[71] (The approach of some officials had been to hive off anything to do with 'women's issues' into the ministry's lap, thereby absolving other ministries of any further obligation. 'What is the need for two Women's Ministries?' one asked me; 'We already have one!'). Another argument raised against the proposed NCSW and its complaint mechanisms was that we were planning a parallel 'government' for women.[72] But the most potent argument was one of finance: the NCSW as envisaged in our draft was said to be too expensive. The statute that finally won approval from the Cabinet and the president was a negotiated document: the Women Ministers Forum had had a choice between a watered-down version without the individual complaint bodies in the provinces, or nothing at all. This is the version that went on the statute book, and the National Commission on the Status of Women came into being in the year 2000.[73]

---

[69] The first of these meetings was held in Islamabad on 26 December 1999 with Dr Atiya Inayatullah in the chair. Those present included Zubaida Jalal, Shahida Jameel, Shaheen Atiqurrehman and myself. My ideas on national machineries for women were also informed by the work of Shirin Rai, including S. Rai (ed.), *Mainstreaming Gender, Democratising the State: Institutional mechanisms for the advancement of women* (Manchester: Manchester University Press, 2003).

[70] The 1999 Optional Protocol to CEDAW (OP-CEDAW) created a mechanism whereby a CEDAW Committee could hear complaints and make enquiries into abuses. The adoption of the CEDAW/OP-CEDAW model as a template meant that women would be able to use the NCSW to complain against violations of their rights within a domestic ambit.

[71] The Eighteenth Constitutional Amendment has delegated Ministries of Women Development to the federating units, i.e. the provinces, and the role of implementing CEDAW has now been assigned to the Human Rights Ministries in the provinces.

[72] Personal communication with relevant civil servants.

[73] Approved by the then president of Pakistan, General Pervez Musharraf, on 17 July 2000, as the National Commission on the Status of Women Ordinance XXVI of 2000. I was appointed the first chair of this commission.

While the NCSW experience was unquestionably informed by the CEDAW/ OP-CEDAW model, another major development was not so directly informed: the constitutional amendment creating reserved seats for women at all levels of government and electoral laws facilitating this change. Our Women Ministers Forum pressed for one-third representation of women in local bodies as well as in Parliament (although at the Parliamentary level the proportion was in the end lower). The views within various constituencies were diverse, ranging from approval of women's political rights to complete disapproval on the basis that this would distort and tear the fabric of society. The constitutional amendment leading to women's reserved seats could not have been achieved without the almost unanimous support of male ministerial colleagues and most of all of General Musharraf himself.

In 2012, twelve years after the NCSW Ordinance was adopted, the Pakistan Parliament approved an amended version of the original law. This law, named the National Commission on the Status of Women Act 2012, received the assent of the president of Pakistan on 8 March 2012.[74] For the first time, a Pakistani law cited as one of its objectives fulfilment of obligations under CEDAW in the preamble:

> Whereas it is expedient to set up a National Commission on the Status of Women for the promotion of social, economic, political and legal rights of women, as provided in the Constitution of the Islamic Republic of Pakistan and in accordance with international declarations, conventions, treaties, covenants and agreements relating to women, including the Convention on the Elimination of All Forms of Discrimination Against Women (CEDAW) and for matters connected therewith or incidental thereto . . . [75]

This groundbreaking milestone entrenched CEDAW within national law adopted by the Majlis-e-Shoora (Parliament), giving it a status that was heretofore only ambiguously placed within national policy and implementation structures and invoked by a few CEDAW enthusiasts. CEDAW also acquired more visibility as the NCSW placed materials and reports related to it on its website.

6.8 Domesticating CEDAW within the Superior Judiciary

As touched upon above, one indicator of CEDAW's domestication would be the use of its provisions in judicial contexts.[76] The judiciary is, of course, potentially an effective vehicle for implementing human rights norms. Yet in the reported case law of Pakistan's superior judiciary (five high courts and

---

[74] Issued in the Gazette of Pakistan Extraordinary on 10 March 2012 (No F. 9(4)/2012-Legis) as the National Commission on the Status of Women Act 2012, Act No VIII of 2012.

[75] Preamble to the National Commission on the Status of Women, Act No VIII of 2012.

[76] I draw more widely upon the case law of the superior judiciary where human rights principles and instruments have been invoked in Ali, 'Interpretative Strategies'.

the Supreme Court), from accession in 1996 through to 2010, there are only four judgments where the court specifically alluded to CEDAW, two delivered by the same judge, Justice Tassadaq Hussain Jilani of the Lahore High Court.[77] The third is a judgment of the High Court of Azad Jammu & Kashmir, citing the Jilani judgment, while the fourth is a Federal Shariat Court judgment in 2007 where the court took *suo moto* notice of Section 10 of the Pakistan Citizenship Act 1951, declaring it discriminatory as it 'negates gender equality and is in violation of Articles 2-A (Objectives Resolution) and 25 (equality of citizens) of the Constitution, also against international commitments of Pakistan and, most importantly, is repugnant to Holy Quran and Sunnah'.[78]

The most widely cited case is *Mst Humaira Mehmood* v. *The State*,[79] a case of alleged *zina* and abduction registered by a father (a sitting member of the Punjab Provincial Assembly) against the husband of his daughter, sparked by her having married of her own choice. The father knew, at the time of his complaint, that his daughter and the accused were lawfully married but went ahead and filed a case of *zina* nonetheless, as a result of which they fled. The police took the daughter home against her will, and her family faked a 'suitable' marriage ceremony which they filmed and later produced in court as evidence of a prior marriage. The judgment against the father was a landmark decision in several ways, drawing as it did on a combination of Islamic law, the Constitution, human rights instruments emanating from the UN, and comparable documents from Islamic forums. The judge emphasized the duty of state institutions to respect, protect and promote the fundamental rights of every person, reminded the parties that Pakistan was a UN member and a party to CEDAW, and drew attention to Article 16, which enjoins all member states to respect the right of women to family life on a basis of equality with men. Justice Jilani also referred to Article 5 of the Cairo Declaration on Human Rights in Islam to reinforce his argument of women's rights within an Islamic framework. He condemned in no uncertain language the 'alliance' of state, society and family in undermining women's rights.

The second case where CEDAW was specifically cited is the case of *Mst Saima and 4 Others* v. *The State*,[80] in which a Christian woman contended that she was lawfully wedded to her husband with her full consent and that the marriage had been performed by a Methodist minister. This was challenged by her mother, who argued that the minister did not hold a valid licence. As a consequence, the mother argued that her daughter was committing *zina*, and invoked the Hudood Ordinance 1979. Justice Jilani ruled that where a couple believe themselves to be married a prima facie case of *zina* does not arise, even within the reading of the Hudood Ordinance. Quoting in particular Article 16 of CEDAW, he also stated,

---

[77] Since elevated to the Supreme Court.   [78] Suo Moto No 1/K of 2006, at para. 28.
[79] PLD 1999 Lah 494.   [80] PLD 2003 Lah 747.

The Court is also conscious of the protection given to marriage and the institutions of the family under the Constitution of the Islamic Republic of Pakistan and the UN Convention on the Elimination of all Forms of Discrimination Against Women. Article 35 of the Constitution enjoins the State to protect the marriage and the family.[81]

In *Mst Sarwar Jan* v. *Abdur Rehman* the court referred to the *Humaira* case,[82] approvingly quoting the Cairo Declaration on Human Rights in Islam and CEDAW and arguing that the government is under obligations under Qur'an and Sunna and international conventions to ensure the rights of women during marriage and at its dissolution. The case was regarding a Muslim wife who applied for dissolution of marriage on the basis of cruel and inhumane behaviour. The court discussing women's right to divorce under Islamic law declared that equality is maintained between the spouses by allowing the wife this right through intervention of the court.

In the fourth case, Suo Moto No 1/K of 2006, civil society organizations, including the Human Rights Commission of Pakistan and the Aurat Foundation, as well as the National Commission on the Status of Women, made submissions and became parties in view of the case's implications for women's rights. The Federal Shariat Court took objection to the Citizenship Act 1951, under which Pakistani men could obtain citizenship for foreign wives but not vice versa, observing that gender inequality violated the Constitution and 'most importantly is repugnant to the Holy Qur'an and Sunnah'.

The court, invoking its jurisdiction to examine laws regarding their Islamic legitimacy, declared it a basic principle of Islamic law to fulfil obligations and noted that Pakistan had made commitments to the international community by becoming a signatory to the UDHR, as well as the Convention on the Nationality of Married Women and CEDAW.[83] The judgment followed Justice Jilani's style of drawing upon plural legal norms: the Constitution, Islamic law and international human rights law. A fascinating aspect is how its use of both Islamic law and CEDAW supports a key argument of this chapter – that Islamic law may be used *for* as well as *against* women's rights to equality and non-discrimination.

Whilst in these cases CEDAW was specifically cited in arriving at a woman-friendly decision, there is a wider body of case law where human rights in general have been used to support a judgment where women's rights have been threatened and/or violated, but in which no specific reference has been made to CEDAW.[84] Why is this? It would appear that judges employ what they perceive

81 *Mst Humaira Mehmood* v. *The State* PLD 1999 Lah 494, at 751–52.   82 2004 CLC 17.
83 Suo Moto No. 1/K of 2006, para. 23. The court also cited Oppenheim's definition of international law as the 'body of customary and treaty rules which are considered legally binding by civilised States in their intercourse with each other'.
84 See, for instance, *Shirin Dokht* v. *Pakistan International Airlines Corporation* 1995 PLC (C.S) 251; *Sameena Masood* v. *Pakistan International Airlines Corporation* PLD 2005 SC 831; *Shrin Munir* v. *Government of Punjab* PLD 1990 SC 295.

as the most relevant laws and legal norms to support their decisions; an invisible 'hierarchy' of laws seems to be at play. Constitutional provisions, Islamic law and other statutory laws are placed above international human rights laws, including CEDAW. It also appears that using human rights in general and CEDAW in particular is an individual choice dependent upon the values and preferences of any given judge. In the Pakistani judiciary, CEDAW's 'champion' seems to be Justice Jilani, but his decisions, though widely cited abroad in human rights circles,[85] do not find a similarly enthusiastic following at home.

6.9 The Impact of CEDAW in Pakistan: Some Concluding Thoughts

Pakistan's decision to accede to CEDAW was a complex one politically and legally, dependent upon champions within government as well as among the public. The processes and discourse of CEDAW ratification clearly demonstrate that the Pakistani government found itself having to play simultaneously to two very different 'galleries'. Accession to a women's rights treaty within Pakistan's pluralist Muslim polity was complicated by the plurality of views regarding what constitutes 'Islamically' and culturally acceptable human rights and the question whether international rights instruments are compatible with rights in the Islamic legal traditions. At a governmental level, acceptance of CEDAW was a top-down process driven by a conscious desire to acquire a place among the international comity of nations. Striking a balance between the domestic and the international was always going to be a challenge.

The question of the extent to which and at what levels CEDAW has found a place within national structures and institutions and within civil society is thus a difficult one to answer. The first point to make is that from a governmental level down to the grass roots the conflict between *sharia* and international human rights law in general, and CEDAW in particular, has tended to be overstated. Significantly, there has been little systematic discussion of those articles of various treaties that clearly fall within the *norms* of Islamic law and *sharia*. Education, for example, which is an issue for CEDAW, is also considered an obligation of every Muslim under interpretations of Islamic law, a Muslim state being in theory accountable for any lapses in providing this right to all its people. But this theme does not find a place on the government's agenda and it is still not held accountable by those individuals and groups who subscribe to an 'Islamic' human rights agenda. Had those many provisions within CEDAW which chimed with an 'Islamic' human rights agenda formed the starting point of the ratification debate, and had compliance with these been demanded of the government by Islamists, then the outcome for domesticating CEDAW in Pakistan would have been quite different. The selective use of 'Islamic' conceptions

---

[85] For example, the Centre for Women's Research, *CEDAW: A Manual* (Colombo: Cenwor, 2006), p. 35; Asia Pacific Forum on Women, Law and Development, *A Digest of Case Law on the Human Rights of Women (Asia Pacific)*, reprint (Chiangmai: APWLD, 2006), p. 22.

of human rights by various constituencies occurs both at home and by delegates representing Pakistan (and other Muslim countries). Delegates of Pakistan to the CEDAW drafting forum, along with other Muslim women delegates, argued for women's rights to education, whereas the government of Pakistan falls short of her obligations to protect these same rights.[86]

In fact, 'playing the Islamic card' to trump women's rights may be a strategy on the part of those in positions of authority to deflect attention from a range of social and legal shortcomings that have little to do with religion. For example, the government has an obligation to ensure adequate provision for spending on basics which impact on the quality of life of all citizens, male and female. The Qur'an and Sunna demand implementation of these entitlements for all Muslims, but 'cultural Islam', especially in the sphere of the family, tends to undermine the rights of women in respect of health, education and economic empowerment. If women are to be kept from going to school for their own 'protection', the need to provide schools for girls – and the cost of so doing – is removed.

There has also been a process of resistance to ideas of women's rights from some religio-political parties and sections of society who perceived (and still perceive) CEDAW as an alien, Western imposition. The present sociopolitical environment in Pakistan is pushing women back into their traditional, disad-vantaged roles, and a rising tide of Islamic fundamentalism in recent years has put women's place in the public and private spheres under pressure. Armed conflict in the north-west of the country especially has had as one of its central agendas women's place in an Islamic society, as defined by a literalist, patriar-chal reading of religious texts. The burning of girls' schools and threats against health professionals, for example, have led to parts of society demanding of females that they stay at home. Genuine security concerns have meant that even those sections of society who do not subscribe to keeping women at home and restraining their activity in the public sphere have been obliged to do so in the interest of safety. How state and society will respond to this latest challenge to women's rights, and whether CEDAW is used as a mobilizing vehicle, remains to be seen.

More positively, we find individuals and groups at the NGO, academic and civil society levels making robust demands for the use of CEDAW as a ref-erence point and lobbying to advance the women's rights and development agenda. Unlike neighbouring India's CEDAW story, demands for accession to CEDAW were initiated and strongly articulated by civil groups as well as in some governmental and political quarters. The accession process also opened up spaces for mounting challenges to fossilized notions of customary as well as religious laws. Advancing women's rights and CEDAW at a national level will, however, require a critical mass of dedicated individuals in the right place

---

[86] For example, with minimal allocation to the education sector in her annual budgets. The figure for the 2015–16 budget for education is 2.11% of the total budget.

at the right time. The National Commission on the Status of Women and the Women Ministers Forum may be looked upon as first steps on the road to internalizing the equality paradigm in a state and society not naturally inclined to non-discrimination.

In conclusion, there is not in Pakistan at the present time a distinct trend toward effectively domesticating CEDAW and women's rights instruments more generally. In many ways, the actors are lone persons or groups of persons committed to CEDAW, playing specific roles at various moments in time. Initiatives by such actors might have made their mark upon the national landscape of women's rights, but the first shoots of equality are yet very fragile. The minimal implementation of the substantive provisions of CEDAW is as much an issue of governance as it is of divergent ideological, political and socio-economic positions on women's rights and entitlements. The way forward includes a multiple approach of challenging the status quo of male–female inequality in the name of religion, culture and tradition; of accountable and transparent governance where men and women are equally facilitated and empowered; and of the opening up of discursive space to engage with varying interpretations of women's human rights in Islam.

7

'Between the Devil and the Deep Blue Sea': *Sharia* Councils and Muslim Women's Rights in the British Muslim Diaspora

7.1 Introduction

A significant articulation of plurality and evolution within the Islamic legal traditions and conceptions of *sharia* came about with large numbers of Muslims migrating to non-Muslim-majority jurisdictions and putting down roots there. In the United Kingdom, for instance, the application of Islamic law and *sharia* is continuously undergoing a transformative process, emerging and evolving as what has been called *Angrezi* ('English' in Urdu) *sharia* – a hybrid of Islamic law and UK law.[1] In common with Muslim-majority jurisdictions, the focus of Islamic law lies in the sphere of family law, this being central to group identity and cultural preservation through control of members of the group, especially women.[2] An example of such control comes in the form of dispute resolution, focusing on family matters, in *Sharia* Councils.

The fact that British Muslim communities' interest in Islamic law and *sharia* lies foremost in being able to control the outcome of marriage and divorce disputes resonates with how the wider British public and state institutions perceive Islamic law. In 2008, the then Archbishop of Canterbury, Dr Rowan Williams, famously declared that Muslim communities sought the freedom to live under *sharia* law, and that there needs to be 'access to recognised authority acting for a religious group: there is already, of course, an Islamic Shari'a Council, much in demand for rulings on marital questions in the UK'.[3] He then qualified this by cautioning that 'recognition of "supplementary jurisdiction" in some areas, especially family law, could have the effect of reinforcing in minority communities some of the most repressive or retrograde elements in them, with particularly serious consequences for the role and liberties of women'.[4]

---

[1] Coined by Menski: Pearl and Menski, *Muslim Family Law*, pp. 58–9. British Muslim communities 'have built the requirements of English law into their traditional legal structures' (ibid., p. 75).

[2] See M. Malik, 'The Branch on Which We Sit: Multiculturalism, Minority Women and Family Law', in A. Diduck and K. O'Donovan (eds.), *Feminist Perspectives on Family Law* (Abingdon: Routledge, 2006), p. 215. See also F. Ahmed and J. Norton, 'Religious Tribunals, Religious Freedom, and Concern for Vulnerable Women', *Child & Family Law Quarterly* 24 (2012), 381–2.

[3] Foundation lecture, Temple Festival, Royal Courts of Justice, 7 February 2008.   [4] Ibid.

Lord Bach, speaking in the House of Lords a year after Dr Williams's speech, was of the view that we

cannot prevent individuals seeking to regulate their lives through religious beliefs or cultural tradition. Communities and other groups have the option to use religious councils or any other system of alternative dispute resolution and agree to abide by their decisions. Nothing in the law of England and Wales prevents people abiding by Sharia principles if they wish, provided that their actions do not conflict with the law in England and Wales. If they do, the law in England and Wales prevails.[5]

Again in response to Dr Williams's lecture, Bano reminded us of the complexity of applying Islamic law and *sharia* in the British Muslim diaspora, observing that

Muslim engagement with sharia cannot be understood merely in terms of the need for legal rights and obligations to be reformulated to make faith-based minority communities more legally and socially inclusive. It is also necessary to understand the specific ways in which such legal orders emerge in the British context and, mostly importantly, the rights and motivations of those members of communities who seek faith-based dispute resolution mechanisms – in this case, focusing particularly on Muslim women.'[6]

This chapter, conscious of Bano's observation, focuses on the role and rationale of *Sharia* Councils and considers questions of authority and authenticity in their operative frameworks from an Islamic jurisprudential perspective. These councils have been established in Britain on the premise that they are manifestations of the Muslim diaspora's 'need' for forums adjudicating on Islamic law, in particular Islamic family law. As stated by the institutions themselves and documented in academic studies on the subject,[7] 'Shariah Councils have been set up specifically to issue Muslim women with Muslim divorce certificates on occasions where Muslim husbands may fail to issue Muslim women with the unilateral Muslim divorce, *talaq*.'[8] In fact, 95 per cent of the caseload for *Sharia* Councils emanates from women seeking religious divorce,[9] the majority

---

[5] *Hansard*, Lords Debates, vol. 711, col. 296–7 (4 June 2009).

[6] S. Bano, 'In Pursuit of Religious and Legal Diversity: A Response to the Archbishop of Canterbury and the "Sharia debate" in Britain', *Ecclesiastical Law Journal* 10(3) (2008), 283.

[7] S. Shah-Kazemi, *Untying the Knot: Muslim Women, Divorce and the Shariah* (London: Nuffield, 2001); S. Bano, 'Islamic Family Arbitration, Justice and Human Rights in Britain', *Law, Social Justice and Global Development Journal* 1 (2007), 1–26; and *An Exploratory Study of Shariah Councils in England with Respect to Family Law* (Reading: Reading University and MoJ, 2012); G. Douglas *et al.*, *Social Cohesion and Civil Law: Marriage, Divorce and Religious Courts* (report of a research study funded by the AHRC) (Cardiff: Cardiff University, 2011); J. Bowen, 'How Could English Courts Recognise Sharia?', *University of St Thomas Law Journal* 7(3) (2010), 411–35.

[8] Bano, *An Exploratory Study*, p. 7.

[9] K. Moore, *The Unfamiliar Abode: Islamic Law in the United States and Britain* (Oxford: Oxford University Press, 2010), p. 117; Bano, *An Exploratory Study*, p. 23.

of these being women in (legally unrecognized) 'Islamic' marriages.[10] But since 'Islamic laws' are susceptible to interpretative plurality, who determines what constitutes 'authentic' Islamic law in the absence of an identifiable authority? Is there a tangible need or requirement for British Muslim communities to have a quasi-legal dispute-resolution system? What are the alternatives?

This chapter focuses on British Muslims who are ethnically Pakistani and who adhere to Sunni traditions – the majority of Britain's Muslim population. Critical questions are addressed which contribute to contemporary debates on the limits of liberal multiculturalism in Britain in its interface with law, religion and society.[11] I advance the view that acceding to demands for accommodating diverse religious and cultural traditions is a slippery slope, since the ingredients of this accommodation are contested, undefined and boundaryless. Considered from a feminist perspective, the agenda for the multiculturalist 'project' is being dominated by those in positions of authority within some ethnic, cultural and religious traditions, and these positions of power have historically excluded women. Who speaks for whom, and who defines culture, religion and tradition, are questions of power play and domination. In the context of *Sharia* Councils, this chapter argues that, whilst some will approach these institutions entirely of their own volition exercising agency, autonomy and/or fulfilment of their religious obligations, their very existence and lack of 'Islamic' alternatives pressurizes women to use such forums to obtain 'acceptance' from their families and communities.[12]

After briefly looking at multiculturalism, minority legal orderings and the types of marriage contracted by British Muslim women, the first section examines how Islamic law conceptualizes Muslims' moral and legal engagement with the non-Muslim-majority state. I argue that, whilst seeking the opinion of *Sharia* Councils or of individual Muslim scholars is the prerogative of every British Muslim, it is neither mandatory under Islamic law nor in accordance with the Islamic understandings of all British Muslim communities. This examination sets the parameters for the Islamic rationale by virtue of which British Muslims can legitimately concede to the requirements of UK law.

The next section goes on to consider why *Sharia* Councils have nevertheless developed in Britain. I argue that claims to Islamic 'authenticity' behind the operation of *Sharia* Councils as the only means of 'Islamic' dispute resolution are obscuring the plurality of approaches to dispute resolution within

---

[10] For ancillary relief (including payment of *mahr*) English courts have nevertheless accepted jurisdiction on the basis of contractual obligations arising from the provisions of the *nikah* marriage contract: for example, *Uddin* v. *Choudhury* [2009] EWCA Civ 1205; and earlier cases such as *Shahnaz* v. *Rizwan* (1964) 1 QBD 390; (1964) 2AllER 993; (1964) 3 WLR 1506.

[11] There is a rich body of work on multiculturalism. This chapter draws upon, among others, Kymlicka, *Multicultural Citizenship*; Parekh, *Rethinking Multiculturalism*; Shachar, *Multicultural Jurisdictions*; Phillips, *Multiculturalism without Culture*; Modood *et al.*, *Multiculturalism, Muslims and Citizenship*; Modood, *Multiculturalism*.

[12] Alternatives would include, for instance, inserting a *talaq-i-tafwid* clause in a *nikah* marriage contract, whereby the wife is delegated the right to divorce her husband.

culturally disparate communities. What is being presented as 'authentic' Islamic dispute resolution is in fact in any given case a contingent product of social norms and the literalist religious justifications of some community members, legitimated by a lack of credible alternative voices from within Muslim communities and a retreat of state engagement under governmental policies on liberal multiculturalism.[13] In a very real – and worrying – way, *Sharia* Councils in their British incarnation may result in being directly antagonistic to Muslim women's interests when offered to them as the only 'Islamically legitimate' exit from a marriage based on the dominant position of the husband.

Finally, I suggest that neither Muslim communities nor governmental institutions are taking the lead in constructively addressing the plurality of Islamic legal traditions and the interpretative complexity inherent within them. On the part of British Muslim communities there is a lack of acceptance that plurality within the Islamic legal traditions makes a single, clear, consistent set of 'authentically Islamic' rules unobtainable; on the part of successive governments there has been a policy (subtly executed, almost by default) of abandoning Muslim communities to 'get on with it', sporadically and vaguely enjoining them to integrate into 'the British way of life'.[14] In the English courts, too, there is no consistent approach to the treatment of Islamic law and little recognition of its plurality and cultural context.[15]

The present enquiry differs significantly from existing literature which has adopted a *Sharia* Council users' perspective and/or procedural analysis,[16] and

---

[13] As Malik states in *Minority Legal Orders in the UK: Minorities, Pluralism and the Law* (London: British Academy, 2012), p. 36, 'In some situations there may be benign neglect where the state does not feel that there are sufficient interests at stake to justify regulating the minority legal order'.

[14] As well as through legislative and other measures, including laws against forced marriage and the recent attempt to prohibit faith-based dispute resolution as seen in the Arbitration and Mediation (Equality) Bill. I am grateful to Professor Shirin Rai for this point.

[15] Trends in those cases where Islamic law has been discussed would be a book in themselves, and they are not directly addressed here.

[16] Shah-Kazemi, *Untying the Knot*; and S. Bano, 'Complexity, Difference and Muslim Personal Law: Rethinking Relationships between Shari'ah Councils and South Asian Muslim Women in Britain' (Warwick University PhD thesis, 2004), are perhaps the two most detailed on the subject. See also S. Bano, *Muslim Women and Shari'ah Councils: Transcending the Boundaries of Community and the Law* (London: Palgrave, 2012); 'Legal Pluralism and Muslim Family Law in Britain', *Journal of South Pacific Law* 4(6) (2000), 1–32; 'Muslim Family Justice and Human Rights', *Journal of Comparative Law* 2(2) (2007), 1–29; and 'Asking the Law Questions: Islamophobia, Agency and Muslim Women', in S. Sayyid and A. Vakil (eds.), *Thinking through Islamophobia: Global Perspectives* (London: Hurst, 2010), pp. 135–56. Douglas *et al.*'s *Social Cohesion* focuses on the structure and operation of the Birmingham Mosque *Sharia* Council (as well as two other faith-based dispute-resolution institutions). Carroll's research on Muslim women's divorce rights and *Sharia* Councils is thorough and offers important insights (L. Carroll, 'Muslim Women and "Islamic Divorce" in England', *Women Living under Muslim Laws*, Dossier 19 (1998), 51–74). Bowen's initial work on interviews with *Sharia* Councils and MATs is a welcome addition (J. Bowen, 'Private Arrangements: "Recognizing Sharia" in England', *Boston Review* 15 (2009), n.p. The Ministry of Justice has undertaken a mapping exercise of *Sharia* Councils: *An Exploratory Study of Shariah Councils in England and Wales*

seeks instead to ascertain the extent to which the councils' services and procedures are framed within a pluralist Islamic jurisprudence and whether there
can be discerned in them any discussion of the distinctive position of Muslims
residing in non-Muslim jurisdictions and seeking engagement and resolution
within such jurisdictions' mainstream legal systems.[17]

7.2 Multiculturalism, Minority Legal Orderings and British Muslim Women

As an evolving and fluid concept denoting the recognition and celebration
of cultural, ethnic, racial and religious diversity, the impact of multiculturalism on Muslim communities in Britain is controversial and contested terrain,
mainly due to what may be seen as a lack of sensitivity towards the vulnerable
within minority communities. Since 9/11 and, especially, the bombings of 7 July
2005, British multiculturalism has lost ground in the face of rising antagonism
towards Islam and Islamic law.[18] 'Multiculturalism' is not easy to define, and the
term lends itself to varying meanings and interpretative debates. In the opinion
of Mehdi *et al.*, 'a case has been made for the view that the term is appropriate not for an empirical description of societal diversity, but only to designate
an ideology or policy designed to overcome some of the conflicts related to
societal diversity'.[19] Others have distinguished between the use of the term
as a demographic variable as opposed to a normative one.[20] A vigorous academic debate on multiculturalism as a political theory has been ongoing since
the 1980s.[21] From Modood's 'multicultural citizenship',[22] challenging cultural
assimilation models, to Parekh's 'open and equal dialogue' between multiple
cultures,[23] it has stretched beyond the territorial and conceptual boundaries
within which it began in Canada. Meer and Modood note in a recent critique that multiculturalism no longer enjoys widespread advocacy yet is still
more vibrant than 'interculturalism'.[24] Introducing the less-explored concept of

with Respect to Family Law was published in October 2012 and is available at the University of
Reading's website.

[17] See my earlier articles: 'Resurrecting Siyar through Fatwas? (Re)Constructing Islamic
International Law in a Post-(Iraq) Invasion World', *Journal of Conflict and Security Law* 14(1)
(2009), 115–44, and 'Religious Pluralism, Human Rights and Citizenship in Europe', in M. L. P.
Leonon and J. E. Goldschmidt (eds.), *Religious Pluralism and Human Rights in Europe*
(Utrecht: Intersentia, 2007), pp. 57–79.

[18] N. Meer and T. Modood, 'How does Interculturalism Contrast with Multiculturalism?', *Journal
of Intercultural Studies* 33(2) (2012), 175–96.

[19] R. Mehdi, H. Petersen, E. Sand and G. Woodman (eds.), *Law and Religion in Multicultural
Societies* (Copenhagen: DJOF, 2008), p. 17.

[20] E. A. Tiryakian, 'Assessing Multiculturalism Theoretically: *E Pluribus Unum, Sic et Non*', in J.
Rex and G. Singh (eds.), *Governance in Multicultural Societies* (Aldershot: Ashgate, 2004),
pp. 1–18. 'Normative multiculturalism' recognizes the unique and distinct needs of particular
cultural groups rather than the individuals in those groups.

[21] See Kymlicka, *Multicultural Citizenship.*   [22] Modood, *Multiculturalism.*

[23] Parekh, *Rethinking Multiculturalism.*

[24] Meer and Modood, 'How Does Interculturalism Contrast?', 176.

'intercultural dialogue',[25] they distinguish it from multiculturalism in terms of its greater endorsement of dialogue and interaction, its holistic consideration of citizenship and cohesion, and its permission of a critical dialogue over cultural practices.[26] It can reasonably be argued that interculturalism allows for greater critical engagement between cultural groups (including between groups within Muslim communities), and the critiquing of *Sharia* Councils, for example, has been a practical result.

Closer to the focus of the present chapter, feminist engagement with multiculturalism has been influential in mounting a robust challenge to gender-neutral perspectives. From Okin's declaring multiculturalism as simply 'bad' for minority women,[27] to Phillips's nuanced preference for 'individual' over 'group' expressions of culture,[28] significant conceptual ground has been covered. Cultural practices are one of a range of identity markers and ways of being where Phillips draws the important distinction between 'understanding cultural pressures, but not assuming that culture dictates',[29] an observation that appreciates the heterogeneity of minority groups, including British Muslim women. Shachar's propositions of 'joint governance' and 'transformative accommodation' offer insights into how the 'paradox of multicultural vulnerability' might find resolution.[30] As she observes,[31] where the elements of multiculturalist discourse consist of society, the group and the individual, the costs of liberal accommodation are likely to be borne by vulnerable individuals. With these complexities in mind, this chapter will start by considering the parameters for engagement with *Sharia* Councils in light of the different possible constructions of Muslim marriages.

7.3 Types of Marriage Contracted, and Their Impact on Choice of Divorce Forum

The need for an 'Islamic' divorce (and hence *Sharia* Councils) arises from the nature of the contract of marriage entered into by British Muslims. There are three possible formulations for an 'Islamic' marriage. (i) A *nikah* ceremony and no engagement with the formal legal system. In this scenario, the marriage is unrecognized by the state and any recourse to civil law is restricted to contractual obligations under the *nikah*, such as *mahr* provisions.[32] (ii) Two ceremonies – the *nikah* ceremony and a separate civil marriage ceremony – resulting in recognition of the marriage in both religious and legal terms. (iii) A

---

[25] Ibid.   [26] Ibid., at 177.

[27] S. M. Okin, 'Is Multiculturalism Bad for Women?', in J. Cohen, M. Howard and M. C. Nussbaum (eds.), *Is Multiculturalism Bad for Women?* (Princeton: Princeton University Press, 1999), pp. 9–24.

[28] Phillips, *Multiculturalism without Culture.*   [29] Ibid., p. 41.

[30] Shachar, *Multicultural Jurisdictions*, p. 3.   [31] Ibid., p. 42.

[32] *Mahr* is given by the groom to the bride when the contract of marriage is made, and becomes her property: also see Mannan, *D. F. Mulla's Principles*, pp. 426–48.

dual ceremony which simultaneously fulfils both the formal legal requirements and religious sanctioning. Such a ceremony must be conducted in a building registered both as a place of worship and as a place for the registration of civil marriages.[33]

Women who go through *nikah*-only marriages,[34] having no status with which to approach a formal divorce court, form the majority of cases seen by *Sharia* Councils. When such *nikah*-only marriages appear before a council, a significant question that might be asked is why the delegated right to divorce under the principle of *tafwid* was not included within the *nikah* contract. If such a clause had existed, it would have negated the need for such women to approach a *Sharia* Council for a divorce (and also offset the need for a *khul'* divorce, which compromises the right to *mahr*, as will be seen later in this chapter). While in the US increasing numbers of mosques and Muslim communities are requiring *imams* to have proof of a civil marriage before performing a *nikah*, and are declaring *mahr* to be an unreturnable gift, such trends do not seem to be apparent in the UK.

7.4 *Siyar*, and the Jurisprudence of Muslims in the Non-Muslim World

Although Muslim migration to Britain is centuries old, large-scale voluntary and permanent settlement was unknown before the second half of the twentieth century. Settled communities of Muslims established themselves as an integral part of the Western social landscape only from about the mid-twentieth century, and this has led to the creation of diaspora communities with multiple identities cutting across fixed categories of 'migrant' and 'host' populations, of which, in Britain, Muslims of Pakistani origin are by far the largest group.[35] Against the backdrop of Muslim mass migration to non-Muslim majority jurisdictions,[36] and in view of the importance of Islamic law to the identities of such diasporas,

---

[33] In accordance with the Places of Worship Registration Act 1855 and s. 41 of the Marriage Act 1949.

[34] For a detailed discussion of possible reasons why Muslims refrain from registering their marriages see R. D. Grillo, 'In the Shadow of the Law: Muslim Marriage and Divorce in the UK', in Mehdi *et al.* (eds.), *Interpreting Divorce Laws in Islam* (Copenhagen: DJOF, 2012), pp. 211–16.

[35] In the 2011 census, Britain's Muslim population stood at 2.6 million. Ethnic breakdown is not yet available for 2011, but in 2001 Muslims of Pakistani origin constituted 43 per cent of Muslims in England, 33 per cent in Wales, and 67 per cent in Scotland (see R. Gale and P. Hopkins (eds.), *Muslims in Britain: Race, Place and Identities* (Edinburgh: Edinburgh University Press, 2009), pp. 4–12).

[36] The distinction between Muslim- and non-Muslim-majority jurisdictions in the present chapter focuses on the notion of whether or not Islam is the religion of the majority population and whether or not Islamic law is part of the 'formal' law of that country. Historically Muslims have captured non-Muslim nations in military ventures and subsequently settled in these jurisdictions as minorities. India, Spain, the Balkans, parts of Africa and other places have undergone such experiences, with subsequent juristic challenges. However, these territories are not the subject of the present enquiry.

the burden on Islamic scholars to respond to the challenges and deeply consider the legal ramifications of interactions between Muslims and their non-Muslim environment increases. Some pertinent enquiries in this regard include: under what circumstances does Islamic law permit Muslims to live in non-Muslim countries, and how are they to organize their lives there so that they remain in accordance with *sharia*? Responses to these fundamental questions have been sought in *siyar* ('Islamic international law') and, more recently, in the burgeoning field of *fiqh al-aqalliyat* ('jurisprudence of minorities').

7.4.1 *Siyar* and the Classification of Modern Britain

At a fundamental level, classical Islamic law, as developed utilizing the principles of *fiqh* (of which *siyar* is a component),[37] simply does not provide a uniform or clear indication of whether it is permissible for a Muslim to migrate voluntarily and permanently to a non-Muslim-majority territory.[38] Most classical Muslim jurists wrote on the subject in the early centuries of Islam, when Muslim conquests brought non-Muslims under Muslim rule,[39] resulting in the development of detailed discourse on rules of law governing non-Muslims living in Muslim jurisdictions. Conversely, the question of Muslims living under non-Muslim rule seldom arose and thus received only fleeting attention in early juristic writings on *siyar*. If anything, the essence of *siyar* on the subject of Muslims in non-Muslim lands was no more than: 'return to a Muslim country as soon as possible!'[40]

An alternative view, though, and one which is of interest in our examination of the Islamic legitimacy of *Sharia* Councils, extended a more liberal approach, allowing a Muslim implicitly to accept *aman* ('protection') from non-Muslim governments. The acceptance of *aman* was subject to certain conditions, the most important being that a Muslim be able to 'manifest signs of Islam' whilst residing in non-Muslim territory.[41] These aspects of *siyar* have,

---

[37] For a comprehensive overview of *siyar*, see S. Mahmassani, 'International Law in the Light of Islamic Discourse', *Recueil de cours* 117 (1996), 201; M. Khadduri, *The Islamic Law of Nations: Shaybani's Siyar* (Baltimore: Johns Hopkins University Press, 1966); M. Hamidullah, *Muslim Conduct of State* (Lahore: Sh. Muhammad Ashraf, 1977).

[38] The two main examples of migration to non-Muslim territories from early Muslim history are the migration to Ethiopia to escape the harassment of the Makkan non-Muslims and the migration to non-Muslim Medina by the Prophet Muhammad. This too was to escape the aggression of the Makkans.

[39] See B. Lewis, 'Legal and Historical Reflections on the Position of Muslim Populations under Non-Muslim Rule', *Journal of the Institute of Muslim Minority Affairs* 13 (1992), 6.

[40] Classical *siyar* did contend with a Muslim travelling temporarily to a non-Muslim land, for example to trade. The various schools of juristic thought offered different approaches to the resultant rights and responsibilities, including a blanket prohibition on engaging with non-Muslims and qualified permission if interaction became a necessity, neither of which is of practical application for a modern diaspora which has perforce to interact with its 'host'.

[41] Lewis, 'Legal and Historical Reflections', 6–7.

however, remained largely unexplored, and Islamic legal scholarship has not been appropriately responsive in developing these possibilities in any significant depth. El Fadl highlights this by stating that, despite the fact that around one-third of all Muslims worldwide now live in non-Muslim countries,

> [t]he ambivalence characteristic of the pre-modern age continues. Few modern Muslims attempt to deal with the principles that should guide the behaviour of Muslims residing in non-Muslim territory. Few modern scholars have attempted to maintain and develop the traditional discourse on the affiliation and inviolability of Muslim minorities.[42]

So classical Muslim jurists never envisaged a situation whereby Muslims would *voluntarily* and *permanently* choose to live in non-Muslim countries, and the discussion has only commenced in the last few decades. The most common jurisprudential argument that is advanced in favour of this modern phenomenon is that of *darura* ('necessity' or 'need'): Muslims forced by *darura* to leave Muslim lands because of economic or sociopolitical difficulties may find a justification in Islamic jurisprudence for engaging with the host nation. We will look at *darura* as a basis for Muslims' interaction with a host state's legal system below; for the moment, it will suffice to say that it is controversial.

But an alternative foundation upon which British Muslims might construct an Islamically legitimate acceptance of the laws of their host nation is to rethink how Britain itself might be classified. The jurisprudence of *siyar* classically used a dichotomy which divided the world into *dar-al-Islam* ('the abode of Islam') and *dar-al-harb* ('the abode of war').[43] Some jurists make the point that such a division was necessitated by the prevailing conditions and sense of insecurity among the fledgling Muslim community.[44] But Britain is now not, in the eyes of all but a few, at war with Islam, and so cannot be categorized as *dar-al-harb*. What, then, of the possibility of Britain being *dar-al-Islam*? A broad definition of *dar-al-Islam* might be 'any territory whose inhabitants observe Islamic law'. This then raises a number of questions: how many people need to observe Islamic law for a territory to qualify? Are Muslims able to freely fulfil their religious obligations and the requirements of prayer? Can Muslims comply with the five pillars of Islam? Is *halal* meat available? By way of a benchmark, and due to the fact that Indian Muslims could comply with the five pillars of Islam and practice fundamental elements of their faith, British India was considered

---

[42] K. A. El Fadl, 'Islamic Law and Muslim Minorities', *Islamic Law and Society* 1(2) (1994), 141–87, 185.

[43] See, for example, M. Khadduri, 'Islam and the Modern Law of Nations', *American Journal of International Law* 50 (1956), 359. *Dar al-harb* was extended to all states and communities not Muslim-ruled. Imam Shafi'i, founder of the Shafi'i school, is said to have formulated these categories.

[44] See, for example, H. Kruse, 'The Foundations of Islamic International Jurisprudence', *Journal of the Pakistan Historical Society* 3 (1955), 232.

by some Muslim scholars as *dar-al-Islam*, though its Muslim population was in the minority.[45] On the basis of this analogy, we might argue that Britain qualifies as *dar-al-Islam*. This, however, is not uncontroversial, since some contend that the central ingredient of *dar-al-Islam* is the *supremacy* of Islamic law in a jurisdiction or, at the very least, the ability of the political authority to advance legal formulations on that basis, including levying special taxes on non-Muslim citizens such as Christians and Jews.[46] Furthermore, colonial India does not mirror contemporary Britain as Indian Muslims were not equal citizens of the Crown but 'native' subjects under colonial rule with limited rights and entitlements. The reason for allowing all natives to comply with their religious obligations, including application of their 'personal laws', was a colonial strategy to rule as painlessly as possible. The same situation cannot be transposed onto contemporary Britain, where Muslims live as equal citizens of the United Kingdom and claim rights to religious freedom and expression on that basis.

Moreover, a changed world scenario dictates a different classification, and the dichotomy of a world either 'of Islam' or 'of war' is no longer, for most jurists, valid.[47] Islamic law now recognizes the existence of non-Muslim states in peaceful relations with Muslim states, and categorizes them as *dar-al-sulh*, 'the lands of peaceful coexistence', and this would include Britain.[48] Significantly, that such states have the authority to make laws which apply to Muslims living within them is recognized.[49]

A number of mechanisms exist in Islamic jurisprudence to inform and facilitate acceptance of the laws of such a non-Muslim state, including the concepts of *ikrah* ('duress'), *maslaha* ('public welfare'), and, as mentioned above, *darura* ('necessity'). Under the principles of Islamic law, Muslims are required to fulfil their obligations to a state which has offered them *aman* ('protection'); they are under the laws of *dar-al-sulh* and subject to them so long as they are living within its territory. Hamidullah, in his treatise *Muslim Conduct of State*, makes the point that,

---

[45] A. Rahim, *Muhammadan Jurisprudence* (Lahore: Mansoor, 1995), pp. 396–7.

[46] Z. Badawi, 'New Fiqh for Minorities' (paper presented at the Muslims of Europe in the New Millenium conference, Regent's College, London, 9–10 September 2000), cited in I. Yilmaz, *Muslim Laws, Politics and Society in Modern Nation States* (Aldershot: Ashgate, 2005), p. 39. On this point see also Mahmassani, 'International Law', 250–2.

[47] For detailed Arabic sources on this point see K. A. Kavanaugh, 'Speaking Law to War', *Journal of Conflict and Security Law* 17(1) (2012), 3–24; for a contemporary discussion see A. A. An-Na'im, 'Why Should Muslims Abandon Jihad?', *Third World Quarterly* 27 (2006), 786; T. Ramadan, *Western Muslims and the Future of Islam* (Oxford: Oxford University Press, 2004); K. A. El Fadl, 'The Rules of Killing at War: An Inquiry into Classical Sources', *Muslim World* 89 (1999), 144.

[48] The terms *dar-al-aman* ('the lands of security') and *dar-al-darura* ('the lands of necessity') could also be explored, and have similar connotations. This section draws upon S. S. Ali and J. Rehman, 'The Concept of Jihad in Islamic International Law', *Journal of Conflict and Security Law* 10(3) (2005), 321–43.

[49] Hamidullah, *Muslim Conduct of State*, p. 130.

> In general, Muslims temporarily residing in a foreign country are recommended very strongly . . . to behave in an exemplary and law abiding manner; to observe fully the conditions of their permit or passport and to refrain from any act of treachery.[50]

It is suggested that if the above obligations are a starting point applicable to temporary Muslim residents, then it might well be assumed that permanent citizens would be imbued with a higher set of obligations. From an Islamic standpoint, then, whether Britain is constructed as *dar-al-Islam* or, less controversially, as *dar-al-sulh*, there is little to prevent Muslim communities in Britain engaging with and abiding by its laws. As An-Na'im observes, 'Islamic law normally requires and sanctions obedience to State law'.[51]

7.4.2 Contemporary *Fiqh al-Aqalliyat* as a Legal Theory for Muslim Minorities

But rather than simply make this observation and move on, an alternative and – for the purposes of critical multiculturalism – potentially more fruitful way of thinking about the legal implications for Muslims living in non-Muslim jurisdictions such as Britain is the contemporary understanding of what is termed 'jurisprudence of (Muslim) minorities' (*fiqh al-aqalliyat*), in particular as expounded and formalized from the 1990s onward by Dr Taha Jabir al-Alwani[52] and the Egyptian theologian Dr Yusuf Al-Qaradawi.[53]

The two main premises of this contemporary *fiqh al-aqalliyat* are (i) Islam's global application and the irrelevance of territorial boundaries to its practice, and (ii) the application of the juristic principle of *maqasid al-sharia* ('ruling according to the intention of Islamic law'). The implication of these premises is that it is possible for a contemporary *fiqh al-aqalliyat* to signify the application of Islamic law within a globalized and contextual framework. Drawing inspiration from verse 22:78 of the Qur'an ('He has not placed any hardship upon you in religion'), this contemporary *fiqh al-aqalliyat* attempts to facilitate plural identities for Muslims living in non-Muslim jurisdictions and mutual relationships between Muslim and non-Muslim communities, as well as create linkages of citizenship and common interests. To this end, it responds from within the Islamic legal tradition to questions that encompass sociopolitical and economic issues, including dispute resolution. Al-Qaradawi, one of

---

[50] Ibid., p. 128.   [51] An-Na'im, 'The Compatibility Dialectic', 3.

[52] Al-Alwani, president of Cordoba University, Virginia, believes that it is time to develop a new jurisprudence for Muslim minorities in the West. He advances detailed contours for a new *fiqh al-aqalliyat* in T. J. Al-Alwani, *Towards a Fiqh for Minorities: Some Basic Reflections* (Herndon, VA: International Institute of Islamic Thought, 2003).

[53] Dr Al-Qaradawi is one of the most influential Muslim scholars of recent times. He is a founding member of the ECFR and has evolved his ideas on *fiqh al-aqalliyat* through the various *fatawa* delivered during its sessions. See Y. Al-Qaradawi, *On Muslim Minority Jurisprudence: The Life of Muslims in Other Societies* (Cairo: Dar-al-Shuruq, 2001); and *The Lawful and the Prohibited in Islam* (London: al-Birr Foundation, 1960).

contemporary *fiqh al-aqalliyat*'s founders, claims that this legal theory 'looks at the Islamic heritage with one eye and the social and cultural reality with the other'.[54] Al-Alwani defines such a '*fiqh* for minorities' as 'a specific discipline which takes into account the relationship between the religious ruling and the conditions of the community and the location where it exists'.[55] An important aspect of *fiqh al-aqalliyat* lies in its proponents' claim that the methodology employed is one of *ijtihad* or 'exertion'; that is to say, in broad terms, rather than being based upon the previous decisions of a religious expert belonging to a school of jurisprudential thought, it has been reached through direct interpretation of the Qur'an and *ahadith*. Based upon traditional *fiqh* rules, contemporary *fiqh al-aqalliyat* is therefore presented as an integrated and integral part of *fiqh*.[56] Fishman states that '[t]his doctrine asserts that Muslim minorities, especially those residing in the West, deserve a special new legal discipline to address their unique religious needs, which differ from those of Muslims residing in Muslim countries.'[57] Muhammad Khalid Masud, a renowned Muslim scholar and former chair of the Council of Islamic Ideology, Pakistan, believes that this fast-growing, contemporary understanding of the jurisprudence applicable to Muslim minorities will impact significantly on the future of Muslims in the West.[58] The late Sheikh ad-Darsh, a prominent scholar, former *imam* of the Regent's Park mosque, and head of the Islamic Sharia Council, sympathizes: in an interview with the scholar Anne-Sophie Roald, he has argued that

> [s]ocial changes are the reasons why Muslims today talk of *fiqh al-aqalliyat*... In the past Muslim scholars worked with the *fiqh* of the Muslim State. Now we Muslims are a minority. Thus, we have to consider these changes in order to be able to reflect the new situation and clarify our attitude. We have to know what is cultural and what is Islamic to be able to make valued judgements.[59]

Although an attractive proposition to some, this contemporary understanding of *fiqh al-aqalliyat* has its outspoken critics. In particular, it is contested by scholars and adherents of juristic schools which consider any modification in the thresholds of legal application to be *bida* ('(unacceptable) innovation').[60] Notions of 'necessity' are considered by such scholars to be an exception rather than the rule, and the very basic question is asked as to why Muslims in the West should have a special dispensatory *fiqh* unavailable to Muslims living in

---

[54] L. Larsen, 'Islamic Jurisprudence and Transnational Flows', in A. Hellum, S. S. Ali and A. Griffiths (eds.), *From Transnational Relations to Transnational Laws: Northern European Laws at the Crossroads* (London: Ashgate, 2011), p. 152.

[55] Al-Alwani, *Towards a Fiqh for Minorities*, p. 3.   [56] Larsen, 'Islamic Jurisprudence', p. 152.

[57] S. Fishman, 'Fiqh al-Aqalliyyat: A Legal Theory for Muslim Minorities', Center on Islam, Democracy, and the Future of the Muslim World, series no 1, paper 2 (2006), p. 1.

[58] Masud, cited in Larsen, 'Islamic Jurisprudence', p. 151.

[59] A. S. Roald, *Women in Islam: The Western Experience* (London: Routledge, 2001), p. 116.

[60] Saudi Arabia's conservative Wahabi scholars form the main critics of *fiqh al-aqalliyat*.

Muslim jurisdictions.[61] It is important to appreciate that, while on the Continent and elsewhere discourse on *fiqh al-aqalliyat* is gaining ground among diaspora scholars and students of Islamic law, in the British context *fiqh al-aqalliyat* is conspicuous by its absence among discussions and decisions of the *Sharia* Councils, as are references to bodies such as the ECFR (see below) which engage with *fiqh al-aqalliyat*[62] (the views of Sheikh ad-Darsh being the exception).[63]

One visible application of *fiqh al-aqalliyat* is to be found in the work of organizations such as the European Council for Fatwa and Research (ECFR), founded in London in 1997 but now based in Dublin. The ECFR aims to help European Muslims confront the specific jurisprudential and practical challenges which arise as a consequence of being a Muslim minority in a non-Muslim jurisdiction. One of the most important *fatawa* to have been handed down by the ECFR, and one which is crucial to questioning the 'need' for *Sharia* Councils in Britain, is headed 'Ruling on a Divorce Issued by a Non-Muslim Judge'. Prompted by the numerous 'limping marriages' in non-Muslim jurisdictions, where husbands have refused to pronounce the word *talaq* ('divorce') on wives who had been granted a civil divorce, this ECFR *fatwa* held that 'due to the absence of an Islamic judicial system in non-Muslim countries, it is imperative that a Muslim who conducted his marriage by virtue of those countries' respective laws, complies with the rulings of a non-Muslim judge in the event of divorce'.[64] In other words, the ECFR was setting out its belief, based – vitally – on Islamic jurisprudence, that there is room (though, it should be added, no mandatory requirement) within a sovereign, non-Muslim country for Muslims to refer legal disputes to the non-Muslim legal system and accept the rulings of a non-Muslim judge.

So it can be demonstrated that there exists within Islamic jurisprudence a sanction for British Muslims to accept the rulings of a non-Muslim court. Historically, *fiqh al-aqalliyat* existed mainly in juristic discourse on the Indian subcontinent as well as among jurists in Andalusia,[65] but it has long been a legitimate topic of juristic thought and hence may validly be extended to

[61] Fishman, 'Fiqh al-aqalliyyat', p. 12. Proponents of *fiqh al-aqalliyat* respond by arguing that this is not *bida* but a use of *maslaha* ('public interest'), and that *fiqh al-aqalliyat* is a methodology for making Muslim minorities more secure and comfortable in their non-Muslim-majority environment and with their multiple identities.

[62] It is telling that none of the works cited in note 7 make any mention of the ECFR or *fiqh al-aqalliyat* when discussing multiculturalism, even in a Muslim context.

[63] For an overview of Sheikh Darsh's views on the subject see G. Wiegers, 'Dr Sayyid Mutawalli ad-Darsh's *Fatwas* for Muslims in Great Britain: The Voice of Official Islam?', in G. Maclean (ed.), *Britain and the Muslim World* (Cambridge: Scholar Press, 2010), pp. 1–18.

[64] ECFR, Fatwa (17), resolution 3/5, in European Council for Fatwa and Research, *First and Second Collection of Fatwas (Qarārat wa fatāwa li-l-majlis al-'urubi li-l-iftā' wa-l-buhūth)* (Cairo: Islamic INC/Al-Falah Foundation, 2002).

[65] Roald, *Women in Islam*, p. 309; Roald also refers to N. H. M. Keller, 'Which of the Four Orthodox Madhabs Has the Most Developed Fiqh for Muslims Living as Minorities?' (available at sunnah.org).

Britain. Yet, as the discussion on *Sharia* Councils below will illustrate, British Muslim communities have by and large chosen not to engage with *fiqh al-aqalliyat*, preferring instead to evolve private legal orderings. We turn now to consider why separate *Sharia* Councils developed as a parallel, quasi-judicial system here, and how they operate in practice today.

7.5 The Origins and Operations of *Sharia* Councils in Britain

The overwhelming majority of Muslims in Britain are of Pakistani, Bangladeshi and Indian origin, and therefore (broadly speaking) Sunni Muslims who follow the juristic traditions of the Hanafi school of thought, yet this apparent homogeneity is not reflected in their differing practices of Islam and varying understandings of Islamic law. Amongst British South Asian Muslims, multiple layered identities mean that *Sharia* Councils are in fact heavily influenced by geographical localities within their countries of origin: a Punjabi or Kashmiri Muslim will differ significantly from an Indian or Bangladeshi, despite their nominal common affiliation as Hanafi Sunnis. A number of other factors, too, have made Britain different from other Muslim diasporas. Large populations of Muslims from rural parts of Pakistan (as well as from Bangladesh and India) arrived in the post-war period to work mainly in factories. As family members set up home close to their relatives, communities laid down roots mostly in the Midlands, the North, and the North West of England. But with the decline of industry and jobs in those regions, subsequent generations are living in large numbers in concentrated pockets of post-industrial cities, with relatively serious problems of health, education and unemployment. Self-contained British Muslim communities have emerged, resulting, in some places, in large-scale withdrawal from the 'mainstream' of British life.

Meanwhile, governmental actors, working within an environment informed by liberal multiculturalist policies, often fearful of accusations of racism, and lately of Islamophobia if cultural practices are questioned, have tended to allow communities free rein to 'police' themselves in cultural matters. While some intervention has been witnessed in the form of (ill-advised) legislation tackling identified problems such as forced marriage, positive initiatives presented in a culturally sensitive manner, including raising awareness of rights as British citizens, are not easily forthcoming. Community ideas of 'justice', under the auspices of *Sharia* Councils, have come to co-exist in an increasingly uneasy relationship with the state and its institutions. The state, in the garb of liberal multiculturalism, has tended to countenance *Sharia* Councils as manifestations of community organizations or as informal extensions of mosques and therefore as aspects of 'religious freedom', yet no formal interaction takes place between the state and a *Sharia* Council except when a member of a *Sharia* Council is sought to appear in court as an 'expert witness' in a case where Islamic law is at issue. A sizeable proportion of communities continue to be regulated by 'private ordering' in the form of local mosque committees, influenced by *imams* hailing from the villages and towns of rural Pakistan, with the sheer number of Muslims in certain cities and regions facilitating (as Ballard describes it) a *desh pardesh* ('home away from home').[66] They form a critical mass of the population,[67] and are hence in a position to impact on the wider local and national landscape, including development of their own version of *sharia* – *Angrezi sharia* or 'English *sharia*'. *Angrezi sharia*, a hybrid of Islamic law and UK law, operates at the intersection of state and society, attempting conformity with both religious and state law.[68] Undergoing two sets of marriage and two sets of divorce but accepting English law on financial matters are examples of *Angrezi sharia*: a pick-and-mix of English, Islamic and local South Asian norms. But it is within the sphere of the *Sharia* Councils especially that we find *Angrezi sharia* being applied most vigorously.

7.5.1 The Rise of Britain's *Sharia* Councils

Responding to the situation in which British Muslims found themselves, from the 1970s onwards a range of organizations came into being, making Muslims' presence felt by their engagement in British public life, participation in policy- and law-making consultations, and their making of demands on behalf of Muslims as a community. Organizations including the Union of Muslim Organisations (founded in 1970), the Muslim Parliament of Britain (1992), the Muslim Council of Britain (1997), the British Muslim Forum (2005), the Muslim Arbitration Tribunal (2007) and,[69] most importantly for present purposes, numerous *Sharia* Councils have been founded in the past few decades.

Sharia Councils, of which there are about eighty to eighty-five in Britain,[70] were established in close alliance with mosques and have been said to represent

---

[66] R. Ballard (ed.), *Desh Pardesh: The South Asian Presence in Britain* (London: Hurst, 1994).

[67] Muslims constitute more than one-third of the population in Tower Hamlets, one-quarter in Newham, and over 10 per cent in Bradford, Birmingham and Leicester, with wards in some cities seeing far higher concentrations. In parts of the West Midlands, Asian communities (of which Muslims are a majority) form 40 per cent of the population. It can, of course, be pointed out that other European countries have Muslim populations which are larger in absolute and proportional terms, but these are very different from the British diaspora and do not provide good comparators: two-thirds of Germany's Muslims trace their roots to Turkey, a secular democracy with a distinct relationship between Islam and the state. The scope and nature of state-endorsed multiculturalism in Germany (and also in France, with its high proportion of Algerian Muslims) differs radically from Britain's.

[68] For a definition and further explanation see Pearl and Menski, *Muslim Family Law*, in particular pp. 58–9.

[69] In recent literature (and tabloid reporting) *Sharia* Councils and MATs have sometimes been conflated, creating the misleading impression that *Sharia* Councils operate under the legal cover of statute law. The two, though, are quite distinct: *Sharia* Councils are informal, while MATs have to comply with provisions of the Arbitration Act 1996. While MATs are not permitted to offer arbitration on, for example, arrangements for children, *Sharia* Councils appear to deal with such matters on a quasi-legal basis. Evidence for this was found by Bano during her fieldwork: Bano, 'Complexity, Difference and Muslim Personal Law', pp. 168–9.

[70] Ibid., p. 117.

a shift 'within the migrants' self-perception from being sojourners to settlers'.[71] They are unofficial, extra-legal entities providing advice and assistance to Muslim communities and undertaking a range of functions including mediation, reconciliation, the issuing of divorce certificates and the production of expert reports on Muslim family law and other matters.[72]

7.5.2 *Sharia* Councils and British Muslim Women

It is not possible to consider the scope and indeed the presence of *Sharia* Councils in Britain without recognizing the centrality of their differing treatment of men and women, and it is this gender inequality, implicitly overlooked by liberal multiculturalism, which lies at the heart of this chapter. Day-to-day activities and engagement with a range of public institutions and service providers, including the NHS, Social Security and banks, to name a few, are just as much prone to 'Islamic' and 'non-Islamic' practices. Yet British Muslims appear far more amenable to engaging with these institutions as compared to family law issues. Malik so aptly identifies one of the main factors for choosing to focus on dispute resolution in family law as follows: 'Minority legal orders often focus on family law precisely because these norms control women and enable the preservation of group identity'.[73]

That the desire to preserve control over women was instrumental in setting up early *Sharia* Councils in Britain is supported by Lucy Carroll. She was of the view that their creation was a response to the belief that a proposed law would have afforded Muslim ex-wives ancillary relief after obtaining a divorce overseas:

> By no means was it a coincidence that just when it appeared clear that legislation would be passed empowering the English Courts to grant ancillary relief in cases where the marriage had been dissolved by a foreign divorce entitled to recognition under English law, spokesmen for male Muslim interests . . . began putting it about that under Muslim law a woman is not entitled to a divorce

---

[71] Lewis, 'Legal and Historical Reflections', 56.

[72] Not without controversy, *Sharia* Councils have presented legal challenges to many jurisdictions in the non-Muslim-majority world. In Canada, for instance, a protracted and very public debate on faith-based arbitration preceded the government banning all such forums, even against the advice of an independent commission. A significant body of literature on the so-called '*sharia* debates' in Canada is now in the public domain, including N. Bakht, 'Family Arbitration Using Shari'a Law', *Muslim World Journal of Human Rights* 1 (2004), 1–24; and *Arbitration, Religion and Family Law: Private Justice on the Back of Women* (Ottawa: NAWL, 2005), p. 64; A. M. Emon, 'Conceiving Islamic Law in a Pluralist Society', *Singapore Journal of Legal Studies* (Dec. 2006), 331–55; M. Boyd, 'Dispute Resolution in Family Law' (2004) (available at attorneygeneral.jus.gov.on.ca); S. Razack, 'The "Sharia Law Debate" in Ontario', *Feminist Legal Studies* 15 (2007), 3–32; and 'Between a Rock and a Hard Place: Canadian Muslim Women's Responses to Faith-Based Arbitration', in Mehdi *et al.*, *Law and Religion*, pp. 83–94; A. Korteweg and J. Selby (eds.), *Debating Shariah: Islam, Gender Politics and Family Law Arbitration* (Toronto: University of Toronto Press, 2012).

[73] Malik, *Minority Legal Orders*, p. 30.

without her husband's consent, and that no Muslim marriage can be dissolved in a 'religious' sense unless the husband pronounces a *talaq*.[74]

Islamic law accepts dissolution of a marriage when (i) the husband pronounces *talaq*; (ii) a judge accepts the wife's request to dissolve the marriage (*khul'*), generally in return for relinquishing her right to *mahr*; (iii) a judge, on the application of the wife, declares the marriage dissolved on grounds acceptable in Islamic law (*faskh*); (iv) the wife exercises a right to divorce if delegated to her in the marriage contract (*talaq-i-tafwid*);[75] or (v) the marriage is dissolved by mutual consent (*mubara't*).[76]

Khalid Masud advances the view that the various categories of a Muslim divorce were informed by patriarchal social practices where women became the less-than-equal partner in dissolution of marriage.[77] The Qur'anic verses on divorce require men not to hold women against their will (verse 4:19), expressly forbid unjust *khul'* practices obliging husbands not to take back what they had given as *mahr* to their spouses (verse 4.21) and so lend support to the argument in this chapter that civil divorces are evidence of breakdown of marriage and thus 'Islamically' recognized dissolution.

Talaq-i-tafwid in particular has been a standard provision of *nikah* contracts in Pakistan since the Muslim Family Laws Ordinance 1961 (MFLO).[78] However, it is curious that this norm has not been adopted within the Diasporic communities in Britain as an 'Islamic' form of divorce nor actively canvassed by *Sharia* Councils, and Muslim leaders do not encourage it. Bano sets out the views of one participant in her research, who on learning about this option, opined,

---

[74] Carroll, 'Muslim Women', p. 5. This possibility triggered fears that women would seek divorces for petty grievances, leaving communities in disarray.

[75] The dissolution of the marriage by *talaq-i-tafwid* means that the husband can exercise the right to divorce, or the wife can exercise her husband's right to divorce. As elaborated by Carroll, 'Since the wife's pronouncement of *talaq*, under the delegated right to do so, is regarded as, and takes effect as, a pronouncement of divorce by the husband, the wife is not divorcing her husband or repudiating her husband, but divorcing herself, repudiating herself, on behalf of her husband.' L. Carroll, 'Talaq-i-Tafwid and Stipulations in a Muslim Marriage Contract: Important Means of Protecting the Position of the South Asian Muslim Wife', *Modern Asian Studies* 16(2) (1982), 283.

[76] Further detail on Muslim family law is available in numerous texts including D. F. Mulla, *Principles of Mohammedan Law* (various editions); Pearl and Menski, *Muslim Family Law*; Doi, *Shariah*.

[77] M. K. Masud, 'Interpreting Divorce Laws in Pakistan: Debates on Shari'a and Gender Equality in 2008', in R. Mehdi, W. Menski and J. S. Nielsen (eds.), *Interpreting Divorce Laws in Islam* (Copenhagen: DJOF Publishing, 2012), pp. 51–3.

[78] Ordinance VIII of 1961 of Pakistan (and Bangladesh since 1971). Section 8 of the MFLO states: 'Where the right to divorce has been duly delegated to the wife and she wishes to exercise that right . . . the provisions of section 7 shall, *mutatis mutandis* . . . apply' (section 7 refers to the *talaq* mode of divorce). Under the rules of the MFLO, the marriage contract at section 18 asks specifically whether the right to divorce has been delegated to the wife and, if so, under what conditions (see Form II, WP Rules under the Muslim Family Laws Ordinance 1961, which British Muslims marrying in Pakistan use as evidence of marriage when seeking clearance for a Pakistani spouse to enter Britain).

> I remember saying to my uncle why didn't you ever tell me about this before and he said well you know . . . it wasn't really important that a woman can divorce her husband in the first place. But for me it was.   (Yasmin, London)[79]

It is imperative to question why there is a lack of knowledge about a right which could easily terminate the need for Muslim women ever approaching a *Sharia* Council for the authentication of a divorce. *Riwaj* and *'urf* ('custom' and 'customary practices', often local and ethnic in origin and patriarchal in nature) are the most likely cause for selective sharing of women's rights in Islamic family law. Ballard sums this up succinctly when he states that

> it is in terms of the ideas and expectations arising from this locally- and community-specific sphere of *riwaj*, rather than those set out in the much more religiously and politically distant arenas of *sharia* and *qanun* (secular law), to which South Asian settlers in Britain have turned for inspiration as they have set about to establish themselves overseas.[80]

7.5.3 British *Sharia* Councils in Practice

Despite their importance as a subject for debate in intra- and inter-community issues, there is very little empirical data on *Sharia* Councils, and this has been the cause of overgeneralizations as to their operation and impact. The challenges of doing fieldwork have been described by the handful of researchers who have conducted empirical research[81] on the subject in the past two decades.[82] The councils occupy a highly secluded sphere, operate at an informal level, may be reluctant to share records, and are introverted in their interaction with 'outsiders', and their function in family dispute resolution only hinders public scrutiny and, therefore, research.[83] The present chapter draws upon published studies of *Sharia* Councils, upon discussions with women who have experienced the workings of the councils, and upon the positions of the councils themselves. To ascertain the last of these three, I approached *Sharia* Councils as many British Muslim women would: through their websites.[84] After studying

---

[79] Bano, 'Complexity, Difference and "Muslim Personal Law"', p. 242.

[80] R. Ballard, 'Ethnic Diversity and the Delivery of Justice', in P. Shah and W. Menski (eds.), *Migration, Diaspora and Legal Systems in Europe* (London and New York: Routledge, 2006), pp. 50–1.

[81] Bano, *An Exploratory Study*; Douglas *et al.*, *Social Cohesion*; Bowen, 'How Could English Courts Recognise Sharia?'.

[82] See, for example, Shah-Kazemi, *Untying the Knot*; Bano, 'Complexity, Difference and "Muslim Personal Law"'.

[83] Nevertheless, the BBC has succeeded in filming the workings of some *Sharia* Councils, and both Shah-Kazemi and Bano were, as Muslim women, able to develop a relationship of trust with some of the councils, as was the research team of Douglas *et al.*

[84] I adopted this course of action based on findings from my 2010 study 'Cyberspace as Emerging Muslim Discursive Space? Online Fatawa on Women and Gender Relations and Its Impact on Muslim Family Law Norms', *International Journal of Law, Policy and the Family* 24(3) (2010), 338–60. This work was supplemented by conversations with members of British Muslim

the websites of the three most prominent *Sharia* Councils – the Islamic Sharia Council (ISC) based in Leyton, East London; the Sharia Council of Birmingham Central Mosque (SCBCM); and the Muslim Law (Shariah) Council UK (MLSCUK)[85] – some interesting questions unfolded regarding their remit as well as their interpretative approaches to Islamic law.

Two striking aspects of the three *Sharia* Councils' work were the subject matter of the cases brought before them and the fact that users were mostly female: all three institutions acknowledge the fact that the vast majority (as much as 95 per cent) of cases before them consist of matrimonial matters, of which Muslim women seeking divorce constitute the largest group. The councils' websites do not present a breakdown of those women who had obtained a civil divorce and now wanted an 'Islamic' one, and those who had married in a religious ceremony alone and for whom an 'Islamic' divorce was necessary only in community terms (they were, legally speaking, merely cohabitants). Case files are confidential, and researchers including Shah-Kazemi and Bano report that it is difficult to obtain exact breakdowns. One researcher who has engaged with *Sharia* Councils and tried to find a more definitive answer says,

> With the breakdown – again I will ask them, but they are likely to provide a generic percentage which they spoke to me about – I think in the region of 90% related to divorce, the vast majority of whom are women. Unfortunately they do not really seem to see the merit in having real solid statistics![86]

While this statistic could be seen as an indication that Muslim women acting upon their own agency find the provision of such services helpful, the gender bias toward women, along with other observations on the exact nature of the rulings given, makes it possible to conclude that *Sharia* Councils, created by Muslim men, are limiting women's autonomy and choice in the field of family law by directing them toward sanctioned forums. However, it is fair to say that perhaps the way in which Islamic laws on divorce are understood and interpreted in largely patriarchal social environments, including resistance to female-instigated divorce within Islamic law itself, gives this power to male-dominated *Sharia* Councils.

Clearly, the objective of *Sharia* Councils is limited, as any wider remit, such as facilitating the practice and operation of Islamic law in non-Muslim jurisdictions, would result in councils' caseloads reflecting a far wider range of issues and involving more male applicants. The practical expression of Islamic law is

---

communities, lawyers, social workers and council users, and interviews with S. Bano (University of Reading), Dr R. Akhtar, Dr Z. Maranlou, Dr H. Bata and M. R. Walji (Al-Mahdi Institute, Birmingham). I am grateful to them for their time and for sharing their ideas with me.

[85] All three councils serve Sunni communities. Only 15 per cent of Britain's Muslim population is Shia. Though there are considerable differences between the two traditions as far as *Sharia* Councils are concerned, this added layer of complexity is beyond the scope of this chapter.

[86] Personal interview (transcript on file).

clearly not confined only to Muslim women and family rights alone. If being allowed to practise Islam in a non-Muslim jurisdiction is a matter of freedom of religion and minority rights, then Muslim men and women ought to be equally keen to access such forums and to raise questions covering the entire spectrum of Muslim life. As *Sharia* Councils do not reflect such a set-up, it can be concluded that their functions and remit are specific and limited.

Setting aside this observation for the moment, an important question which this study looked at (bearing in mind the background of *siyar* and *fiqh al-aqalliyat* outlined above) was whether the *Sharia* Councils drew upon the basic jurisprudential concepts which relate to Muslims living in non-Muslim jurisdictions: *darar* ('harm'), *maqasid-al-sharia* (the 'objectives of *sharia*'), *maslaha* ('public interest') and *darura* ('necessity'). Most *Sharia* Councils' websites have a section where users can pose questions and seek responses from scholars of Islamic law. While many aspects of Islamic family law were discussed in the Q&A forums of the three websites studied, there was scant evidence in the material available to the public that *darar*, *maqasid-al-sharia*, *maslaha* and *darura* were drawn upon in answering questions. This major omission evidences the lack of interaction between the theological parameters of citizenship in places like Britain and the rule of Islamic law being advised and implemented. Thus it would be reasonable to conclude that these *Sharia* Councils, despite their assertion that they offer expert Islamic legal advice and guidance, lean heavily toward an 'operative Islamic law'; that is to say, a version of Islamic law which is culturally inclined rather than doctrinal, and focused on specific limited issues.

While the *Sharia* Councils studied illustrated the pluralist nature of the legal traditions amongst British Muslims, they also reflected the predominance of conservative and literalist interpretations of Islamic family law, imbued with popular cultural understandings, which are evident amongst Hanafi Sunnis of Pakistani origin.[87] The ISC website, for example, propounds a man's superiority over his wife, justified by the belief that the man in turn bears financial responsibility for his wife and family, and upon this assertion hangs the ISC's position that a husband has a unilateral right to pronounce *talaq*; on the other hand, women seeking a *khul'* divorce without 'good cause' are reminded that the Prophet Muhammad called such women 'hypocrites'. Yet the Supreme Court of Pakistan as far back as 1967, in the landmark case of *Khurshid Bibi* v. *Muhammad Amin*,[88] declared unequivocally that a woman's right to *khul'* was established, and that she did not have to give any 'cause', good or bad, to obtain it. The late Cassandra Balchin summed up the British situation aptly when she suggested,

What is being applied in Britain by the 'Sharia Councils' is an interpretation which fuses the worst aspects of a Hanafi Muslim tradition (that is no longer

---

[87] This is corroborated by the composition and users of many *Sharia* Councils and supported by the few empirical studies on the subject referred to previously.

[88] PLD 1967 SC 97.

the law in Bangladesh, Pakistan or Egypt), with the worst aspects of traditions from non-Hanafi schools (which they counter-balanced with other provisions), to produce something that is uniquely discriminatory, uniquely British and that is unrecognizable for Muslims in contexts outside Europe.[89]

Another example of the 'operative Islamic law' underlying the positions of the *Sharia* Councils studied is the extent to which they present options for stipulating conditions in marriage contracts intended to afford the Muslim wife the right to exit an unsatisfactory marriage.[90] Thus, for example, if *Sharia* Councils specify conditions which would circumvent the argument that a husband must consent to a civil divorce before an Islamic divorce can be obtained, this would prevent women (with civil marriage contracts) from being caught within limping marriages as well as women in *nikah*-only marriages. *Sharia* Councils may encourage *talaq-i-tafwid* (delegating right of divorce to the wife), which, as mentioned above, is an established right that a Muslim wife may negotiate and enter into her marriage contract. Alone amongst the councils studied, the MLSCUK provides forms whereby a couple can enter into an agreement for a monogamous marriage. If this agreement is broken by the man's taking a second wife,[91] his first wife can divorce him unilaterally in a civil, but Islamically valid, divorce. The only forms available from the ISC and SCBCM, however, are those for 'standard' Islamic marriage and divorce. The ISC's position is that a civil divorce which the husband has neither instigated nor acquiesced to is 'Islamically' invalid,[92] obliging the wife to apply to the ISC for an additional *khul'* divorce.

While the ISC's avowed position is that it seeks to offer marriage and divorce services and does not wish to engage with the formal court system, the SCBCM is aligned to the Birmingham Central Mosque, which is registered for marriage. On the one hand, the SCBCM presents an attitude of openness to formal legal and judicial structures and to bringing its members within mainstream British life; on the other, its failure to offer a 'monogamous marriage' form as well as a *talaq-i-tafwid* form (delegating to the wife the right to pronounce divorce) is at odds with this stance. The provision by the MLSCUK (the third *Sharia* Council studied here) of a form for the delegation of a power of divorce (here in the case of polygamy) is noteworthy, since if all Muslim marriages (monogamous and polygamous) contained such a clause then the husband's consent to civil divorce

---

[89] C. Balchin, 'Divorce in Classical Muslim Jurisprudence and the Differences between Jewish and Muslim Divorce' (2009) (available at muslimmarriagecontract.org), p. 3.

[90] For a detailed discussion of possible 'Islamic' stipulations entered by a wife for her right of divorce, see Mannan, *D. F. Mulla's Principles*, pp. 461–4.

[91] In an Islamic ceremony – the marriage would, of course, not be valid if contracted in the UK.

[92] Acquiescence may be implied or constructive. The fact that most civil divorces are uncontested ought to mean that the Muslim husband has by default agreed to the proceedings and the outcome, thereby making it 'Islamically' valid and not requiring another procedure under a *Sharia* Council. The ISC, however, requires the written consent of the husband for a civil divorce to be Islamically valid.

would be legally presumed and a second, 'Islamic' divorce would be unnecessary, with the claims to jurisdiction by *Sharia* Councils over the provision of 'Islamically' valid divorces then being wholly undermined.[93]

All three *Sharia* Councils issue a 'disclaimer' on their websites regarding legal standing in a court of law, stating, as does the ISC, that the 'divorce certificate' issued by them

> nullifies an Islamic marriage to which it applies only and has no bearing on the status of any coexistent civil contract (one which is recognised as legally binding under UK Law); for a civil divorce, applicants are advised to refer to the UK legal system for assistance in this area.

Finally, it is telling that a divorce certificate issued by the *Sharia* Councils (without an accompanying decree from an English court) is not recognized by any court in the Muslim world, whereas a civil decree absolute without a *Sharia* Council divorce certificate *is* recognized.

7.5.4 *Sharia* Councils as Contrary to British Muslim Women's Interests?

As indicated earlier, the main reason for the existence of *Sharia* Councils is that they offer women an 'Islamic' exit from 'limping marriages' already terminated by the civil courts, or, in case of *nikah*-only marriages, *Sharia* Council intervention is Muslim women's only exit as they are not classed as 'married' for purposes of English law.[94] With the ideological support of a *Sharia* Council, many husbands appear to use community sanction to act to their wife's detriment by not pronouncing *talaq*. Lewis, in his study of Bradford Muslims, describes how *pir* (religious elders) are inundated by community members asking for guidance on whether a marriage created and then dissolved under English law without the husband's consent/acquiescence is validly dissolved under Islamic law;[95] *Sharia* Councils are regularly approached by ex-wives (according to state law) to seek a subsequent 'Islamic' divorce. But it is clear that demands for Islamic divorce are contingent upon the insecurities and lack of confidence and knowledge of Muslim communities in general and of women in particular, rather than being rooted in uncontested Islamic requirements. One of the avowed objectives of *Sharia* Councils is to provide assistance to women in a safe, secure environment; it is said that these women are reluctant to speak about intimate and personal

---

[93] An important initiative was undertaken by the Muslim Institute in 2008 when it developed a Model Muslim Marriage Contract, including stipulations such as *talaq-i-tafwid*; a prohibition on polygamy; a mandatory civil ceremony; the entering into marriage of only adult women, without the consent and presence of a *wali* being necessary; and recourse to civil divorce courts. There is no information available in existing literature of the take-up of the model contract.

[94] In this regard the observation that the 'Shariah Council stressed how it always advised women to register their marriage under state law' is telling: R. Sandberg, G. Douglas, N. Doe and A. Khan, 'Britain's Religious Tribunals: Joint Governance in Practice', *Oxford Journal of Legal Studies* 33(2) (2013), 263–91.

[95] Lewis, 'Legal and Historical Reflections', 83.

matters to 'strange men'.[96] Yet *Sharia* Councils are usually all-male organizations which one would expect to count precisely as strangers in the eyes of Muslim women.[97] Whilst some Muslim women no doubt have a personal desire to have the divorce confirmed by a perceived 'authoritative' religious person or body, others are also led by family and community pressure to adhere to what are misleadingly portrayed as 'Islamic' requirements. As one *Sharia* Council user confided,

> I was abused to a point where I could not take it any more. My family did not support a divorce as they thought it would bring shame upon them. But I went to court and got a divorce. Yet no one in the community and even my family believed that I was divorced and they said that I would have to go to an *imam* or a *Sharia* Council to get a true Islamic divorce. Otherwise I would remain his wife forever.[98]

A *de jure* ex-wife, desperate to be acknowledged socially as an 'Islamically' divorced woman, is thus at the mercy of her ex-husband and of the negotiating prowess of a *Sharia* Council. She must first pay a fee to initiate her case, and the negotiation may end with the husband demanding money or other privileges in return for declaring *talaq*. If he refuses to declare *talaq*, there is little that the *Sharia* Council can do to compel him, reflecting the true limitation of their powers. As a possible solution to such an impasse, the *Sharia* Councils, in difficult cases, might encourage the ex-wife to opt for *khul'*, which means giving up her *mahr* in return for dissolution of the Islamic marriage.[99] This compromises the wife's legitimate claim to divorce, where she is not required to relinquish her *mahr*.[100]

Shah-Kazemi and Bano point to the dilemma confronted by women desperate to end a violent marriage, who see in a *Sharia* Council their only way out because that is what they have been warned is the only 'legitimate' way out. (Although there is evidence that some women will actively strategize to do this, simply to get rid of an undesirable marriage.)[101] There is also evidence that some will '*Sharia* Council-shop' until they are satisfied that they will achieve the outcome they seek.[102] It has been suggested that women have been known to

---

[96] A phrase used on the website of the ISC.

[97] At the time of writing, two *Sharia* Councils have included women on their panels: the SCBCM has one female official 'second to a judge', as well as Mrs Amra Bone, an Islamic studies academic.

[98] Confidential communication with 'Ms A' from Birmingham, on file.

[99] Personal communication with S. Bano with reference to her empirical study of *Sharia* Councils.

[100] Where the husband is at fault, the wife has the right to divorce and to retain *mahr*. Dissolution of Muslim Marriages Act 1939 (applicable in India, Bangladesh and Pakistan), Muslim Family Laws Ordinance 1961 (Pakistan) and Moroccan Family Code 2004. Cases where *Sharia* Councils are known to declare a *faskh* (dissolution on fault grounds) are very few and further research is required to disaggregate the various forms of divorce issued by these councils.

[101] Bano, 'Muslim Family Justice', 22–3.   [102] Ibid.

tolerate the intolerable through 'adaptive preferences':[103] accessing *Sharia* Councils to obtain a certificate of divorce is perceived by many women as an undesirable experience, but one to which they will acquiesce in order to end an undesirable marriage.[104] Thus, in conclusion, it can be stated that *Sharia* Councils reinforce the patriarchal understandings and interpretation of Islamic laws through the lens of culture and tradition; however, in the absence of alternative 'Islamically' authentic institutions, they provide Muslim women with an 'Islamic' avenue to exercise their right to a divorce.

7.6 Conclusion

I have argued in this chapter that the modes and mechanisms of engagement between British Muslims and the state and her institutions require intra- as well as inter-community discourses juxtaposed with equality and mutual self-respect and awareness of the inherent challenges. Such discourses commence with locating concrete commonalities and 'fault lines' and accepting that sociocultural and religious norms as practised by individuals and communities reflect human-constructed understandings, fluid and evolving, simultaneously performed and resisted. For instance, popularly perceived fault lines including polygamy, unequal divorce rights, inheritance and child custody rights for Muslim women are often seen in definitive and simplistic terms. Closer scrutiny of Muslim communities, however, reflects a more complex and nuanced reality: alongside some acceptance, there exist robust resistance and contestation of these practices presenting opportunities for a shared space for discussion.[105]

In a multicultural and heterogeneous society like Britain, a delimited policy is unlikely to be successful and a nuanced and deeper understanding within the legal establishment of the normative bases of 'other' legal systems, including Islamic law, is required. These minority systems coexist quite effectively within informal space, providing guidance for individuals and communities. The dominant legal system is in a position to apply its overarching power and discretion in determining the extent to which it accords recognition to these minority legal orders, if at all. This selectivity is evident in the phenomenal interest and interaction with Islamic financial law (mortgages, insurance, wills etc.), Islamic banks being some of the fastest-growing institutions worldwide.[106] Phillips's perceptive observations of striking a balance between the individual as more than a bearer of some monolithic culture and an autonomous being engaging with other (socio-legal) orderings offer important insights into how

---

[103] M. Nussbaum, *Women and Human Development* (Cambridge: Cambridge University Press, 2000), pp. 116–18.

[104] That is not to say that all women approach a *Sharia* Council unwillingly.

[105] As is evident in the laws of most Muslim jurisdictions, including Pakistan, Bangladesh, Morocco, Tunisia and others.

[106] A similarly inquisitive attitude is not always demonstrated in the area of Islamic family law.

multiculturalist societies might resolve normative conflicts.[107] Certain reforms and legal developments could help bridge the gap between the courts, Muslim communities wishing to satisfy the demands of religious conscience and British citizenship, and the wider interests of a society demanding equal treatment for women. One such development could be the simple registration of more mosques as places where a marriage can be legally solemnized.[108] Another could be that *imams* (holding the requisite authority to conduct the civil ceremony of marriage) be permitted to celebrate *nikah* (and simultaneously issue a civil certificate).

Recent developments have drawn English law closer to Islamic law, arguably smoothing the way to decisions which are friendlier to Muslim women. Since *Radmacher* v. *Granatino*,[109] where an English court accepted prenuptial agreements (conceptually a close relative of *mahr*) as capable of being given effect, it has become possible to hope that such developments will enable larger numbers of British Muslims to engage with the civil law. Maleiha Malik proposes the route of 'cultural voluntarism' and 'severance' in her report, *Minority Legal Orders in the UK: Minorities, Pluralism and the Law*,[110] as a positive way forward to allow selective minority legal orders to function so long as these specific norms do not go against public policy considerations.

Considering the particular focus of the present chapter, interpretative plurality of Islamic family law, informed by different cultures and traditions, makes it neither possible nor feasible to describe *Sharia* Councils as the sole 'legitimate' and 'authoritative' 'Islamic' dispute-resolution forum. It is important to stress that entrenching dual procedures for marriage and divorce is not the only 'Islamic' option available to *Sharia* Councils. By applying the jurisprudence of contemporary *fiqh al-aqalliyat*, they could equally well highlight an Islamically acceptable policy of fulfilling perceived religious duties within the formal legal system, sending out to Muslim communities clear signals of adaptability and engagement to this effect.[111] Theoretically, British Muslims have the choice of approaching either a *Sharia* Council or a court of law in fulfilling their legal and religious obligations as they perceive them; in practice, the very availability of 'Islamic' dispute-resolution forums has placed Muslim communities under great pressure to revert to them for preference.

The discourse on *siyar* and *fiqh al-aqalliyat* reflects the manner in which these options have been employed (or not) and highlights the plurality of the Islamic

---

[107] Phillips, *Multiculturalism without Culture*, p. 41.

[108] For example, a national campaign entitled 'Register our Marriage', initiated by Aina Khan, is under way at the time of writing.

[109] [2010] UKSC 42.   [110] Malik, *Minority Legal Orders*.

[111] For instance, encouraging mosques to obtain a licence to conduct marriages in accordance with civil law, or including a clause in the *nikah* for accepting the civil court as the forum for divorce. In the area of inheritance and succession, British Muslims readily accept the requirements of civil law, and in the field of financial matters great strides have been made in creating 'Islamic' mortgages and financial products.

legal tradition in opening up spaces for individual and community choices. Most British Muslims today would not contemplate turning directly to *siyar*, as the traditional aspect of the Islamic jurisprudence in this area requires them to return to a Muslim-majority jurisdiction except for temporary residence or travel in non-Muslim jurisdictions. *Fiqh al-aqalliyat* holds more promise, and has found supporters in Europe and North America, but few in Britain. Unanimity of opinion is not easily forthcoming, and unless the concepts of *darura* and *maqasid al-sharia* are understood as an ongoing 'necessity' requiring Muslims to remain in non-Muslim jurisdictions, wholesale adoption of this theory of minority jurisprudence is unlikely. Britain's Muslim communities have not, on the whole, as yet gone any great distance down the road to exploring an 'Islamic' rationale for their presence in contemporary Britain. If serious efforts are made, however, it *is* possible for all Muslim communities to agree upon a common core of principles, including Islamic conceptions of justice and the moral obligations of Muslims towards non-Muslims found in classical Islamic jurisprudence.[112] Such an exploration is necessary if the landscape underlying the mindset of diaspora communities is to encompass a justification of the need (or otherwise) for Muslim dispute-resolution forums.

Muslims, like the majority population, are too busy with everyday life to spend time theorizing about these questions. When confronted with matters touching upon family law, families and communities tend to extemporize solutions, often approaching family or community members or a respected *imam* rather than debate the underlying issues and agreeing on a coherent 'Islamic' response. This improvisation and lack of overall direction, when added to the tendency under liberal multiculturalism for communities to yield authority to the conservative voices of *Angrezi shariat*, has resulted in the rise of *Sharia* Councils applying discriminatory versions of Islamic law undermining the rights of women. *Sharia* Councils emerged to fill a gap (real or perceived) of access to justice for a community which feared the encroachment of secular Western morals, but they were also an expression of a deliberate strategy of raising religion as a marker of identity and in so doing perpetuating other markers of identity, including patriarchal and elitist domination over the less articulate and less empowered. Effective challenges will therefore have to come from within these very constituencies.

The main challenges highlighted within this chapter do not stem simply from differences in law but run much deeper into matters of ideology, identity and authority. *Sharia* Councils in one sense are simply the boldest expression of issues whose solution will require great political will on both sides. Answers will not be found in the form of simplistic binaries – Muslim/non-Muslim, *sharia*/civil law – but must take account of the layered and complex identities of

---

[112] On this point, the discussion in A. F. March, 'Sources of Moral Obligation to Non-Muslims in Fiqh al-aqalliyyat (Jurisprudence of Muslim Minorities) Discourse', *Islamic Law and Society* 16 (2009), 34–94, is illuminating.

individual Muslims and communities. In the short term, though, *Sharia* Councils are not going away anytime soon, and attempts at legislation to prohibit faith-based dispute resolution represent a dangerous trend which Parliament must refrain from following.[113] One possible way forward is to engage them in a dialogue from an Islamic legal perspective, as the present chapter attempts to do. Another response would be to empower Muslim women with knowledge relating to Islamically valid options and alternatives available within family law, including the option of approaching the English courts. A simply constructed handbook outlining how some 'mainstream' options are nevertheless Islamically valid could be one strategy to empower Muslim women in this regard.[114]

In closing, it would be fair to state that while a number of strategies and policy initiatives would be useful, addressing issues of Muslim identities requires engagement as equal citizens of a democratic, multicultural, multi-religious polity. A proactive Muslim civil society facilitating dialogue and debate among Muslim communities as well as with government is imperative, so that competing voices may be heard and mutual accommodation fostered.[115] The foundation for mutual engagement between British Muslims and the English legal system lies in nurturing a common core of moral and ethical normative values through respectful and honest dialogue.

---

[113] I refer here to the Private Member's Arbitration and Mediation (Equality) Bill introduced by Baroness Cox of Queensbury. For a concise analysis see R. D. Grillo, *Muslim Families, Politics and the Law: A Legal Industry in Multicultural Britain* (London: Ashgate, 2015). Likewise, rumours that government proposals are afoot to scrutinize the workings of *Sharia* Councils in the UK with a view to restrict or even ban some of these institutions will only drive many such underground and further alienate Muslim communities.

[114] Mediation is an option under English law and is 'becoming more important for all family law disputes and there is evidence that new Muslim groups (often led by Muslim women) are emerging trying to address questions of consent and coercion but facing a backlash from some sections of the Muslim community' (personal email from Bano, 23 July 2015).

[115] See Emon, 'Conceiving Islamic Law', 331.

8

Internet *Fatawa*: Challenging Tradition and Modernity in Women and Gender Issues

8.1 Introduction

One of the main arguments advanced in this book is the inherent dynamism of the Islamic legal traditions and their responsiveness to social realities through various juristic techniques, mechanisms and institutions. Historically, one such mechanism has been the *fatwa* (plural *fatawa*) through which an individual, a *qadi* (judge) or a ruler sought a non-binding response to a specific legal issue. Over time these opinions grew into an imposing body of materials, some of which was incorporated into legal textbooks and manuals for future reference. As a flexible vehicle of legal interpretation, *fatawa* are a reflection of evolving norms of Islamic law and society in language comprehensible to lay members of Muslim communities.

Today, in an age of print and electronic media, the institution of *ifta* (the act of issuing *fatawa*) has undergone significant transformation whilst retaining its core function. Beyond the mediums of newspaper, radio and television, *fatawa* in their latest manifestation are being issued by 'Internet *muftis*' to a growing, Internet-savvy population of *fatwa*-seekers. Discourse on Internet *fatawa* as an interpretative and pedagogical tool, as well as an emerging discursive space in a virtual environment, is an ever-expanding field of investigation.

The present chapter looks at the idea that, in employing a combination of traditional *ifta* tools as well as the virtual environment of the World Wide Web, Internet *fatawa* simultaneously challenge tradition and modernity. Tradition is being challenged by a fragmentation of authority and a democratizing of knowledge, making it more accessible to individuals and communities at the national, transnational and international levels; while modernity is being challenged in the way Internet *fatawa* are legitimating and reviving historical formulations of legal interpretations.

Drawing upon a selection of *fatawa* on women, gender and family law norms from selected Internet sites, this chapter makes a number of observations.[1] Most

---

[1] The opportunity to undertake research in this area initially arose through the CULCOM project in Oslo, with which I was involved in my position as Professor II at the University of Oslo. This resulted in two publications which informed this chapter. Building on primary research undertaken in 2009–10 and published as 'Behind the Cyberspace Veil: Online *Fatwas* on

basically, the arrival of Internet *fatawa* has led to a dislocation of traditional forms of authority within the Islamic legal traditions. Internet *fatawa* exist within a virtual space, available within the privacy of the home, that makes women in particular more confident in raising questions which they would not pose face-to-face. The plurality within the Islamic legal traditions readily lends itself to providing answers through this new medium, and Internet *fatawa* are proving to be an enabling and empowering mechanism for Muslim women to decide for themselves how to act. The Internet has provided Muslim women with opportunities to inquire about issues not usually posed, due to societal norms on what may or may not be discussed in public. Women have, for instance, asked whether it is permitted to have breast augmentation surgery to please a husband, the nature of a relationship with a fiancé, whether or not one can engage in body piercing, and so on.[2] At the same time, though, this does not necessarily equate to Muslim women being 'liberated' from what might be called 'patriarchal' interpretations of Islamic law: it is evident that amongst the proliferation of Internet *fatawa* are those which would aim to channel women towards a particular interpretation of Islam, with an element of sermonizing on how a Muslim woman ought to conduct herself.

The study shows that, in their *fatawa*, *muftis* try to be inclusive of all schools of juristic thought in Sunni Islam, insofar as most of the *fatawa* proceed by laying out what the various schools say on the subject before pronouncing on what the *mufti* himself considers the best option. The Internet format is serving as a new, global space for discourse among Muslims of very different traditions and views, resulting in a cross-fertilization of ideas across the various schools of juristic thought. This is an important finding for the present research, since on most topics there is significant disparity and only rarely absolute consensus. (For instance, on dress code, some *muftis* say only the head covering is required; others say the face also ought to be covered, and so on.) The notable exceptions to this trend are the triple *talaq* and *tahlil* marriage, where all Sunni schools of juristic thought speak with one voice. These two 'uncomfortable' aspects of Islamic family law have been, and still are, widely considered unjust, and Muslims throughout history have been uncomfortable in 'owning' these legal concepts and have strategized against their implementation. The tension here is between what might, according to certain textual exegesis, be considered 'legally valid', and what is not permitted on the grounds that it is unjust.

Cyberspace has impacted on the development of the Islamic legal traditions by opening up to a vast audience the potential for enquiring about and responding to contemporary issues and the challenges of modernity: how, especially, Muslims should negotiate the 'necessity' of wearing Muslim dress in a non-Muslim country, or difficult questions on divorce or *tahlil* marriage.

Women's Family Rights', in Hellum, Ali and Griffiths, *From Transnational Relations to Transnational Laws*, pp. 125–46; and 'Cyberspace as Emerging Muslim Discursive Space?'.

[2] Examples from the Internet *fatawa* are studied and set out below.

As Muslims seek online answers from within the Islamic legal traditions, Internet *fatawa* are proving to be a modern manifestation of the ever-present tension between 'doctrinal' law from above and 'living law' from below. Increasing access to the Internet is challenging the historical conception that only states and governments are the legitimate arbiters of legal disputes, and that the traditional sources of interpretative authority – the local *aalim* or the *imam* of the neighbourhood mosque – are the only repositories of Islamic law.

8.2 Contextualizing *Fatawa* in the Islamic Legal Traditions

What, then, is the normative status of *fatawa* across territorial borders and boundaries? As discussed in Chapter 1, 'Islamic law' (or, more broadly, the Islamic legal traditions) is an extremely complex web and hierarchy of sources and juristic techniques developed over time and in varied places. Most scholars are agreed on the hierarchy of sources – the Qur'an and Sunna as primary sources, and *ijma* (consensus) and *qiyas* (analogy) as secondary sources, along with a host of juristic techniques.[3] Historically, *fatawa* collections show that, in issuing a *fatwa*, the *mufti* was mindful of employing these sources as well as local custom (*'urf, ta'amul,* or *adah*). *Fatawa* issued by *muftis* in diverse social and historical settings 'served to stimulate the development of the *shari'a* from below, in response to the specific needs of particular Muslim communities'.[4] In other words, customary practices were reflected through *fatawa*, bringing communities and the legal system (the formalized procedures of state, judiciary and legislature) closer together.[5] It is important to recognize the connection and interface, both juristic and historical, between *ijtihad, 'urf* and *ifta* as well as the nuanced distance between these three concepts.[6] For present purposes, the point to be noted is that *fatawa* were, historically speaking, as much 'bottom-up' as 'top-down' law, reacting to real-life situations and practice – just as we can now observe in their Internet manifestation.

At its most basic, a *fatwa* is a response to a real or hypothetical question by a questioner. It reflects the personal interpretation of the *mufti*, based on his personal opinion and interpretation of the religious texts, as well as the rulings and *fatawa* of earlier scholars on the subject. The *fatwa* is a non-binding, advisory opinion of a *mufti* to an individual questioner, who may be a *qadi* (judge), a private individual, or an institution,[7] and consists of a question (*sua'al,* or *istifta*) together with an answer (*jawab*). The *fatwa* is perceived by many as a multi-functional 'meeting point between legal theory and social

---

[3] Including *ijtihad, taqlid, ikhtilaf, takhhayur, talfiq, darura, istishab, istihsan* and *sadd al-dharai.*

[4] W. Hallaq, 'From *Fatwas* to *Furu*: Growth and Change in Islamic Substantive Law', in *Islamic Law and Society* 1 (1994), 29–65.

[5] Masud, Messick and Powers, *Islamic Legal Interpretation*, p. 4.

[6] Although not the focus of the present chapter, there is debate as to the qualifications of *mufti* and whether they ought also to be qualified as *mujtahid.*

[7] Masud, Messick and Powers, 'Muftis, Fatwas, and Islamic Legal Interpretation'.

practice'.[8] These include employing *fatwa* as a legal tool in assisting the adjudication process, as a social instrument in the form of questions by persons in the community, as inputs to political discourse in relation to an act of state or government (either within the state or vis-à-vis another state or states), or as a device for reform (where a *mufti* presents his viewpoint for reform in existing practice). *Fatawa* historically 'formed the vital link between academic theories of pure scholarship and the influences of practical life, and through them the dictates of the doctrine were gradually adapted to the changing needs of Muslim society'.[9] Masud, Messick and Powers are of the view that 'the accumulation of fatwas issued by muftis in diverse social and historical settings served to stimulate the development of the shari'a from below, in response to the specific needs of particular Muslim communities'.[10] Hallaq, too, is of the view that the interplay between substantive Islamic law (*furu ul fiqh*) and *fatawa* nourished a vitality and responsiveness that was central to the continuing dynamism of Islamic law and Muslim societies.[11]

The institution of *ifta* has had a profound effect upon the development of the Islamic legal traditions.[12] Voluminous compilations of the *fatawa* of reputable *muftis* have established a place for themselves as definitive legal texts and made clear the connection between this knowledge and the evolution of Islamic law:[13]

> Our enquiry suggests that the juridical genre of the *fatwa* was chiefly responsible for the growth and change of legal doctrine in the schools, and that our current perception of Islamic law as a jurists' law must now be further defined as a *muftis'* law. Any enquiry into the historical evolution and later development of substantive legal doctrine must take account of the *mufti* and his *fatwa*.[14]

[8] A. Caeiro, 'The Shifitng Moral Universe of the Tradition of Ifta: A Diachronic Study of Four Adab-al Fatwa Manuals', *Muslim World* 96(4) (October 2006), 661.

[9] Coulson, *History of Islamic Law*, p. 142.

[10] Masud, Messick and Powers, 'Muftis, Fatwas, and Islamic Legal Interpretation', p. 4.

[11] Hallaq, 'From *Fatwas* to *Furu*'.

[12] English-language literature based on historical records of *fatawa* is on the rise and offers rich insights into the role of this institution in the development of the Islamic legal traditions. For an excellent collection of case studies in the premodern, colonial and contemporary era, see Masud, Messick and Powers, *Islamic Legal Interpretation*; D. Powers, 'Kadijustiz or Qadi-Justice? A Paternity Dispute from Fourteenth-Century Morocco', *Islamic Law and Society* 1(3) (1994), 332–66; J. Tucker, 'Muftis and Matrimony: Islamic Law and Gender in Ottoman Syria and Palestine', *Islamic Law and Society* 1(3) (1994), 265–300; K. A. Miller, 'Muslim Minorities and the Obligation to Migrate to Islamic Territory: Two Fatwas from Fifteenth-Century Granada', *Islamic Law and Society* 7(2) (2000), 256–85; B. Stowasser and Z. Abul-Magd, 'Tahlil Marriage in Shari'a: Legal Codes, and the Contemporary *Fatwa* Literature', in Haddad and Stowasser, *Islamic Law*, pp. 161–81.

[13] Some of the better-known *fatawa* collections include *Kitab al-Nawazil*, compiled by Abu Layth al-Samarqandi; *Majma' al-nawazil wa'l-waqiy'at* by al-Natifi; *Fatawa Qadikhan* by Qadikhan; *Fatawa Ibn Rushd*; *Kitab al-Mi'yar* by Ahmad al-Wansharisi; and *Al-Fatawa al-Alamgiriyya* by Shaykh Nizam of Burhanpur.

[14] Hallaq, 'From *Fatwas* to *Furu*', p. 65. For a good historical and comparative account of the role of *ifta*, particularly in its state-linked manifestation, see J. Skovgaard-Petersen, 'A Typology of State *Muftis*', in Haddad and Stowasser, *Islamic Law*, pp. 81–98.

The substantive observation here for our purposes is that *fatawa* have always been an essential part of a 'genuine' and evolving Islamic law.

The institutional forms taken by the *mufti*-ship have historically been diverse, too, just like the requirements as to who could be a *mufti*, the requisite qualifications, and the relationship between *mufti* and questioner. There are, indeed, specific compilations elaborating on the above questions.[15] An indicator of the high standards of ability, integrity and competence required of a *mufti* is that some early Muslim scholars were of the view that in order to be a *mufti* one had to be a *mujtahid* (i.e. one who can make *ijtihad*). In other words, a *mufti* ought to be capable of both *ijtihad* and *fatawa* – a tall order, and a consideration that poses challenges to Internet *fatawa* insofar as they are a modern manifestation of *ifta*.

8.3 Internet *Fatawa*: Challenging Tradition and Democratizing Knowledge

From its starting point as an inherently one-to-one response by a *mufti* to a questioner, the *fatwa* in its Internet incarnation has gripped the attention of many different constituencies.[16] Muslim *fatwa*-seekers, as well as academics, social and political institutions, states and governments, and organizations watching over cyberspace are engaged in exploring websites issuing *fatawa* on a wide range of subjects. Enquiry into various aspects of what Bunt terms the 'cyber-Islamic environment'[17] forms a burgeoning field of study.[18] As a socio-legal advisory process, the institution of *ifta* has undergone a transformation in being applied in cyberspace. El-Nawawy and Khamis note that Internet technology leads to audience segmentation, moving people away from a unitary and coherent public sphere and closer to scattered, isolated and fragmented 'public sphericules'.[19] The mode of transmission of Internet *fatawa* has changed the *mufti*–questioner relationship from being face-to-face and

---

[15]   See Masud, Messick and Powers, *Islamic Legal Interpretation*, p. 333, note 13, for a list of some of the treatises addressing this matter.

[16]   Cyberspace has, for example, been used by individuals and institutions to enhance their visibility and to disseminate information about Islam and Islamic law, as well as by radical organizations seeking to publicize their political agenda, including recruiting for illegal activities. Watching over such Internet sites is also of integral interest to the security services.

[17]   G. Bunt, *iMuslims: Rewiring the House of Islam* (Chapel Hill: University of North Carolina Press, 2009), p. 1.

[18]   Among the many studies, see in particular G. Bunt, *Islam in the Digital Age: E-Jihad, Online Fatwas and Cyber Islamic Environments* (London: Pluto Press, 2003); M. El-Nawawy and S. Khamis, *Islam Dot Com: Contemporary Islamic Discourses in Cyberspace* (New York: Macmillan, 2009); Black *et al.*, *Modern Perspectives*; A. El-Tahawy, 'The Internet Is the New Mosque: Fatwa at the Click of a Mouse', *Arab Insight: Emerging Social and Legal Trends* 2(1) (2008), 11–19; M. Furber, 'Ranking Confidence in the Validity of Contemporary Fatwas and Their Dissemination Channels', Tabah Foundation Analytic Brief No 13 (2013) (available at tabahfoundation.org); V. Sisler, 'The Internet and the Construction of Islamic Knowledge in Europe', *Masaryk University Journal of Law and Technology* 1(2) (2007), 205–18.

[19]   El-Nawawy and Khamis, *Islam Dot Com*, p. 72, citing Gitlin.

one-to-one to being distant, impersonal and between one speaker and many possible hearers.

8.4 The Form, Content and Features of Internet *Fatawa*

One interesting aspect of Internet *fatawa* is that they faithfully follow the traditional prototype. First, the *mufti* recites the name of Allah and His Prophet and indicates that this opinion is delivered from an Islamic perspective, drawing upon Islamic sources, and to the best of his knowledge and competence. The substance of the *fatwa* then sets out the opinions of other jurists and offers evidence of the plural norms operating within the Islamic legal traditions, after which the *mufti* sets out his specific answer. The *fatwa* closes with an acknowledgement that this opinion is not a claim to the only truth, as only Allah knows best. (This apparently religious invocation can also be construed as the *mufti*'s 'disclaimer': he has done his best within the realm of human reason, but there might be other truths that he has not been able to extract given his knowledge of the legal sources.)

Cross-fertilization of ideas, opinions and arguments drawn from the four juristic schools of Sunni thought are a common feature of Internet *fatawa*.[20] Thus a single *fatwa* will encapsulate and recall viewpoints of a number of *muftis* from various parts and institutions of the Muslim world as well as scholars of the Muslim diaspora.[21] (It is worth mentioning here the clear difference between the plurality of opinions cited in Internet *fatawa* and the relative legal insularity of *fatawa* issued by the numerous Muslim *Sharia* Councils operating in the UK, which do not appear to cross-fertilize their decisions with those of similar institutions in other parts of the world.[22])

Internet *fatawa* highlight the many shades of opinion across the various juristic schools of thought. The range of opinions offered on the same subject is very broad, and close attention is paid to this by young Muslims living in the West. For instance, in the case of the 'correct' dress code for women, advice ranges from just a headscarf, to the *niqab* face veil, to a full-body covering including hands and feet. On whether it is sufficient for women to use sporting helmets in place of headscarves, on whether it is permissible to take the *hijab* off to pursue education in countries where this is banned, and suchlike questions, *fatawa* opinions vary widely, reflecting the diverse opinions of scholars and commentators of the Qur'an and *ahadith*. So which opinion ought a questioner to adopt? Will questioners respect the variety and diversity of opinions as a 'positive' that offers choices and options, or will they tend to migrate toward a rather more conservative norm? For many young, Internet-savvy Muslims living in the West, their search is increasingly for a 'pure', 'pristine' Islam, 'uncontaminated' by the

---

[20] The present study is confined to *fatawa* rendered by Sunni *muftis*.
[21] Stowasser and Abul-Magd, 'Tahlil Marriage in Shari'a', p. 162.
[22] See the discussion in the chapter on *Sharia* Councils in this book.

cultural Islam of their parents. In the global context, this cyberspace environment 'has contributed to "essentialism" and "homogenization" of religion',[23] quite alien to the Islamic traditions. So we can observe inherently contradictory trends – on the one hand, Internet *fatawa* are setting out a broad range of juristic opinions for a global audience, yet at the same time they are narrowing the field in pointing toward a more restrictive conclusion as to the opinion that ought to be adopted.

8.5 Internet *Fatawa* on Questions of Women and Gender

The findings of this chapter are based on a study of *fatawa*-issuing websites initially undertaken in 2009 and followed up in 2014, and triggered by the phenomenal proliferation of *fatwa* websites and Internet *muftis*, and by increasing access to and interest in the Internet among Muslim communities. In 2009, three websites – islamonline.net, islamonline.com, and islamtoday.com – were chosen. During the follow-up research in 2014, onislam.net was added. All four sites state their main objective as information dissemination on Islam and Muslims, all include a dedicated section for *fatawa*, and all are Sunni (the Shia have a very different structure for seeking *fatawa*, which is beyond the scope of this study).

(i) islamonline.net has offices in Doha and Cairo. Its stated aim is 'to provide information about Islam and its civilizations, the universe and its changes, current affairs and their analyses, and general information and services that one cannot do without in the 21st century'. It 'aims to present the unified and lively nature of Islam that is keeping up with modern times in all areas'. It asserts that it engages 'experts from all over the world and from all religions, ethnicities, and cultures specializing in politics, economics, the media, sociology, technology, the arts, and other fields'. The site regards its audience as being 'all people, Muslim and non-Muslim, regardless of geographic boundaries, race, religion, language, background, culture or gender', and sees its approach as 'balanced', 'adopting the middle ground of Islam, avoiding extremism or negligence, rejecting deviant or eccentric opinions'. The site appears open to sharing information regarding the specialists who sit at the keyboard, and has a commercial aspect which is visible from the advertisements displayed on its homepage.

(ii) Owned and operated by Aljazeera Publishing, islamonline.com is based in Dubai and describes itself as 'the leading and original Islamic portal on the Internet' and 'the number one source for Islamic content in the Islamic world'. Its stated objective is 'to portray a positive and accurate picture of Islam to the world as well as providing support services for Muslims as

---

[23]   Sisler, 'Internet and the Construction of Islamic Knowledge', 211.

well as for non Muslims wishing to explore Islam'. The site carries a large number of advertisements, in particular on jobs in the Middle East.

(iii) islamtoday.com has since 2001 been directed by Sheikh Salman al-Oadah, an influential Saudi cleric, Islamic scholar and media personality, whose influence comes from 'his innovative reach in the Muslim world propagated via islamtoday.com and his persistent efforts at ministering to the needs of the global Muslim community'. Sheikh Salman is described as an 'advocate of peaceful coexistence' and an 'ambassador of non-violence' who 'is outspoken about the importance of inculcating love and mercy as opposed to violence in the daily life of Muslims', and he notably rebuked Al-Qaeda and Osama bin Laden over their use of violence. islamtoday.com provides resources in English, Arabic, French and Chinese and 'brings together a diverse range of Islamic scholars and educators to provide guidance in Islamic thought'. The site notes that Sheikh Salman's work 'has far-reaching impact in an age when religion is spread through media and technology'. The site has no advertisements, and appears to be purely of an information-sharing and pedagogical nature. It has not proved possible to identify its offices' physical location.

(iv) onislam.net was launched in 2014 by the founders of islamonline.net after a disagreement with its Qatari financiers. In the view of onislam.net, the original islamonline.net site

> had enjoyed editorial independence since its birth in 1999 under the auspices of prominent scholar Sheikh Yusuf Al-Qaradawi, by separating its editorial content from its funding. The equation changed a year ago after the new board started interfering in the editorial process and showing discomfort with the moderate message of the website.

> onislam.net was launched under the umbrella of an Egyptian non-profit civil organization for media development.

> It seeks to review and renew contemporary Islamic discourses and help reach common grounds among people of different faiths and cultures. onislam will have a special focus on the institution of the family and the challenges facing Muslim families, especially in non Muslim-majority countries.[24]

There are, inevitably, commonalities shared by all four sites as well as subtler differences. Addressing a global audience is a common feature, and all highlight news items relating to Muslims worldwide. None of the four restricts itself to the viewpoint of any single juristic school. In fact, all four adopt what is in their view an inclusive, holistic, middle-ground approach to Islam. Whilst I generally agree that the approach is balanced, streaks of patriarchal, male dominance are often to be seen. All four offer users the option of reading contents in, at a minimum, Arabic or English and identify the theme(s) they wish to seek

---

[24] 'IslamOnline Founders Launch OnIslam', onislam.net, 9 October 2010.

guidance on. Of course, accessing the Internet and being able to communicate in Arabic or English are limiting factors of this process, ruling out all those Muslims who are unable to do either.

When we come to examine the *fatawa* presented on the four sites, they cover an extremely wide range of issues, but what stands out is the fact that they are almost all concerned with what we might call issues of women and gender. There are, for example, fewer *fatawa* on issues relating to mercantile law, Islamic finance or criminal law. Guidance on Islamic finance has been institutionalized through Islamic finance advisory boards in Muslim and non-Muslim countries, which may be the reason for the few questioners on the interest sites studied. Subjects of Internet *fatawa* and the numbers also depend upon particular national and international situations. So, for instance, during the two Iraq wars, as well as the invasion of Afghanistan, many *fatawa* came into the public domain from Muslims seeking guidance on whether this situation called for *jihad*.[25] Instead, we are overwhelmed with topics such as the interactions with those who are *mahram* and non-*mahram*, the etiquette of social interaction between the sexes (both online and face-to-face, and whether engaged or not), women's education, women's employment in a mixed environment, the parameters of love between opposite sexes, the pre-marital relationship among engaged couples, the pre-consummation relationship between those who have been married by *nikah*, the domain of activities for girls and women and their overall status within the family, negotiating and resolving conflicts between outdoor activities and responsibilities within the home, the marital rights of husband and wife, the right to divorce in different circumstances (e.g., if the wife refuses to wear *hijab* or *niqab*), the right of a wife to seek divorce if her husband does not observe religious dictates, women's consent and guardians' authority in matters of marriage, women's participation in religious ceremonies, women's role in politics, personal bodily matters including menstruation and its effect on sexual and religious matters, the right to abortion, the due spacing between children, women's involvement in sexual practices such as fornication and masturbation, a husband's obligation to provide sexual satisfaction, female circumcision and its validity in the Islamic legal tradition, women employing artificial or medical means to enhance their beauty, paternity testing, breast augmentation, body piercing, and, finally, differences in the legal status of men and women – but three topics in particular stood out because of the frequency with which they were raised: (i) the issue of 'Islamic' dress in a non-Muslim country, (ii) the triple *talaq* and (iii) the question of the necessity of a *tahlil* marriage between divorce and remarriage. These are set out by frequency in Table 8.1.

It must be stressed that these figures are only an approximation of the total number of *fatawa* on these three major topics. It is in fact impossible to tease out the *fatawa* into discrete units: they were handed down across a ten-year

---

[25] For details see Ali, 'Resurrecting Siyar through Fatwas?'.

Table 8.1 Selected Internet *fatawa* by frequency

Dress code	Divorce	*Tahlil*	Total
156	62	63	281

period from 2004 to 2014, and any given *fatwa* was liable to be presented more than once and, in effect, cut and pasted and replicated across multiple websites to support the advice given by different *muftis*. There was, indeed, significant overlap and repetition of *fatawa* even on the same site.

In the initial phase of the research, a list of approximately 100 *fatawa* relating to the three major topics was developed, rising to 281 in 2014. These were examined in order to compile a summary of the issues raised, to ascertain similarities between the questions, to highlight trends and patterns in the questions and the responses, to identify the countries from which the questions were being asked, and, finally, to discern which were the most 'burning' questions. As to the identities of the interlocutors – the *mufti* and the *fatwa*-seeker (or *mustafti*) – though we can never be certain of anybody's true identity in an online context, we can at least say who they claim to be, if we take them at their word. Historically it was a well-known *mufti* or *aalim* who was the sole source of authority (validated often by a *qadi* who used the *fatwa* as a basis for his decision). In this study, each of the *fatawa* either gave the name and credentials of the *mufti* or (in the case of onislam.net) simply stated that they were a 'consultant'. Credentials consisted of graduate of Al-Azhar University, Cairo, Egypt; professor of Shari'a, Cairo University; *imam* of Calgary mosque, Alberta, Canada; and former professor of King Saud University, Riyadh, Saudi Arabia. I did not come across any female *muftis* in this sample, although some websites do appear to have female advisers who communicate the *fatwa* to the questioner. As for the *fatwa*-seekers, again, the Internet context makes it impossible to determine accurately their provenance. Many do not give a location, while others state or imply that they are in a non-Muslim country. Overall, the strong impression gained is that the majority are based in English-speaking diaspora nations such as the UK, the US, Australia and Canada, but also other Western countries such as France and Germany, and, to a lesser degree, Muslim nations such as Egypt, Kuwait, Nigeria, the Maldives, India, Pakistan, Egypt and Saudi Arabia. Since only the name and place of the questioner (at most) appear on the *fatawa*, it was not possible to develop a detailed profile by socio-economic level or by religious and political convictions, etc. Although, by virtue of the Internet's very nature, it was impossible to ascertain *definitively* the origin, gender, etc. of the questioner or the identity of the respondent, the vast majority (95 per cent) of questioners self-asserted as women. Despite this acknowledged limitation, there at least appeared to be a spread of *fatawa* whose questioners were from many different countries, and consequently the questions and responses encompassed a rich spectrum of subjects and themes broadly falling into the area of family law, women and gender.[26]

8.6 Muslim Women's Legal Position as Seen through the Lens of Internet *Fatawa*

The issue of the position of Muslim women within the Islamic legal tradition generates complex and diverse understandings of the primary and secondary sources of Islamic law discussed above. Concentric circles of plural normative frameworks based upon cultural, traditional, socio-economic and political practices inform Muslim women's status and rights. In recent decades a further circle has been added – the demands of life in a non-Muslim diaspora and as members of transnational families and communities.[27] Demands on the Islamic legal traditions to interpret Muslim women's status and entitlements in this changing global environment are, unsurprisingly, increasing.

Based on the Qur'an and Sunna, the position of Muslim women is one of complete equality and dignity in the ethical, moral and reward/punishment paradigm (*ibadaat*). At the level of socio-economic, political and family life (*muamalaat*), however, they are placed at a lower hierarchical level, in the belief that women are in need of protection. It is this hierarchy of status that continues to inform perceptions regarding Muslim women and their place in society, both in traditional and in Internet *fatawa*. I have elsewhere presented a detailed categorization and hierarchization of women's rights in Islam, arguing that these categories are fluid and evolving and not set in watertight compartments.[28] The *fatawa* discussed in the present chapter bring this fluidity into relief by using language and terminology that may be interpreted as discriminatory by some and protective and/or corrective by others.

Two areas appear to be foremost in the minds of questioners seeking *fatawa* – norms regulating a Muslim woman's dress and demeanour, and her rights and entitlements in family life (mostly vis-à-vis her spouse). This is hardly surprising, as both are fertile grounds for an interpretative discourse, placed as they are at the intersection of culture, tradition and religion. In specific terms, the laws relating to Muslim women's status and entitlements and how she is required to conduct herself draw largely upon just a few verses of the Qur'an. The focus of contestation arises from literal, patriarchal and historical understandings of these verses, arguably creating and upholding a hierarchy on the basis of sex:

(i) 2:228: 'Divorced women shall wait concerning themselves for three monthly periods. Nor is it lawful for them to hide what Allah hath created

---

[26] These are not presented in order of importance or frequency of *fatawa* pronounced but rather as they were encountered during the study.

[27] See the discussion in Chapter 7.

[28] Ali, *Gender and Human Rights*, in particular Chapter 2.

in their wombs, if they have faith in Allah and the Last Day. And their husbands have the better right to take them back in that period, if they wish for reconciliation. And women shall have rights similar to the rights against them, according to what is equitable; but men have a degree [of advantage] over them.' This 'degree [of advantage]' has been commonly interpreted as alluding to the superior right of the husband to divorce his wife.

(ii) 2:282: '...and get two witnesses, out of your own men, and if there are not two men, then a man and two women, such as ye choose, for witnesses, so that if one of them errs, the other can remind her'. In this verse (which establishes procedures for transcribing contracts and obligations into writing), women have been prescribed as witnesses, but with an evidentiary value half that of men.

(iii) 4:3: 'If ye fear that ye shall not be able to deal justly with the orphans, Marry women of your choice, Two or three or four; but if ye fear that ye shall not be able to deal justly [with them], then only one, or [a captive] that your right hands possess, that will be more suitable, to prevent you from doing injustice.' This 'polygamy verse' is taken as permitting a man to marry more than one wife. Progressive, reformist and feminist interpretations of the verse look, however, at its context and argue that it is an exception rather than a rule. Verse 4:129 can also read together with this verse to make the 'right' to polygamy more restrictive.

(iv) 4:11: '...To the male, a portion equal to that of two females: if only daughters, two or more, their share is two-thirds of the inheritance; if only one, her share is a half. For parents, a sixth share of the inheritance to each, if the deceased left children; if no children, and the parents are the [only] heirs, the mother has a third; if the deceased left brothers [or sisters] the mother has a sixth'. This verse sets out some of the rules on inheritance, under which women are allocated half-shares in comparison to men standing in similar relationship.

(v) 4:34: 'Men are the protectors and maintainers of women, because Allah has given the one more [strength] than the other, and because they support them from their means. Therefore the righteous women are devoutly obedient, and guard in [the husband's] absence what Allah would have them guard. As to those women on whose part ye fear disloyalty and ill-conduct, admonish them [first], [Next], refuse to share their beds, [And last] beat them [lightly]; but if they return to obedience, seek not against them means [of annoyance].' The contents of this verse are perhaps the most challenging for Muslim women. Despite a number of woman-friendly interpretations canvassed over the years to 'blunt' its impact, the reality is that it has entrenched patriarchy and relegated women to an inferior position.

(vi) 24:30–1: 'Say to the believing men that they should lower their gaze and guard their modesty: that will make for greater purity for them ... And say to the believing women that they should lower their gaze and guard their modesty; that they should not display their beauty and ornaments except what [must ordinarily] appear thereof; that they should draw their veils over their bosoms and not display their beauty except to [those relations set out in detail]; and that they should not strike their feet in order to draw attention to their hidden ornaments.' This verse sets out norms regulating dress codes. Highly contextual in nature, they are taken literally by the vast majority of Muslims who consider covering the head, neck and chest to be compulsory for Muslim women, and, further, that an outer covering must be worn to ensure coverage down to the feet.

(vii) 33:59: 'O Prophet, tell your wives and your daughters and the women of the believers to bring down over themselves [part] of their outer garments. That is more suitable that they will be known and not be abused?'

A number of scholars have challenged restrictive interpretations of these verses, adopting the position that what have become the only benchmark for women's position and rights in Islam are in fact susceptible to multiple interpretations and are contested terrain.[29] The questioning and clarifications linked to these verses continues unabated across Muslim communities in transnational and international settings, as is evident from the Internet *fatawa* presented below.

8.7 Women's Dress Code and Demeanour

In the present study, the largest single number of questions on all the websites studied related to clarification on Muslim women's dress and demeanour. In the first phase, of the 100 *fatawa*, fifty-six related to this subject. In the second phase, a similar trend brought up a further 100 *fatawa*.[30] These *fatawa* can be subdivided into three areas: (i) wearing the *hijab*, and why; (ii) whether the *niqab* is obligatory, and whether a husband may require his wife to wear it (or not wear it); (iii) special dispensation when the *niqab* is likely to conflict with the law in non-Muslim jurisdictions. To provide a feel for the questions initially raised, a sample will suffice:

> 'My question relates to *hijab*; some people claim that *hijab* poses a restriction to women's liberty. What is your opinion on that?'
>
> 'This issue of *hijab* has reached a very serious stage. Could you please clarify whether *hijab* is a religious symbol or not?'
>
> 'Why should women only cover their body and face, even on a hot day? How is it possible for women and not for men?'
>
> 'How does Islam respect a woman by letting her wear *hijab*? Could you please give me the answer in a logical and rational way?'

[29] F. Rehman, A. A. An-Na'im, R Hassan, A. Wadud, F. Mernissi, A. Barlas, Z. Mir-Hoseini, A. Al-Hibri, L. Ahmed, H. Afshar, S. Haeri and S. S. Ali to name a few.

[30] The number of overall *fatawa* available on this subject is far higher: onislam.net alone lists about 130 *fatawa* on 'Dress Code & Adornment' given between 2004 and 2014.

'*Hijab* (as a dress code) for women in Islam, does it concern women only? Do men have nothing to bear in this? Secondly, I hear a lot of confusing things about *hijab*. While some say one does not need to cover the hair, others say that one must also cover one's face and hands besides the rest of the body. If a person refuses to cover her head, can others call her a non-Muslim simply for baring her head?'

Let us, then, look at one question and its answer: 'I am a Muslim teenager who is considering wearing *hijab*. However, I'd like to ask a few questions regarding this topic. What is the purpose of wearing *hijab*? Are there any advantages or benefits?'[31] The question is answered by Sheikh Riyad al-Musaymiri, a professor at Al-Imam University in Riyadh, as follows:

I am glad to read about your concern for what would please your Lord, though you are young. May Allah bless you. I hope that, by the will of Allah, you will be a pious Muslim woman throughout your life and keep seeking knowledge and endeavoring to please your Lord. Regarding your questions, these are the answers:

1. The purpose of wearing *hijab* is, first and foremost, out of obedience to Allah and His Messenger (peace be upon him). Allah says: 'And when you ask them for anything, ask them from before a screen.' One of the main objectives of *hijab* is to safeguard women from the gazes of people of weak morals and from those seeking to indulge in unlawful worldly pleasures. 2. The benefits of *hijab* are numerous. In addition to what I have already mentioned above, it protects the girl from being physically attacked or her reputation being injured. The Muslim woman is distinguished from the impious woman, for which she deserves respect. Last but not least, *hijab* also saves men from undergoing trials and temptations due to the beauty of women, just like the rules for modest male dress are there to save women from undergoing trials from the temptation of provocatively dressed men. Modest dress must be observed by men. Men are not allowed to wear shorts or wear tight fitting clothes. One of the reasons for this is that it protects women from temptation. May Allah protect you and guide you.

On the subject of whether a Muslim wife ought to wear the *hijab* on her husband's orders, the questions raised included the following, from a man: 'What should I do if my wife refuses to cover her hands, even though I asked her to do that from the beginning, then I commanded her to, but she refuses? What do you say if I threaten her with divorce?' The reply comes:

Allah has enjoined woman to be obedient to her husband, and has made men *qawwamun* (protectors and maintainers) of women. They are supposed to direct and look after women as a leader directs and looks after his people, because of the physical and mental characteristics with which Allah has distinguished them, as well as the financial duties that he has enjoined upon them. Allah says 'Men are the protectors and maintainers of women' (Verse 4:34). You can seek help in

---

[31] See en.islamtoday.net/node/1130.

admonishing her and advising her through useful tapes and books which speak of the obligation of *hijab* for Muslim women . . .

A female questioner asks,

I wear *hijab* but do not wear *niqab*, my husband says that if I do not start covering my face then he will divorce me. He says that whatever he asks me to do I should do. I do not want to disobey my husband but to wear *niqab* would cause me great hardship and sadden me deeply.

The reply comes:

So you have to fear Allah in this matter and respond to two commands: the command of Allah and the command of your husband. Undoubtedly this will be very good for you. This matter will make your husband happy and bring happiness to your home. Feelings of difficulty will pass if you are patient and get used to it . . . You will be responding to Islamic commands and the command of your husband which is in accordance with the laws of Allah . . .

Quite different to these rather conservative responses, though, is that to a question from a woman living in the US. She sets out her story in a long email: married less than a month earlier, her husband wants her to wear the *niqab*. He has shown her Islamic teaching videos to support his request, and cites verse 33:59 as evidence. He is very upset and angry at her refusal and has said he will not see her until she wears it, even though before marriage he had said he would not force her. She is now a social worker, and when she previously wore a *niqab* it only created problems in a society where it is not the norm, and in an area with scarcely any other Muslims. She knows his children will be teased and bullied.

The response:

at your age and experience, 'it is NOT to do . . . ' what your husband is imposing on you. You are still very young. You are still at the very start of your marriage. No kids in the marriage. The man promised you before marriage that he will not 'force' you to do it. Then, why would you want to start your life by teaching him that he can always change his word by 'punishing you' whenever he wants to get away with what he wants?! . . . Your husband, at a certain stage of time, when he was not yet your husband, wanted to become your husband and to have you as a wife. At that point of time, he gave you a promise. Then, now, today, when you are his, he completely forgets about that promise and imposes on you his desire by all means. He tries to convince you. He emotionally tries to affect you. He religiously tries to convince you by giving you videos and scholarly opinions. Then, he decides to punish you by staying away from you for three months! What kind of marital dialogue is this?! This is his attitude and 'policy' in solving a marital conflict after being 'recently married'. Ask yourself, how will he reach his goals after nine years of marriage? How will he resolve any of your conflicts when your opinions differ in relation to which school you take the kids to?

The *mufti* admits that he cannot give a straightforward yes or no answer, but advises that she should look carefully at her marriage and how she would like it to continue. As for the *niqab*, it is a choice which has to be made solely for the sake of Allah. He acknowledges that the issue is contested between scholars:

> Some agree that it is obligatory, some agree that it is preferred and some see that it is simply cultural and has nothing to do with religion. In this answer, I will not provide you a *fatwa* whether it is obligatory or not. This issue has been long discussed between great scholars and you can make your own research.

In language which would not be out of place in the advice column of a women's magazine, he reassures her,

> Being a good wife does not mean that he imposes on you what he promised he would not, particularly what he has previously promised that he won't. But, being a good wife means that you succeed in making him happy ... Let him know that you love and respect him. Keep your feelings, love, smile and respect for him. Talk to him softly and ask him to keep his promise. Tell him how heavy you feel this step is for you now and promise him to be more conservative with strangers. Tell him that you love him and that you want to continue your life with him, but that you don't see that you will be a faithful Muslim if you do it now. Promise him to read and study more about *niqab*. If you are ever convinced, then do it for the sake of Allah. If you are not, then never do it. If your husband ever takes it to the edge, that you will have to choose between him and *niqab* on one side, or letting go completely on the other side, then it will be your choice. Try never to take it that far. But if it is ever there, then think carefully if you really want to continue life with a man who solves marital conflicts through this attitude.

A third *fatwa* on dress raises issues of multiple identities, divided loyalties and legal obligations. The question is posed by an American Muslim who has heard about the case of a Muslim woman suing the State of Florida because it asked her to remove her *niqab* for an ID photo. It had been argued before the court that her *niqab* could only be removed if she were dead:

> What would you say to Muslim women who live in the West generally and in the US particularly about the issue of *niqab*? Is it so difficult to remove the *niqab* that she must file a case against the state, which doesn't even require her to uncover her hair, as some states do require for the drivers' license?

The response is balanced:

> As for your question, bear in mind that the majority of imams – including those of the four schools of *fiqh* as well as others – hold the opinion that a woman is not obliged to cover her face and hands. However, a group of scholars, the majority of whom belong to the Hanbali School, teach that a woman must cover her face and hands as well. It goes without saying that Muslims precede others in keeping the public interest and security of the nation. Therefore, if the law governing a given country requires uncovering the face of the woman for genuine reasons,

such as identification, the Muslim woman, like all other women, abides by the
law.

The scholar Sheikh Muhammad Iqbal Nadvi (*imam* of Calgary Mosque, Alberta,
and former professor at King Saud University, Riyadh), is quoted:

> The issue of *niqab* (covering the whole body including the face and hands) is a
> basic condition of *hijab* (Muslim woman's dress) in one school of *fiqh*, while it
> is recommended part of *hijab* in other schools. But what is agreed upon in all
> schools is to remove the *niqab* [i.e. to uncover the face] for some genuine reasons
> such as identification or medical purpose. The case you mentioned may be a
> reason to remove the *niqab* if the police officer is in need to do so, and there is
> a legal requirement by the law to show the face, regardless of the faith and this
> applies to all faiths. However, this should not be a way of discrimination against
> a veiled woman just to tease her. Therefore, the sister has to insist on her right to
> use *niqab* and fight for this right if she is targeted for discrimination and the law
> does not require showing the face.

Another professor of *sharia* at Cairo University is similarly cited:

> It is permissible, as far as *sharia* is concerned, to remove the *niqab* for some
> genuine reasons such as identification or to get a photo for ID or driving license.
> Therefore, if a Muslim woman is asked to remove the face cover to get a photo
> for such genuine reasons, then she is permitted to do so and Almighty Allah will
> forgive such matters.[32]

All three *fatawa* emphasize the wearing of the *hijab* and modest clothing for
Muslim women. Although verse 24:30 outlines a dress code for men, in the
hundreds of *fatawa* on the subject there is no *fatwa* regarding this. There may
be different reasons behind this silence regarding Muslim men's obligation to
dress modestly: lack of pressure to conform to a certain dress code, or the
spotlight being on Muslim women as 'visible' bearers of Muslim identity, or
it may also be the case that as maintainers and protectors of women in their
households (recalling verse 4:34), men are acting as monitoring agents for them
but are not monitored in return.

While some of the *fatawa* reveal a degree of contestation over women's dress,
there is little contestation on the basic principles of the code. They advised that
there is no choice when it comes to covering the head, neck and chest, and the
basic question of the contextual nature of this very rule remains unchallenged
and untouched in the discussions. Difference of opinion only arises in whether
the *niqab* is compulsory or not, and whether context plays a role in how a
woman ought to appear in the public sphere. The discursive element arises
both in the way in which some questions are framed and in responses provided.
Some women forced by their husbands against their will to wear the *niqab* seek
an Islamically authoritative response. In one instance, a husband seeks guidance

---

[32] See www.islamawareness.net/Hijab/Niqab/questions.html, collected from live *fatawas* of
www.islamonline.net.

regarding the limits of his authority over a wife who refuses to cover her hands. Whilst the responses differ in their detail, all these responses agree that the wife ought to obey her husband, even though a *niqab* is not universally agreed upon as compulsory. One *fatwa*, though, adopts a different standpoint, arguing that *forcing* a wife to do something is un-Islamic, in that wearing a *niqab* is supposed to be for Allah and not for the happiness of humans. It highlights the husband's unreasonableness and makes it clear that this does not bode well for the marriage. In comparison to the other *fatawa* studied, this stands out in the challenge it throws at the patriarchal stance of most *muftis*, both on and off the Internet.

The *fatwa* regarding ID photographs raises issues regarding the dress code for women but in a transnational and international context, and especially within a Muslim diaspora where laws are increasingly being adopted to prohibit face coverings. The *muftis* here lay out the plurality of interpretations on the *niqab*, then locate the question within the specific minority setting, arguing that Muslims must abide by the law of the land and that they ought therefore to remove a veil for identification in accordance with the law. *Fiqh al-aqalliyat* is invoked, where necessity (*darura*) may make the prohibited permissible.

In the Islamic traditions, veiling represents the ultimate dichotomy between the public and private spheres through a pronounced dress code for Muslim women. What usually does not come across in general debate, though, is the Qur'anic emphasis on 'recognition' and visibility of identity through dress as a protective measure in a politically and socially hostile and unfriendly environment. Were this aspect of the context to be highlighted, it would be clear that time, place, context and situation inform the dress code as much as the text. For instance, when in the politically hostile environment after 9/11 Muslim women wearing headscarves were harassed in public places, some scholars questioned the 'protective' nature of this dress code, and called on Muslim women to be cautious and conscious of their safety. A questioner from the USA, for example, sought a *fatwa* in 2003: 'Following what happened in the US lately, my wife can't go outside because she is scared. Can she take off her *hijab* when she goes out or not?' In response, the *fatwa* states that while covering the hair is non-controversial and that all schools of thought agree that a woman must cover her hair, in cases of a threat to her life she may remove it, if only temporarily. This *fatwa* is an example of the pragmatism that is being invoked in some quarters through application of *fiqh al-aqalliyat* and *maqasid al-sharia*. An example of this line of thinking is one *fatwa* responding to the question 'is the face veil compulsory?': 'I do not recommend the *niqab* for women who live in the West since they will attract unnecessary attention and people are less likely to easily communicate with them'.[33] Responding to a similar question about appropriate head covering for Muslim girls, Sheikh Muhammad Salim 'Abd al-Wadud cites the renowned Hanbali scholar Ibn Taymiyyah:

---

[33] 'Is Face Veil (Niqab) Compulsory?', onislam.net, 2 June 2014.

If the Muslim lives in a non-Muslim country, regardless of whether or not that country is hostile with the Muslim countries, he will not be obligated to make himself appear different than them. This is on account of the difficulties that doing so can pose. Indeed, it might be preferable or even obligatory for him to conform to their outward standards of appearance if there is a benefit.[34]

Another interesting example is the wish of a British-Pakistani bride-to-be expected to wear the traditional bridal outfit befitting her ethnic heritage ('embroidered scarf, tunic & long, baggy skirt (*lengha*)') to instead be more 'Islamically' attired on her wedding day:

Initially, I had no qualms about wearing this outfit as I would be covered according to the Islamic requirements for a woman. However, I was talking to a few sisters who have commented that for me to wear such an outfit would not be acceptable in Islam as it would be bright, and some non-*mahram* men would see me in it.

In response, the *mufti* told her that a woman's clothes should not be an adornment in themselves, that they should be wide and loose to cover all the body, and thick so that they are not transparent: 'You should advise your family and explain to them the necessity of adhering to that which Allah has prescribed and enjoined. Explain that to your husband also, for he is responsible before Allah and is required to protect you and have protective jealousy concerning you.'

It is clear, then, that Internet *fatawa* on women's dress code reflect the divergence of opinion among scholars of Islamic law and varied interpretations of general and vaguely phrased Qur'anic verses. As may be gleaned from those verses, their objective is to set out a code of conduct and dress for Muslims (both male and female), adding specific rules for women in vulnerable social and political environments.[35] The first rule relates to the lowering of the gaze in interactions with men, which leads one to extrapolate the possibility of a gender-desegregated environment and women's role in the public space. Second, women have the added responsibility of covering their bodies except 'what is apparent' or what 'is acceptable', a latitude naturally leading to varying interpretations. Although the difference in practical terms only extends to whether the face should be covered or just the hair, a truly modern contextual interpretation of what constitutes 'apparent' and 'acceptable' would certainly lead us to ask more piercing questions. Does a head or face covering identifying the woman as a Muslim not leave her susceptible to harassment in an age of

---

34 Iqtida al-Sirat al-Mustaqim 176, cited in the *fatwa* at en.islamtoday.net/node/712.

35 For instance, when in the early days of Islam there were incidents of harassment against Muslim women, the Prophet asked women to identify themselves in public by wearing an outer garment. But where sociopolitical considerations now require that Muslim women 'blend in' with the wider population, this is instead advisable. Finally, where covering the head, face etc. is against the law in the country where a Muslim woman resides, and adhering to the *hijab/niqab* endangers access to basic education, health, employment and so on, a judgement has to be made whether it is advisable to confront the law, and to what end.

Islamophobia? The proposition I would make here is this: if the purpose of covering in a specific manner is to protect the woman, then it may well be that by *not* identifying herself by a particular manner of dress she is better protected. This perhaps is a step too far for Muslim individuals and communities, but is nevertheless one that has to be taken if the challenge of modernity is to be addressed from *within* the Islamic legal traditions.

8.8 The Triple *Talaq* Form of Divorce

The Prophetic *hadith* 'Of all things permitted in the eyes of Allah, divorce is the most abhorrent' sets the tone and tenor of the negative connotations of divorce in the Islamic legal traditions. It is considered as an absolute last resort and one that must follow certain procedures allowing for reconciliation as far as is possible. This is set out in several Qur'anic verses:

 (i) 2:228 (see above).
 (ii) 2:229: 'A divorce is only permissible twice: after that, the parties should either hold together on equitable terms, or separate with kindness. It is not lawful for you [men] to take back any of your gifts [from your wives], except when both parties fear that they would be unable to keep the limits ordained by Allah. If ye [judges] do indeed fear that they would be unable to keep the limits ordained by Allah, there is no blame on either of them if she give something for her freedom.'
(iii) 2:230: 'So if a husband divorces his wife [irrevocably], he cannot, after that, remarry her until after she has married another husband and he has divorced her. In that case there is no blame on either of them if they reunite, provided they feel that they can keep the limits ordained by Allah.'
 (iv) 2:231: 'When ye divorce women, and they fulfil the term of their [*iddat*], either take them back on equitable terms or set them free on equitable terms; but do not take them back to injure them, [or] to take undue advantage; if any one does that, he wrongs his own soul.'
 (v) 2:232: 'When ye divorce women, and they fulfil the term of their [*iddat*], do not prevent them from marrying their [former] husbands, if they mutually agree on equitable terms.'

On the face of it, these verses create a clear set of rules for terminating the marriage contract. Yet, in keeping with the interpretative plurality at play in most areas of the Islamic legal traditions, they have been subject to multiple ways of understanding and application. The main area of contention lies in whether a single pronouncement stating that the wife stands 'divorced thrice' or that she is divorced 'irrevocably' indeed has that effect. Prescribed procedure on divorce has been divided into the *ahsan* and *hasan* modes. By the former, a husband makes one pronouncement of divorce during his wife's *tuhr*,[36] and abstains

---

[36] That is, the period between two menstrual cycles when it is permitted for the husband to have sexual intercourse with his wife.

from sex with her throughout the period of *iddat*,[37] during which he may revert to her (and the divorce does not take effect). By the latter, the husband must pronounce a single *talaq* during the wife's *tuhr* for three consecutive months, while refraining from sex with her. This, too, allows reconciliation until the end of the third month. The verses state that only if a divorce procedure has been repeated thrice does it become irrevocable, and so a husband cannot then take his wife back. (Ithna Ashari Shia law only allows divorce in accordance with the prescribed *ahsan* and *hasan* modes, and does not recognize the triple *talaq*.)[38]

However, as is recognized in the Islamic legal scholarship, it was the second caliph Umar ibn Al-Khattab (reigned 634–44) who ruled that a triple *talaq* amounts to a valid, irrevocable divorce.[39] This form of divorce, although validated only under specific and special circumstances, nevertheless became part of Muslim practice. Contested throughout Muslim history for its summary and unjust manner of terminating a marriage, it is known as *talaq ul-biddat* (*biddat* means 'innovation', but in the sense of it being unauthorized or undesirable) and has been the subject of much scholarly as well as popular debate. In an almost fatalistic presentation, scholars have described the triple *talaq* as theologically bad but legally valid, implying that, despite its negative and unjust consequences, it is legally effective. Frank Vogel notes this ambivalence:

> Early in Muslim history the practice arose of issuing three divorces at once, the husband ridding himself of his wife in one dramatic, fatal stroke. Historically, Sunni *fiqh* authorities have almost universally held that such a triple divorce has full effect as triple, even though they decry it as sinful and even forbidden. However sinful, this form seems always to have been in common use, to the extent that many Muslim men today seem to know of no other form.[40]

The process of law reform and codification in the Muslim world set about allaying this sense of lingering injustice and disquiet with the triple *talaq*. The personal status codes of many Muslim jurisdictions have attempted to curtail it by expressly declaring its three pronouncements as equivalent to just one, in the spirit of the Qur'anic verses. For example, Jordan's Personal Status Law holds,

---

[37] The prescribed waiting period after a pronouncement of divorce. This is primarily to ascertain whether the wife is pregnant so that, if she is, paternity is established and the child ascribed to the father.

[38] El-Alami and Hinchcliffe, *Islamic Marriage and Divorce Laws*, pp. 23–4. For a discussion of the impact of triple *talaq* on women's rights in Oman (Ibadi school), see K. Al-Azri, 'One or Three? Exploring the Scholarly Conflict over the Question of Triple Talaq (Divorce) in Islamic Law with Particular Emphasis on Oman', *Arab Law Quarterly* 25(3) (2011), 277–96.

[39] N. Ahmad, 'A Critical Appraisal of "Triple Talaq" in Islamic Law', *International Journal of Law, Policy and the Family* 23(1) (2009), 53–61.

[40] F. E. Vogel, 'The Complementarity of *Ifta* and *Qada*: Three Saudi *Fatwas* on Divorce', in Masud, Messick and Powers, *Islamic Legal Interpretation*, p. 265. Historical court records too provide evidence that the triple *talaq* was accepted as legally enforceable. See, for instance, I. Agmon, 'Muslim Women in Court According to the Sijill of Late Ottoman Jaffa and Haifa: Some Methodological Notes', in A. A. Sonbol (ed.), *Women, the Family, and Divorce Laws in Islamic History* (Syracuse: Syracuse University Press, 1996), pp. 130–1.

'*Talaq* to which a number is attached verbally or by gesture and *talaq* repeated at a single session shall take effect only as a single *talaq*.'[41] And Pakistan's Muslim Family Laws Ordinance 1961 'reinstates' the *ahsan* mode of divorce, stating, 'Save as provided in sub-section (5), *talaq* unless revoked earlier, expressly or otherwise, shall not be effective until the expiration of 90 days from the day on which notice under sub-section (1) is delivered'.

As a result of these statutory prohibitions regarding the triple *talaq*, a disconnect has arisen between the laws of divorce as enunciated by classical scholars and the personal status codes of modern-day Muslim jurisdictions. The 'sinfulness' of the triple *talaq*, which severs the marriage contract in less than one minute, is a challenge that modern Muslims have taken on. Interestingly, Internet *fatawa* reinforce the legislatures' approach and reflect their position. Of all the *fatawa* studied, not a single one ruled in favour of a triple *talaq*. New alliances are being forged between various constituencies of Muslims to resolve questions of Islamic law in a manner they believe are in keeping with *'adl* (justice). What *is* surprising, however, is that this aggressive campaign from law-makers as well as Internet *muftis* has not dissuaded Muslim communities from continuing this practice. Muslims continue to remain unsure of the validity of the triple *talaq*, as demonstrated by the large numbers of questions on the subject. Furthermore, one consequence of a 'valid' triple *talaq* is that most abhorrent of practices, the *tahlil* (or *halala*) marriage.

A survey of the sixty-two *fatawa* on the triple *talaq* shows that it had generally been pronounced in a fit of anger, when the husband was not in control of himself. Fearful for the fate of his marriage, he then typically reaches out to the *mufti* in the hope that he will declare his divorce ineffective. One question was posed by a British convert to Islam; he and his wife had been married for three months, and he had on many occasions pronounced a single *talaq* during arguments. He explained,

> now people are telling me that I must leave my wife who I love and she has to be married to another and have sexual intercourse with another man and divorce or he dies before we can remarry, which she finds disgusting and I believe seems very un-Islamic . . .

The response explained first that 'were it not for the anger he would not have issued the divorce, then it does not count as a divorce'. Second, it was noted that the legal opinions of *fuqaha* differ concerning the triple *talaq*, the most correct opinion being that it only counts as one divorce.

> By the same token, if he issued a divorce then he repeated it during the *iddat*, the divorce before taking her back is part of the first divorce, because it only happens once, and divorce can only happen again after a marriage contract or after taking the wife back.

[41] El-Alami and Hinchcliffe, *Islamic Marriage and Divorce Laws*, p. 99.

The *mufti* also gave his opinion on the matter of lack of witnesses, since the questioner had hoped that his pronouncements might not be valid; the *mufti* noted the scholarly consensus that a pronouncement of *talaq* is valid without witnesses. His advice ended, 'We advise you to be careful and avoid using the word *talaq* altogether.' Another question regarding validity of the triple *talaq* turned on whether the husband had been threatened with violence and imprisonment on false charges if he did not pronounce divorce on his wife. The *mufti* quoted a number of scholars – Zaad al-Mustaqni, Ibn al-Qayyim, Zaad al-Ma'aad, Sunan Ibn Maajah, Ibn Abbaas and I'laam al-Muwaqqi'een – in support, and recommended that the questioner take the case to a *sharia* court to cancel the divorce.

It is clear, then, from its portrayal in Internet *fatawa* that the triple *talaq* as a valid form of divorce is understood to be problematic within Muslim society and within the Islamic legal traditions; unjustly resulting in a summary severance of the marital tie, it has always sat uncomfortably on the fringes of Islamic legality. Muslim jurisdictions have legislated to prohibit the practice; yet it is evoked by husbands across the world. Muslim popular consciousness has always raised it as an issue of severe injustice: it is a recurrent trope in South Asian fiction, and popular Urdu and Hindi movies have made it their central theme, with pronouncement of the triple *talaq* highlighted along with all the attendant negative consequences for the family.[42] It is therefore especially interesting that Internet *fatawa* on the subject appear without exception to challenge its validity and legitimacy, presenting instead a unified position, declaring it simply invalid from an Islamic legal perspective.

8.9 *Tahlil* Marriage

As observed in sixty-three of the Internet *fatawa* studied, the status of *tahlil* marriage (an intervening marriage between the divorce and remarriage of the same two people, intended to make the remarriage permissible) proved to be an excellent example of how the Internet *fatwa* is challenging modernity and tradition. The status of *tahlil* marriage has certainly been contested historically, with the Qur'anic text susceptible to varying interpretations resulting in more than one possible legal formulation, a fact recognized and set out in Internet *fatawa*. A *tahlil* marriage undertaken solely with the intent of marrying the first husband is only considered valid by a small minority of Hanafi scholars. Furthermore, the Qur'anic verses incorporate social and ethical dimensions alongside the legal norm. What passes on as Islamic law in a certain jurisdiction, community or court rests upon understanding of the religious text in that particular time, place and locality, and in the institution from which it draws its legitimacy. Yet despite these variations, one factor remains resistant to change – an all-encompassing patriarchal mindset which, despite centuries of discussion,

---

[42] Indeed, one of the best-known Hindi films on the topic is simply titled *Talaq*.

has shifted little, manifesting itself in a default position of superiority and stewardship for men, and subservience for women.

This patriarchal lens is evident in the manner in which the relevant verse (2:230: 'So if he divorces her she shall not be lawful to him afterwards until she marries another husband; then if he divorces her there is no blame on them both if they return to each other [by marriage] . . . ') is construed within the legal traditions and among communities. A second translation of the same verse, by Abdullah Yusaf Ali, states, 'And if he has divorced her [for the third time], then she is not lawful to him afterward until [after] she marries a husband other than him. And if the latter husband divorces her [or dies], there is no blame upon the woman and her former husband for returning to each other'. The commentary that follows describes the woman's remarriage and the second husband's act of divorcing her as setting 'an almost impossible condition. The lesson is: if a man loves a woman he should not allow a sudden gust of temper or anger to induce him to take hasty action'.[43]

Even during the lifetime of the Prophet, at least two possible interpretations of verse 2:230 were floated. The more widely accepted and practised is that the intervening *tahlil* marriage is conducted solely to facilitate the remarriage of the former spouses and make the woman *halal* to her former husband; the more religiously and ethically plausible interpretation is that the rationale behind verse 2:230 is to afford the permissibility and possibility of a valid remarriage between divorced couples should they *perchance* have had an intervening marriage and divorce, rather than denying this possibility to the couple. Two seemingly opposing *ahadith* add to this debate. The first is where he is said to have stated, 'Allah has cursed the *muhallil* [a man who marries a woman and divorces her so that she can go back to her first husband] and the *muhallal lahu* [the first husband]' (narrated from Abu Dawud, one of the six authentic *hadith* collections).[44] But another *hadith* declared that the woman 'is not lawful for the first [husband] until she tastes the honey of the other husband and he tastes her honey'.[45] Reconciling the two *ahadith* on the basis of their different contexts, it is obvious that the first was a general principle of interpreting verse 2:230: no one would be allowed to marry with the *intention* of acting as a temporary spouse and divorcing the wife to enable a remarriage. The second, however, relates to a woman who, after an irrevocable divorce, remarried and then, without consummating the remarriage, demanded to be divorced so she could remarry her former husband. What is prohibited is an intervening marriage for the sole purpose of fulfilling the requirements of verse 2:230.

[43]   *The Holy Qur'an, Text, Translation & Commentary by Abdullah Yusuf Ali* (Lahore: Sheikh Muhammad Ashraf, 1990), p. 91.
[44]   See http://islamqa.info/en/159041. A similar *hadith* is narrated from the collection *Ibn Majah*, in which the Prophet is stated to have declared, 'Shall I not tell you of a borrowed billy-goat? He is the *muhallil*. May Allah curse *al-muhallil* and *al-muhallallahu*.'
[45]   Abu Dawud, Book 12, *Hadith* 2302, narrated by Ummul Mominin Aisha, available at http://slamqa.info/en/159041.

Muslim communities have historically been uncomfortable with *tahlil* marriage, as is evident from the manner in which it is discussed and approached in Islamic history, in legal construction, and in questions posed to *muftis* to solicit *fatawa*, as well as in case law. It has been perceived as a 'punishment' for the first husband, since his wife becomes the wife of another man, a serious insult in a male-dominated society. What I have personally always found puzzling is the absence of discussion or mention of the intervening marriage as a punishment for the wife. After all, it is she who is made to agree (by popular understandings of the concept) to a fake and temporary marriage in order that her husband may marry her again. The divorce itself has in all probability been the result of a *talaq* pronounced by a husband who has since regretted it and wants to reconcile. This line of investigation leads one down a path of gendered, male-dominant aspects of Islamic family law and a near absence of women's voices or gender-neutral interpretation of the religious text. Whatever its interpretation, verse 2:230 has created a legal barrier between a divorced couple's ability to remarry without an intervening marriage that has been consummated.

In an age of codified family law, where the family is considered the cornerstone of society, *tahlil* marriage is largely excluded from Arab legal codes. Any contract that would impose conditions on the duration of the marriage is invalid under, for example, Egyptian law.[46] *Tahlil* marriage is 'squeezed out . . . between the now code-driven definition of marriage as a lasting contract and the prohibition of any kind of temporary marital arrangement'.[47] Similar articulations appear in Jordanian law:

> absolute irrevocability [of divorce] shall be negated by the marriage of the irrevocably divorced woman who has completed the waiting period to another husband, without the intention of *tahlil*. This shall be on the condition that the marriage is consummated, and after she is divorced from the second husband and has completed the waiting period she shall be lawful to the first husband.

In Moroccan law, too, a remarriage 'is required . . . to restitute an irrevocably divorced wife to her former husband but must be concluded without intent of time limitation, and must be consummated'.[48]

The legal historian Judith Tucker has traced popular conceptions of Islamic family law as presented in the courts of the *qadi* and in the *fatawa* of *muftis* through her archival research in the Middle East.[49] Discussing *talaq* and remarriage to the same spouse, she refers to a historical *fatwa* clarifying the validity of a *tahlil* marriage, in which the husband had had his wife married to his adolescent slave, with minimal sexual contact before being divorced, and

---

[46] El-Alami, *The Marriage Contract in Islamic Law: The Shariah and Personal Status Laws of Egypt and Morocco* (London: Graham & Trotman, 1992), p. 24, cited in Stowasser and Abul-Magd, 'Tahlil Marriage in Shari'a'.

[47] Stowasser and Abul-Magd, 'Tahlil Marriage in Shari'a', p. 170.   [48] Ibid., p. 174.

[49] J. Tucker, *In the House of the Law: Gender and Islamic Law in Ottoman Syria and Palestine* (Berkeley: University of California Press, 1998).

then remarried to him. The *mufti* declared this to be a valid procedure making the wife *halal*.[50] In a more recent work, Tucker also highlights the variety of interpretations applied to verse 2:230 that have created confusion around the validity of *tahlil* marriage. Citing classical Islamic law scholars[51] of the different schools of juristic thought, *muftis* and *fatawa*, she shows that discourse on this point has not engaged from a woman's perspective, legal history simply presenting women with a fait accompli.[52] Seeking to remove this ambiguity through *fatawa* is therefore not confined to Internet websites but runs deep in legal history.

The sixty-three Internet *fatawa* appear to have adopted a strong line on the validity of an 'instrumental' *tahlil* marriage, describing it as *haram*. In this, they are in line with a wider debate it is possible to see on the Internet. A straightforward question was asked at islamonline.com: 'My friend has divorced his wife the third and final divorce. Is it permissible that I marry her then divorce her so that she can return to her first husband?' The *fatwa* cited verse 2:230 in finding that the wife indeed could not remarry the same man without an intervening marriage, but also insisted that the remarriage had to be valid, not a (temporary) *muta* marriage or an (instrumental) *tahlil* marriage. This insistence that *tahlil* marriage was *haram* was grounded in *ahadith* ('Abu Dawood (2076) narrated that the Prophet (peace and blessings of Allah be upon him) said: Allah has cursed the *muhallil* [a man who marries a woman and divorces her so that she can go back to her first husband] and the *muhallal lahu* [the first husband]. This was classed as *saheeh* by al-Albaani in Sunan Abi Dawood'[53]) and in the rulings of subsequent legal scholars (Ibn Majaah, Abd al-Razzaaq, Al-Haakim, Naafia, Imam Ahmad). Similar *fatawa* issued from the other websites in the study also categorically denounced *tahlil* marriage as prohibited.

It is evident, then, that a new form of homogenization of opinion has emerged regarding *tahlil* marriages across the four Sunni schools of juristic thought. Originally, solely the minority Hanafi opinion declared a *tahlil* marriage valid at an abstract level, without interrogating the details of the parties' intentions or the duration of marriage, while the Malik, Shafi'i and Hanbali schools established stringent rules to reflect *ahadith* on the subject. Yet Internet *fatawa*, in line with the personal status codes of Muslim jurisdictions, are now invariably ruling against the institution of *tahlil* marriage, and supporting only the 'permanent' contract of marriage, a new trend in an inherently pluralistic matter.

8.10 Reflections and Conclusions on Internet *Fatawa* as Counterhegemonic Discursive Sites

Internet *fatawa* relating to women and gender issues offer interesting insights into how legal traditions are responding to changing societal understandings.

[50] Ibid., p. 88.
[51] Al-Marghinani, Al-Hedaya, 2:589, cited in Tucker, *Women, Family, and Gender in Islamic Law*, p. 88.
[52] Ibid.   [53] See http://islamqa.info/en/109245.

From the outset, it is clear that the websites studied (as well as others not forming the subject of this study) have situated themselves in a global and universal framework and context, recalling the universal nature of the Muslim *ummah*. Having said that, most of the questions and responses have been framed within the lived experiences of what we might broadly call 'Western' or diaspora Muslims (unsurprisingly, given that access to the Internet and fluency in its predominant languages have so far created much less of a 'virtual' Muslim audience in the non-West). The websites appear to have an agenda of 'Islamizing' these diaspora Muslims, which accounts for the ethical and moral emphasis and tenor which are presented alongside the legal content of the *fatawa*. Finally, it is easy to detect the strongly pedagogical aim of the *fatawa*. Based on the range of themes, questions posed and responses received from *muftis* in the present sample, *fatawa* websites have swiftly come to occupy a new niche as places for the dissemination of a counterhegemonic discourse on socio-legal, political, and religious issues. By arching across national boundaries and ethnicities, they are challenging existing norms based on localized traditions and schools of juristic thought. British Muslims of South Asian descent, for example, are seeking affirmation of a 'pure' or 'pristine' Islam by challenging their parents' ethnically rooted notions of Islam manifested in, say, divorce by triple *talaq*, dress codes and so on.

Internet *fatawa* on women and gender issues appear to run counter to the mainstream, male-dominated discourse within the legal traditions by seeking 'logical' or 'rational' reasons for what is asserted. Simultaneously, these sites are in themselves hegemonic in that they are a form of regulation of family and of family formations through religion rather than through secular or 'humanist' mores. The *fatawa* in the study also highlight a counterhegemony in their resistance to the dominant 'Western' discourse on these matters, ensuring that the discussion remains within an Islamic framework, by and for Muslim communities.

Muslims globally are increasingly referring to Internet *fatawa* to raise questions and address issues affecting their lives, communities and countries, and the world at large. We have only focused on *fatawa* that have generated a discourse on the Islamic legal traditions, relating to women and gender issues and, more broadly, to family law in contemporary transnational settings, but Internet *fatawa* cover all manner of subjects. The *fatawa* we have looked at raise a number of important points in informing our understandings of views of Muslims on norms and principles impacting on the status of women and the role and obligations of Muslims, individually and collectively. But of course just a brief reflection should also alert us to the dangers of engagement with faceless, shadowy figures and entities whose credentials we do not know. We have no way of knowing whether the questioners and the *muftis* are 'real' persons, or what their qualifications are to assert what they do. It might be argued that Muslim women seeking insights into their most intimate and critical dilemmas are caught in a controlling mechanism which is merely dressed in the garb of autonomy. Following on from this is another concern: in the absence of a uniform, agreed, global, authoritative voice across the Muslim world regarding the accuracy or otherwise of a *fatwa*, how might *fatwa* pronouncements be regulated, if at all? We still stand at the dawn of the Internet *fatawa*, and what their implication might be for law- and policy-making in Muslim countries, as well as for regulatory norms for diaspora Muslims, is as yet unknown. Historically, questions relating to family law have been formulated within the confines of particular communities, and *muftis* were rarely called upon to address and develop comprehensive norms and guidance regarding plural identities, e.g. a Muslim also being Pakistani and British, or an American of Syrian origin. The Islamic legal traditions are under pressure to respond to the anxieties of Muslims in Muslim-majority countries as well as in the West, who need to make decisions impacting on their lives and those of their families and communities. This discourse has found a variety of contemporary manifestations, of which the use of Internet discussions, chat rooms, email and *fatawa* is just one.

Other trends emerge from this study. For instance, the number of *fatawa* on triple *talaq* divorce and *tahlil* marriage are far fewer than those on dress. This is partly because discussions on the two former topics are generally interlinked and, in quite a few cases, the *fatawa* on *tahlil* are preceded by a discussion on Islamic rulings on *talaq*. From a closer analysis of islamonline.net, a marked rise in 2011 in the number of queries on dress (especially *niqab* and *hijab*) can be noted compared to the preceding years.[54] This increase might best be explained by the fact that these queries coincided with the ban on face coverings implemented in France in the preceding months. The dress-code *fatawa* of this period clearly engage with the legal debates in France, while also touching upon the topics of secularism and human rights, as well as the relationship between religious commandments and state laws.

Finally, there is the role of these websites to consider in the evolution and development of national and international laws, norms and regulatory mechanisms on women and gender. Have Muslims in France, for instance, decided to adhere to a *fatwa* that requires them to register their marriages within the mainstream French legal system? Why is there not a *fatwa* from a UK-based *mufti* enabling British Muslim women to register their marriages within the British legal system, saving them the difficulties arising from non-recognition of their 'religious' marriage contracts in English courts? Have Muslim women in Norway accepted the un-Islamic-ness of the triple *talaq* and acknowledged that Pakistan's statute (the country of origin of many Norwegian Muslims) prohibiting it is Islamically valid? Have women reading these *fatawa* refused to enter into *tahlil* marriages on the basis of their illegality in Islamic law? These and many other questions need yet to be addressed. It is not immediately apparent whether Internet *fatawa* are moving beyond their websites to impact upon Islamic law as practised by globalized Muslim communities and upon state

---

[54] islamonline.com presented ten *fatawa* about *niqab/hijab* in 2011 alone, compared to just twenty-one on the same issues between 2003 and 2010.

practice, or whether they will remain within the confines of a 'cyber-Islamic environment'. In Western Europe, in the absence of institutionalized Muslim authorities, *muftis* and their *fatawa* play a significant role in the construction of Islamic knowledge.[55] Internet websites regularly respond to questions of Muslims from Muslim and non-Muslim countries, mainly Europe and the United States. Sisler concludes that a new paradigm has emerged in the construction of Islamic knowledge.[56] However, this is qualified by cautioning that, despite the phenomenal number of hits on these websites, 'there is no proof that the Internet itself is an antidote to authoritarianism and could radically reshape the foundations of the decision-making process. The construction of Islamic knowledge in Europe is a complex matter . . . and cannot be understood solely within a media-centric logic'.[57] Musa Furber's study highlights the complexity inherent in the role of Internet *fatawa* in the development of Islamic law, an important finding being that increase in distance from the source of the *fatwa* (the *mufti*) leads to a decrease in confidence in the validity of the transmitted *fatwa*.[58] Hence a much longer timespan is required to assess the impact of Internet *fatawa* on Islamic law and existing studies are only indicative of trends and possible directions.

The Internet *fatawa* studied illustrate their two-sided nature, challenging both tradition and modernity. They also testify to the dynamism of the Islamic legal traditions in responding to contemporary challenges by attempting to move beyond interpretative plurality when the situation demands unanimity. The closing of ranks among all the Sunni schools in relation to the triple *talaq* and *tahlil* marriage testifies to a new paradigm of an inter-*madhhab* and inter-sect (Sunni–Shia) alliance.

---

[55] Sisler, 'Internet and the Construction of Islamic Knowledge', 206. Caeiro has noted that 'in Europe the *fatwa* is the only useful mechanism in dealing with normative issues'.
[56] Sisler, 'Internet and the Construction of Islamic Knowledge', 208.
[57] Ibid., 210.   [58] Furber, 'Ranking Confidence', p. 3.

Conclusion

Reflecting at the *Dihliz*

The sheikh of the land of Halba removed his turban and rubbed his hand across his head, then put it back and said, 'Freedom is the sacred value accepted by everyone.'

I protested: '*This* freedom has overstepped the boundaries of Islam!'

'But it is also sacred to the Islam of Halba.'

Frustrated, I said: 'If our Prophet were to be resurrected today, he would reject this side of your Islam!'

'And were he to be, may the blessings and peace of Allah be upon him. Would he not reject the whole of *your* Islam?'

Naguib Mahfouz, the Journey of Ibn Fattouma

As we reach the concluding pages of *Modern Challenges*, the vantage point from where I stand at the *dihliz* enables me to look back at the ground covered and offer some reflections. My vantage point has opened up for me panoramic views of wide-ranging pluralities within the Islamic legal traditions, especially when I have looked through the lens of culture and tradition. When I have shifted my sightline to look from a Western and a global angle, I have been able to see the multiple challenges and opportunities posed to Islamic law and *sharia* by tradition and modernity.

The *dihliz*, this in-between place, is both interior and exterior to the traditions I have sought to explore.[1] Critically placed at the intersection of overlapping discourses and intellectual universes, the *dihliz* has for me facilitated insights into various texts and interpretations and cultural frameworks. Privileged to have grown up with multiple identities and languages,[2] and with lived experiences from Muslim-majority and non-Muslim jurisdictions, crossing and negotiating boundaries has always come naturally to me. At times and

---

[1] The *dihliz* is conceptualized differently by others. Moosa observes that it is 'neither active nor passive; interior or exterior'. Moosa, *Ghazali*, p. 67.

[2] The ability to draw upon literature from Pashto, Urdu, Persian and Arabic has been a huge advantage.

places where civilizations and cultures meet, interact and are transformed, language and terminology assume a great importance. The richness and depth of the Islamic traditions, steeped in so many cultures, can only be captured by listening to 'linguistic communities' other than those of the academy.[3] The vital and living oral traditions of Muslim communities continue to inform the day-to-day dynamics of the Islamic legal traditions, and they cannot remain unheeded.

Poised at the *dihliz*, I conceptualized the *sharia* as a flowing stream composed of varying currents – intertwined, dynamic, vibrant, and responsive to changing place and time. Simultaneously, the vantage point of the *dihliz* has presented me with varying visions of the stream, of which some appear in particularly sharp relief; it would be fair to say that what appear to me as vibrant and self-renewing waters from one angle may be seen as something quite different by others. Not every student of the Islamic traditions will discern motion and evolution in *sharia*, but will instead conflate it with the divine word, the Qur'an, unchangeable and immutable. So *sharia* may equally be presented as static and fossilized, and uncritically followed. In *Modern Challenges*, looking out from the *dihliz*, I have tried to portray diverse Muslim communities, each one laying claim to the authenticity of their own *sharia*, and with little resolution in sight.

The existing uncritical approach towards *sharia*, as well as broad generalizations on the subject, are being increasingly questioned. Ibrahim Warde, for example, has observed,

> Any religion that has survived for fourteen centuries, and that has some 1.2 billion followers spread in every part of the globe must have some measure of flexibility and diversity. Any such religion should be resistant to broad-brush generalizations. Statements to the effect that 'Islam says . . .' or 'Muslims believe . . .' must include significant qualifiers and caveats.[4]

An-Na'im's pronouncements on *sharia* have been the boldest presented from within an Islamic legal perspective. Seizing on contradictions and anachronisms within historical *sharia*, he has made the claim that *sharia* is not, and was never intended to be, 'law' but instead a set of non-binding norms. I agree, and *Modern Challenges* has described *sharia* as regulatory norms extending to all spheres of life, informed by the Qur'an and Sunna, as well as human understandings of these primary sources of Islamic law. *Sharia*, I submit, has both moving and fixed components, each of which is susceptible to varying interpretations.

For those asking whether *sharia* exists, or whether it disappeared during colonial times, I would reiterate here that while elements of historical *sharia* have

---

[3] This phrase is borrowed from Muhammad Qasim Zaman, and is employed here to denote modes of expression from various constituencies claiming knowledge of Islamic law and *sharia*. These include scholars both religious and secular, as well as the lay population.

[4] Warde, *Islamic Finance*, pp. 12–13.

indeed become redundant, the flowing stream has brought forth new elements.[5] One question arising from *Modern Challenges* (and not one that can be answered in full here) is how much more evidence is required to demonstrate that, in reality, *sharia*, the Islamic legal traditions, and Islamic law have responded to changing circumstances by changing from within? How else does one explain the advent of the prohibition of slavery, of the sovereign Muslim nation state, of statutory legislation, and of accession to international treaties and agreements by Muslim states? What is at question is not *whether* there has been evolution; the question is *why* is there this resistance to acknowledging that change?[6] This state of denial of – and resistance to – change has thus far prevented alternative methodologies from within the Islamic traditions from taking root.

A way forward may lie in a perceptive observation from Anver Emon. Regarding freedom of religion, governance and constitutionalism, he has remarked,

> Arguably, before one can use accommodation or integration models to reform rules of pre-modern Shari'a, I argue that one needs to first rethink how Shari'a values can be implemented in light of a normative framework in which the past becomes relevant for defining the present and sketching the future amidst changed modes of political organization and governance.[7]

Flagging up differences among the various schools of juristic thought, Emon has argued that contemporary states have plucked aspects of the historical *sharia* out of their original context and placed them piecemeal into a nation-state context to grant it Islamic content. But of course the determination of what is 'Islamic' relies on an assumed objectivity, a determinacy, and even an inevitability as God's law; yet 'the legal rules were the product of a juristic process that used authority of Shari'a-based language to prioritize some readings over others'.[8] In other words, a contextual and historical approach to develop methodologies for reform is critical. Contemporary 'Islamization' programmes in a number of Muslim jurisdictions suffer from what Hallaq has described as 'an irredeemable state of denial' and are an example of this non-contextual approach.[9] It demonstrates exactly how *not* to take Islamic law and *sharia* forward. It is a denial of where *sharia* and the Islamic legal traditions more broadly stand in the twenty-first century. Ignoring the contingencies, order and meaning of historical *sharia* and implanting irrelevant norms has only resulted in dissonance.[10]

A challenging aspect of exploring from the vantage point of the *dihliz* is the interpretative plurality of the Islamic legal traditions and the intricate interplay

---

[5] The most prominent examples include norms relating to the regulation of slavery, *aman*, taxes paid by non-Muslims in return for protection (*jizya*) and the conceptual dichotomy of a world comprising the abodes of Islam and of war.

[6] N. Anderson, *Law Reform in the Muslim World* (London: Athlone, 1976), p. 36.

[7] Emon, 'The Limits of Constitutionalism', p. 34.   [8] Ibid.

[9] Hallaq, 'Can the *Sharia* Be Restored?', p. 22.

[10] Emon, 'The Limits of Constitutionalism', pp. 35–6.

between doctrinal and cultural Islam. And then, of course, there is the mutual challenge of tradition and modernity to the Islamic legal traditions in various spheres of life. And so another question arising from *Modern Challenges* is – *which sharia* are Muslims expected to follow, as interpreted *by* whom, and *for* whom?

In the various themes I have explored in *Modern Challenges*, a multi-layered and complex process of pluralism has been visible. Muslim communities have embraced the advent of the modern nation state, but with plural understandings of how to articulate (or not) their 'Islamic' nature and credentials. Some states describe themselves as 'Islamic' or 'Muslim', others remain silent on this point. Likewise there is little similarity on positions regarding what constitutes an 'Islamic state'. This plurality leads to paradoxes. On the one hand, states might include 'Islamic' articulations of governance in the form of 'Islamic' clauses in constitutional provisions as well as in equal-rights provisions; on the other, these very provisions stand disregarded in practice or negated by contrary laws. In a number of jurisdictions, women must seek the permission of their male guardian in order to travel,[11] and so any constitutional provisions on equality are undermined by opposing formulations. Are such legal paradoxes simply reflective of a duality of approaches to rights and obligations in Muslim states and societies? In light of the multifaceted reality of Muslim states, and with such groups as ISIS, Al-Qaeda and the Taliban espousing their various ideas, what hope is there for any universal *umma* espousing equality and non-discrimination any time soon?[12]

I have repeatedly highlighted the plurality that exists where tradition challenges modernity in the new formulations of classical *ifta*. *Muftis* in their new incarnations have made a comeback as Internet *muftis* and members of Islamic finance *sharia* compliance boards. Modernity is simultaneously challenging tradition by demanding clarity and uniformity in statutory legislation and by moving away from the jurist-informed, case-by-case decisions of *qadis*. Plurality, too, has played a role in the multiple identities of Muslim women and in how they have represented their governments in treaty-making in international forums. The contribution of Muslim women to the drafting of CEDAW was a fascinating example of how tradition and modernity have colluded and collided, with delegates highlighting divergences between their understandings of Islamic law and the proposed articles, yet equally being willing and able to challenge discriminatory understandings of their religious and cultural traditions. CEDAW's reception within state and society, too, displayed a distinct plurality, as has been evident in Pakistan.

Another significant plurality has emerged in transnational forms of the Islamic legal traditions as a result of migration to the non-Muslim nations

---

[11] Saudi Arabia requires a male relative within the prohibited degrees to accompany a woman on her travels.

[12] Bearing in mind that historical *sharia* did not espouse this doctrine.

of the West. Dispute-resolution forums such as the UK's *Sharia* Councils and the European Council of Fatwa and Research (ECFR) are examples of 'travelling' Islam – of cultures appropriating their preferred legal tradition. British *Sharia* Councils dispense an Islamic law that has the clear stamp of South Asia, whereas the ECFR has a wider but arguably more Middle Eastern inclination. This plurality is underlain by the acquisition of control and authority over diaspora communities.[13]

But is it enough to conclude that the Islamic tradition is plural and leave it at that? To observe that local culture, politics and economics intertwine with Islam to construct a living Islam that varies with time and place? That increasing access to knowledge, technology and communication are engendering a novel trans-local and transnational Islam, and that lay Muslims are now able to articulate their understandings of what constitutes legal tradition? A number of challenges have been highlighted and debated in *Modern Challenges*, though not necessarily resolved – as is their nature.

By far the most important issue in *Modern Challenges* has been the plurality of understandings regarding what constitutes real Islamic law. But who is to determine what constitutes pristine Islam, and who is to reject its tainted versions? Defining what constitutes true Islam is itself a struggle for authority and authoritarianism, a struggle evident since Islam's arrival fourteen centuries ago. Theory and practice offer differing responses. Textual norms of governance hold the accountability of those in positions of authority to be extremely important; yet Islam as practised by the nations which are home to the vast majority of Muslims barely recognize this point.[14] It is the legal obligation of rulers of Muslim states to ensure basic rights and necessities to all within their jurisdictions – access to health, education, employment, safety and security – yet the reality is utterly different. One possible way of explaining this chasm lies in the simple observation that when Muslims behave in a certain fashion, good or bad, they do not do so on behalf of Islam. Muslims behave as any other humans would, in accordance with the dictates of their conscience, and their sense of right and wrong, but mostly in self-interest; Islamic law and *sharia* are not, it needs to be conceded, guiding their every action.

Who gets to draw up the checklist of what constitutes authentic Islamic law is critical to this discourse. Classical conservative views, as well as extremist groups operating in the name of Islam, all have their particularities in this regard. In their view, Islamic law is expressed in terms that are held to be the opposite of Western conceptions:[15] authentic Islamic law must not display any convergence with its Western counterparts. In the real and imagined struggle

---

[13] See Hellum, Ali and Griffiths, *From Transnational Relations to Transnational Laws*, p. 23.

[14] Some Muslim-majority jurisdictions, such as Nigeria and Pakistan, are amongst the most corrupt countries on Earth!

[15] K. Hossain, 'Pluralism and the Law: Evolving Legal Frameworks for Change in Muslim Societies: Some Reflections', in A. Soeteman (ed.), *Pluralism and Law: Proceedings of the 20th IVR World Congress*, Amsterdam, 2001, p. 71.

between Western and Islamic conceptions of law the boundaries are blurred, but popular conceptions and elite interests keep the myth of divergence alive. What *Modern Challenges* has shown is that areas of convergence between Islamic and Western conceptions are plentiful: whether it is a matter of approaching the glass as half empty or half full is a political question and not a religious one. In the conservative and extremist camps, any movement and evolution are regarded as evidence of taint, and any plurality of understandings is overruled. Their hegemonic process of defining and appropriating authenticity and of rejecting competing authenticities has become the norm and will be difficult to dismantle.

At a theoretical level, it has been correctly observed that authenticity and originality do not necessarily depend on purity and that 'pure' and 'mixed' (i.e. hybrid) traditions can be unique. 'Authenticity must be seen as a construct rendered by rhetorics of power and persuasion.'[16] The difference between authority and authoritarianism is relevant, as authoritarianism goes well beyond authority, appropriating for itself the sole authority to define the authentic to the exclusion of all other renderings. Uprisings and terrorism today reflect this relentless authoritarianism. The only answer to this dictatorship of ideas is to open up a discursive space where, rather than speak of 'authenticity' and 'authority' in the singular, plural authenticities are accepted, respected and recognized. This is only ever likely to succeed if the silent majority of Muslims around the world make their voices heard.

A possible such discursive space might prove to be the various Muslim diasporas. Most South Asian Muslims arriving in Britain bring a version of Sunni Hanafi Islam, enculturated in the customary practices of Pakistan, and they believe it to be *the* Islam, and *the* Islamic law. Encountering a French Muslim from Morocco is often a shock to the system, as his or her Maliki Islam tinged with North African customs is founded upon differences they had been unaware of. Travelling from the local to the trans-local and the transnational environment generates challenges for the traveller over the religious–cultural baggage they carry, but it equally exposes them to other Islams. Globalization and its technologies, too, have played a parallel role in unifying and harmonizing aspects of the Islamic legal traditions across the *madahhab*. Imperceptibly, a process of metamorphosis can occur in diasporas. Exposure to alternative understandings becomes a reality of life – that people may or may not choose to accept and engage with. Simultaneously, traditions absorb some of the attributes of the soil in which they are transplanted. While some Muslims in multicultural Britain invoke their right to have only an unregistered *nikah* marriage, French Muslims do the exact opposite and go through a civil ceremony that does not preclude a *nikah*. Roald's work on Muslim women in Europe is evidence that a slow but sure evolution in the field of women's rights and in perceptions of the rights

---

[16] P. Manderville, *Transnational Muslim Politics: Reimagining the Umma* (London: Routledge, 2001), p. 180.

and obligations of husband and wife is indeed occurring.[17] Difficult though
it appears in the present moment, this must be flagged up as an opportunity
for the emergence of a dynamic approach to a tolerant and plural Islamic law.
Whether diaspora communities can and will become the torchbearers of a tolerant, inclusive, democratic and egalitarian Islamic tradition is a question for
another day.

Modern Challenges has not approached Islamic law as a discrete legal order
but as a dynamic, fluid and evolving normative framework that generates and
is generated by social, economic and political compulsions. Islamic law is not
dependent upon territoriality, is relatively autonomous, and is equally porous
in nature so as to absorb influences from the environment in which it operates and is employed. Although the word 'secular' is anathema to many Muslim
ears, this repulsion is largely the result of mistranslation. Translated mostly with
the negative connotations as 'irreligious' or 'atheist' rather than neutrally 'non-
religious', secularization of laws is read as anti-Islamic. Due to the highly sensitive nature of this debate, those in positions of power and authority, ranging
from religious scholars to governmental elites, use this as a pretext to disregard,
for instance, human rights treaties. Secularization is also equated with Westernization and held up as the undesirable 'other' to be shunned at all costs. The
history of fourteen centuries of Islam, however, tell a different story. After the
death of the Prophet Muhammad and with the expansion of Muslim rule, a rich
array of laws was generated, mostly by rulers whose authority to legislate was
and is accepted by jurists as a legitimate exercise within the Islamic traditions.
Known as *siyasa sharia*, the resultant *qanun* (cognate with the English word
'canon') has been an established practice of Muslim communities and lately of
nation states for over a millennium, the proviso remaining that no law should
violate clear injunctions of the Qur'an or Sunna. This critical aspect of the legal
traditions as practised for centuries is an important way forward for legislating
in Muslim jurisdictions and sidestepping the ambiguity of the historical *sharia*.
But this practice is not being flagged up to the lay population, arguably because
of the challenge it brings to existing power structures and elites.

A final issue in these concluding reflections relates to the emergence of
new constituencies claiming and/or desiring knowledge of Islamic law and
jurisprudence, among them the 'new religious intellectuals', to use Eickelman's
description.[18] Competing with the traditionally trained *ulama* who until a few
generations ago maintained a complete monopoly over law-making and the
interpretation of Islamic law and *sharia*, they challenge tradition from within
the tradition itself.[19] These new constituencies – the *aalim*, the modernist

---

[17] Roald, *Women in Islam*.

[18] D. Eickelman and J. Piscatori, *Muslim Politics* (Princeton: Princeton University Press, 1996),
pp. 13, 43–74, cited in M. Zaman, 'Religious Discourse and the Public Sphere in Pakistan',
Revue des Mondes Musulmans et de la Méditerranée 123 (2008), 55–73.

[19] Zaman distinguishes between *ulama* who inhabit their own discursive space built on
traditional, historical formulations and methodologies of *fiqh*; modernists who concentrate on

scholar, the Islamist, the knowledgeable lay Muslim – do not subscribe to the same linguistic community, in the sense that their modes of expression differ. The discourse between and among these constituencies, and the linguistics of that discourse, are, to borrow Zaman's phrase, 'incommensurable' at best. The moral philosopher Alasdair MacIntyre, in reflecting upon the inherent difficulties of translating the ideas of one linguistic community so that they might be comprehensible to others, has rightly observed that the manner in which these ideas get translated and understood results in them being rejected.[20] Defined and distilled from distinct traditions, even similar ideas appear to be translated and read differently among different linguistic communities. For any fruitful progress to be made on any aspect of Islamic law and *sharia*, all constituencies need to speak *to* each other, and not *over* or *at* each other.

At present, however, this is not the case, and the various constituencies appear to have little more than contempt for each other's legal acumen and knowledge. Jealously guarding a tradition 'constituted by a long and complex history of commentary, debate, agreements, and disagreements about the foundational texts and about all matters Islamic', the *ulama* use their own particular knowledge base as their sole reference point. 'Modernist' scholars such as Rahman have scant chance of recognition and have been angrily accused of 'undermining' Islam and its traditions.[21] Many of Rahman's views (including doubts as to the authenticity of certain *ahadith*, a view of the Qur'an that posits a more active role for the Prophet in the revelatory process than orthodox tradition allows, and a denial that Qur'anic legal norms were meant for all times) have garnered fierce opposition.[22] Here, for example, is an excerpt from the monthly magazine of the Dar-ul-Uloom Haqqania, a major Deobandi *madrasa* in Pakistan,[23] with advice for Rahman and his Institute of Islamic Research on what Islamic scholarship should or should not be about:

the 'spirit' of Islamic law; and Islamists who go straight to the foundational text. See Zaman, 'Religious Discourse'.

[20] A. MacIntyre, 'Relativism, Power, and Philosophy', in K. Baynes, J. Bohman and T. McCarthy (eds.), *After Philosophy: End or Transformation?* (Cambridge, MA: MIT Press, 1987), p. 390, cited in Zaman, 'Religious Discourse'.

[21] Fazlur Rahman obtained his DPhil in medieval Islamic philosophy from Oxford University and was subsequently a professor of Islamic studies at McGill University, Montreal. In 1962, he returned to Pakistan to become the director of the recently founded Institute of Islamic Research, established under the presidency of Ayub Khan (1958–69) to assist the government in reinterpreting Islamic norms in order to make them compatible with its modernizing initiatives.

[22] F. Rahman, 'Some Islamic Issues in the Ayyub Khan Era', in D. P. Little (ed.), *Essays on Islamic Civilization Presented to Niyazi Berkes* (Leiden: E. J. Brill, 1976), pp. 286–8, 299–301, cited in Zaman, 'Religious Discourse'.

[23] 'Deobandi' indicates *ulama* or institutions broadly following the approach of the nineteenth-century *madrasa* in the Indian town of Deoband which aimed to reform Islam on the Indian subcontinent by emphasizing the teachings of the Qur'an and *ahadith*. Thousands of *madaris* of this viewpoint exist in Pakistan today. The Dar-ul-Uloom Haqqania in the Khyber Pakhtunkhwa province has gained notoriety for its close ties with those who emerged as the Taliban in Afghanistan.

> If you really wish to establish the supremacy of Islam in every age and if you gen-
> uinely believe that . . . Islam can provide alternative solutions to the illegitimate
> social and economic problems created by the West, then the goal of your research
> should not be to turn Islam's 'prohibitions' into its 'permissions' as a way of
> justifying illegitimate Western practices . . . You ought to seek solutions to new
> problems within specific limits, according to specific conditions, and in light of
> the Qur'an, the Sunna, the ways of the Prophet's companions and the judgments
> of the forebears, rather than make the sharia itself subservient to reason, giving
> the latter a free rein to 'veto' the entire textually-based sharia.[24]

In closing, one of the main challenges to the Islamic legal traditions remains the
continuing and escalating tensions between traditional *ulama*, Islamists (so-
called), and modernist scholars. Rahman's calls for an alternative methodology
for interpreting Islam, by critiquing it from within and focusing on the spirit
rather than the text alone, have died a silent death in contemporary Pakistan.
Persuasive calls by An-Na'im for a secular state, argued from within an Islamic
tradition, to facilitate the practice of Islam in Muslims' personal lives, remain
within confined circles. The antagonism of traditional *ulama* against what they
perceive to be Western-inspired ideas, and a resistance to engage across linguistic
communities, are incessant. Then again, the tone of modernist scholars when
talking about the traditional *ulama* is derisive. The crucial difference between
the debates going on in the twenty-first century and those of a century earlier
lies in the critical mass of Muslims that now live within the Western diaspora,
and in increasing numbers of educated lay Muslims. When and if we finally
get beyond mutual undermining and derision, a firmly grounded, serious and
well-researched argument over how best to advance the evolution of Islamic
law and *sharia* will be needed. A keenly interested lay population will ensure
that challenges to both tradition and modernity from within the plural Islamic
legal traditions are mounted and responded to.

Amongst its many shades of meaning, *dihliz* also denotes ideas of new beginnings of life, new vistas and new horizons. I hope I have depicted some of
these new beginnings by offering some reflexive and self-critical ideas affecting
the Islamic legal traditions. My personal understanding of Islam is just one of
different ways of thinking about the subject, and many more questions may be
posed and answers sought. As the present conversation comes to a close, new
ones are in the making, and the journey and the narratives of the flowing stream
of *sharia* continue.

[24] Abd al-Haqq *et al.*, *Fatawa Haqqaniyya*, compiled by Mukhtar Allah Haqqani, 6 vols. (Akora
Khattak: Jami'a Dar al-'Ulum Haqqaniyya, 2002), vol. 1. pp. 579–80.

Bibilography

The Holy Qur'an: English Translation of the Meanings and Commentary (Mecca: Presidency of Islamic Researches, Ifta, Call and Guidance, 1411 AH)

The Holy Qur'an, Text, Translation & Commentary by Abdullah Yusuf Ali (Lahore: Sheikh Muhammad Ashraf, 1990)

The Koran (trans. A. J. Arberry) (London: George Allen and Unwin, 1966)

The Qur'an: Basic Teachings (trans. and ed. T. B. Irving, K. Ahmad, and M. M. Ahsan) (Leicester: Islamic Foundation, 1979)

Abd al-Haqq *et al.*, *Fatawa Haqqaniyya*, compiled by Mukhtar Allah Haqqani, 6 vols. (Akora Khattak: Jami'a Dar al-'Ulum Haqqaniyya, 2002)

Abdul Gafoor, A., *Interest-Free Commercial Banking* (Groningen: APPTEC, 1995)

Abiad, N., *Sharia, Muslim States and International Human Rights Treaty Obligations: A Comparative Study* (London: BIICL, 2008)

Afshar, H., *Islam and Feminisms: An Iranian Case Study*, Women's Studies in York (Basingstoke: Macmillan Press, 1998)

Afshari, R., 'On Historiography of Human Rights: Reflections on Paul Gordon Lauren's *The Evolution of International Human Rights: Visions Seen*', *Human Rights Quarterly* 29(1) (2007), 1–67

Afzalur-Rahman, M. A., *Economic Doctrines of Islam* (Lahore: Islamic Publications, 1974)

Agmon, I., 'Muslim Women in Court According to the Sijill of Late Ottoman Jaffa and Haifa: Some Methodological Notes', in A. A. Sonbol (ed.), *Women, the Family, and Divorce Laws in Islamic History* (Syracuse: Syracuse University Press, 1996), pp. 126–40

Ahmad, K., 'Islamic Finance and Banking: The Challenge and Prospects', *Review of Islamic Economics* 9 (2000), 57–82

Ahmad, M., (ed.), *State, Politics, and Islam* (Indianapolis: American Trust Publications, 1986)

Ahmad, N., 'A Critical Appraisal of "Triple Talaq" in Islamic Law', *International Journal of Law, Policy and the Family* 23(1) (2009), 53–61

Ahmed, D., and Ginsburg, T., 'Constitutional Islamization and Human Rights: The Surprising Origin and Spread of Islamic Supremacy in Constitutions', *Virginia Journal of International Law* 54(3) (2013), 615–95

Ahmed, D., and Gouda, M., 'Measuring Constitutional Islamization: The Islamic Constitutions Index', *Hastings International & Comparative Law Review* 38(1) (2015), 1–76

Ahmed, F., and Norton, J., 'Religious Tribunals, Religious Freedom, and Concern for Vulnerable Women', *Child & Family Law Quarterly* 24 (2012), 363–88

Ahmed, J. (ed), *Speeches and Writings of Mr. Jinnah* (Lahore: Sh. Muhammad Ashraf, 1964)

Ahmed, L., *Women and Gender in Islam: Historical Roots of a Modern Debate* (New Haven: Yale University Press, 1992)

Ahmed, S. M., 'Economics of Islam', in S. M. Ahmed, *Social Justice in Islam* (Lahore: Institute of Islamic Culture, 1975)

Al-Alwani, T. J., *Towards a Fiqh for Minorities: Some Basic Reflections* (Herndon, VA: International Institute of Islamic Thought, 2003)

Al-Awa, M. S., *On the Political System of the Islamic States* (Indianapolis: American Trust Publications, 1980)

Al-Azri, K., 'One or Three? Exploring the Scholarly Conflict over the Question of Triple Talaq (Divorce) in Islamic Law with Particular Emphasis on Oman', *Arab Law Quarterly* 25(3) (2011), 277–96

Al-Diwany, T., *Islamic Finance: What It Is and What It Could Be* (Bolton: 1st Ethical Trust, 2010)

Al-Hibri, A., 'Islamic and American Constitutional Law: Borrowing Possibilities or a History of Borrowing?', *University of Pennsylvania Journal of Constitutional Law* 1 (1999), 492–527

Al-Hibri, A., 'Islamic Constitutionalism and the Concept of Democracy', *Case Western Reserve Journal of International Law* 24(1) (1992), 3–10

Al-Hibri, A., 'Islamic Constitutionalism and the Concept of Democracy', in F. Dallmayr (ed.), *Border Crossings: Toward a Comparative Political Theory* (Lanham, MD: Lexington Books, 1999), pp. 61–88

Al-Hibri, A., 'Muslim Women's Rights in the Global Village: Opportunities and Challenges', *Journal of Law and Religion* 15 (2001), 37–66

Al-Hibri, A., 'A Study of Islamic Herstory: Or How Did We Ever get into This Mess?', *Women's Studies International Forum* 5(2) (1982), pp. 201–19

Al-Jassar, J., 'Regulatory Environment and Strategic Directions in Islamic Finance' (Proceedings of the Fifth Harvard University Forum on Islamic Finance, Center for Middle Eastern Studies, 2000)

Al-Nagar *et al.*, *One Hundred Questions & One Hundred Answers Concerning Islamic Banks* (Cairo: IAIB, 1980)

Al-Qaradawi, Y., *The Lawful and the Prohibited in Islam* (London: al-Birr Foundation, 1960)

Al-Qaradawi, Y., *On Muslim Minority Jurisprudence: The Life of Muslims in Other Societies* (Cairo: Dar-al-Shuruq, 2001)

Al-Qurtubi, *Al-Kafi fi Fiqh Ahl-al-Madinah*

Al-Tahir Al-Haddad, *Our Women in the Law and in Society* (ed. R. Husni and D. Newman) (Routledge, 2007)

Ali, S. S., 'Authority and Authenticity: Sharia Councils, Muslim Women's Rights and the English Courts', *Child and Family Law Quarterly* 25(2) (2013), 113–37

Ali, S. S., 'Behind the Cyberspace Veil: Online Fatwas on Women's Family Rights', in S. Hellum, S. S. Ali and A. Griffiths (eds.), *From Transnational Relations to Transnational Laws: Northern European Law at the Crossroads* (London: Ashgate, 2010), pp. 125–46

Ali, S. S., 'A Comparative Perspective of the Convention on the Rights of the Child and the Principles of Islamic Law', in *Protecting the World's Children: Impact of the Convention of the Rights of the Child in Diverse Legal Systems* (Cambridge: Cambridge University Press, 2007), pp. 142–208

Ali, S. S., *A Comparative Study of the United Nations Convention on the Elimination of All Forms of Discrimination against Women: Islamic Law and Laws of Pakistan* (Peshawar: Shaheen, 1995)

Ali, S. S. (ed.), *Conceptualising Islamic Law: CEDAW and Women's Human Rights in Plural Legal Settings: A Comparative Analysis of the Application of CEDAW in Bangladesh, India and Pakistan* (Delhi: UNIFEM Regional Office, 2006)

Ali, S. S., 'Cyberspace as Emerging Muslim Discursive Space? Online Fatawa on Women and Gender Relations and Its Impact on Muslim Family Law Norms', *International Journal of Law, Policy and the Family* 24(3) (2010), 338–60

Ali, S. S., 'From Muslim Migrants to Muslim Citizens: Islamic Law and Muslims in a Multi-faith Britain', in R. Griffiths-Jones (ed.), *Islam in English Law: Rights and Responsibilities and the Role of Shari'a* (Cambridge: Cambridge University Press, 2012), pp. 157–75

Ali, S. S., *Gender and Human Rights in Islam and International Law: Equal before Allah, Unequal before Man?* (The Hague: Kluwer Law International, 2000)

Ali, S. S., 'Interpretative Strategies for Women's Human Rights in a Plural Legal Framework: Exploring Judicial and State Responses to Hudood Laws in Pakistan', A. Hellum, J. Stewart, S. S. Ali and A. Tsanga (eds.), *Human Rights, Plural Legalities and Gendered Realities: Paths are Made by Walking* (Harare: Weaver Books, 2006), pp. 381–406

Ali, S. S., 'Is an Adult Muslim Woman *Sui Juris*? Some Reflections on the Concept of "Consent in Marriage" without a *Wali* (with Particular Reference to the Saima Waheed Case)', *Yearbook of Islamic and Middle Eastern Law* 3 (1996), 156–74

Ali, S. S., 'Law, Islam and the Women's Movement in Pakistan', in S. M. Rai (ed.), *Gender and Democratisation: International Perspectives* (London: Routledge, 2000), pp. 41–63

Ali, S. S., 'Overlapping Discursive Terrains of Culture, Law and Women's Rights: An Exploratory Study on Legal Pluralism at Play in Pakistan', in J. Bennett (ed.), *Scratching the Surface: Democracy, Traditions, Gender* (Lahore: Heinrich Böll, 2007), pp. 77–8

Ali, S. S., 'Religious Pluralism, Human Rights and Citizenship in Europe', in M. L. P. Leonon and J. E. Goldschmidt (eds.), *Religious Pluralism and Human Rights in Europe* (Utrecht: Intersentia, 2007), pp. 57–79

Ali, S. S., 'Resurrecting Siyar through Fatwas? (Re)Constructing Islamic International Law in a Post-(Iraq) Invasion World', *Journal of Conflict and Security Law* 14(1) (2009), 115–44

Ali, S. S., 'Testing the Limits of Family Law Reform in Pakistan: A Critical Analysis of the Muslim Family Laws Ordinance 1961', in A. Bainham (ed.), *International Survey of Family Law* (Bristol: Jordan, 2002), pp. 317–35

Ali, S. S., 'Women's Rights, CEDAW and International Human Rights Debates: Toward Empowerment?', in J. L. Parpart, S. M. Rai and K. Staudt (eds.), *Gender and Empowerment in a Local Global World* (London: Routledge, 2002), pp. 61–78

Ali, S. S., and Rehman, J., 'The Concept of Jihad in Islamic International Law', *Journal of Conflict and Security Law* 10(3) (2005), 321–43

Ali, S. S., and Rehman, J., *Indigenous Peoples and Ethnic Minorities of Pakistan: Constitutional and Legal Perspectives* (Richmond: Curzon, 2001)

Alrasheed, A., 'Sudanese Women in Exile: Islam, Politics and the State', conference proceedings: Thinking Gender – the NEXT generation, 21–2 June 2006, e-paper no 1

An-Na'im, A. A., *African Constitutionalism and the Role of Islam* (Pennsylvania: Philadelphia University Press, 2006)

An-Na'im, A. A., 'The Compatibility Dialectic: Mediating the Legitimate Coexistence of Islamic Law and State Law', *Modern Law Review* 73(1) (2010), 1–29

An-Na'im, A. A., 'Human Rights in the Arab World: A Regional Perspective', *Human Rights Quarterly* 23 (2001), 701–32

An-Na'im, A. A., 'An Inclusive Approach to the Mediation of Competing Human Rights Claims', *Constellations* 20(1) (2013), 7–17

An-Na'im, A. A., *Islam and the Secular State: Negotiating the Future of Sharia* (Cambridge, MA: Harvard University Press, 2008)

An-Na'im, A. A., 'Islam, Islamic Law and the Dilemma of Cultural Legitimacy for Universal Human Rights', in C. Welch and V. Leary (eds.), *Asian Perspectives on Human Rights* (Boulder, CO: Westview Press, 1990), pp. 31–54

An-Na'im, A. A., 'Islam, State and Politics', paper presented at the Human Rights and Renewing of Religious Discourse conference, 18–20 April 2006, at the Swedish Institute, Alexandria

An-Na'im, A. A. (ed.), *Islamic Family Law in a Changing World: A Global Resource Book* (London: Zed Press, 2002)

An-Na'im, A. A., 'A New Islamic Politics: Faith and Human Rights in the Middle East', *Foreign Affairs* 75(3) (1996), 122–6

An-Na'im, A. A., *Towards an Islamic Reformation: Civil Liberties, Human Rights and International Law* (Syracuse: Syracuse University Press, 1990)

An-Na'im, A. A., *What Is an American Muslim? Embracing Faith and Citizenship* (Oxford: Oxford University Press, 2014)

An-Na'im, A. A., 'Why Should Muslims Abandon Jihad?', *Third World Quarterly* 27 (2006), 785–97

Anderson, M. R., 'Islamic Law and the Colonial Encounter in British India', in C. Mallat and J. Connors (eds.), *Islamic Family Law* (London: Graham & Trotman, 1990), pp. 205–23

Anderson, N., *Law Reform in the Muslim World* (London: Athlone, 1976)

Arjomand, S. A., 'The Constitution of Medina: A Sociolegal Interpretation of Muhammad's Acts of Foundation of the Umma', *International Journal of Middle East Studies* 41 (2009), 555–75

Arjomand, S. A., 'Islamic Constitutionalism', *Annual Review of Law and Social Sciences* 3 (2007), 115–40

Arjomand, S. A., 'Religion and Constitutionalism in Western History and in Modern Iran and Pakistan', in S. A. Arjomand (ed.), *The Political Dimensions of Religion* (Albany: State University of New York Press, 1993), pp. 69–99

Arjomand, S. A., *The Shadow of God and the Hidden Imam: Religion, Political Organization and Societal Change in Shi'ite Iran from the Beginning to 1890* (Chicago: The University of Chicago Press, 1984)

Arkoun, M., *Rethinking Islam: Common Questions, Uncommon Answers* (Boulder, CO: Westview Press, 1994)

Asad, M., *The Principles of State and Government in Islam* (Kuala Lumpur: Islamic Book Trust, 1980)

Asad, T., *Genealogies of Religion: Discipline and Reasons of Power in Christianity and Islam* (Baltimore: Johns Hopkins University Press, 1993)

Asad, T., 'The Idea of an Anthropology of Islam', Center for Contemporary Arab Studies, Washington, DC, occasional papers 14, 1986

Asia Pacific Forum on Women, Law and Development, *A Digest of Case Law on the Human Rights of Women (Asia Pacific)* (Chiangmai: APWLD, 2006, reprint)

Asutay, M., 'Conceptualising and Locating the Social Failure of Islamic Finance: Aspirations of Islamic Moral Economy vs the Realities of Islamic Finance', *Asian and African Studies* 11(2) (2012), 93–113

Asutay, M., 'Political Economy Approach to Islamic Economics: Systemic Understanding for an Alternative Economic System', *Kyoto Bulletin of Islamic Area Studies* 1(2) (2007), 3–18

Ayub, M., *Understanding Islamic Finance* (Chichester: John Wiley and Sons Limited, 2007)

Badawi, Z., 'New Fiqh for Minorities', paper presented at the Muslims of Europe in the New Millennium conference, Regent's College, London, 9–10 September 2000

Baderin, M. A., 'Human Rights and Islamic Law: The Myth of Discord', *European Human Rights Law Review* 2 (2005), 165–85

Baderin, M. A., *International Human Rights and Islamic Law* (New York: Oxford University Press, 2003)

Baillie, N., *Baillie's Digest of Moohammudan Law* (1865)

Bakht, N., *Arbitration, Religion and Family Law: Private Justice on the Back of Women* (Ottawa: NAWL, 2005)

Bakht, N., 'Family Arbitration Using Shari'a Law', *Muslim World Journal of Human Rights* 1 (2004), 1–24

Baki, F., 'Islam and Modernity: Nurcholish Madjid's Interpretation of Civil Society, Pluralism, Secularization and Democracy', *Asian Journal of Social Sciences* 33 (2005), 492–5

Balchin, C., 'Divorce in Classical Muslim Jurisprudence and the Differences between Jewish and Muslim Divorce' (2009), available at muslimmarriagecontract.org

Ballard, R. (ed.), *Desh Pardesh: The South Asian Presence in Britain* (London: Hurst, 1994)

Ballard, R., 'Ethnic Diversity and the Delivery of Justice', in P. Shah and W. Menski (eds.), *Migration, Diaspora and Legal Systems in Europe* (London and New York: Routledge, 2006), pp. 39–56

Bano, S., 'Asking the Law Questions: Islamophobia, Agency and Muslim Women', in S. Sayyid and A. Vakil (eds.), *Thinking through Islamophobia: Global Perspectives* (London: Hurst, 2010), pp. 135–56

Bano, S., 'Complexity, Difference and Muslim Personal Law: Rethinking Relationships between Shari'ah Councils and South Asian Muslim Women in Britain', Warwick University PhD thesis, 2004

Bano, S., *An Exploratory Study of Shariah Councils in England with Respect to Family Law* (Reading: Reading University and MoJ, 2012)

Bano, S., 'In Pursuit of Religious and Legal Diversity: A Response to the Archbishop of Canterbury and the "Sharia Debate" in Britain', *Ecclesiastical Law Journal* 10(3) (2008), 283–309

Bano, S., 'Islamic Family Arbitration, Justice and Human Rights in Britain', *Law, Social Justice and Global Development Journal* 1 (2007), 1–26

Bano, S., 'Legal Pluralism and Muslim Family Law in Britain', *Journal of South Pacific Law* 4(6) (2000), 1–32

Bano, S., 'Muslim Family Justice and Human Rights', *Journal of Comparative Law* 2(2) (2007), 1–29

Bano, S., *Muslim Women and Shari'ah Councils: Transcending the Boundaries of Community and the Law* (London: Palgrave, 2012)

Banuri, T., and Mahmood, M., 'Learning from Failure: Institutional Reform for Human Resource Development', in T. Banuri, S. R. Khan and M. Mahmood (eds.), *Just Development: Beyond Adjustment with a Human Face* (Oxford: Oxford University Press, 1998), pp. 3–16

Barlas, A., *Believing Women in Islam: Unreading Patriarchal Interpretations of the Qur'an* (Austin: University of Texas Press, 2002)

Baxi, U., 'From Human Rights to the Right to Be Human: Some Heresies', *India International Centre Quarterly* 13(3–4) (1986), 185–200

Bellamy, R. (ed.), *Constitutionalism and Democracy* (Farnham: Ashgate, 2006)

Berger, M. S., 'Sharia and the Nation State', in R. Peters and P. Bearman (eds.), *The Ashgate Research Companion to Islamic Law* (Farnham: Ashgate, 2014), pp. 223–34

Binder, L., *Religion and Politics in Pakistan* (Berkeley and Los Angeles: University of California Press, 1963)

Black, A., Esmaeili, H., and Hosen, N., *Modern Perspectives on Islamic Law* (Cheltenham: Edward Elgar, 2013)

Bowen, J., 'How Could English Courts Recognise Sharia?', *University of St. Thomas Law Journal* 7(3) (2010), 411–35

Bowen, J., 'Private Arrangements: "Recognizing Sharia" in England', *Boston Review* 15 (2009), n.p.

Boyd, M., 'Dispute Resolution in Family Law' (2004), available at attorneygeneral.jus.gov.on.ca

Brown, N. J., *Constitutions in a Non-constitutional World: Arab Basic Laws and the Prospects for Accountable Government* (Albany: State University of New York Press, 2002)

Brown, N. J., 'Islamic Constitutionalism in Theory and Practice', in E. Cotran and A. O. Sherif (eds.), *Democracy, the Rule of Law and Islam* (London: Kluwer, 1999), 491–506

Brown, N. J., and Sherif, A. O., 'Inscribing the Islamic Shari'a in Arab Constitutional Law', in Y. Y. Haddad and B. Stowasser (eds.), *Islamic Law and the Challenges of Modernity* (Walnut Creek, CA: Altamira Press, 2004), pp. 55–80

Buehler, M., 'The Rise of Shari'a By-laws in Indonesian Districts: An Indication of Changing Patterns of Power Accumulation and Political Corruption', *South-East Asia Research* 16(2) (2008), 255–85

Bunt, G., *iMuslims: Rewiring the House of Islam* (Chapel Hill: University of North Carolina Press, 2009)

Bunt, G., *Islam in the Digital Age: E-jihad, Online Fatwas and Cyber Islamic Environments* (London: Pluto Press, 2003)

Burrows, N., 'The 1979 Convention on the Elimination of All Forms of Discrimination against Women', *Netherlands International Law Review* 32 (1985), 419–60

Buskens, L., 'Recent Debates on Family Law Reform in Morocco: Islamic Law as Politics in an Emerging Public Sphere', *Islamic Law & Society* 10 (2003), 70–131

Calder, N., 'Law', in *Oxford Encyclopaedia of the Modern Islamic World*, vol. 2 (New York: Oxford University Press, 1995), available online at www.oxfordislamicstudies.com/article/opr/t236/e0473#e0473-s1

Carroll, L., 'Muslim Women and "Islamic Divorce" in England', *Women Living under Muslim Laws*, Dossier 19 (1998), 51–74

Carroll, L., 'The Pakistan Federal Shariat Court, Section 4 of the Muslim Family Laws Ordinance, and the Orphaned Grandchild', *Islamic Law and Society* 9 (2002), 70–82

Carroll, L., 'Talaq-i-Tafwid and Stipulations in a Muslim Marriage Contract: Important Means of Protecting the Position of the South Asian Muslim Wife', *Modern Asian Studies* 16(2) (1982), 277–309

Centre for Women's Research, *CEDAW: A Manual* (Colombo: Cenwor, 2006)

Chapra, M. U., *The Future of Economics: An Islamic Perspective* (Leicester: Islamic Foundation, 2000)

Chaudhary, G. W., *Constitutional Development in Pakistan* (London: Lowe and Brydone, 1971)

Chaudhary, G. W., 'Religious Minorities in Pakistan', *Muslim World* 46 (1956), 313–23

Cheema, S. A., '*Problematizing "Authenticity": A Critical Appraisal of the Jamaat-i-Islami Gender Discourse*', Warwick University PhD thesis, 2011

Chinkin, C., 'Reservations and Objections to the Convention on the Elimination of All Forms of Discrimination against Women', in J. P. Gardner (ed.), *Human Rights as General Norms and a State's Right to Opt Out* (London: BIICL, 1997), pp. 64–84

Choudhoury, M., *The Foundation of Islamic Political Economy* (London: Macmillan, 1987)

Cizakca, M., 'Can There Be Innovation in Islamic Finance? Case Study: Esham', paper presented at the 11th IFSB Summit, 20 May 2014, Mauritius

Clark, B., 'The Vienna Convention Reservations Regime and the Convention on Discrimination against Women', *American Journal of International Law* 85 (1991), 281–321

Connors, J., 'The Women's Convention in the Muslim World', in M. Yamani (ed.), *Feminism and Islam: Legal and Literary Perspectives* (Reading: Ithaca, 1996), pp. 351–71

Coulson, N. J., *Conflicts and Tensions in Islamic Jurisprudence* (Chicago: The University of Chicago Press, 1969)

Coulson, N. J., *A History of Islamic Law* (Edinburgh: Edinburgh University Press, 1964)

Coulson, N. J., 'The State and the Individual in Islamic Law', *International and Comparative Law Quarterly* 6 (1957), 49–60

Crone, P., *Slaves on Horses: The Evolution of the Islamic Polity* (Cambridge: Cambridge University Press, 1980)

Derrett, J., 'Justice, Equity and Good Conscience', in J. Anderson (ed.), *Changing Laws in Developing Countries* (London: Allen & Unwin, 1963), 114–53

Devji, F., *Muslim Zion: Pakistan as a Political Idea* (London: Hurst, 2013)

Diduck, A., and O'Donovan, K. (eds.), *Feminist Perspectives on Family Law* (Abingdon: Routledge, 2006)

Doi, A. R. I., *Shariah: The Islamic Law* (London: Ta-Ha, 1984)

Donnelly, J., *Universal Human Rights in Theory and Practice* (Ithaca: Cornell University Press, 1989)

Donnelly, J., 'Western Perspectives', in E. A. Kolodziej (ed.), *A Force Profonde: The Power, Politics and Promise of Human Rights* (Philadelphia: University of Pennsylvania Press, 2003), pp. 31–44

Douglas, G., Doe, N., Gilliat-Ray, S., Sandberg, R., and Khan, A., *Social Cohesion and Civil Law: Marriage, Divorce and Religious Courts* (report of a research study funded by the AHRC) (Cardiff: Cardiff University, 2011)

Dupret, B., 'Legal Pluralism, Plurality of Laws, and Legal Practices: Theories, Critiques and Praxeological Re-specification', *European Journal of Legal Studies* 1 (2007), 1–26

Dusuki, A. W., 'Corporate Social Responsibility of Islamic Banking in Malaysia: A Synthesis of Islamic and Stakeholders' Perspectives', Loughborough University PhD thesis, 2005

El Fadl, K. A., 'The Centrality of Shariah to Government and Constitutionalism in Islam', in R. Grote and T. Röder (eds.), *Constitutionalism in Islamic Countries: Between Upheaval and Continuity* (Oxford: Oxford University Press, 2012), pp. 35–61

El Fadl, K. A., *Islam and the Challenge of Democracy* (Princeton: Princeton University Press, 2004)

El Fadl, K. A., 'Islamic Law and Muslim Minorities', *Islamic Law and Society* 1:(2) (1994), 141–87

El Fadl, K. A., 'The Rules of Killing at War: An Inquiry into Classical Sources', *Muslim World* 89 (1999), 144–57

El Fadl, K. A., *Speaking in God's Name: Islamic Law, Authority and Women* (Oxford: One World, 2001)

El-Alami, D., and Hinchcliffe, D., *Islamic Marriage and Divorce Laws in the Arab World* (The Hague: Kluwer, 1996)

El-Alami, D., *The Marriage Contract in Islamic Law: The Shariah and Personal Status Laws of Egypt and Morocco* (London: Graham & Trotman, 1992)

El-Azhary Sonbol, A., *Women, the Family, and Divorce Laws in Islamic History* (Syracuse: Syracuse University Press, 1996)

El-Gamal, M. A., , 'A Basic Guide to Contemporary Islamic Banking and Finance' (2000), available at www.lariba.com/dev/knowledge-center/islamic-banking-guide.pdf

El-Gamal, M. A., 'An Economic Explication of the Prohibition of Riba in Classical Islamic Jurisprudence', proceedings of the Third Harvard University Forum on Islamic Finance, 2000

El-Gamal, M. A., *Islamic Finance: Law, Economics, and Practice* (New York: Cambridge University Press, 2006)

El-Gamal, M. A., 'Limits and Dangers of Sharia Arbitrage', in N. Ali (ed.), *Islamic Finance: Current Legal and Regulatory Issues* (Cambridge, MA: Islamic Finance Project, Islamic Legal Studies Program, Harvard University, 2005), pp. 127–31

El-Nawawy, M., and Khamis, S., *Islam Dot Com: Contemporary Islamic Discourses in Cyberspace* (New York: Macmillan, 2009)

El-Tahawy, A., 'The Internet Is the New Mosque: Fatwa at the Click of a Mouse', *Arab Insight: Emerging Social and Legal Trends* 2(1) (2008), 11–19

Elias, J., and Rethel, L. (eds.), *The Everyday Political Economy of Southeast Asia* (Cambridge University Press, forthcoming 2016)

Emon, A. M., 'Comment: Reflections on the "Constitution of Medina": An Essay on Methodology and Ideology in Islamic Legal History', *UCLA Journal of Islamic & Near Eastern Law* 1 (2002), 103–33

Emon, A. M., 'Conceiving Islamic Law in a Pluralist Society', *Singapore Journal of Legal Studies* (Dec. 2006), 331–55

Emon, A. M., *Islamic Natural Law Theories* (Oxford: Oxford University Press, 2010)

Emon, A. M., 'The Limits of Constitutionalism in the Muslim World: History and Identity in Islamic Law', in Islamic Law and Law of the Muslim World, paper no 08-09

Emon, A. M., 'The Paradox of Equality and the Politics of Difference: Gender Equality, Islamic Law and the Modern State', in Z. Mir-Husseini, K. Vogt, L. Larsen and C. Moe (eds.), *Gender and Equality in Muslim Family Law: Justice and Ethics in the Islamic Legal Tradition* (London: I. B. Tauris, 2013), pp. 237–58

Emon, A. M., Ellis, M., and Glahn, B. (eds.), *Islamic Law and International Human Rights Law: Searching for Common Ground?* (Oxford: Oxford University Press, 2010)

Ercanbrack, J., *The Transformation of Islamic Law in Global Financial Markets* (Cambridge: Cambridge University Press, 2015)

Esposito, J., and DeLong-Bas, N. J., *Women in Muslim Family Law*, 2nd edn (Syracuse: Syracuse University Press, 2001)

European Council for Fatwa and Research, *First and Second Collection of Fatwas (Qarārat wa fatāwa li-l-majlis al-'urubi li-l-iftā' wa-l-buhūth)* (Cairo: Islamic INC/Al-Falah Foundation, 2002)

Farooq, M. U., 'Riba, Interest and Six Hadiths: Do We Have a Definition or a Conundrum?', *Review of Islamic Economics* 13(1) (2009), 105–41

Feldman, N., and Martinez, R., 'Constitutional Politics and Texts in the New Iraq: An Experiment in Islamic Democracy', *Fordham Law Review* 75 (2006), 883–920

Fishman, S., 'Fiqh Al-Aqalliyyat: A Legal Theory for Muslim Minorities', Center on Islam, Democracy, and the Future of the Muslim World, series no 1, paper 2 (2006)

Foster, N., and Archer, S. (forthcoming), 'Islamic Financial Law: Law without a Legal System', conference paper, Business Inbetween Cultures: The Development of Islamic Finance, European Association for Banking and Financial History e.V., Sarajevo, 15–16 November 2012

Freeman, M. A., Chinkin, C., and Rudolf, B. (eds.), *The UN Convention on the Elimination of All Forms of Discrimination against Women: A Commentary* (Oxford: Oxford University Press, 2013)

Furber, M., 'Ranking Confidence in the Validity of Contemporary Fatwas and Their Dissemination Channels', *Tabah Foundation analytic brief no 13* (2013), available at tabahfoundation.org

Fyzee, A. A. A., *Outlines of Muhammadan Law*, 4th edn (Oxford: Oxford University Press, 1974)

Gale, R., and Hopkins, P. (eds.), *Muslims in Britain: Race, Place and Identities* (Edinburgh: Edinburgh University Press, 2009)

Gardner, J. P. (ed.), *Human Rights as General Norms and a State's Right to Opt Out* (London: BIICL, 1997)

Giddens, A., *The Consequences of Modernity* (Cambridge: Polity Press, 1990)

Gilani, R., 'A Note on Islamic Family Law and Islamization in Pakistan', in C. Mallat and J. Connors (eds.), *Islamic Family Law* (London: Graham & Trotman, 1990), pp. 339–46

Glenn, H. P., *Legal Traditions of the World: Sustainable Diversity in Law* (Oxford: Oxford University Press, 2000)

Grillo, R. D., 'In the Shadow of the Law: Muslim Marriage and Divorce in the UK', in R. Mehdi, W. Menski and J. Nielsen (eds.), *Interpreting Divorce Laws in Islam* (Copenhagen: DJOF, 2012), pp. 211–16

Grillo, R. D., *Muslim Families, Politics and the Law: A Legal Industry in Multicultural Britain* (London: Ashgate, 2015)

Grote, R., and Röder, T. (eds.), *Constitutionalism in Islamic Countries: Between Upheaval and Continuity* (Oxford: Oxford University Press, 2012)

Haddad, Y. Y., and Stowasser, B. (eds.), *Islamic Law and the Challenges of Modernity* (Walnut Creek, CA: Altamira Press, 2004)

Haddad, Y. Y., and Stowasser, B., 'Islamic Law and the Challenge of Modernity', in Y. Y. Haddad and B. Stowasser (eds.), *Islamic Law and the Challenges of Modernity* (Walnut Creek, CA: Altamira Press, 2004), pp. 1–17

Haeri, S., *Law of Desire: Temporary Marriage in Shi'i Iran* (Syracuse: Syracuse University Press, 1989)

Haikal, M. H., *Abu Bakr al-Siddiq* (Cairo: Matba's Masdar Shirka Musahim Misriyya, 1958)

Hajjar, L., 'Domestic Violence and Shari'a: A Comparative Study of Muslim Societies in the Middle East, Africa and Asia', in L. Welchman (ed.), *Women's Rights and Islamic Family Law: Perspectives on Reform* (London: Zed, 2004), pp. 233–68

Hallaq, W., 'Can the *Sharia* Be Restored?', in Y. Y. Haddad and B. Stowasser (eds.), *Islamic Law and the Challenges of Modernity* (Walnut Creek, CA: Altamira Press, 2004), pp. 21–53

Hallaq, W., 'From *Fatwas* to *Furu*: Growth and Change in Islamic Substantive Law', *Islamic Law and Society* 1 (1994), 29–65

Hallaq, W., *An Introduction to Islamic Law* (Cambridge: Cambridge University Press, 2009)

Hallaq, W., *Sharia: Theory, Practice, Transformations* (Cambridge: Cambridge University Press, 2009)

Halliday, F., and Alavi, H. (eds.), *State and Ideology in the Middle East and Pakistan* (London: Macmillan Educational, 1988)

Hamidullah, M., *The First Written Constitution in the World*, 2nd edn (Lahore: Sheikh Muhammad Ashraf, 1968)

Hamidullah, M., *Muslim Conduct of State* (Lahore: Sh. Muhammad Ashraf, 1977)

Hamilton, W., 'Constitutionalism', in E. Seligman and A. Johnson (eds.), *Encyclopedia of the Social Sciences*, vol. 4 (Cambridge: Cambridge University Press, 1931), pp. 255–9

Hamoudi, H. A., 'The Death of Islamic Law', *Georgia Journal of International and Comparative Law* 38 (2010), 293–337

Hamoudi, H. A., 'The Impossible, Highly Desired Islamic Bank', *William & Mary Business Law Review* 5 (2014), 105–58

Hamoudi, H. A., 'Jurisprudential Schizophrenia: On Form and Function in Islamic Finance', *Chicago Journal of International Law* 7(2) (2007), 605–22

Hamoudi, H. A., 'Repugnancy in the Arab World', *Williamette Law Review* 48 (2012), 427–50

Hassan, R., 'An Islamic Perspective', in J. Belcher (ed.), *Women, Religion and Sexuality* (Geneva: WCC, 1990), pp. 93–128

Hassan, R., 'On Human Rights and the Quranic Perspective', in A. Swidler (ed.), *Human Rights in Religious Traditions* (New York: Pilgrim Press, 1982), pp. 51–66

Hassan, R., 'The Role and Responsibilities of Women in the Legal and Ritual Tradition of Islam', paper presented to the Trialogue of Jewish–Christian–Muslim scholars at the Joseph and Rose Kennedy Institute for Ethics, Washington, DC, 1980

Haugestad, A., *Reservations to the United Nations Women's Convention, with special focus on Reservations Submitted by Muslim Countries, Studies in Women's Law*, 39 (Oslo, 1995)

Haydar, A., 'From the Anglo-Muhammadan Law to the Shariah: The Pakistan Experiment', *Journal of South Asian and Middle Eastern Studies* 10(4) (1987), 33–50

Hellum, A., Ali, S. S., and Griffiths, A. (eds.), *From Transnational Relations to Transnational Laws: Northern European Law at the Crossroads* (London: Ashgate, 2010)

Henkin, L., 'Elements of Constitutionalism', Center for the Study of Human Rights, occasional paper series, 1994

Hevener, N., *International Law and the Status of Women* (Boulder, CO: Westview Press, 1983)

Hosen, N., 'In Search of Islamic Constitutionalism', *American Journal of Social Sciences* 21(2) (2004), 1–24.

Hosen, N., *Shari'a and Constitutional Reform in Indonesia* (Singapore: Institute of South East Asian Studies, 2007)

Hossain, K., 'Pluralism and the Law: Evolving Legal Frameworks for Change in Muslim Societies: Some Reflections', in A. Soeteman (ed.), *Pluralism and Law: Proceedings of the 20th IVR World Congress*, Amsterdam, 2001 (Stuttgart: Franz Steiner Verlag, 2004), pp. 71–76

Howard, R., 'Human Rights and the Search for Community', *Journal of Peace Research* 32(1) (1995), 1–8

Huq, A., 'Section 4 of the Muslim Family Laws Ordinance 1961: A Critic', *Northern University Journal of Law* 1 (2010), 7–13

Ibn Ishaq, M., *Sirat Rasul Allah*, translated from Guillaume's *The Life of Muhammad: A Translation of Ishaq's Sirat Rasul Allah* (Karachi: Oxford University Press, 1955)

International Association of Islamic Banks, *Islamic Handbook of Islamic Banking*, 6 vols. (Cairo: IAIB, 1977–86)

Iqbal, Z., and Mirakhor, A., *An Introduction to Islamic Finance: Theory and Practice* (Singapore: Wiley Finance, 2007)

Jung, M. U. ibn S., *The Administration of Justice in Islam* (Lahore: Law Publishing, 1980)

Kamali, M. H., 'Constitutionalism in Islamic Countries: A Contemporary Perspective of Islamic Law', in R. Grote and T. Röder (eds.), *Constitutionalism in Islamic Countries: Between Upheaval and Continuity* (Oxford: Oxford University Press, 2012), pp. 19–33

Kamali, M. H., *Principles of Islamic Jurisprudence*, 3rd edn (Cambridge: Islamic Texts Society, 2003)

Kavanaugh, K., 'Narrating Law', in A. M. Emon, M. Ellis and B. Glahn (eds.), *Islamic Law and International Human Rights Law: Searching for Common Ground?* (Oxford: Oxford University Press, 2010), pp. 17–51

Kavanaugh, K., 'Speaking Law to War', *Journal of Conflict and Security Law* 17(1) (2012), 3–24

Kedourie, E., *Democracy and Arab Political Culture* (London: Frank Cass, 1992)

Khadduri, M., 'Islam and the Modern Law of Nations', *American Journal of International Law* 50 (1956), 358–72

Khadduri, M., *The Islamic Law of Nations: Shaybani's Siyar* (Baltimore: Johns Hopkins University Press, 1966)

Klabbers, J., Peters, A., and Ulfstein, G. (eds.), *The Constitutionalization of International Law* (Oxford: Oxford University Press, 2011)

Kolodziej, E.A. (ed.), *A Force Profonde: The Power, Politics and Promise of Human Rights* (Philadelphia: University of Pennsylvania Press, 2003)

Korteweg, A., and Selby, J. (eds.), *Debating Shariah: Islam, Gender Politics and Family Law Arbitration* (Toronto: University of Toronto Press, 2012)

Koskenniemi, M., 'International Law and Hegemony: A Reconfiguration', *Cambridge Review of International Affairs* 17(2) (2004), 197–218

Krisch, N., *Beyond Constitutionalism: The Pluralist Structure of Postnational Law* (Oxford: Oxford University Press, 2010)

Krivenko, E. Y., *Women, Islam and International Law: Within the Context of the Convention on the Elimination of All Forms of Discrimination against Women* (Leiden: Martinus Nijhoff, 2009)

Kruse, H., 'The Foundations of Islamic International Jurisprudence', *Journal of the Pakistan Historical Society* 3 (1955), 231–67

Kugle, S. A., 'Framed, Blamed and Renamed: The Recasting of Islamic Jurisprudence in Colonial South Asia', *Modern Asian Studies* 35 (2001), 257–313

Kymlicka, W., *Multicultural Citizenship: A Liberal Theory of Minority Rights* (Oxford: Clarendon Press, 1995)

Laqueur, W., and Rubin, B. (eds.), *The Human Rights Reader* (New York: New American Library, 1979)

Larsen, L., 'Islamic Jurisprudence and Transnational Flows', in S. Hellum, S. S. Ali and A. Griffiths (eds.), *From Transnational Relations to Transnational Laws: Northern European Laws at the Crossroads* (London: Ashgate, 2010), pp. 139–63

Latief, H., 'Islamic Charities and Social Activism: Welfare, Dakwah and Politics in Indonesia', Utrecht University PhD thesis, 2012

Lau, M., *The Role of Islam in the Legal System of Pakistan* (Leiden: Nijhoff, 2006)

Lau, M., 'Sharia and National Law in Pakistan', in J. M. Otto (ed.), *Sharia Incorporated: A Comparative Overview of the Legal Systems of Twelve Muslim Countries in the Past and Present* (Leiden: Leiden University Press, 2010), 373–432

Lauren, P. G., *The Evolution of International Human Rights: Visions Seen*, 2nd edn (Philadelphia: University of Pennsylvania Press, 2003)

Lecker, M., *The 'Constitution of Medina': Muhammad's First Legal Document* (Princeton: Darwin, 2004)

Levy, R., *The Social Structure of Islam* (Cambridge: Cambridge University Press, 1979, reprint)

Lewis, B., 'Freedom and Justice in the Modern Middle East', *Foreign Affairs* (May–June 2005), online

Lewis, B., 'Legal and Historical Reflections on the Position of Muslim Populations under Non-Muslim Rule', *Journal of the Institute of Muslim Minority Affairs* 13 (1992), 1–15

Lijznaad, L., *Reservations to UN Human Rights Treaties: Ratify and Ruin?* (Dordrecht: Martinus Nijhoff, 1995)

Lombardi, C. B., *State Law as Islamic Law in Modern Egypt: The Incorporation of the Shari'a into Egyptian Constitutional Law* (Leiden: Brill, 2006)

Loughlin, M., and Walker, N. (eds.), *The Paradox of Constitutionalism: Constituent Power and Constitutional Form* (Oxford: Oxford University Press, 2008)

Macfarlane, J., *Islamic Divorce in North America: A Shari'a Path in a Secular Society* (Oxford: Oxford University Press, 2012)

MacIntyre, A., 'Relativism, Power, and Philosophy', in K. Baynes, J. Bohman, and T. McCarthy (eds.), *After Philosophy: End or Transformation?* (Cambridge, MA: MIT Press, 1987), pp. 385–411

Mahmassani, S., 'International Law in the Light of Islamic Discourse', *Recueil de cours* 117 (1996), 201–328

Mahmood, S., *The Politics of Piety: The Islamic Revival and the Feminist Subject* (Princeton: Princeton University Press, 2011)

Malik, M., 'The Branch on Which We Sit: Multiculturalism, Minority Women and Family Law', in A. Diduck and K. O'Donovan (eds.), *Feminist Perspectives on Family Law* (Abingdon: Routledge, 2006), pp. 211–34

Malik, M., *Minority Legal Orders in the UK: Minorities, Pluralism and the Law* (London: British Academy, 2012)

Mallat, C., 'The Debate on Riba and Interest in Twentieth Century Egypt', in C. Mallat (ed.), *Islamic Law and Finance* (London: Graham & Trotman, 1998), pp. 69–88

Mallat, C. (ed.), *Islam and Public Law: Classical and Contemporary Studies* (London: Graham & Trotman, 1993)

Mallat, C. (ed.), *Islamic Law and Finance* (London: Graham & Trotman, 1998)

Mallat, C., *The Renewal of Islamic Law: Muhammad Baqer as-Sadr, Najaf and the Shi'i International* (Cambridge: Cambridge University Press, 2004)

Mallat, C., 'Tantawi on Banking Operations in Egypt', in M. Masud, B. Messick and D. Powers (eds.), *Islamic Legal Interpretation: Muftis and Their Fatwas* (Karachi: Oxford University Press, 2005), pp. 286–96

Mallat, C., and Connors, J. (eds.), *Islamic Family Law* (London: Graham & Trotman, 1990)

Manderville, P., *Transnational Muslim Politics: Reimagining the Umma* (London: Routledge, 2001)

Mannan, M. A. (ed.), *D. F. Mulla's Principles of Mahomedan Law* (Lahore: PLD Publishers, 1995)

March, A. F., 'Sources of Moral Obligation to Non-Muslims in Fiqh al-Aqalliyyat (Jurisprudence of Muslim Minorities) Discourse', *Islamic Law and Society* 16 (2009), 34–94

March, A. F., 'Taking People as They Are: Islam as a "Realistic Utopia" in the Political Theory of Sayyid Qutb', *American Political Science Review* 104(1) (2000), 189–207

Marshall, P., *Radical Islam's Rules: The Worldwide Spread of Extreme Shari'a Law* (Lanham, MD: Rowman and Littlefield, 2005)

Masud, M., 'Gender Equality and the Doctrine of Wilaya', in Z. Mir-Husseini, K. Vogt, L. Larsen and C. Moe (eds.), *Gender and Equality in Muslim Family Law: Justice and Ethics in the Islamic Legal Tradition* (London: I. B. Tauris, 2013), pp. 127–52

Masud, M., Messick, B., and Powers, D. (eds.), *Islamic Legal Interpretation: Muftis and Their Fatwas* (Karachi: Oxford University Press, 2005)

Masud, M., Messick, B., and Powers, D., 'Muftis, Fatwas, and Islamic Legal Interpretation', in M. Masud, B. Messick and D. Powers (eds.), *Islamic Legal Interpretation: Muftis and Their Fatwas* (Karachi: Oxford University Press, 2005), pp. 3–32

Masud, M., Salvatore, A., and van Bruinessen, M. (eds.), *Islam and Modernity: Key Issues and Debates* (Edinburgh: Edinburgh University Press, 2009)

Maududi, A. A., *The Economic System of Islam* (Lahore: Islamic Publications, 1970)

Maududi, A. A., *Haquq uz Zojjain* (Lahore: Idara Tarjumanul Quran, 1943)

Maududi, A. A., *The Islamic Law and Constitution*, 4th edn (Lahore: Islamic Publications, 1969)

Maududi, A. A., *Khawateen aur Deeni Masayl* (Lahore: Islamic Publications, 2000)

Maududi, A. A., *Political Theory of Islam* (Lahore: Islamic Publications, 1985)

Maududi, A. A., *Purdah* (Lahore: Islamic Publications, 2003)

Maududi, A. A., *Purdah and the Status of Woman in Islam* (ed. and trans. Al-Ashari) (Lahore: Islamic Publications, 1975)

Maurer, B., 'The Disunity of Finance: Alternative Practices to Western Finance', in K. Knorr Cetina and A. Preda (eds.), *The Oxford Handbook of the Sociology of Finance* (Oxford: Oxford University Press, 2012), pp. 413–30

Maurer, B. (2008), 'Re-socialising Finance? Or Dressing It in Mufti? Calculating Alternatives for Cultural Economies', *Journal of Cultural Economy* 1(1), 65–78

Mayer, A. E., 'The Convention on the Elimination of All Forms of Discrimination against Women: The Political Nature of "Religious" Reservations' (online paper)

Mayer, A. E., *Islam and Human Rights: Tradition and Politics*, 3rd edn (Boulder, CO: Westview Press, 1999)

Meer, N., and Modood, T., 'How Does Interculturalism Contrast with Multiculturalism?', *Journal of Intercultural Studies* 33(2) (2012), 175–96

Mehdi, R., *Islamisation of the Law in Pakistan* (Richmond: Curzon, 1994)

Mehdi, R., Petersen, H., Sand, E., and Woodman, G. (eds.), *Law and Religion in Multicultural Societies* (Copenhagen: DJOF, 2008)

Mernissi, F., *Women and Islam* (trans. M. J. Lakeland) (Oxford: Blackwell, 1991)

Meron, T., *Human Rights Law-Making in the United Nations: A Critique of Instruments and Process* (Oxford: Clarendon Press, 1986)

Meron, T., 'Iran's Challenge to the International Law of Human Rights', *Human Rights Reporter* 13(8) (1989), 8–13

Merry, S. E., 'Legal Pluralism', *Law & Society Review* 22 (1988), 869–96

Metcalf, B., 'Islamic Arguments in Contemporary Pakistan', in W. Roff (ed.), *Islam and the Political Economy of Meaning* (London: Routledge, 1987), pp. 132–59

Miller, K. A., 'Muslim Minorities and the Obligation to Migrate to Islamic Territory: Two Fatwas from Fifteenth-Century Granada', *Islamic Law and Society* 7(2) (2000), 256–85

Mir-Husseini, Z., *Islam and Gender: The Religious Debate in Contemporary Islam* (Princeton: Princeton University Press, 1999)

Mir-Husseini, Z., 'Justice, Equality and Muslim Family Laws', in Z. Mir-Husseini, K. Vogt, L. Larsen and C. Moe (eds.), *Gender and Equality in Muslim Family Law: Justice and Ethics in the Islamic Legal Tradition* (London: I. B. Tauris, 2013), pp. 7–34

Mir-Husseini, Z., *Marriage on Trial. A Study of Islamic Family Law: Iran and Morocco Compared* (London: I. B. Tauris, 1993)

Mir-Husseini, Z., Vogt, K., Larsen, L., and Moe, C. (eds.), *Gender and Equality in Muslim Family Law: Justice and Ethics in the Islamic Legal Tradition* (London: I. B. Tauris, 2013)

Modood, T., *Multiculturalism* (Themes for the 21st Century Series) (Cambridge: Polity Press, 2007)

Modood, T., Triandafyllidou, A., and Zapata-Barrero, R. (eds.), *Multiculturalism, Muslims and Citizenship* (Oxford: Routledge, 2006)

Mohd, M. B., *Principles and Practice of Takaful and Insurance Compared* (Malaysia: International Islamic University, 2001)

Moore, K., *The Unfamiliar Abode: Islamic Law in the United States and Britain* (Oxford: Oxford University Press, 2010)

Moors, A., *Women, Property and Islam* (Cambridge: Cambridge University Press, 1995)

Moosa, E., *Ghazali and the Poetics of Imagination* (Chapel Hill: University of North Carolina Press, 2005)

Morsink, J., *The Universal Declaration of Human Rights: Origins, Drafting and Intent* (Philadelphia: University of Pennsylvania Press, 1999)

Moustafa, T., *The Struggle for Political Power: Law, Politics and Economic Development in Egypt* (Cambridge: Cambridge University Press, 2009)

Mullally, S., '"As Nearly as May Be": Debating Women's Human Rights in Pakistan', *Social and Legal Studies* 14 (2005), 341–58

Mumtaz, K., and Shaheed, F., *Women of Pakistan: Two Steps Forward, One Step Back?* (Lahore: Vanguard, 1987)

Naqvi, S., *Ethics and Economics: An Islamic Synthesis* (Leicester: Islamic Foundation, 1981)

National Commission for Justice and Peace, *Discrimination Lingers on . . . A Report on the Compliance of CEDAW in Pakistan* (Lahore, 2007)

Nielsen, J. S., 'Sharia between Renewal and Tradition', in J. S. Nielsen and L. Christoffersen (eds.), *Sharia as Discourse: Legal Traditions and the Encounter with Europe* (Farnham: Ashgate, 2010), pp. 1–16

Nu'mani, M. S., *Safarnama* (Lahore: Ghulam Ali and Sons, 1961)

Nussbaum, M., *Women and Human Development* (Cambridge: Cambridge University Press, 2000)

Okin, S. M., 'Is Multiculturalism Bad for Women?', in J. Cohen, M. Howard and M. C. Nussbaum (eds.), *Is Multiculturalism Bad for Women?* (Princeton: Princeton University Press, 1999), pp. 9–24

Pakistan, Government of, *Report of the Pakistan Commission on the Status of Women* (Islamabad: Government of Pakistan Printing Press, 1986)

Pakistan, Government of, *Working Paper: The Convention on Elimination of All Forms of Discrimination against Women* (Islamabad: Government of Pakistan, Ministry of Foreign Affairs, 1994)

Pannikar, R., 'Is Human Rights a Western Construct?', *Diogenes* 120 (1982), 75–102

Parekh, B., *Rethinking Multiculturalism: Cultural Diversity and Political Theory* (Cambridge, MA: Harvard University Press, 2002)

Pearl, D., and Menski, W., *Muslim Family Law*, 3rd edn (London: Sweet and Maxwell, 1998)

Peters, R., and Bearman, P. (eds.), *The Ashgate Research Companion to Islamic Law* (Farnham: Ashgate, 2014)

Philipp, T., 'The Idea of Islamic Economics', *Die Welt des Islams* 30 (1990), 117–39

Phillips, A., *Multiculturalism without Culture* (Princeton: Princeton University Press, 2007)

Pickthall, M., *The Meaning of the Glorious Koran: An Explanatory Translation* (London: Knopf, 1930)

Pipes, D., 'Cartoons and Islamic Imperialism' (2006), available at danielpipes.org/article/3360

Pollis, A., and Schwab, P., 'Human Rights: A Western Construct with Limited Applicability', in A. Pollis and P. Schwab (eds.), *Human Rights: Cultural and Ideological Perspectives* (New York: Praeger, 1979), pp. 1–18

Pomeranz, F., 'Business Ethics: The Perspective of Islam', *American Journal of Islamic Social Sciences* 12(3) (1995), 400–4

Powers, D., 'Kadijustiz or Qadi-Justice? A Paternity Dispute from Fourteenth-Century Morocco', *Islamic Law and Society* 1(3) (1994), 332–66

Pruitt, L. R., 'CEDAW and Rural Development: Empowering Women with Law from the Top Down, Activism from the Bottom Up', *Baltimore Law Review* 41 (2011), 263–320

Pruitt, L. R., 'Migration, Development, and the Promise of CEDAW for Rural Women', *Michigan Journal of International Law* 30 (2009), 707–63

Quraishi, A., 'What if Sharia Weren't the Enemy? Rethinking International Women's Rights Advocacy on Islamic Law', *Columbia Journal of Gender and Law* 22 (2011), 173–249

Quraishi, A., and Vogel, F. (eds.), *The Islamic Marriage Contract* (Cambridge, MA: Harvard University Press, 2008)

Qutb, S., *Milestones* (trans. A. Z. Hammad) (Indianapolis: American Trust, 1990)

Qutb, S., *Social Justice in Islam* (ed. H. Algar, trans. J. R. Hardie and H. Algar) (Oneonta, NY: Islamic Publications International, 2000)

Rab, A., *Exploring Islam in a New Light: A View from the Quranic Perspective* (Brainbow, 2010)

Rabb, I., '"We the Jurists": Islamic Constitutionalism in Iraq', *Journal of Constitutional Law* 10(3) (2008), 527–79

Raday, F., 'Gender and Democratic Citizenship: The Impact of CEDAW', *International Journal of Constitutional Law* 10(2) (2012), 512–30

Rahim, A., *Muhammadan Jurisprudence* (Lahore: Mansoor, 1995)

Rahman, F., *Islam*, 2nd edn (Chicago: University of Chicago Press, 1979)

Rahman, F., *Islam and Modernity: Transformation of an Intellectual Tradition* (Chicago: The University of Chicago Press, 1982)

Rahman, F., *Islamic Methodology in History* (Karachi: Central Institute of Islamic Research, 1965)

Rahman, F., 'Riba and Interest', *Islamic Studies* 3 (1964), 1–43

Rahman, F., 'Some Islamic Issues in the Ayyub Khan Era', in D. P. Little (ed.), *Essays on Islamic Civilization Presented to Niyazi Berkes* (Leiden: EJ Brill, 1976), pp. 284–302

Rahman, F., 'The Status of Women in Islam: A Modernist Interpretation', in H. Papanek and G. Minault (eds.), *Separate Worlds: Studies of Purdah in South Asia* (Delhi: Chanakya, 1982), pp. 285–310; also (revised) in G. Nashat (ed.), *Women and Revolution in Iran* (Boulder, CO: Westview Press, 1983), pp. 37–54

Rai, S., *Gender and the Political Economy of Development* (Cambridge: Polity Press, 2002)

Rai, S. (ed.), *Mainstreaming Gender, Democratising the State: Institutional Mechanisms for the Advancement of Women* (Manchester: Manchester University Press, 2003)

Ramadan, T., *Western Muslims and the Future of Islam* (Oxford: Oxford University Press, 2004)

Razack, S., 'Between a Rock and a Hard Place: Canadian Muslim Women's Responses to Faith-Based Arbitration', in R. Mehdi, H. Petersen, E. Sand and G. Woodman (eds.), *Law and Religion in Multicultural Societies* (Copenhagen: DJOF, 2008), pp. 83–94

Razack, S., 'The "Sharia Law Debate" in Ontario', *Feminist Legal Studies* 15 (2007), 3–32

Redding, J. A., 'Constitutionalizing Islam: Theory and Practice', *Virginia Journal of International Law* 44 (2004), 773–97

Rehof, L. A., Guide to the Travaux Preparatoires of the United Nations Convention on the Elimination of All Forms of Discrimination against Women *(International Studies in Human Rights 29)* (Dordrecht: Martinus Nijhoff, 1993)

Reinhart, A. K., 'Islamic Law as Islamic Ethics', *Journal of Religious Ethics* 11(2) (1983), 186–203

Reisman, M. H. A., 'Islamic Fundamentalism and Its Impact on International Law and Politics', in M. Janis (ed.), *The Influence of Religion on the Development of International Law* (The Hague: Kluwer, 1991), pp. 107–34

Resnik, J., 'Comparative Inequalities: CEDAW, the Jurisdiction of Gender, and the Heterogeneity of Transnational Law Production', *International Journal of Constitutional Law* 10(2) (2012), 531–50

Rethal, L., 'Global Ambitions, Local Realities: The Everyday Political Economy of Islamic Finance in Malaysia', in J. Elias and L. Rethel (eds.), *The Everyday Political Economy of Southeast Asia* (Cambridge: Cambridge University Press, forthcoming 2016)

Rethal, L., 'Whose Legitimacy? Islamic Finance and the Global Financial Order', *Review of International Political Economy* 18(1) (2010), 75–98

Roald, A. S., *Women in Islam: The Western Experience* (London: Routledge, 2001)

Rohe, M., *Islamic Law in Past and Present* (trans. Gwendolin Goldbloom) (Leiden: Brill, 2014)

Rohe, M., 'Sharia and the Muslim Diaspora', in R. Peters and P. Bearman (eds.), *The Ashgate Research Companion to Islamic Law* (Farnham: Ashgate, 2014), pp. 261–76

Rose, P. L., 'Muhammad, the Jews and the Constitution of Medina: Retrieving the Historical Kernel', *Der Islam* 86 (2011), 1–29

Roy, O., *The Failure of Political Islam* (Cambridge, MA: Harvard University Press, 1996)

Ryan, N., 'The Rise and Rise of Islamic Finance', *The Market*, 2 August 2008

Sachedina, A., *Islam and the Challenge of Human Rights* (Oxford: Oxford University Press, 2009)

Saeed, A., 'Sharia and Finance', in R. Peters and P. Bearman (eds.), *The Ashgate Research Companion to Islamic Law* (Farnham: Ashgate, 2014), 249–59

Safi, L. M., 'The Islamic State: A Conceptual Framework', *American Journal of Islamic Social Sciences* (September 1999), 221–34

Said, A. A., 'Precept and Practice of Human Rights in Islam', *Universal Human Rights* 1 (April 1979), 63–80

Saleh, N. A., *Unlawful Gain and Legitimate Profit in Islamic Law: Riba, Gharar and Islamic Banking* (Cambridge: Cambridge University Press, 1986)

Salem, N., 'Islam and the Status of Women in Tunisia', in F. Hussain (ed.), *Muslim Women* (New York: St Martin's, 1984)

Salim, A., *Challenging the Secular State: The Islamization of Law in Modern Indonesia* (Honolulu: University of Hawaii, 2008)

Salim, A., *The Shift in Zakat Practice in Indonesia: From Piety to an Islamic Socio-Political-Economic System* (Chiang Mai: Asian Muslim Action Network and Silkworm Books, 2008)

Sandberg, R., Douglas, G., Doe, N., and Khan, A., 'Britain's Religious Tribunals: Joint Governance in Practice', *Oxford Journal of Legal Studies* 33(2) (2013), 263–91

Sarker, M. A. A., 'Islamic Business Contracts, Agency Problem and the Theory of the Islamic Firm', *International Journal of Islamic Financial Services* 1(2) (1999), available at www.iiibf.org/journals/journal2/art2.pdf

Sayeh, L. P., and Morse, A. M., 'Islam and the Treatment of Women: An Incomplete Understanding of Gradualism', *Texas International Law Journal* 30 (1995), 311–34

Schacht, J., *Introduction to Islamic Law* (Oxford: Clarendon Press, 1964)

Schneider, I., *Women in the Islamic World: From Earliest Times to the Arab Spring* (trans. S. Rendall) (Princeton: Markus Wiener, 2014)

Scott, G., *Controlling the State: Constitutionalism from Ancient Athens to Today* (Cambridge, MA: Harvard University Press, 1999)

Scruton, R., *A Dictionary of Political Thought* (London: Macmillan, 1982)

Sepper, E., 'Confronting the "Sacred and Unchangeable": The Obligation to Modify Cultural Patterns under the Women's Discrimination Treaty', in S. Kouvo and Z. Pearson (eds.), *Gender and International Law* (Abingdon: Routledge, 2014), pp. 169–212

Serjeant, R. B., 'The Constitution of Medina', *Islamic Law Quarterly* 8 (1964), 3–16

Serjeant, R. B., 'The Sunnah Jami'a Pacts with the Yathrib Jews, and the Tahrim of Yathrib: Analysis and Translation of the Documents Comprised in the So-Called "Constitution of Medina"', *Bulletin of the School of Oriental and African Studies* 41 (1978), 1–41

Shachar, A., *Multicultural Jurisdictions: Cultural Differences and Women's Rights* (Cambridge: Cambridge University Press, 2005)

Shah-Kazemi, S., *Untying the Knot: Muslim Women, Divorce and the Shariah* (London: Nuffield, 2001)

Shahab, R., *Muslim Women in Political Power* (Lahore: Maqbool Academy, 1993)

Shaheed, F., 'Citizenship and the Nuanced Belonging of Women', in J. Bennett (ed.), *Scratching the Surface: Democracy, Traditions, Gender* (Lahore: Heinrich Böll, 2007), pp. 23–37

Shaheed, F., 'Engagements of Culture, Customs and Law: Women's Lives and Activism', in F. Shaheed, S. Warraich, C. Balchin and A. Guzdar (eds.), *Shaping Women's Lives* (Lahore: Shirkatgah, 1998), pp. 61–80

Shahid, A., 'Post-divorce Maintenance for Muslim Women in Pakistan and Bangladesh: A Comparative Perspective', *International Journal of Law, Policy & the Family* 27 (2013), 197–215

Shirkat Gah Women's Resource Centre, *Talibanisation and Poor Governance: Undermining CEDAW in Pakistan* (Lahore, 2007)

Shirkat Gah Women's Resource Centre, 'Women's Rights in Muslim Family Law in Pakistan: 45 Years of Recommendations vs. the FSC Judgement', January 2000 special bulletin, February 2000

Siddique, O., *Pakistan's Experience with Formal Law: An Alien Justice* (Cambridge: Cambridge University Press, 2013)

Siddiqui, N., *Partnership in Islamic Banking* (Leicester: Islamic Foundation, 1985)

Sikand, Y., 'Reforming Muslim Personal Laws in India: The Fyzee Formula', *Women Living under Muslim Laws*, Dossier 27 (2005), available at www.wluml.org/node/499

Sisler, V., 'The Internet and the Construction of Islamic Knowledge in Europe', *Masaryk University Journal of Law and Technology* 1(2) (2007), 205–18

Skovgaard-Petersen, J., 'A Typology of State *Muftis*', in Y. Y. Haddad and B. Stowasser (eds.), *Islamic Law and the Challenges of Modernity* (Walnut Creek, CA: Altamira Press, 2004), pp. 81–98

Sonbol, A. A., 'A Response to Muslim Countries' Reservations against Full Implementation of CEDAW', *Journal of Women of the Middle East & the Islamic World* 8 (2010), 348–67

Sousa Santos, B. de, 'Law: A Map of Misreading: Towards a Postmodern Conception of Law', *Journal of Law & Society* 14 (1989), 279–302

Sousa Santos, B. de, *Toward a New Common Sense* (New York: Routledge, 1995)

Stahnke, T., and Blitt, R., *The Religion–State Relationship and the Right to Freedom of Religion or Belief: A Comparative Textual Analysis of the Constitutions of Predominantly Muslim Countries* (Washington, DC: USCIRF, 2005)

Stilt, K. A., 'Contextualizing Constitutional Islam: The Malaysian Experience', *International Journal of Constitutional Law* 13 (2015), 407–33

Stilt, K. A., 'Islam Is the Solution: Constitutional Visions of the Egyptian Muslim Brotherhood', *Texas International Law Journal* 46 (2010), 73–108

Stout, J., 'Commitments and Traditions in the Study of Religious Ethics', *Journal of Religious Ethics* 25(3) (1998) 25th anniversary supplement, 23–56

Stowasser, B., 'The Status of Women in Early Islam', in F. Hussain (ed.), *Muslim Women* (New York: St Martin's Press, 1984), 11–43

Stowasser, B., *Women in the Qur'an: Traditions and Interpretation* (Oxford: Oxford University Press, 1994)

Stowasser, B., and Abul-Magd, Z., 'Tahlil Marriage in Shari'a: Legal Codes, and the Contemporary *Fatwa* Literature', in Y. Y. Haddad and B. Stowasser (eds.), *Islamic*

Law and the Challenges of Modernity (Walnut Creek, CA: Altamira Press, 2004), pp. 161–81

Strauss, D., *The Living Constitution* (New York: Oxford University Press, 2010)

Strawson, J., 'Reflections on the West's Question: "Is there a Human Rights Discourse in Islam?"', paper presented at the Critical Legal Conference, University of Edinburgh, 8–10 September 1995

Sultany, N., 'Religion and Constitutionalism: Lessons from American and Islamic Constitutionalism', *Emory International Law Review* 28 (2014), 345–424

Taha, M. M., *The Second Message of Islam* (trans. An-Na'im) (Syracuse: Syracuse University Press, 1987)

Timm, H., 'The Cultural and Demographic Aspects of the Islamic Financial System and the Potential for Islamic Products in the German Market', Stralsund University PhD thesis, 2005

Tiryakian, E. A., 'Assessing Multiculturalism Theoretically: E Pluribus Unum, Sic et Non', in J. Rex and G. Singh (eds.), *Governance in Multicultural Societies* (Aldershot: Ashgate, 2004), pp. 1–18

Tucker, J., *In the House of the Law: Gender and Islamic Law in Ottoman Syria and Palestine* (Berkeley: UC, 1998)

Tucker, J., 'Muftis and Matrimony: Islamic Law and Gender in Ottoman Syria and Palestine', *Islamic Law and Society* 1(3) (1994), 265–300

Tucker, J., *Women, Family, and Gender in Islamic Law* (Cambridge: Cambridge University Press, 2008)

Turner, B., *Weber and Islam: A Critical Study* (London and Boston: Routledge and Kegan Paul, 1974)

Twining, W., *Globalisation and Legal Theory* (London: Butterworths, 2000)

Twining, W., *Human Rights, Southern Voices: Francis Deng, Abdullahi An-Na'im, Yash Ghai, and Upendra Baxi* (Cambridge: Cambridge University Press, 2009)

Umar Farooq, M., 'Exploitation, Profit and the Riba-Interest Reductionism', paper presented at the Annual Conference of the Eastern Economic Association, New York, 23–6 February 2007

Vasak, K., 'Toward a Specific International Human Rights Law', in K. Vasak (ed.), *The International Dimension of Human Rights*, vol. 2 (Westport, CT: Greenwood Press, 1982)

Venardos, A. M., *Islamic Banking and Finance in Southeast Asia: Its Development and Future* (Singapore: World Scientific, 2006)

Vikor, K., 'Origins of the Sharia', in R. Peters and P. Bearman (eds.), *The Ashgate Research Companion to Islamic Law* (Farnham: Ashgate, 2014), pp. 13–25

Visser, H., *Islamic Finance: Principles and Practice* (Cheltenham: Edward Elgar, 2009)

Vogel, F. E., 'The Complementarity of *Ifta* and *Qada*: Three Saudi *Fatwas* on Divorce', in M. Masud, B. Messick and D. Powers (eds.), *Islamic Legal Interpretation: Muftis and Their Fatwas* (Karachi: Oxford University Press, 2005), pp. 262–9

Vogel, F. E., and Hayes, S. L., *Islamic Law and Finance: Religion, Risk and Return* (London: Kluwer, 1998)

Wadud, A., *Inside the Gender Jihad: Women's Reform in Islam* (Oxford: Oneworld, 2006)

Waldron, J., 'Constitutionalism: A Skeptical View', in Christiano and Christman (eds.), *Contemporary Debates in Political Theory* (Oxford: Wiley-Blackwell, 2009), doi: 10.1002/9781444310399.ch15

Walker, N., 'Constitutionalism and the Incompleteness of Democracy: An Iterative Relationship', *Journal of Legal Philosophy* 3 (2010), 206–33

Waltz, S., 'Universal Human Rights: The Contribution of Muslim States', *Human Rights Quarterly* 6(4) (2004), 799–844

Waluchow, W., 'Constitutional Interpretation', in A. Marmor (ed.), *The Routledge Companion to Philosophy of Law* (New York: Routledge, 2012), pp. 417–33

Waluchow, W., 'Constitutionalism', *Stanford Encyclopedia of Philosophy* (Spring 2014), pp. 21–9

Waluchow, W., 'Constitutions as Living Trees: An Idiot Defends', *Canadian Journal of Law and Jurisprudence* 18(2) (2005), n.p.

Warde, I., *Islamic Finance in the Global Economy*, 2nd edn (Edinburgh: Edinburgh University Press, 2010)

Washbrook, D., 'Law, State, and Agrarian Society in Colonial India', *Modern Asian Studies* 15 (1981), 649–721

Weiss, A. M., 'Interpreting Islam and Women's Rights: Implementing CEDAW in Pakistan', *International Sociology* 18(3) (2003), 581–601

Weiss, A. M. (ed.), *Islamic Reassertion in Pakistan* (Syracuse: Syracuse University Press, 1986)

Weissbrodt, D., 'Human Rights: An Historical Perspective', in P. Davies (ed.), *Human Rights* (London: Routledge, 1988), pp. 1–20

Welch, C. E., 'Human Rights and African Women: A Comparison of Protection under Two Major Treaties', *Human Rights Quarterly* 15 (1993), 853–906

Welchman, L. *Beyond the Code: Muslim Family Law and the Shari'a Judiciary in the Palestinian West Bank* (The Hague: Kluwer, 2000)

Welchman, L., (ed.), *Women's Rights and Islamic Family Law: Perspectives on Reform* (London: Zed, 2004)

Wellhausen, J., 'Muhammads Gemeindeordnung von Medina', in *Skizzen und Vorarbeiten*, vol. 4 (Berlin: Reimer, 1889), pp. 65–83

Welton, M. D., 'Review of Hallaq's *The Impossible State: Islam, Politics, and Modernity's Moral Predicament*', *Middle East Journal* 67(3) (2013), 492–3

Wiegers, G., 'Dr Sayyid Mutawalli ad-Darsh's Fatwas for Muslims in Great Britain: The Voice of Official Islam?', in G. Maclean (ed.), *Britain and the Muslim World* (Cambridge: Scholar Press, 2010), pp. 1–18

Wilson, R., *The Development of Islamic Finance in the GCC* (London: LSE, 2009)

Wohlers-Scharf, T., *Arab and Islamic Banks: New Business Partners for Developing Countries* (Paris: OECD, 1983)

Woodman, G. R., 'The Idea of Legal Pluralism', in B. Dupret, M. Berger, and L. Al-Zwaini (eds.), *Legal Pluralism in the Arab World* (The Hague: Kluwer, 1999), pp. 3–19

Wormuth, F. D., *The Origins of Modern Constitutionalism* (New York: Harper and Brothers, 1949)

Wright, J. W., 'Islamic Banking in Practice: Problems in Jordan and Saudi Arabia', Centre for Middle Eastern and Islamic Studies, University of Durham, occasional paper 48, 1995

Yasin, M., and Banuri, T. (eds.), *Dispensation of Justice in Pakistan* (Oxford: Oxford University Press, 2003)

Yildirim, Y., 'Peace and Conflict Resolution in the Medina Charter', *Peace Review* 18(1) (2006), 109–17

Yilmaz, I., *Muslim Laws, Politics and Society in Modern Nation States* (Aldershot: Ashgate, 2005)

Zaidi, Y., 'The Interplay of CEDAW, National Laws and Customary Practices in Pakistan: A Literature Review', in S. S. Ali (ed.), *Conceptualising Islamic Law: CEDAW and Women's Human Rights in Plural Legal Settings: A Comparative Analysis of the Application of CEDAW in Bangladesh, India and Pakistan* (Delhi: UNIFEM Regional Office, 2006), pp. 199–263

Zaman, M., 'Religious Discourse and the Public Sphere in Pakistan', *Revue des mondes musulmans et de la Méditerranée* 123 (2008), 55–73

Zaman, M., *The Ulama in Contemporary Islam: Custodians of Change* (Princeton: Princeton University Press, 2007)

Zaman, S., *Economic Functions of an Islamic State: The Early Experience* (Leicester: Islamic Foundation, 1991)

Index